D1304909

It makes me very happy to join
with the West Philadelphia Womens
Committee for the Philadelphia Orchestra
in dedicating this book to my dear
beloved friend Maestro Eugene Ormandy,
who has given Philadelphia and the
World so much joy through his
superb musicianship!

With deep admiration
and gratitude,

Rudolf Serkin.

RFD #3 BRATTLEBORO, VERMONT 05301

The Philadelphia Orchestra Cookbook

Published by
The West Philadelphia Committee
For
The Philadelphia Orchestra

P.O. Box 685
Bryn Mawr, Pennsylvania 19010
1980

First Printing	October 1980	10,000 Books
Second Printing	April 1981	10,000 Books
Third Printing	April 1982	15,000 Books
Fourth Printing	June 1983	15,000 Books
Fifth Printing	October 1986	10,000 Books
Sixth Printing	October 1988	10,000 Books
Seventh Printing	October 1991	10,000 Books
Eighth Printing	February 1994	10,000 Books

Copies of **The Philadelphia Orchestra Cookbook** may be obtained by addressing **The Philadelphia Orchestra Cookbook**, Box 685, Bryn Mawr, Pennsylvania 19010. Price $16.00 per copy, $3.00 postage and handling. Pennsylvania residents pay $.96 sales tax per copy.

The recipes in this cookbook were selected, tested and edited by the members of The West Philadelphia Committee for The Philadelphia Orchestra and The Evening Associates.

International Standard Book Number 0-918544-46-7

Printed in the USA by

WIMMER
The Wimmer Companies, Inc.
Memphis • Dallas

THE ACADEMY OF MUSIC

Opened at a grand promenade-concert and ball on January 26, 1857, the Academy of Music has been the home of The Philadelphia Orchestra since the first appearance of the orchestra in 1900.

A comprehensive array of cultural entertainment—concert, opera, the dance, recital, rock and lectures—is offered from the stage of the Academy of Music. It also is the scene of ceremonial and political events. The roster of the world's leading performers, orators, lecturers and public figures who have appeared on stage is a veritable "Who's Who" of the last century. The lavish auditorium offers every advantage for displaying the talents of each performer.

The scientific explanation for the "sonic patina" in the Academy of Music is undetermined. There are numerous factors contributing to the quality of the sound. The room is surrounded by a curved, three-foot thick brick wall. Its lavish ornamentation is gilded, carved wood. The stage is raked two and one-half feet toward the rear. Beneath the parquet floor there is a dry well. Above the dazzling crystal chandelier, the center of the ornately painted ceiling is saucer-shaped. The architectural features of this imposing building combine to create a superb environment for virtually perfect sound. Undistorted and uninterrupted, this is enjoyed by an audience of nearly three thousand.

Limited funds compelled architects Napoleon E. H. C. Le Brun and Gustavus Runge to keep the exterior of the building "as plain as a market place" making it possible to concentrate on a lavish interior "giving (that) all possible efficiency, convenience and luxury."

Concurrent events may be held in the Academy of Music for it contains a soundproof ballroom, elegantly fashioned in 1922, after the Hall of Mirrors at Versailles. A richly furnished reception room adjoins the stage. Dignitaries may receive guests here after performances.

Since 1957, a gala concert and ball is held in Philadelphia each January for the benefit of the Academy of Music. The overwhelming popularity of these occasions provides substantial funds for the restoration and modernization of the building.

Designated a National Historic Monument in 1963 by the federal government and a registered historic building by Philadelphia, the Academy of Music is a year-round working theatre. Thus, the "Grand Old Lady of Locust Street" continues its century-old tradition of providing Philadelphia a cultural center of artistic and historic distinction.

THE PHILADELPHIA ORCHESTRA

January 1757

> *"On Tuesday next, the 25th inst, at the Assembly Room in Lodge Allez will be performed a Concert of Music, under the direction of Mr. John Palma; to begin exactly at six o'clock. Tickets to be had at the London Coffee House at One Dollar each; and no person to be admitted without a ticket."*

This was the first recorded public concert in Philadelphia. Public concerts were not given during the period of the Revolution and were not resumed until 1820 when the Philadelphia Musical Fund Society, sponsoring an orchestra and chorus, was founded. Forty years later, the orchestra having disbanded, the musicians organized the Germania Orchestra which gave concerts not only at the Musical Fund, but also at the Academy of Fine Arts and the recently opened Academy of Music. The musicians of the Germania Orchestra reorganized in 1893 as the Philadelphia Symphony which in 1900 sold its assets—a music library, a set of kettledrums and its music desks—to the Executive Committee of The Philadelphia Orchestra. The first Philadelphia Orchestra concert was performed November 16 of that year with Fritz Scheel conducting.

Maestro Scheel was intent on the artistic development of the Orchestra and brought together musicians of the highest quality. By the time of his death in 1907, The Philadelphia Orchestra was acclaimed wherever it performed. His vision undoubtedly gave the Orchestra its wonderful foundation.

Further progress was made during the next several years under Carl Pohlig who resigned in 1912 and was replaced by Leopold Stokowski who had been conductor of the Cincinnati Symphony. As Music Director of The Philadelphia Orchestra he led his opening concert October 12, 1912.

The fourth Music Director, Eugene Ormandy, observed his 45th Anniversary during the 1979-80 season. Maestros Stokowski and Ormandy are credited with having built The Philadelphia Orchestra into a world renowned ensemble.

In the 1980-81 season the Orchestra's respected and beloved Maestro, Eugene Ormandy, became Conductor Laureate and handed over the baton to Riccardo Muti, who, as the fifth Music Director, led the Orchestra until 1993.

Wolfgang Sawallisch began his tenure as the sixth Music Director of The Philadelphia Orchestra during the 1993-94 season. He has been a frequent guest conductor since his initial appearance with the Orchestra in 1966. Maestro Sawallisch was General Director and Music Director of the Bavarian State Opera in Munich and he is the Honorary Conductor of the NHK Symphony Orchestra in Tokyo.

THE PHILADELPHIA ORCHESTRA COOKBOOK

HONORARY CHAIRMAN
MRS. EUGENE ORMANDY

CHAIRMAN
MRS. JOHN V. CALHOUN, JR.

ARTIST
HELEN LOWDEN EVANS

EDITORS-IN-CHIEF	Mrs. John E. Krout
	Mrs. A. Addison Roberts
CONTRIBUTING EDITORS	Mrs. E. Dyson Herting
	Mrs. H. Ober Hess
ART EDITOR	Mrs. Robert Alan Swift
CIRCULATION	Mrs. George M. Ahrens
	Mrs. Revere Counselman
MARKETING	Mrs. Craig W. Cullen
	Mrs. Stevan Simich
PUBLICITY	Mrs. B. Herbert Lee
RECIPE TESTING	Mrs. J. Mahlon Buck, Jr.
	Mrs. Louis Hood
NEW YORK AREA REPRESENTATIVE	Mrs. Rodney D. Day, III
SPECIAL SALES REPRESENTATIVE	Mrs. Henry Wendt
TREASURER	Mrs. William W. Lander
HONORARY MEMBER	Mr. John V. Calhoun, Jr.

Every member of The West Philadelphia Committee promotes and sells **The Philadelphia Orchestra Cookbook.**

ACKNOWLEDGEMENT

To the many friends of The Philadelphia Orchestra who have shared treasured recipes for this volume, The Cookbook Committee expresses heartfelt thanks. Recipes indicated with the ♩ have been contributed by members of The Philadelphia Orchestra, their families and guest artists. The ♔ denotes recipes from chefs and culinary notables. We regret that duplication and similarity prevented our using some of the recipes submitted. We are ever grateful for the imaginative recipes from our contributors.

TABLE OF CONTENTS

A NOTE ON QUANTITIES

When ordering foods that are served in individual portions, such as small whole fish, escalopes of veal, and the like, allow one or two over the number of people being catered for. This would apply when cooking a dish of eggs mollet for example—have one more on the dish for appearance. In fact one should never have an 'exact fit' for any dish.

Soups. Three people to a pint of soup is a good average. If plates are used, instead of cups or bowls, less can be allowed—say, four to a pint.

Fish. Fish is less satisfying than butcher's meat. Allow ½ pound of white fish per head when bought and cooked on the bone. When fillets of fish are served as a first course, one is sufficient if the recipe is elaborate and contains a garnish, but if the dish is simple, such as meuniere, allow two; for a main course allow two fillets from a large fish if the meal is a three-course one.

Meat. 4 to 6 ounces per head for stewing or grilling meat without bone. With bone, a middle neck of lamb, for example, not less than ½ pound a head. Generally speaking the more bone the greater quantity of meat required. For a roast, a minimum of 3½ pounds for four people; this allows for bone weight and should be sufficient for two meals.

Rice. 1 ounce per head for boiled rice for a salad; 1½ ounces for a risotto or pilaf; and 2 ounces per head for rice to serve with curry.

Pasta. 6 to 8 ounces for 4 people is generally sufficient.

Many of the recipes used in this section were generously donated by K. Carol Carlson, vice president of the ARA Food Services of Philadelphia, Pennsylvania.

Repertoire

cooking for a crowd

GALA DINNER PRECEDING OPENING CONCERT

Spinach-Cheese Squares
Mushroom Mousse   Bacon-Pineapple Bits
Consommé with Aromatic Spices
Mousseline de Saumon and Sauce Verte
Butterflied Leg of Lamb
with
Herbal Mustard Coating
Dinner Rolls
Tomato Soufflé   Spinach, Broccoli, Artichoke Combo
Green Salad
Chocolate Bourbon Cake
Coffee   Barclay After Dinner Mints   Cafe Brûlot

HUNT BREAKFAST

Foxy Hot and Spicy Cider
Baked Virginia Ham   Seafood au Gratin
Quiche for a Crowd
Creamed Eggs and Asparagus Casserole
Toasted English Muffins   Sally Lunn
Citrus Marmalade
Coffee   Tea

MORNING MUSICALES COMMITTEE MEETING

German Coffee Cake   Cinnamon Flop
Cream Cheese Braids
Russian Tea   Coffee

BOARD OF DIRECTORS' LUNCHEON MEETING

Snapper Soup with Sherry
Provençale Beef Salad with Anchovy Vinaigrette
Popovers
French Mint Dessert

MUMMERS DAY PARADE BRUNCH

Glögg
University City Historical Society Punch
Punch for a Crowd
Chicken Supreme   Ham Loaf
Javanese Salad   Zingy Tomato Aspic
Philadelphia Sticky Buns
Fresh Fruit Compote

WEST PHILADELPHIA WOMEN'S COMMITTEE
OPEN REHEARSAL BRUNCH
OCTOBER 1979

Cider   Sherry
Ramequin Fôrestière
Spiced Fruit Mix
Strawberry Nut Bread   Oregon Apple Bread
Pumpkin Bread
Coffee   Tea

PICNIC AT THE DELL

Gazpacho   Cold Deviled Shrimp
Benné Seed Biscuits
Chicken and Ham Loaf Chadds Ford
Marinated Carrots
Lemon Squares   Potato Chip and Corn Flake Cookies
Super Lemonade
Spiced Iced Tea

ARMY-NAVY FOOTBALL GAME LUNCHEON

Gin or Vodka Punch   Union League Specials
Richmond Whiskey Sours
Moussaka
Green Bean Salad
Gougère
Bavarian Melon
Coffee

WEST PHILADELPHIA WOMEN'S COMMITTEE
OPEN REHEARSAL LUNCHEON
MARCH 1978

Sherry   Clamato Juice
"Our Chicken Salad"
"What Is It" Salad
Cheese Beoregs
Cheese Cake   Cherry Tarts
Coffee   Tea

TAILGATE PICNIC BEFORE
PHILADELPHIA EAGLES GAME

Winter Alfresco "Brew-ha-ha"
Purée of Carrot Soup
Gold Green Veal Loaf   Meat Barags
"Aunt Carolyn's Elegant Picnic"
Assorted Fruit
Peanut Butter Sticks   Hello Dollies
Coffee

SUPPER FOLLOWING
OLD PHILADELPHIA WALKING TOUR

Lamb Curry   Peach Chutney   Biscuits
Asparagus Vinaigrette
Apricot and Lemon Sherbet
Billy's Crunchy Cookies   Blond Brownies
Coffee

MEMBERSHIP CAMPAIGN
KICK-OFF LUNCHEON

Champagne Punch
Mandarin Walnut Chicken
Rice Salad with Chutney Dressing   Whole Green Beans
Apricot Bread
Lemon Mousse   Amaretti

CHRISTMAS IN OLD PHILADELPHIA

Eggnog   Fish House Punch, Old Philadelphia   Wassail
Pepper Pot Soup
Roast Turkey   Oyster Cornmeal Stuffing
Cranberry Salad
Twice-Baked Yams   Baked Potatoes in Cream
Peas and Black Olives
Different Banana Bread   Zucchini Bread
Mincemeat Chiffon Pie   Indian Pudding
Syllabub

CHAMPAGNE SUPPER FOLLOWING
NEW YEAR'S EVE CONCERT

Lobster Newburg
Wild Rice Casserole   Mushroom and Spinach Salad
Herb Toast
Pêche Melba

Tuning up

appetizers

DIPPER NUGGETS

Easy
Freeze

Serves: 8-10
Preparing: 30 minutes
Baking: 20 minutes

2 whole chicken breasts,
  skinned and boned
1 egg, beaten
⅓ cup water

⅓ cup flour
2 teaspoons sesame seeds
½ teaspoon salt
1 pint corn oil

Cut chicken into 1"x1"x½" nuggets. Mix egg and water. Add flour, sesame seeds and salt to make a batter (very runny). Pour oil into an electric fry pan and heat oil to 375° (on top of range, medium high). Dip the nuggets into the batter; drain off excess batter. Carefully add nuggets a few at a time. Fry for three to five mintues, or until golden brown. Drain on paper towels. Serve with Nippy Pineapple Sauce, Creamy Dill Sauce or Savory Sauce. If frozen, thaw before heating at 350°-400° for 20 minutes.

Mrs. Donald W. Belcher
Radnor, Pennyslvania

SAUCES FOR DIPPER NUGGETS

Nippy Pineapple Sauce

Makes: ½ cup

½ cup pineapple preserves
2 tablespoons prepared
  mustard

2 tablespoons horseradish

Heat over low heat until well blended.

Creamy Dill Sauce

Makes: 1 cup

½ cup sour cream
½ cup mayonnaise
1 teaspoon dill weed

2 tablespoons finely chopped dill
  pickles

Let stand at room temperature for 1 hour to blend flavors.

Savory Sauce

Makes: 1 cup

1 cup catsup
½ teaspoon dry mustard
1 tablespoon brown sugar

2 tablespoons vinegar
6 tablespoons butter

Combine all ingredients, cook, stirring constantly for four to five minutes.

Mrs. Donald W. Belcher
Radnor, Pennsylvania

CREAM CHEESE MOUSSE

Easy
Do ahead

Serves: 4
Preparing: 5-10 minutes
Chilling: 24 hours

**6 ounces Philadelphia cream
  cheese, at room
  temperature
1 can Campbell's consommé**

**1 teaspoon curry powder
1 teaspoon lemon juice
salt and pepper
pimiento or olive**

Put cheese and 14 tablespoons consommé, the curry powder, lemon juice, salt and freshly ground black pepper into a blender or food processor. Blend or process until very well mixed. Pour into four ramekins and leave to set overnight. The next day pour remaining consommé on top of ramekins. Allow to set and decorate with finely sliced pimiento or olives.

Mrs. William C. Ferguson
Philadelphia, Pennsylvania

Mrs. Patrick P. J. Stephenson
Warwick, Bermuda

BAKED CLAMS WITH WALNUTS

Easy
Partial do ahead

Serves: 4
Preparing: 15 minutes
Baking: 5 minutes

16 littleneck or cherry stone clams on half shell

Topping:

**2 shallots, minced
10 walnut halves
¼ cup parsley
3 tablespoons vermouth,
  white wine or Pernod**

**4 tablespoons unsalted butter
¼ cup fresh fine bread crumbs
Parmesan cheese (freshly grated)**

Chop and mash together shallots, walnut halves, parsley, vermouth or white wine. Knead in butter, bread crumbs, Parmesan cheese. Spoon topping on each clam. Cover with freshly grated Parmesan cheese (best quality). Make a bed of loosely crumpled aluminum foil on a pan. Set filled clams in their shells on foil. Bake in 450° oven (very hot), loosely covered with foil for 3-5 minutes. When just barely done, brown close to hot broiler.

Mrs. John W. Eckman
Philadelphia, Pennsylvania

FRENCH FRIED SWISS CHEESE NUGGETS

Easy
Partial do ahead

Makes: 40
Preparing: ½ hour plus
Chilling: 12 hours
Frying: 2 minutes

¼ cup butter
½ cup all-purpose flour
⅛ teaspoon salt
dash of cayenne
1 egg, slightly beaten
½ cup hot milk

3 cups finely grated Swiss
  cheese
½ cup all-purpose flour
melted shortening for deep fat
  frying
1 cup dry bread crumbs

Egg Dip

1 egg
¾ cup milk

½ teaspoon salt

Melt butter in saucepan. Add flour, salt and cayenne. Blend well. Cook over low heat 2 to 3 minutes, stirring constantly. Remove from heat. Add egg and beat with a wire whisk several minutes until well blended. Add hot milk slowly, continuing to beat with wire whisk until mixture is smooth and creamy. Add cheese and beat to combine thoroughly. Chill overnight or several hours until mixture is firm. Using a tablespoon, shape little rounds of mixture into balls (about ½ ounce each). Roll lightly in flour. Combine egg, milk and salt to make the egg dip. Dip the floured cheese balls into the egg dip and drain. Roll in bread crumbs; chill until ready to cook. Fry in deep fat at 350° for 2 minutes. Drain. Serve hot. Makes 40 ½ ounce cheese balls.

K. Carol Carlson
ARA Services, Incorporated
Philadelphia, Pennsylvania

QUICHE PETITES

Average
Do ahead
Freeze

Makes:24 pieces
Preparing: 15-20 minutes
Baking: 30 minutes

1 cup unsifted flour
½ cup butter
3 ounces cream cheese
1 egg, slightly beaten
½ cup milk

¼ teaspoon salt
½ pound mushrooms, diced
1 cup grated Swiss cheese
½ cup real bacon bits
1 small onion, grated (optional)

Cream butter and cream cheese. Work in flour. Roll into 24 balls and press into miniature muffin pans. Sauté diced mushrooms and onion. Spread into tins. Divide Swiss cheese and bacon bits into tins. Pour mixture of egg, milk and salt over the above. Bake at 350° for 30 minutes.

Mrs. Victor Johnson
Madison, Wisconsin

CHEESE COOKIES

Easy   *Makes: 60*
Do ahead   *Preparing: 15 minutes*
Freeze   *Baking: 10 minutes*

These go with cocktails, salad, soup, etc. They have been used many times at our West Philadelphia luncheons and Morning Musicales.

2 cups grated sharp cheese   **2 cups Rice Krispies**
2 cups flour   **½ teaspoon cayenne pepper**
2 sticks margarine

Mix all ingredients by hand and form into small balls. Place on ungreased cookie sheet, flatten with heel of hand or fork. Bake at 350° for 10 minutes or until slightly browned. Cool and place in covered tin. Can be frozen and reheated as needed.

The Committee

SHRIMP DIP

Easy   *Serves: 12*
Do ahead   *Preparing: 20 minutes*

1 package cream cheese (8   **1 tablespoon diced onion**
  ounces)   **1 tablespoon minced celery**
¾ cup mayonnaise   **1 tablespoon minced green**
1 pound cooked shrimp,   **pepper**
  diced (or 3 4½ ounce cans   **2 tablespoons lemon juice**
  large, deveined shrimp)   **¼ teaspoon salt**
                                              4 drops Tabasco

Mix all ingredients with electric mixer or use blender for smoother dip.

Mrs. Richard S. Schweiker
Washington, D.C.

HOT CRAB FONDUE

Easy
Do ahead
Freeze

Serves: 20
Preparing: 10 minutes
Cooking: 10 minutes

3 8-ounce packages
  Philadelphia cream cheese
2 8-ounce cans crabmeat,
  drained
2 cloves minced garlic
½ cup Hellman's mayonnaise

2 teaspoons prepared mustard
¼ cup dry white wine
2 teaspoons powdered sugar
2 teaspoons minced onion
dash or two Lawry's seasoned
  salt

Put all ingredients in top of double boiler. Heat until ingredients are hot and well blended. Serve with rosemary melba toast.

Barbara W. Trimmer
Hopetown, Abaco, Bahamas

OYSTER ROLL O'BOYLE

Easy
Do ahead

Serves: 20
Preparing: 20 minutes
Chilling: 30 minutes

2 8-ounce packages cream
  cheese
2 tins smoked oysters,
  drained and chopped
2 tablespoons Worcestershire
  sauce

2 tablespoons mayonnaise
1 garlic clove, crushed
2 tablespoons onion, finely
  chopped
salt and pepper (optional)

Cream mayonnaise into cream cheese. Add garlic, Worcestershire and onion and cream until fluffy. Spread ½ inch on wax paper, spread oysters on top and roll like jelly roll, and chill ½ hour at least. If your "dough" is too soft at first, chill flat and then roll. Slice to serve on crackers.

Mrs. John J. Hosey IV
Flourtown, Pennsylvania

WENDY BROWN'S GUACAMOLE DIP

Easy

Serves: 12
Preparing: 20 minutes
Chilling: 1 hour

2 ripe avocados peeled,
  pitted and mashed
½ cup mayonnaise
2 teaspoons fresh lemon
  juice
1 package taco seasoning
  mix

¾ cup sour cream
3 scallions, chopped
1 tomato, diced and drained of
  excess juice
½ can medium, pitted ripe olives,
  drained
4 ounces cheddar cheese, grated

Mix first three ingredients and spread in large base layer on a dinner plate. Mix next two ingredients separately and spread in smaller second layer, on top of avocado mixture. Sprinkle scallions around green base layer's edge. Arrange diced tomato and olives on inner layer. Sprinkle shredded cheese over all. Serve with tortilla chips.

Mrs. Donald Van Roden
Malvern, Pennsylvania

SPINACH CHEESE SQUARES

Easy
Do ahead
Freeze

Serves: 38-45 pieces
Preparing: 20 minutes
Baking: 35 minutes

4 tablespoons butter
3 eggs
1 cup flour
1 cup milk
1 teaspoon salt
few dashes pepper
1 teaspoon baking powder

1 pound Monterey Jack cheese,
  grated
2 packages frozen chopped
  spinach, thawed and drained
1 heaping teaspoon minced
  onion

Preheat oven to 350°. In a 9"x13" casserole, melt butter in oven. Remove. In large bowl beat eggs; add flour, milk and seasonings. Mix well. Add cheese, thawed spinach and onion. Pour all into oblong baking dish and bake 35 minutes. Remove and cool 45 minutes to set. Cut into bite-sized pieces. To freeze, place on cookie sheet. When frozen, transfer to plastic bag. To reheat, bake at 325° for 12 minutes.

Mrs. Robert S. Woodcock
Gladwyne, Pennsylvania

CURRY DIP

Easy
Do ahead

Makes: 2 cups
Preparing: 15 minutes
Chilling: 4 hours

2 cups mayonnaise
3 teaspoons curry powder
3 tablespoons chili sauce
1 tablespoon Worcestershire
  sauce

½ teaspoon salt
pepper
½ teaspoon garlic salt
1 teaspoon instant onion

Blend all ingredients. Refrigerate to chill. Serve with raw vegetables.

Mrs. Dick Thornburgh
Harrisburg, Pennsylvania

LILY CUP HORS D'OEUVRES

Average
Partial do ahead

Serves: 6
Preparing: 30 minutes

Obviously my favorite recipe must contain flowers. Could serve as a centerpiece in lieu of flowers.

18 freshly picked day lily
  florets, choose your
  favorite color (the stamens
  and pistils must be
  removed)
½ cup finely chopped
  nasturtium blooms
3 or 4 finely chopped
  nasturtium leaves
2½ cups finely cubed cooked
  white meat of chicken

2 tablespoons minced onion
2 tablespoons minced parsley
½ cup olive oil
2 tablespoons wine vinegar
¼ teaspoon chervil
½ teaspoon Dijon mustard
salt and pepper to taste
crisp lettuce leaves

Combine diced chicken, nasturtium blooms and leaves, onion, parsley, salt and pepper. Moisten with dressing made by blending olive oil, vinegar, chervil, mustard, salt and pepper. Spoon a tablespoon of salad mix into the center of each day lily blossom. Arrange lilies on lettuce-lined plates, three to a serving. Makes six servings. The entire concoction may be eaten as a gourmet as well as an horticultural delight.

J. Liddon Pennock, Jr.
Meadowbrook, Pennsylvania

TANGO VEGETABLE DIP

Easy

Preparing: 10 minutes
Chilling: 3 hours

2 cups mayonnaise
1 cup cottage cheese
¾ cup chopped green onions
1 tablespoon plus 1½
** teaspoons horseradish**
1 tablespoon plus 1½
** teaspoons Worcestershire**
** sauce**

1½ teaspoons caraway seeds
1½ teaspoons celery seeds
1 tablespoon garlic salt or
** powder**
1 teaspoon salt
1 teaspoon Tabasco
½ teaspoon seasoned salt

Mix all ingredients together and chill. Great as a vegetable dip or over hot vegetables!

Mrs. René Slemmer
Moorestown, New Jersey

SHRIMP AND ARTICHOKE APPETIZER

Preparing: 15 minutes

There are no exact proportions; tasting is essential. V.I.P. brand artichoke bottoms work well in this recipe.

canned artichoke bottoms, 1
** per person**
medium sized shrimp, fresh,
** frozen or tinned**
mayonnaise flavored with
** lemon juice, curry powder**

capers
minced parsley
lemon wedges

Rinse shrimp if canned; rinse artichoke bottoms. Mix shrimp with enough flavored mayonnaise to bind. Mound shrimp on artichoke bottoms; decorate with capers, parsley and lemon wedges.

Mrs. M. Todd Cooke
Media, Pennsylvania

SPINACH DIP

Easy
Do ahead

Serves: 12
Preparing: 10 minutes

4 10-ounce packages frozen
chopped spinach
1 cup mayonnaise, (low fat,
lower calorie imitation
mayonnaise substitutes
easily)

2 tablespoons dehydrated
chopped dried onion
various dried seasonings to
taste, such as oregano,
pepper, salt, garlic salt

Cook frozen spinach. Drain. Mix all ingredients well. Should be moist and of "dipping" consistency. May be used immediately or chilled for later use. Serve with crisp raw vegetables, i.e., carrot sticks, broccoli cuts, cauliflower cuts, etc.

Mrs. Seymour Rosenfeld
Merion, Pennsylvania

DIP STAUTBERG

Easy
Do ahead

Serves: 6-8
Preparing: 20 minutes

1 large container sour cream
1 package Lipton onion soup
2 packages frozen avocados
or 3 ripe avocados
(mashed)

1 to 2 tablespoons horseradish
cayenne pepper to taste

Mix and serve wtih fresh vegetables and chips.

Susan Schiffer Stautberg
Philadelphia, Pennsylvania

CHEESE MUSHROOM CANAPES

Easy
Freeze

Preparing: 30 minutes
Broiling: 2-3 minutes

¼ pound mushrooms
1 tablespoon butter
1 8-ounce package softened
cream cheese

1 teaspoon minced onion
salt and pepper to taste
pinch of thyme
bread rounds

Dice mushrooms in very small pieces and sauté quickly in the butter. Mix mushrooms, onions and seasonings with cream cheese. Toast small rounds of bread on one side. Spread untoasted side with mushroom mixture. Refrigerate or freeze. Place on cookie sheet to thaw. When ready to serve, place under broiler until puffy and brown.

Mrs. John F. Lloyd
Ardmore, Pennsylvania

HERB TOAST

Easy
Do ahead
Freeze

Makes: 50-60
Preparing: 10 minutes
Cooking: 15 minutes

¼ pound butter
¼ teaspoon thyme
salt, to taste
black pepper, to taste
1 tablespoon lemon juice

1 teaspoon fresh parsley,
 chopped
¼ teaspoon chopped garlic
½ teaspoon chopped shallots
stale bread, cut into "fingers"

Mix together in a small bowl, butter, thyme, salt, black pepper, lemon juice, freshly chopped parsley, chopped garlic and chopped shallots. Place in saucepan and melt over slow fire. Dip fingers of stale bread into herb mixture. Place on baking sheet and bake at 350° until brown, turning once.

Julie Dannenbaum
Philadelphia, Pennsylvania

SESAME MUSHROOMS

Easy

Makes: 20 pieces
Preparing: 10 minutes

sesame crackers
8 ounces cream cheese
3 egg yolks
½ teaspoon garlic salt

10 fresh mushrooms, chopped,
 sauteed in small amount of
 butter

Mix cream cheese, egg yolks, garlic salt. Sauté chopped mushrooms in small amount of butter. Blend both preparations. Mound on sesame crackers. Important to cover crackers to the very edge. Broil one to two minutes until brown and bubbly. Mixture should be "mounded" on crackers at the last minute; otherwise crackers become soggy.

Mrs. Robert Watson
Charlotte, North Carolina

SPANAKOPITES

Average
Do ahead
Freeze

Makes: approximately 110 pieces
Preparing: 90 minutes
Baking: 20 minutes

Pastry

2 cups flour
8 ounces softened cream
  cheese

8 ounces softened butter or
  margarine

Filling

1 package frozen chopped
  spinach
6 ounces frozen chopped
  onions, or 1 large onion,
  chopped
5 tablespoons oil
salt and pepper to taste

1 teaspoon dill weed
½ pound Feta cheese crumbled*
½ cup grated sharp cheese
  (Kefalotiri or Locatelli
  cheese)*
4 eggs, slightly beaten

Pastry
Cut flour into cheese and shortening; then work with hands until it gathers into a ball. Refrigerate at least two hours.

Filling
Prepare spinach according to package directions. Drain well. Place in large mixing bowl. Sauté onions in oil until transparent. Add to spinach. Add salt and pepper, dill weed, and cheeses. Mix well. Add eggs and mix again. Roll out part of pastry on well-floured board until about ⅛" thick. Using water glass or cookie cutter, make circles about 2¾ inches in diameter. Put about ½ tablespoon filling in each circle and fold pastry in half, carefully sealing edges by pressing with tines of fork. Bake now on ungreased cookie sheet or freeze until quite firm on cookie sheet; then transfer to plastic storage bags until used. Cook in preheated 375° oven, whether fresh or frozen, for 20 minutes or until golden brown.

*If there is no Feta cheese available, ½ pound cottage cheese may be substituted and the grated cheese increased to 1 cup or more.

Anne Lagos
Media, Pennsylvania

Chill raw vegetables in juice from dill pickle jar to make a crunchy, low-calorie snack.

MUSHROOM MOUSSE

Average
Do ahead

Serves: 10
Preparing: 20 minutes
Chilling: 2 hours

½ **pound fresh mushrooms,**
 chopped
1 **tablespoon butter**
1½ **teaspoons gelatine**
1 **tablespoon sherry**
¼ **cup cold chicken broth**
1 **egg, separated**
1½ **drops Tabasco sauce**

¼ **cup mayonnaise**
1 **teaspoon drained capers**
1½ **tablespoons onion, chopped**
½ **teaspoon lemon juice**
pinch white ground pepper
½ **cup heavy cream**
¼ **teaspoon garlic salt**

Brown the mushrooms in butter in a large skillet. Set aside. Soften the gelatine in the sherry and broth in the container of a blender for a minute or two. Blend briefly. Add mushrooms, egg yolk, Tabasco, mayonnaise, capers, onion, lemon juice, garlic, salt and pepper. Blend until smooth; add the cream, blend again. In a small bowl beat the egg white until stiff. Fold lightly into the mushroom mixture. Pour into a 2-cup mold and refrigerate until ready to serve. Unmold and serve with melba toast, water biscuits or white toast points. Or, spoon into lightly poached mushroom caps.

Mrs. Louis Hood
Wayne, Pennsylvania

CRAB MEAT MOLD AND SPREAD

Easy
Do ahead

Makes: 48-50
Preparing: 20 minutes
Chilling: 6 hours

1 **can cream of shrimp soup,**
 undiluted
2 **3-ounce packages cream**
 cheese
¼ **cup onion, chopped fine**

1 **cup mayonnaise**
2 **envelopes unflavored gelatine**
1 **cup cold water**
1 **can crab meat, drained**
1 **cup celery, chopped fine**

In medium saucepan combine soup, cheese and onion. Heat until cheese is melted, stir. Blend in mayonnaise and remove from heat. In small pan sprinkle gelatine over water, on low heat, until dissolved. Stir into soup mixture, add crab meat and celery. Pour into 6 cup mold and refrigerate at least 6 hours. Unmold on plate and serve with crackers.

Mrs. Paul A. Bowers
Bala Cynwyd, Pennsylvania

MUSHROOM STRUDEL

Average
Freeze

Serves: 16
Preparing: 30 minutes
Baking: 20-30 minutes

1 pound sweet Italian
  sausage
1 pound mushrooms, cleaned
  and minced
2 tablespoons minced
  shallots
3 tablespoons butter
1 tablespoon oil

salt and pepper to taste
¼ teaspoon thyme
8 ounces cream cheese, softened
8 phyllo leaves
½ cup melted butter or
  margarine
½ cup bread crumbs

Sauté sausage until cooked through. Crumble. Sauté minced mushrooms and shallots in butter and oil until dry. Season to taste with salt, pepper and thyme. In a bowl, mix together sausage, mushrooms and cream cheese. Spread on a table a sheet of phyllo dough, long end toward you. Brush with melted butter and sprinkle lightly with bread crumbs. Repeat with 2nd and 3rd sheets. Add 4th sheet, butter but do not add crumbs. (Note—there are approximately 20 leaves in a box of phyllo leaves.) Place half of the sausage mixture along the edge, about 1½ inches in. Fold in sides and roll up tightly as for a jelly roll. Brush with butter and bake at 400° for about 20-30 minutes, or until brown. The roll can be frozen unbaked if wrapped very well. Bake without defrosting. This recipe will fill two rolls. To serve, cool slightly. There is no way to keep the crisp phyllo dough from shattering when cut. Cut each roll in 8 pieces and push back together again. Thus filling will not run.

Mrs. Harry Gorodetzer
Narberth, Pennsylvania

LOUISA'S DIP

Easy
Do ahead
Freeze

Serves: 8
Preparing: 5 minutes
Baking: 15 minutes

1 8-ounce package cream
  cheese
2 tablespoons milk
½ cup sour cream
2 tablespoons green pepper,
  minced

2 tablespoons onion, minced
4 ounces dried beef, shredded
¼ cup chopped walnuts
Triscuits or king-size corn chips

Blend cream cheese and milk in blender until smooth. Add sour cream, then green pepper and onion. Fold in dried beef, but don't blend. Pour into heatproof serving dish. Top with walnuts. Heat at 350° for 10-15 minutes or until bubbly. Serve with Triscuits or corn chips.

Mrs. Herbert T. Rorer
Haverford, Pennsylvania

Mrs. Peter A. Hurbet
Rosemont, Pennsylvania

CAVIAR PIE

Easy   *Serves: 10-12*
Partial do ahead   *Preparing: 25 minutes*
                                                         Chilling: 1 hour

6 eggs, hard-boiled   **2 4-ounce jars lumpfish caviar**
1 stick butter, softened   **1 cup sour cream**
6 small white onions,
**   chopped (or equivalent**
**   scallions)**

Finely chop or sieve eggs and mix with butter. Put paste in glass pie pan and refrigerate one hour. Add layer of onions, then a layer of caviar. Top with sour cream, heated slightly for easier spreading. Serve cold with crackers.

Mrs. Roger Decker
Haverford, Pennsylvania

SPICY BEEF DIP

Easy   *Serves: 10*
Do ahead   *Preparing: 20 minutes*
                                                       Cooking: 15 minutes

1 pound ground beef   **1 teaspoon sugar**
½ cup chopped onion   **1 8-ounce package cream cheese**
1 clove garlic, crushed   **⅓ cup Parmesan cheese**
1 8-ounce can tomato sauce   **1 tablespoon butter**
¼ cup catsup   **Fritos**
¾ teaspoon oregano

Brown beef, onions, and garlic in butter. Stir in everything but cheeses, and simmer for 10 minutes. Remove from heat and add cheeses. Stir until cheeses melt. Serve in a chafing dish, surrounded by Fritos.

Mrs. Harry G. Rieger, Jr.
Haverford, Pennsylvania

GARBANZO COCKTAIL DIP

Easy
Do ahead
Freeze

Serves: 8-10
Preparing: 20 minutes

1 15-ounce can chick peas,
  rinsed and drained
1 teaspoon salt
freshly ground pepper,
  several grinds

¼ cup lemon juice
½ cup salad oil
1 to 2 large cloves garlic,
  chopped
2 tablespoons chopped parsley

Pour salt, pepper, lemon juice, salad oil and garlic into a blender. Spin until smooth. Add the peas, one-third at a time, and blend until the mixture is velvety smooth. Add parsley and spin once or twice more. Spread on melba toast.

Mrs. George M. Ahrens
Rosemont, Pennsylvania

OLD ENGLISH CANAPE

Easy
Do ahead
Freeze

Makes: 128 pieces
Preparing: 30 minutes

Use a food processor

1 jar Old English cheese
  spread (5 ounces)
2 small cans tiny shrimp,
  drained
1 stick butter
1 teaspoon lemon juice

dash Tabasco
1 tablespoon mayonnaise
8 English muffins split
1 teaspoon grated onion
  (optional)

Mix all ingredients except shrimp and muffins in food processor with steel blade. Add shrimp. Spread mixture on muffins and cut in eight pieces. Freeze on a baking sheet and then put in plastic bag. Put under broiler, without defrosting, until brown. Can substitute 1 7-ounce can of crabmeat for shrimp.

Mrs. James Humphries
Paget, Burmuda

Mary H. Campbell
Ware, Massachusetts

GRAVLAKS

Easy   *Preparing: ½ hour*
Do ahead   *Marinating: 48 hours*

A Scandinavian recipe for marinated salmon.

2 pounds fresh salmon   **2 tablespoons coarse salt**
  (cross-section from middle **1 tablespoon sugar**
  part of fish)   **1 teaspoon white pepper**
1 large bunch fresh dill

Mustard Sauce

1 tablespoon tarragon vinegar **pepper and/or paprika**
3 tablespoons oil   **1 to 3 tablespoons prepared**
½ teaspoon salt   **French mustard**
chopped dill (lots of it)

Cut salmon in half lengthwise; remove all bones. Rub in salt, sugar, pepper mixture.

Place one half, skin side down, in a glass dish; pile dill on top. Place other half of salmon on top of this, skin side up. Cover with foil. Place weights on top and refrigerate for 24-48 hours. When ready, remove dill and slice very thinly. Serve on dark bread with mustard sauce.

Mrs. Robert Yarnall
Philadelphia, Pennsylvania

PINK POPPY SEED DIP

Easy   *Preparing: 15 minutes*
Do ahead

Use House of Herbs "Pink Poppy Dip" as base.

8 ounces cream cheese   **1 teaspoon paprika**
2 tablespoons olive juice **dash of cracked pepper**
2 teaspoons "Pink Poppy **20 green olives, coarsely**
  Dip"   **chopped**
2 tablespoons finely chopped **sour cream**
  onion

Thin cream cheese with olive juice. Coarsely chop green olives. Combine remaining ingredients. Then add sour cream to achieve "dipping" consistency.

Jane Martin
Berwyn, Pennsylvania

BARAG-MEAT

Easy
Do ahead
Freeze

Makes: approximately 45
Preparing: 2 hours
Baking: 10-15 minutes

2 tablespoons butter
1 pound lean ground round
  steak
2 cloves garlic, minced
2 small onions, finely
  chopped
1 teaspoon salt, or to taste
½ teaspoon pepper

1 teaspoon curry powder
½ teaspoon allspice
¼ teaspoon cinnamon
1 6-ounce can tomato paste
1 cup water
½ pound phyllo pastry sheets
½ pound melted butter

Dampen a dish towel, spread it on the counter, and cover it with waxed paper. Unfold the phyllo leaves and set them on top of the waxed paper. There are approximately 30 leaves per pound. Keep dough stacked, and cut with scissors into 3 equal parts. Seal the first two parts in a plastic bag and refrigerate to allow dough to remain soft and pliable.

In a skillet melt butter and sauté meat, garlic and onions, stirring constantly until meat is well browned. Add spices. Stir in tomato paste mixed with water and bring to a boil, stirring. Cover and cook over low heat for 20 minutes, stirring occasionally. Cool and drain off excess liquid. Cut phyllo sheets into 3 sections. Brush one sheet at a time with melted butter. Place one heaping teaspoon of the meat mixture at one end of the sheet, fold in sides and roll up like a tiny jelly roll. Place on cookie sheet and brush with melted butter. Keep phyllo not being used covered at all times with wax paper and a damp towel. When all pastry and filling are used, freeze the rolls. While still frozen, bake in a preheated 425° oven for 10 to 15 minutes or until rolls are a golden brown. Cool a little and serve warm.

Mrs. Joseph B. Erwin
Berwyn, Pennsylvania

CHEESE OLIVE SPREAD

Easy
Do ahead

Serves: 10
Preparing: 30 minutes
Chilling time

8 ounces cream cheese
8 ounces blue cheese
4 ounces butter
6 ounces pitted ripe olives

3 tablespoons chopped chives,
  fresh or freeze-dried
2 tablespoons brandy
3 ounces slivered almonds

Allow cheeses and butter to soften at room temperature. Chop olives in quarters or smaller. Mix first six ingredients thoroughly. Shape in a mound on serving plate. Place in refrigerator to chill. Place almonds in fry pan with small amount of butter. Toast over medium heat until golden brown, stirring frequently. Allow to cool. Spread almonds over chilled cheese mixture. Serve with your favorite crackers.

Julia de Pasquale
Philadelphia, Pennsylvania

FIVE CHEESE BALL

Easy   *Serves: 25*
Do ahead   *Preparing: 5 minutes*
Freeze

½ **pound blue cheese**   ¼ **teaspoon salt**
½ **pound Mozzarella**   ⅛ **teaspoon pepper**
½ **pound Ricotta**   ½ **pint heavy cream**
½ **pound Gorgonzola**   ½ **teaspoon Worcestershire**
½ **pound Cheshire**   **sauce**

Blend all ingredients together except cream. Then blend in cream slowly. Season. Pour into ice cream mold and freeze at least two hours. Remove from mold ½ hour before serving. Serve with water biscuits.

Mrs. James Birney
Faribault, Minnesota

HONEY CURRY DIP

Easy   *Serves: 12*
Do ahead   *Preparing: 15 minutes*
                                        Chilling: 3 hours

1 **pint mayonnaise**   1 **tablespoon lemon juice**
3 **tablespoons honey**   1 **tablespoon curry**
3 **tablespoons catsup**   **salt and pepper to taste**
3 **tablespoons grated onion,** 9 **drops of Tabasco sauce**
   or less to taste

Mix all the above ingredients and refrigerate for several hours before serving. Serve with Munchos or potato chips.

Mrs. Wallace H. Wallace
Wayne, Pennsylvania

BABA GHANNOOJ
(Arabian Eggplant Dip)

Average
Do ahead
Freeze

Serves: 8-10
Preparing: 40 minutes to 1 hour

1 eggplant, 1-1¼ pound
¼ cup fresh lemon juice
2 tablespoons "Taratoor" sauce,
1 large clove garlic, peeled and finely chopped

1 teaspoon salt
1 tablespoon olive oil
¼ cup finely chopped parsley or 1 teaspoon dried parsley flakes

"Taratoor" sauce

½ cup fresh lemon juice
¾ to 1 cup cold water
1 cup sesame tahini (can be purchased in most gourmet or health food shops)

3 cloves garlic, peeled and finely chopped
1 teaspoon salt

Taratoor sauce—In a deep bowl mash the garlic with the back of a large wooden spoon or pestle. Stir in tahini. With wooden spoon beat in ½ cup of the cold water and lemon juice and salt. Still beating, add up to ½ cup more water, one tablespoon at a time until the sauce has the consistency of thick mayonnaise. Keeps well in tight jar.

Eggplant
Prick the eggplant in 3 or 4 places with the tines of a long handled fork so the steam escapes. Roast the eggplant whole over a gas flame turning it once or twice until done. If you have an electric stove, pierce the eggplant and place it on a baking sheet and broil it 4 inches from the heat for 20 minutes, turning it to char on all sides. When it's done, cut in half lengthwise and let it cool to the point you can pick up a half in your hand. Peel it. Try to get off as much of the burnt particles of skin as you can. Let it rest for a few minutes and then drain it. Run a sharp knife through it several times and then mash it to a fairly smooth pulp with a fork. Mix in the lemon juice, Taratoor, garlic and salt. At this point it can be frozen for up to several weeks and then thawed and completed just prior to serving. To serve, spread the purée on a large dinner plate; sprinkle the top with the olive oil, onions, and parsley. Serve with Pita bread, crackers or vegetable sticks.

Sidney Curtiss
Philadelphia, Pennsylvania

ASPARAGUS-STUFFED EGGS

Easy
Do Ahead
Best if done 24 hours before serving.

Serves: Flexible
Preparing: 30 minutes

hard-boiled eggs (as many as you need to serve, plus 2 extra eggs for every 3 you serve)
canned asparagus (1 spear to each 3 eggs)

mayonnaise and catsup in equal parts
pitted black olives, sliced in half
parsley flakes
seasoned salt

Slice eggs in half lengthwise; chop yolks finely, reserving extra yolks. Chop asparagus finely (use scissors). Mix asparagus with chopped yolks; add catsup and mayonnaise equally, 1 teaspoon at a time, until moist but still firm. Season to taste with salt. Stuff eggs. Sprinkle tops with reserved egg yolks and parsley. Garnish each with ½ olive.

Mrs. Robert Alan Swift
Bryn Mawr, Pennsylvania

FRIED FRENCHY

Easy

Serves: 6
Preparing: 10 minutes
Cooking: 30 minutes

This recipe would be good for a Brie or Camembert that you might have kept too long or is dried out.

1 8-ounce Brie or Camembert
flour
bread crumbs

2 to 3 tablespoons butter
1 egg, beaten

Roll cheese in flour and dip in beaten egg and roll in bread crumbs. Melt butter over medium heat in a small pan and fry cheese, turning to brown on all sides. Be very careful at all times not to puncture the cheese. Serve warm with assorted crackers.

Betts McCoy
The Villanova Cheese Shop
Villanova, Pennsylvania

CURRIED EGG RING WITH PRAWNS

Average
Partial do ahead

Serves: 8-10
Preparing: 30 minutes
Chilling: overnight

12 hard-boiled eggs
½ pint jellied stock or canned
  consommé

8 ounces heavy cream
1 tablespoon gelatine
salt

Curry sauce
2 tablespoons olive oil
1 tablespoon curry powder
1 chopped onion
1 clove garlic, crushed

1 teaspoon apricot jam
2 tablespoons tomato purée
2 slices lemon
¼ pint water

Garnish
½ pound prawns
2 tablespoons vinaigrette
  dressing

½ to 1 cucumber, sliced
parsley, chopped

Curry sauce: Sauté onion in oil with the crushed garlic. Add curry powder and mix well with the onion. Cook together for a few minutes, stirring well. Add tomato purée and water with lemon slices. Cook together for 7 to 10 minutes, and stir in the jam. Bring to a boil. When cool, *strain* into a jam jar with an air-tight lid. It will keep in refrigerator for about a week. Chop hard-boiled eggs coarsely and add salt. Heat consommé with gelatine, stirring well. Pour it into a shallow dish and put in freezer. Remove when nearly set. Whip cream lightly and add the consommé, blending well together. Stir in the chopped eggs, then the curry sauce. Grease a 9½" ring mold and put in the mixture. Allow to set in the refrigerator overnight. Unmold the ring by quickly dipping the sides in hot water, having first loosened the sides with a spatula. Toss the prawns in the dressing and fill the center of the egg mold. Sprinkle with parsley and decorate with slices of cucumber.

Mrs. Peter Few-Brown
Winkfield, Berkshire, England

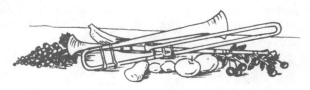

EGG MOLD HAYDEN

Easy
Do ahead

Serves: 12
Preparing: 30 minutes
Chilling: 1 hour

10 hard-boiled eggs, slightly
   cooled
8 ounces cream cheese
2 to 3 scallions or green
   onions
1 teaspoon prepared yellow
   mustard

¼ cup mayonnaise
1 tablespoon lemon juice
1 teaspoon celery seed
1 teaspoon salt
dash Tabasco
caviar (optional)
parsley, chopped

Mix cheese, mustard, mayonnaise, lemon juice, Tabasco and seasonings together. Add chopped onion and eggs and blend briefly. Line small mold with plastic wrap and set small container in bottom to allow for addition of caviar at time of serving. Sprinkle with chopped parsley or desired garnish before adding egg mixture. Unmold at serving time and fill cavity with caviar. Serve with choice of crackers or small rye rounds. This may also be served unmolded, in a dish, as a vegetable dip. Will keep, refrigerated, two weeks.

Food processor method: Put cream cheese, mustard, Tabasco and seasonings in bowl of processor, fitted with steel blade. Add onion, cut in pieces, and eggs, quartered, and process briefly on and off. (Eliminate mayonnaise and lemon as it becomes too creamy to mold.)

Mrs. J. P. Hayden
Cincinnati, Ohio

PEANUT BUTTER STICKS

Easy
Do ahead
Freeze

Serves: 10
Preparing: 30 minutes
Baking: 20 minutes

6 slices white bread, with
   crust removed
½ cup smooth peanut butter

¼ cup Wesson oil
graham crackers

Cut each slice of bread into approximately 5 strips and place on cookie sheet. Bake in 250° oven for about 20 minutes. Mix together the peanut butter and oil and roll the bread sticks in this mixture. Crush graham crackers and roll the moist bread sticks in crumbs and place in a tin. They will keep for a very long time.

E. Jane Thiry
Jenkintown, Pennsylvania

BLUE CHEESE CHEESECAKE

Complicated
Do ahead

Serves: 12-20
Preparing: 1 hour
Baking: 1 hour and 40 minutes
Resting: 3 hours

Basic cheesecake:
3½ 8-ounce packages of cream cheese, at room temperature

4 large eggs
⅓ cup heavy cream

Blue-cheese cheesecake:
basic cheesecake
⅓ cup fine bread crumbs
¼ cup Parmesan cheese
½ pound bacon

1 medium onion, finely chopped
½ pound blue cheese, crumbled
salt and freshly ground pepper
3 drops Tabasco sauce

Preheat oven to 300°. Prepare basic cheesecake; place cream cheese, eggs and heavy cream in bowl of electric mixer and beat ingredients until smooth. Set aside. Butter a metal cheesecake pan (8″ wide and 3″ deep). Sprinkle with combined breadcrumbs and Parmesan cheese. Shake crumbs around bottom and sides until coated. Shake out excess crumbs. Sauté bacon until crisp and chop finely. Sauté the onion in 1 tablespoon bacon fat until wilted. To the basic mixture add bacon, onion, blue cheese, salt and pepper and Tabasco, blending thoroughly. Pour the batter into prepared pan and shake gently to level the mixture. Set pan into slightly larger pan and pour boiling water into it to a depth of 2 inches. Bake in preheated oven 1 hour and 40 minutes. Turn off oven and let cake sit in oven 1 hour longer. Lift cake out of water bath and place on rack to cool 2 hours before unmolding.

Mrs. Robert P. Tyson
West Chester, Pennsylvania

DAFFODIL DIP

Easy
Do ahead

Makes: 2 cups
Preparing: 20 minutes
Chilling time

½ cup mayonnaise
1 8-ounce package cream cheese
½ cup chopped parsley
1 hard boiled egg

2 tablespoons chopped onion
1 small clove garlic, minced
1 tablespoon anchovy paste (scant)
dash of pepper

Add mayonnaise to softened cream cheese; blend well. Add parsley, chopped egg white, onion, garlic, anchovy paste, and pepper. Mix well. When ready to serve, sprinkle with grated egg yolk. Serve with assorted raw vegetables.

Mrs. Samuel Ballam
Haverford, Pennsylvania

CURRIED OLIVE CANAPES

Easy
Do ahead

Makes: 32 small squares
Preparing: 20 minutes

1 4½-ounce can ripe olives, chopped
¼ cup grated onion
¾ cup grated cheddar cheese

¼ cup mayonnaise
¼ teaspoon curry powder
8 slices thin bread

Mix above ingredients together. Remove crusts from bread and toast lightly on one side. Cut into quarters. Spread mixture on untoasted side. Heat under broiler until bubbly, 2 or 3 minutes. Watch closely.

Mrs. Walter Locher
Springfield, Pennsylvania

Mrs. Thomas S. Johnston
West Chester, Pennsylvania

ZUCCHINI APPETIZER

Easy
Do ahead
Freeze

Serves: 12 to 16
Preparing: 20 minutes
Baking: 25 minutes

3 to 4 cups grated zucchini (2 large or 4 small ones)
1 cup Bisquick
½ cup finely chopped onion
½ cup vegetable oil
1 clove garlic

½ teaspoon dried marjoram or oregano
4 medium eggs, lightly beaten
salt and pepper to taste
parsley, snipped

Heat oven to 350°. Oil oblong pan, 13"x9"x2". Mix all ingredients; spread in pan. Bake until golden brown, about 25 minutes. Cut into 2"x1" pieces for approximately 24 appetizers. Garnish with snipped parsley.

Ella R. Torrey
Philadelphia, Pennsylvania

PICKLED FLYING FISH

Average   *Preparing: 1 hour plus*
Do ahead   *Marinating: 7 days*

Use as hors d'oeurves on crackers or rye bread or as first course on lettuce.
Keeps for days.

8 boned flying fish or   **1 cup milk or light cream**
substitute turbot or any   **grated rind of 2 limes**
firm fish   **½ cup vinegar**
juice of 2 limes   **1 stalk celery, chopped**
1½ cups water   **2 carrots, thinly sliced**
2 bay leaves   **2 onions, thinly sliced**
6 crushed peppercorns   **2 teaspoons capers**
2 tablespoons parsley,   **sour cream**
chopped   **bit of fresh onion**

Cut fish into bite-sized pieces. Salt lightly; drizzle with lime juice; add a grind
of pepper. Combine vinegar and water; bring to boil. Add bay leaves,
peppercorns, parsley, celery and carrots. Simmer 20 minutes. Arrange fish
in deep porcelain or glass dish; add onion rings. Add milk or cream to
marinade and pour over fish. Add lime rind and capers. Cover and marinate
refrigerated for seven days. Turn gently with fork every two days. Lift out fish
and vegetables, discard bay leaves and marinade. Mix with sour cream;
add a bit of fresh onion and serve.

Joseph McLaughlin
Robert Thompson
Barbados, West Indies

BOURSIN

Easy   *Serves: 6-8*
Do ahead   *Preparing: 10 minutes*

8 ounces cream cheese   **½ tablespoon oregano, or to**
2 tablespoons butter   **taste**
½ teaspoon lemon juice, or   **⅛ teaspoon cayenne**
to taste   **⅛ teaspoon salt**
2 cloves garlic, mashed   **2 tablespoons parsley, minced**

Combine all ingredients. Can be mixed by hand, but easier in food processor. Serve on crackers.

Bettina Dilworth
New York, New York

SPINACH STRUDEL

Complicated
Do ahead
Freeze

Serves: 10
Preparing: 30 minutes
Baking: 35 minutes

1 package frozen strudel
   leaves
2 pounds fresh spinach
½ cup bread crumbs
⅔ cup parsley leaves, firmly
   packed (⅓ cup minced)
12 scallions (½ cup minced)
4 tablespoons butter

6 ounces Feta cheese, crumbled
   or grated
4 tablespoons fresh dill (or 2
   tablespoons dried dill)
4 large eggs
salt
freshly ground pepper
4 ounces butter

Thaw strudel leaves by removing from freezer 4 hours before using.

Spinach: Wash, cut off stems. Cook quickly in uncovered pot with only the water clinging to leaves. As soon as spinach wilts, refresh in cold water, drain, pat dry and purée.

Filling: Mince parsley and scallions. Sauté in 2 tablespoons butter until wilted. Shred cheese; chop dill and beat eggs. Add parsley, scallions, cheese, dill, spinach and seasonings.

Strudel: Make bread crumbs. Melt 4 ounces butter, and set both aside. Place a strudel leaf on a damp towel (cover remaining leaves with plastic wrap to keep fresh). Brush leaf with melted butter; sprinkle lightly with bread crumbs. Repeat 3 more times as 3 more leaves are added in layers. Place ⅓ of spinach mixture ¼ inch from edge along longer side of dough, (which should be placed nearest you). Roll like a jelly roll, with the assistance of a towel. Place on buttered baking sheet. Brush top lightly with melted butter. This recipe makes 3 strudel rolls, so repeat 2 more times. Bake in preheated 375° oven for 30 to 35 minutes, or until browned.

Unused strudel leaves can be refrozen. The unbaked strudels may be carefully wrapped in aluminum foil and frozen. To serve as appetizers, slice about ½ inch thick while frozen, before baking. Add additional 10 to 15 minutes to baking time.

Mrs. J. P. Hayden
Cincinnati, Ohio

Spread party rye with butter, sprinkle with oregano and toast at 200° for 1 hour.

DILLWORTH MEAT BALLS

Easy
Do ahead
Freeze

Serves: 20
Preparing: 20 minutes

1 lb. hamburger
1 envelope Lipton onion soup
  mix

1 egg
¼ cup seasoned Italian bread
  crumbs

Sauce
1 bottle hot ketchup
1 jar currant jelly

1 bottle regular ketchup

Shape meat into balls and fry. Make sauce. Put meatballs into sauce and serve in chafing dish.

Mrs. John T. Dillworth
Wayne, Pennsylvania

PRINCETON PATÉ

Average
Do ahead

Preparing: 15 minutes

¾ pound chicken livers
3 tablespoons bourbon
¾ cup butter
2 tablespoons chopped onion
¼ teaspoon grated nutmeg
⅛ teaspoon ground cloves

chicken bouillon (to cover livers
  for cooking)
½ teaspoon dry mustard
¼ teaspoon salt
pepper to taste

Cut livers in small pieces and remove fat. Cook slowly in chicken bouillon (small amount). Drain. Put livers and all other ingredients in food processor with steel blade, or use blender, and process until smooth. Pack in two small crocks or tureens and refrigerate until firm.

Mrs. J. Mahlon Buck, Jr.
Haverford, Pennsylvania

BEOREG (Armenian Cheese Pastry)

Average
Do ahead
Freeze

Makes: 50 pastries
Preparing: 1½-2 hours
Baking: 15 minutes

1 pound thin sheets phyllo
 dough
1 pound butter, melted
1 pound Monterey Jack
 cheese, grated

½ pound sharp cheese, grated
½ cup chopped parsley
2 eggs, beaten
pinch of Accent and baking soda

Mix all ingredients together except phyllo dough and butter. Unfold dough. Cut in half. (You will have about 50 sheets.) Put first half in slightly damp towel, wrap and put in refrigerator to allow dough to remain soft and pliable. Keep dough stacked on work board. Using one sheet at a time, brush sheet sparsely with melted butter and place cheese mixture toward top of dough. Fold top of sheet over mixture, then fold sides. Bottom of sheet will be folded about 1½ inches. Roll up and place on cookie sheet side by side. When the cookie sheet is filled, place waxed paper over first layer and place another layer of Beoreg until finished. Freeze. Use these as needed. Take directly from freezer and bake 15 minutes in 375° oven. Allow each guest 2 to 3.

Mrs. Joseph H. Stein, Jr.
Malibu, California

SEAFOOD-SPINACH COMBO

Easy
Partial do ahead

Serves: 10
Preparing: 20 minutes

1 pound cooked scallops, cut
 in quarters if large (or 1
 pound crabmeat)
1 cup Hellman's mayonnaise
1 tablespoon minced parsley
1 tablespoon Maggi
 seasoning
1 teaspoon onion juice
1 teaspoon dry mustard

½ teaspoon curry powder
1 dash red pepper (or Tabasco)
1 dash black pepper
2 or 3 slices pimiento, chopped
½ bunch scallions, chopped
1 package frozen chopped
 spinach, cooked and well
 drained
optional—1 can mussels

Mix everything, except seafood, together several hours ahead of time. Add seafood ½ hour or so before serving.

Mrs. Nathaniel Apter
McKeesport, Pennsylvania

SAUERKRAUT BALLS

Easy

Makes: 50
Preparing: ½ hour
Chilling: 1 hour

⅔ cup finely chopped
  smoked ham
⅔ cup finely chopped cooked
  corned beef
⅓ cup ground pork sausage
3 tablespoons minced onions
1 tablespoon finely chopped
  fresh parsley
3 tablespoons shortening
⅔ cup all-purpose flour

½ cup milk
¼ teaspoon salt
¼ teaspoon dry mustard
1⅔ cups firmly packed, finely
  chopped, drained, sauerkraut
½ cup all-purpose flour
melted shortening for deep fat
  frying
1 cup dry bread crumbs

Egg dip

1 egg
¾ cup milk

½ teaspoon salt

Cook ham, corned beef, sausage, onions and parsley in shortening over medium heat until sausage is golden brown. Add flour. Cook over low heat about 5 minutes, stirring constantly. Add milk, salt and dry mustard. Cook over low heat until mixture is thickened. Remove from heat. Stir in sauerkraut and mix well. Chill mixture thoroughly. Using a tablespoon, shape little rounds of mixture into balls (about ½ ounce each). Roll lightly in flour. Combine egg, milk and salt to make egg dip. Dip the floured sauerkraut balls into the egg dip and drain. Roll in bread crumbs; chill until ready to cook. Fry in deep fat at 375° for 1½ to 2 minutes or until golden brown. Drain. Serve hot. Makes approximately 50 ½ ounce sauerkraut balls.

K. Carol Carlson, Vice president
ARA Services, Inc.
Philadelphia, Pennsylvania

CRAB FINGER ROLLS

Average
Do ahead
Freeze

Makes: 80
Preparing: 1 hour
Baking: 5-7 minutes
Broiling: 2 minutes

4 ounces butter
8 ounces cream cheese

1 pound crab meat
2 loaves thinly sliced white bread

In double boiler melt butter, blend in cream cheese and cool. Add flaked crabmeat. Remove crusts from bread, roll each slice with rolling pin until quite thin. Spread on mixture. Roll up each slice and cut in half. Freeze on trays until firm (unwrapped). Pack in plastic bags.

To serve: Thaw 30-60 minutes. Place rolls on baking tray, brush with melted butter. Bake at 400° 5-7 minutes and broil to brown for 2 minutes.

Mrs. George S. Fabian
Bryn Mawr, Pennsylvania

SHRIMP BUTTER ROUNDS

Easy   *Preparing: 30 minutes*
Do ahead
Freeze

2 cans small shrimp   **1½ sticks butter**
1 tablespoon minced dry   **4 tablespoons mayonnaise**
**   onion**   **1 8-ounce package cream cheese**
3 or 4 tablespoons lemon   **salt to taste**
**   juice**

Soften cream cheese and butter. Mix thoroughly and then add all ingredients but shrimp. Drain and crumble shrimp and add to mixture. Spread thickly on toasted bread rounds. Heat in 350° oven for 20 minutes. (Can be served cold without baking.) If freezing, do so before baking.

The Committee

CHICKEN WINGS

Easy   *Serves: Allow 3 per serving*
Do ahead   *Preparing: 5 minutes*
                                             Baking: 1½ hours

1 cup soy sauce   **1 cup brown sugar**
1 cup white wine   **50 chicken wings**

Mix above marinade. Lay chicken wings flat on a jelly roll pan and cover with marinade. Bake about an hour and a half at 400° until brown and crisp. No need to turn.

Mrs. Edward A. Kammerer
Philadelphia, Pennsylvania

ASPARAGUS ROLLS

Easy
Do ahead
Freeze

Makes: 88 to 100
Preparing: 30 minutes

1 large loaf of thinly sliced white bread, Pepperidge Farm or Arnold's
8 ounces cream cheese, well softened

4 ounces blue cheese, well softened
½ pound melted butter
1 package asparagus spears, cook as directed on package

Count asparagus spears and cut crusts off the same number of pieces of bread. Roll over each piece of bread with a pastry roller to flatten well. Blend softened cream cheese and blue cheese together and spread on each piece of bread. Place an asparagus spear on each piece of bread and roll the bread around the spear. Put some melted butter in shallow dish. Replace the butter as needed. Dip rolled bread in melted butter (do this quickly as the bread soaks the butter very quickly). Place the rolls on cookie sheet and freeze for about an hour. Cut each rolled bread into four pieces and put these in a plastic bag and place in freezer. When ready to use, place in 350° oven for 25 minutes or until golden brown. After cooking, you may use the broiler for a few seconds to get top brown.

Adrienne D. Pacheco
Langhorne, Pennsylvania

Helen R. Kroesser
Ocean City, New Jersey

ARTICHOKES RAMAKI

Easy
Do ahead

Serves: 24
Preparing: 15 minutes
Broiling: 8 minutes

1 package frozen artichoke hearts

onion salt
12 slices bacon

Cook according to package directions one package frozen artichoke hearts. Drain and sprinkle with onion salt. Cut crosswise 12 slices of bacon. Wrap each half slice around artichoke heart. Refrigerate. When ready to serve, broil 6 inches from heat about eight minutes, turning once. Serve on toothpicks.

Radford Beasley
Philadelphia, Pennsylvania

TAPENADE

Easy
Do ahead

Serves: 6
Preparing: 10 minutes

½ cup black olives, oil cured
  if available
¼ cup capers
¼ cup anchovies (6 fillets)
¼ cup tuna
1 clove garlic, peeled and
  crushed

freshly ground pepper
½ teaspoon dry mustard
juice of one lemon
2 tablespoons fresh basil (if not
  available, use parsley)
olive oil as needed

Place all ingredients except the olive oil in the blender or food processor and mix to a paste. Add olive oil if using as a dip. Place in bowl and cover with plastic wrap. This mixture can be used as a spread with fresh French bread or thinned with olive oil as a dip for crudites. Will keep in refrigerator for 10 days.

Mrs. David Acton
Haverford, Pennsylvania

A quickie! Spread a Triscuit with herb cheese and top with a slice of olive. Broil until bubbly and serve.

CAVIAR MOUSSE

Easy
Do ahead

Serves: 20-30
Preparing: 20 minutes
Chilling: 2 hours

9 hard-boiled eggs
1½ envelopes unflavored
  gelatine
3 tablespoons fresh lemon
  juice

1½ cups mayonnaise
1½ teaspoons Sauce Diable
1 tablespoon minced onion
2 3¼-ounce jars lump caviar
3 tablespoons vermouth

Lightly oil 4 cup mold. Rice or finely chop eggs. Place in large mixing bowl. Combine gelatine, lemon juice and vermouth in top of double boiler and heat until gelatine is dissolved. Add mayonnaise, sauce and onion to eggs. Fold in gelatine, blend carefully. Fold in caviar carefully. Pour into mold. Chill. Serve with thin pumpernickel or rusk crackers.

Mrs. R. J. McKain
Rosemont, Pennsylvania

SHRIMP-DILL APPETIZER

Easy
Do ahead

Makes: 24 appetizer portions; 6-8 if
made in a pan for a first course
Preparing: 45 minutes
Chilling: 4 hours

2 envelopes unflavored
  gelatine
1½ cups tomato juice
2 tablespoons lemon juice
¼ cup chili sauce
¼ teaspoon Tabasco

1 teaspoon Worcestershire sauce
1 tablespoon dried dill leaf
1 pint sour cream
2 cups (¾ pound) finely
  chopped, cooked and shelled
  shrimp*

Sprinkle gelatine over tomato juice in saucepan. Place over moderate heat and stir constantly until gelatine is dissolved, 2 to 3 minutes. Remove from heat. Stir in lemon juice, chili sauce, Worcestershire sauce, Tabasco and dill. When mixture is cool, stir in sour cream and beat until smooth. Stir in shrimp. Turn into 5-cup mold or a 9″ square pan. Chill until firm. Unmold; garnish with whole shrimp and sprigs of dill, if desired. (*1¼ pounds fresh shrimp yields approximately ¾ pound cooked and shelled.)

Mrs. Stevan Simich
Wayne, Pennsylvania

JELLIED ROQUEFORT MOUSSE

Easy
Do ahead

Serves: 8
Preparing: 30 minutes
Chilling time

1 tablespoon gelatine
¼ cup cold water
1 cup heavy cream, whipped
½ cup Roquefort or blue
  cheese

8 ounces cream cheese
¼ teaspoon salt
1 teaspoon onion juice
¼ teaspoon paprika

Mix the gelatine and cold water and melt over hot water. Mix the cheese and seasonings with a little milk or cream to make smooth. Add this to the melted gelatine, then fold in the whipped cream. Pour into 1½ quart ring mold and chill until set. Fill center with watercress. This is delicious served as an appetizer with crackers or is lovely served with lettuce and pear halves, sprinkled with French dressing for luncheon.

Mrs. Dana Fernald
Malvern, Pennsylvania

Do, Re, Mi

breads

SPICY PEACH NUT BREAD

Easy

Makes: 20 slices or more
Preparing: 30 minutes
Baking: 60-70 minutes

2 cups flour
⅔ cup sugar
2 teaspoons baking powder
½ teaspoon salt
½ teaspoon soda
¼ teaspoon ground cloves
2 tablespoons margarine

16 ounce can (2 cups) sliced
  peaches
½ cup reserved peach syrup
2 eggs
1 cup chopped walnuts
powdered sugar glaze (optional)

Preheat oven to 350°. Lightly spoon flour into measuring cup, level off. Blend all ingredients at low speed until moistened. Beat 2 minutes at medium speed. Stir batter and pour into generously greased and floured loaf pan. Bake 60 to 70 minutes until toothpick comes out clean. Immediately remove from pan. Cool completely. If desired, drizzle with powdered sugar glaze. Store tightly wrapped in refrigerator.

Mrs. C. Wilbur Ufford
Haverford, Pennsylvania

IRISH SODA BREAD

Easy

Serves: 20
Preparing: 30 minutes
Baking: 1 hour

4 cups flour
1 cup sugar
5 teaspoons baking powder
¼ teaspoon baking soda
1 teaspoon salt
3 eggs, beaten

2 ounces butter, melted
1 teaspoon caraway seeds
1 cup raisins, (coat raisins with
  flour before adding to recipe)
1 cup milk, (more if batter is too
  stiff)

Sift flour with baking powder and salt and baking soda; add raisins, sugar and caraway seeds. Fluff with your hands until mixed. Make a well in the mixture and add milk, butter and eggs. Mix with spoon until everything is moist. Do not beat. Bake at 350° for one hour, using a greased 10¼" cast iron frying pan. Test center with straw to be sure it is completely cooked before removing from oven.

Mrs. Austin Kelly
Philadelphia, Pennsylvania

CORNISH SAFFRON BREAD OR BUNS

Complicated
Do ahead
Freeze

Serves: 3 loaves (braided)
Preparing: 3 hours
Baking: 20 minutes

2 packages active dry yeast
3 cups lukewarm milk
1 teaspoon saffron
1½ cups sugar
¼ teaspoon salt
2 eggs
1 cup melted butter
8 cups all-purpose flour

1 cup seedless raisins
⅓ cup chopped candied lemon
   peel
⅓ cup citron
⅓ cup walnuts (optional)
2 cups currants
2 tablespoons sugar

In a small bowl dissolve yeast in ½ cup lukewarm milk. In a large bowl mix 2½ cups milk, saffron, sugar, salt, 1 egg, butter and small amount of flour. Add yeast and remaining flour. Now add fruits and nuts. Beat with wooden spoon until firm and smooth. Sprinkle with flour. Cover with a towel, let rise in a warm place until doubled in bulk, about 2 hours. Turn out on floured board and knead until smooth. Divide into 9 portions. Roll each piece out with hands until 14" long. Make a loaf by braiding 3 pieces, tuck under ends. Place each loaf on buttered baking sheet or make buns. Cover and let rise. Pre-heat oven, 375° for bread, 425° for buns. Brush with slightly beaten egg, sprinkle with sugar. Bake loaves 15-20 minutes, bake buns 10-12 minutes, slightly longer at high altitudes.

Barbara Bailey
Vail, Colorado

PUMPKIN BREAD

Easy

Preparing: 15 minutes
Baking: 1½ hours

1½ cups sugar
1 teaspoon soda
¼ teaspoon baking powder
¾ teaspoon salt
½ teaspoon cloves
½ teaspoon nutmeg
½ teaspoon cinnamon

1⅔ cups flour
2 eggs
½ cup oil
1 cup canned pumpkin
½ cup water
½ cup chopped nuts
½ cup chopped dates

Sift together the first 8 ingredients. Add eggs, oil, pumpkin and water and mix with beater. Add nuts and dates. Bake at 350° for 1½ hours.

Mrs. Walter Mondale
Washington, D.C.

ALL-BRAN BREAD

Easy
Freeze

Makes: 1 loaf
Preparing: 2 hours
Baking: 1 hour and 10 minutes

1 cup milk
1 cup seedless raisins
1 cup light brown sugar

1 cup All-Bran
1 cup self-rising flour

Mix milk, raisins, sugar and All-Bran in a bowl and leave for 2 hours. Mix in self-rising flour and put dough in a buttered loaf pan. Bake in middle of oven at 350° for 1 hour and 10 minutes. Cool slightly before removing from pan.

Mrs. Alexander Cleland
Musselburgh, Scotland

BEER BREAD

Easy
Do ahead

Serves: 10-12
Preparing: 15 minutes
Baking: 30 minutes

4 cups Bisquick
3 tablespoons sugar

1 12-ounce can of beer at room temperature

Mix all ingredients. Pour into 2 small greased loaf pans. Allow bread to rise for at least 10 minutes. Bake at 375° for 30 minutes.

The Committee

CRANBERRY NUT BREAD

Easy
Do ahead
Freeze

Serves: 4-6
Preparing: 20-30 minutes
Baking: 50-55 minutes

1 egg
1 cup chopped walnuts
1 cup sugar
2 cups sifted all-purpose flour
½ teaspoon salt
½ teaspoon baking soda

1½ teaspoons baking powder
1 tablespoon grated orange rind and fresh orange juice to equal ¾ cup
2 tablespoons shortening
1 cup cranberries, chopped in blender

Sift dry ingredients. Add rind, juice and shortening. Add egg. Mix well. Add walnuts and cranberries. Place in greased loaf pan (9"x5"x3") and bake at 325° for 1 hour. Can use smaller loaf pans and bake about 50-55 minutes.

Mrs. Theodore H. Ashford
Wilmington, Delaware

APRICOT BREAD

Easy
Freeze

Makes: 1 loaf
Preparing: 30 minutes
Baking: 45 minutes

¾ cup dried apricots
¾ cup milk
1 tablespoon butter
½ cup sugar
1 egg

1 teaspoon salt
½ teaspoon soda
1¼ cups flour
1 teaspoon baking powder
grated peel of one orange

Chop apricots and heat in milk, (do not boil); add butter. Set aside to cool. Add sugar, salt and soda to beaten egg. Add apricots and milk mixture. Stir and add to flour and baking powder. Add grated orange peel and mix quickly. Put into greased and floured bread tin. Bake at 350° about 45 minutes, until tester comes out clean.

The Committee

BISCUIT MIX

Easy
Do ahead

Makes up to 60 biscuits
Preparing: 5 minutes
Baking: 12 minutes

Much less expensive than purchased mix. Lasts indefinitely.

3 tablespoons baking powder
6 cups sifted flour

1 tablespoon salt
1 cup vegetable shortening

Sift dry ingredients together. Cut in shortening until mixture looks like coarse corn meal. Store in covered container. No refrigeration required. *Yield:* 6½ cups mix, or, enough for 60 biscuits. *To Use:* add ¾ cup milk to 2½ cups mix. Blend, roll out ½" thick. Cut and bake in 425° oven for 12 minutes.

Adelaide F. Cummings
West Falmouth, Massachusetts

APPLE KUCHEN

Easy

Preparing: 15 minutes
Baking: 35 minutes

1 package yellow cake mix
½ cup butter, softened
1 20-ounce can pie apples,
  drained

1 teaspoon cinnamon
2 egg yolks
1 cup sour cream

Preheat oven to 350°. Cut butter into cake mix (dry) until crumbly. Pat mixture lightly into ungreased 13"x9"x2" pan, building up slightly at edges. Bake 10 minutes. Arrange apple slices on warm crust. Sprinkle cinnamon on apples. Blend sour cream and egg yolks and drizzle over apples. Bake 25 minutes or until edges are lightly brown. Do not overcook. Serve warm with a scoop of ice cream.

Mrs. Danilo M. De Dominicis
Wayne, Pennsylvania

To prevent a hump from rising in the center of quick breads, cut vertically down the center of the dough when it starts to rise during baking.

CRUSTY CHEESE BREAD

Average
Do ahead
Freeze

Serves: 6-8
Preparing: 2 hours
Baking: 25-35 minutes

1 yeast cake
½ cup scalded milk
3 cups flour
1 teaspoon salt
2 tablespoons sugar

⅔ cup cold or warm mashed
  potatoes
⅓ cup butter, melted
1 cup shredded cheese
2 eggs

Soften yeast cake in scalded milk, cooled. Let stand 5 minutes. Mix flour, salt, and sugar. Combine in large bowl mashed potatoes, melted butter, shredded cheese, eggs, yeast and milk. Blend in dry ingredients and mix. Knead on floured board until smooth and satiny. Cover and let rise until double. Then knead again. Shape into long roll and fit into greased 9" ring mold. Let rise. Bake at 375° for 25 to 35 minutes.

Mrs. E. N. Read
Chevy Chase, Maryland

COFFEE RING

Easy

Do ahead

Freeze

Makes: 3 dozen

Preparing: 20 minutes

2 hours to completion

2 cups milk
½ cup sugar
½ cup shortening
1 teaspoon salt
6 cups sifted flour

2 packages yeast
½ cup melted butter
2 tablespoons cinnamon
1½ cups sugar
1 cup chopped pecans

Place milk, sugar and shortening in saucepan. Scald milk. Remove from heat. Add salt, and cool to lukewarm. Dissolve yeast in two tablespoons warm water. Add to mixture. Beat in flour and knead. Let rise to double bulk and knead again. Break dough into balls the size of large marbles. Dip into melted butter. Roll in combined sugar and cinnamon mixture, and then in pecans. Place loosely in greased cake pans. Bake at 350° for 45 minutes. Turn pan upside down on cake plate and cool.

Mrs. Henry Wendt
Devon, Pennsylvania

DIFFERENT BANANA BREAD

Easy

Do ahead

Freeze

Preparing: 30 minutes

Baking: 1 hour and 15 minutes

½ cup shortening or 1 stick
  margarine
1 cup sugar
2 eggs
1½ cups mashed bananas (3
  to 5 bananas)
¾ cup grated carrots

2 cups sifted flour
1 teaspoon salt
½ teaspoon soda
1 teaspoon vanilla
⅔ cup chopped nuts
⅔ cup snipped prunes
1 teaspoon lemon juice

Cream shortening; add sugar slowly; cream well. Add eggs and beat. Mix in bananas, carrots and snipped prunes. Then add flour, salt and soda which have been sifted together. Add nuts and lemon juice. Bake for approximately 1 hour and 15 minutes at 325° in a greased 2-quart loaf pan (or 4 one-pint loaf pans for smaller loaves). Test center for doneness by inserting a toothpick which should come out clean when done. Cool thoroughly; wrap in foil. Store in refrigerator or freezer. Best after one day.

The Committee

RASPBERRY COFFEE CAKE

Average
Do ahead

Preparing: 1 hour
Baking: 25 minutes

Coffee Cake

2 cups sifted flour
3 teaspoons baking powder
½ teaspoon salt
¼ cup sugar

¼ cup shortening
⅔ to ¾ cup milk
melted butter
½ to 1 cup raspberry jam*

Sift together flour, baking powder, salt and sugar. Cut in shortening and enough milk to make a soft dough. Knead on floured board for about ½ minute. Roll out ⅛" thick. Brush with melted butter. Spread with raspberry jam. Roll like a jelly roll and seal edges. Shape roll into a crescent and cut through outer edge at ½" to 1" intervals. Bake at 375° for 25 minutes. While still warm, ice and sprinkle with nuts.

*Strawberry, boysenberry, blackberry, etc., jam may be substituted for raspberry jam.

Icing:

2 cups confectioners' sugar
3 tablespoons butter
¼ teaspoon salt

2 teaspoons vanilla
½ cup chopped nuts

Sift sugar. Heat butter until soft. Add sugar gradually, blending until creamy. Let stand over *(not in)* hot water for 15 minutes. Add salt and vanilla; blend. If icing is too thin, add sugar; if too thick, add a little cream.

Mrs. Robert Alan Swift
Bryn Mawr, Pennsylvania

SPRINKLE BREAD

Easy

Preparing: 20 minutes
Baking: 60 minutes

1½ cups seedless raisins
1 cup boiling water
juice and grated rind of one
   orange
1 egg
1 cup brown sugar

2 tablespoons salad oil
1 cup whole wheat flour
1½ cups enriched flour
2 teaspoons baking powder
½ teaspoon soda
1 teaspoon salt

Combine raisins and boiling water in mixing bowl. Add orange juice and rind. Allow to cool slightly (5 to 10 minutes). Stir in egg, sugar and oil, mixing well. Add dry ingredients, beating thoroughly. Pour into greased 8½"x4½"x2½" loaf pan. Bake at 325° for 60 minutes.

Linda Tulloch
Chadds Ford, Pennsylvania

PHILADELPHIA STICKY BUNS

Complicated　　　　　　　　　　　　　　　　　　*Makes: 18*
Do ahead　　　　　　　　　　　　　　　　*Preparing: 4 hours*
Freeze　　　　　　　　　　　　　　　*Baking: 30 minutes*

6 cups flour (or more as　　　　**2 tablespoons sugar**
needed)　　　　　　　　　　　　**2 teaspoons salt**
1 cup milk　　　　　　　　**1 tablespoon Crisco (heaping)**
1 cup water　　　　　　　**1 tablespoon butter (heaping)**
1 yeast cake, dissolved in ¼
cup warm water

Topping for 18 rolls:

1 pound butter (approximate)　　　**cinnamon**
4 cups light brown sugar
(approximate)

Scald milk and add to butter, Crisco, salt and sugar in a large bowl. When this is dissolved, add 1 cup cold water. Liquid should be lukewarm. Add dissolved yeast and mix. Add 3 cups flour and mix with knife. Cover and let sponge rise 1 hour in warm place (90°). Add 3 or more cups of flour and knead. (Sometimes extra flour is needed to make dough workable.) Divide in half. Let rise in two greased bowls for an hour (warm place 90°). Take half of dough and roll out jelly roll style. Cover generously with butter, brown sugar and cinnamon. Put remaining butter, brown sugar and cinnamon on bottom and sides of 9" square pan. Cut dough in nine pieces and arrange in pan. Let rise in warm place for one hour. Bake at 400° for about 30 minutes or until done. Cool on rack. Turn rolls upside down when serving so that the sticky runs through the rolls.

The other half of the dough can be handled in the same way to make nine more sticky buns. However, if you prefer, you can make a loaf of bread, parker house rolls or the like, leaving out the cinnamon and brown sugar.

Mrs. Frank H. Reichel, Jr.
Villanova, Pennsylvania

PANCAKE PUFF

Easy

Serves: 6
Preparing: 10 minutes
Baking: 30 minutes

4 large eggs
1 cup all-purpose flour
1 cup milk
4 tablespoons butter

2 tablespoons sugar
1 tablespoon lemon juice,
  optional

Preheat oven to 400°. Beat eggs with a fork. Mix in flour, then milk until well blended. Place butter in 9" or 10" ovenproof skillet and melt in oven until sizzling. Pour egg mixture into hot skillet and return to oven for 20 minutes. Remove from oven and quickly sprinkle sugar and lemon juice, if desired, over puff. Return to oven for 10 minutes more, or until well browned. Cut into wedges and serve hot, plain, or with cinnamon sugar or maple syrup.

Mrs. A. Balfour Brehman, Jr.
Villanova, Pennsylvania

Mrs. Henry Zenzie
Princeton, New Jersey

ZUCCHINI NUT BREAD

Easy
Do ahead
Freeze

Preparing: 30 minutes
Baking: 1 hour

3 eggs, beaten
1 cup vegetable oil
1 cup sugar
⅓ cup molasses
2 teaspoons vanilla
2½ cups unsifted flour
1 teaspoon salt

1 teaspoon soda
½ teaspoon baking powder
2 teaspoons cinnamon
2 cups shredded zucchini, skin
  included
1 cup raisins
1 cup chopped walnuts

Combine and mix first five ingredients. Sift together and add flour, salt, soda, baking powder, and cinnamon. Add zucchini, raisins, and nuts. Bake in two 5"x9" greased loaf pans at 350° for one hour. Cool ten minutes in pans; then turn out on racks and finish cooling.

Mrs. Eugene DeVol
Villanova, Pennsylvania

SALLY LUNN

Easy

Makes: 2 loaves
Preparing: 20 minutes
Baking: 35 minutes

**2 cups lukewarm milk
(110° F.)
1 ounce crumbled yeast
½ pound butter
¾ cup sugar**

**1 teaspoon salt
½ teaspoon mace
1½ cups eggs, slightly beaten
8 cups flour**

Place all ingredients in mixer bowl in order listed. Mix on low speed with dough hook or paddle until combined. Mix on medium speed 5 minutes. Remove from mixer and cover. Proof until double in size in warm place free from draft, (approximately 1½ hours). Return to mixer. Mix on medium speed 5 minutes. Pour half into each of two 10″ greased tube pans. Proof until double in size. Bake in 350° oven 35 minutes until golden brown. Slice in 1″ slices and serve while warm.

K. Carol Carlson, Vice-President
ARA Services
Philadelphia, Pennsylvania

POPOVERS

Easy

Serves: 8
Preparing: 15 minutes
Baking: 30-35 minutes

**1 cup milk
⅞ cup flour
½ teaspoon salt**

**1 tablespoon cooking oil
2 eggs**

Combine milk, flour, oil, salt. Beat with mixer on high speed, scraping bowl to include all flour. Generously grease iron muffin pan. Fill ⅔ full. Put in *cold* oven. Turn to 425°. Bake 30 to 35 minutes. Remove when highly puffed and brown. Let stand for a few minutes for easier removal.

These can also be used for a pretty dessert by adding a little sugar to the flour mixture. Fill with rum flavored custard, ice cream with snips of candied ginger, ginger marmalade or sliced berries of the season.

Mrs. Boris Sokoloff
Philadelphia, Pennsylvania

COPENHAGEN DANISH PASTRY

Average
Do ahead
Freeze

Serves: 6
Preparing: 2 hours
Cooking: 12 minutes

Being a Dane I should like my contribution to be an example of *real* Danish pastry. Three things are essential: use a light hand (as we Danish say); keep the ingredients cool; and fold the dough very carefully around the fillings to prevent leaking.

Dough

1 package fresh yeast
5 ounces cold water
2 egg yolks
½ teaspoon salt

1½ teaspoons sugar
½ ounce butter or margarine
   (cold)
2 cups wheat flour

For Rolling: 1⅝ cup margarine

For Glaze: 2 eggs

For Topping: ⅓ cup ground almonds

Fillings

Almond:
2 tablespoons water
¾ cup almond paste

Remonce:
½ cup butter
⅓ cup sugar
1 teaspoon vanilla
¼ cup chopped almonds
¼ cup chopped raisins

Custard:
2 eggs
2 tablespoons sugar
1 tablespoon flour
½ teaspoon vanilla (or
   kirsch, brandy, orange
   liqueur)
½ pint milk

Dough: Put the water and flour in the refrigerator for 1 hour (separately). Mix yeast into water in a large bowl. Beat egg yolks, salt and sugar into mixture. Rub the cold butter into the flour and mix into the yeast liquid. Knead well. Let dough rest 15 minutes. Rolling: Put the margarine between foil and roll to 8"x8" square. Roll dough to 19"x19" square. Place butter on dough, corners touching middle of edges. Fold corners of dough toward center. Roll again in two directions. Fold in three layers and chill for 15 minutes. Fold in three layers and roll twice more, chilling for 15 minutes each time. Finally, roll dough to rectangle ⅜" thick and cut edges straight. If cut edge shows several layers the dough is right. This is basic dough for many kinds of pastry.

Fillings: *Almond Filling:* Soften almond paste with water.

Remonce: Put all ingredients together at room temperature. Store in cool place until ready to mix.

Custard Filling: Beat eggs and sugar together in saucepan. Add margarine and milk. Heat mixture to boiling, beating constantly. Do not boil. Beat occasionally while cooling. Add flavoring when luke-warm.

Pastry Types:

Envelopes: Cut dough in 4"x4" squares. Place 1 teaspoon almond filling or custard filling in center. Fold over four corners. Place on greased pastry sheet. Let rise 20 minutes. Brush with egg. Bake for 12 minutes in 475° oven. When cool, ice with sugar icing.

Pastry Bars: Roll dough to rectangle 8" wide and length of pastry sheet. Spread remonce along center. Fold over one side and brush with egg. Fold over other side. Turn upside down. Brush with egg and sprinkle with sugar and chopped almonds. Place on greased pastry sheet. Let rise for 20 minutes. Bake 12 minutes at 475°. Cut into pieces to serve.

Mrs. Inga Wulff Bech
Virum, Denmark

GERMAN COFFEE CAKE

Average
Do ahead
Freeze

Serves: 16
Preparing: 20 minutes
Baking: 55-60 minutes

1 cup shortening
2 cups sugar
3 cups flour
2 teaspoons baking soda
1 teaspoon salt
4 egg yolks

2 cups sour cream
2 teaspoons vanilla
4 egg whites
¾ cup coconut
1 teaspoon cinnamon
½ cup sugar

Cream together shortening and 2 cups sugar. Sift together flour, baking soda and salt and add to shortening and sugar. Gradually add well beaten egg yolks, sour cream and vanilla. Fold in stiffly beaten egg whites. Mix together in separate bowl coconut, cinnamon and ½ cup sugar. Pour layer of batter into greased and floured tube or Bundt pan. Then sprinkle with some topping mix. Alternate layers of batter and topping, ending with batter. Bake in 375° oven for 55-60 minutes. Cool for 20 minutes before turning out on cake plate.

Mrs. Richard T. Schulze
Great Falls, Virginia

BLUEBERRY CAKE

Easy
Do ahead
Freeze

Serves: 6-8
Preparing: 15 minutes
Baking: 45 minutes

Cake

2 cups sifted flour
2 teaspoons baking powder
½ teaspoon salt
¼ cup butter

¾ cup sugar
1 egg
½ cup milk
2 cups blueberries

Topping

½ cup sugar
⅓ cup flour

1 teaspoon cinnamon
¼ cup butter

Sift dry ingredients. Cream butter and gradually beat in sugar. Add egg and milk, and beat until smooth. Add dry ingredients and fold in berries. Spread in greased and floured 8″ or 9″ round or square pan. Mix dry ingredients for topping and cut in butter. Sprinkle topping over cake and bake in 350° oven for 45 minutes.

Betty Dexter
Philadelphia, Pennsylvania

ZUCCHINI BREAD

Easy
Do ahead
Freeze

Serves: 10-12
Preparing: 20 mintues
Baking: 50 minutes

2 cups Bisquick
1½ cups shredded zucchini
¾ cup sugar
¼ cup vegetable oil
3 eggs

1 teaspoon vanilla
3 teaspoons ground cinnamon
2 teaspoons ground nutmeg
½ cup chopped nuts

Heat oven to 350°. Grease bottom of pan (9″x5″x3″). Beat all ingredients on low speed, scraping bowl constantly, for 30 seconds. Beat at medium speed, scraping bowl occasionally, for 1 minute. Pour into pan. Bake until done, about 50 to 55 minutes. Cool 10 minutes. Remove from pan. Keep stored in refrigerator.

Susan Hilsee
Philadelphia, Pennsylvania

RHUBARB BREAD

Easy
Do ahead
Freeze

Makes: 2 large or 4 small loaves
Preparing: 15-20 minutes
Baking: 45-60 minutes—large loaves
35-45 minutes—small loaves

1½ cups brown sugar
⅔ cup liquid shortening
1 egg
1 cup sour milk or buttermilk
1 teaspoon salt

1 teaspoon soda
1 teaspoon vanilla
2½ cups flour
1½ cups fresh or frozen rhubarb, diced

Topping:

½ cup nuts
½ cup brown sugar

1 tablespoon butter
½ teaspoon cinnamon (optional)

Mix together all ingredients, except topping. Pour into 2 large or 4 small well-greased loaf pans. Combine topping ingredients and sprinkle on top. Bake at 350° for 45 to 60 minutes for large loaves, 35 to 45 minutes for small loaves. Allow to cool before removing from pans.

Mrs. Lee Peterson
Hillsboro, Oregon

GOUGÈRE (CHEESE PUFFS)

Easy
Freeze

Serves: 4-6
Preparing: 15 minutes
Baking: 45-50 minutes

1 cup water
½ cup butter
½ teaspoon salt
dash pepper

1 cup sifted flour
4 eggs
3 ounces shredded Swiss cheese

Combine water, butter, salt, pepper in saucepan. Bring to a boil. Add flour at once. Beat over low heat until mixture leaves sides of pan and does not separate. Remove from heat. Continue beating to cool mixture. Add eggs, one at a time. Beat until mixture has a satiny sheen. Stir in cheese. Spoon out on a buttered baking sheet in a ring design. Bake at 375° for 40 to 50 minutes.

Mrs. A. Balfour Brehman
Villanova, Pennsylvania

MORAVIAN SUGAR CAKES

Average
Freeze

Makes: six or seven 9" cakes
Preparing: 5 hours
Baking: 30 minutes

1 cup cooked, riced potatoes
  (2 medium potatoes)
⅔ cup shortening (Crisco)
½ cup granulated sugar
1 heaping teaspoon salt

2 envelopes yeast
½ cup warm water
2 eggs, beaten
1 cup milk, scalded
5-6 cups flour

Topping

1 pound brown sugar
  mixed with
½ cup flour

½ pound butter, melted

Mix shortening, salt and sugar with warm, riced potatoes in a large bowl. Dissolve yeast in warm water. Add, with beaten eggs, to potato mixture; mix well. Gradually add warm milk and flour alternately. Dough should be slightly sticky. Knead for five minutes until springy. Put dough in greased bowl. Grease top of dough. Cover with cloth. Let rise. May take 3 to 4 hours. Punch down. Let rise again until double. Divide into six or seven pieces. Roll out. Spread in 9" pans. Let rise again (1 hour). Punch small dents with finger in top of dough at regular intervals. Place a bit of butter in each hole. Cover all with generous amount of topping. Drizzle butter over top. Bake 30 minutes at 350° degrees.

Mrs. Harris C. Arnold
Lancaster, Pennsylvania

OREGON APPLE BREAD

Average
Do ahead
Freeze

Serves: 6
Preparing: 20 minutes
Baking: 1 hour

2 cups flour
2 teaspoons baking powder
1 teaspoon salt
½ teaspoon cinnamon
¼ teaspoon nutmeg
½ cup butter or shortening

1¼ cups sugar
2 eggs
1½ cups peeled, finely grated
  apple
½ cup chopped walnuts or
  pecans

Preheat oven to 350°. Sift together the first five ingredients and set aside. Cream the butter and sugar together until light and fluffy. Beat in the eggs one at a time, beating well after each addition. Stir in the dry ingredients and apple, half at a time. Fold in the nuts. Pour into a well-greased and floured 9"x5"x3" loaf pan. Bake for 1 hour or until done. Cool in pan for 10 minutes and turn onto rack. Cool completely before slicing.

Mrs. John E. Krout
Rosemont, Pennsylvania

HAM BISCUITS

Easy   *Makes 20*
Do ahead   *Preparing: 25 minutes*
Freeze   *Baking: 10 minutes*

1 cup flour
1½ teaspoons baking powder
¼ teaspoon salt
1 tablespoon Crisco
**   (heaping)**

1 tablespoon butter (heaping)
⅓ + cup of milk
sliced baked ham, cut into small
**   pieces to fit biscuits**
butter for biscuits

Sift flour, baking powder and salt. Cut in Crisco and butter. Add milk. Mix, handling as little as possible. Roll and cut dough with small biscuit cutter. Place on cookie sheet. Bake at 400° for ten minutes or until slightly brown. Butter and place ham in biscuits. Reheat about 5 minutes in foil before serving.

Mrs. Frank H. Reichel
Villanova, Pennsylvania

CINNAMON FLOP

Easy   *Serves: 8*
Do ahead   *Preparing: 5 minutes*
Freeze   *Baking: 30-40 minutes*

1 package white or yellow
**   cake mix**
1 stick butter or margarine

1 cup brown sugar
2 tablespoons cinnamon

Prepare cake mix according to directions on box. Put in a 13"x9"x2" pan. Dot with butter and sprinkle with brown sugar and cinnamon. Bake according to directions on box.

Mrs. Thomas H. Nicholson
Rosemont, Pennsylvania

REFRIGERATOR BRAN MUFFINS

Easy   *Preparing: 30 minutes*
Do ahead   *Baking: 20 minutes*

Step 1

2 cups All-Bran   2 cups boiling water
1 15-ounce box raisins

Step 2

1 cup white sugar   4 eggs, well beaten
1 cup corn oil   1 quart buttermilk
2 cups molasses   3 cups bran

Step 3

5 cups flour   1 teaspoon salt
5 teaspoons soda

Preheat oven to 400°. Pour water over All-Bran and raisins and cool. In large bowl, add all other ingredients to the sugar listed in Step 2. Stir flour, soda and salt together and add to the sugar mixture. Add all this to the All-Bran, raisin mixture. Pour into buttered muffin tins; fill to ⅔. Bake for 20 minutes, cool and remove. Prepared mixture can be stored, covered, in the refrigerator for two months.

Mrs. Charles Watson
New Canaan, Connecticut

CURRIED ROLLED TOAST

Preparing: 15 minutes
Baking: 20 minutes

1 stick butter, softened   pepper, to taste
curry, to taste   garlic, to taste
salt, to taste   1 loaf thin sliced bread

Cut crusts off bread. Combine butter, curry, salt, pepper, and garlic. Spread on bread; roll up in jelly roll style with seam side down and place on baking sheet. Toast in slow oven (200°) until brown, about 20 minutes.

Mrs. John V. Calhoun, Jr.
Devon, Pennsylvania

OATMEAL RAISIN MUFFINS

Easy

Serves: 12
Preparing: 15 minutes
Baking: 15-20 minutes

1 cup sifted all-purpose flour
3 teaspoons baking powder
¼ cup shortening
1 cup quick cooking rolled
  oats
1 egg

1 cup milk
½ cup brown sugar
½ cup raisins
¼ cup granulated sugar
¼ teaspoon cinnamon
½ teaspoon salt

Sift together flour, baking powder, salt. Cut in the shortening until mixture is like coarse crumbs. Stir in rolled oats. Combine egg, milk and brown sugar. Beat well. Stir into dry ingredients. Add raisins. Spoon into baking cups in muffin pan. Combine sugar and cinnamon and sprinkle over batter. Bake in 425° oven 15 to 20 minutes.

Mrs. Revere G. Counselman
Wayne, Pennsylvania

DINNER ROLLS

Easy
Do ahead
Freeze

Makes 42 3" rolls
Preparing: 2½ hours
Baking: 10-15 minutes

2 large eggs, or 3 small
1 mixing spoon of lard,
  melted
2¾ cups warm water
1 cake yeast or 2 envelopes
  of dry yeast, dissolved in
  ¼ cup warm water

½ cup sugar
1 teaspoon salt
9 cups flour

Mix together eggs and lard in water. Add dissolved yeast or dry yeast. Add sugar and salt. Add flour. Mix thoroughly. Drop onto heavily floured surface, knead until able to handle. Return to mixing bowl, greased with lard or Crisco. Grease surface; cover bowl with damp cloth. Set in warm place until double in bulk, about 2 hours depending on room temperature. Poke down. Dipping fingers in flour, pull off desired roll size; put a small bit of butter in center and fold in; place on greased cookie sheet or pan; set rolls aside in warm place until doubled in size. Put in preheated 350° oven about 10-15 minutes. Cool.

The Committee

CREAM CHEESE BRAIDS

Average
Do ahead
Freeze

Makes: 4 loaves
Preparing: 1 hour
Chilling: overnight
Baking: 12-15 minutes

1 cup sour cream
½ cup granulated sugar
1 teaspoon salt
½ cup melted margarine
Filling:

2 packages dry yeast
½ cup warm water
2 eggs, beaten
4 cups all-purpose flour

2 8-ounce packages cream
  cheese
¾ cup granulated sugar

1 egg, beaten
⅛ teaspoon salt
2 teaspoons vanilla

Glaze:

2 cups confectioners' sugar
4 tablespoons milk

2 teaspoons vanilla

Heat sour cream. Stir in sugar, salt and butter. Cool to lukewarm. Sprinkle yeast over water in a mixing bowl. Stir to dissolve. Add sour cream mixture, eggs and flour. Mix until well blended. Cover tightly and refrigerate overnight. Next day divide dough into 4 parts. Roll out each to a 12"x8" rectangle on a well-floured surface. Spread ¼ of the filling on each rectangle, spreading it to ½ inch from edge. Roll each rectangle up lengthwise. Seal edges and fold ends under slightly. Place seam side down, on a greased cookie sheet. Slit each roll at 2" intervals to resemble a braid. Cover and let rise until doubled in size (about 1 hour). Bake at 375° for 12-15 minutes, or until lightly browned. While still warm, spread with glaze. This recipe makes four loaves, which freeze beautifully. Need only to defrost the night before for a superb breakfast treat, served at room temperature.

Mrs. Robert S. Watson
Charlotte, North Carolina

BENNÉ SEED BISCUITS

Easy
Do ahead

Makes: 4 dozen
Preparing: 30 minutes
Cooking: 25 minutes

1 cup benné seeds (or
  sesame seeds)
2 cups flour
1 teaspoon salt

dash cayenne
1 cup shortening
¼ cup cold water

Place seeds one layer deep on cookie sheet. Roast in 350° oven 10 minutes or until golden brown. Combine flour, salt and pepper. Cut in shortening. Add water. Mix to pie crust consistency. Add seeds. Mix. Roll ¼" thick. Cut into 2" rounds. Place on greased sheet. Bake in 300° oven 25 minutes. Before removing from pan and while hot, sprinkle with salt. Cool and then store in covered tin.

K. Carol Carlson, Vice-President
ARA Services
Philadelphia, Pennsylvania

CHRISTMAS STOLLEN

Average   *Preparing: 1½ hours*
Do ahead   *Baking: 30-40 minutes*
Freeze

1½ cups milk, scalded,   ¼ teaspoon cardamon
   cooled to lukewarm   ½ teaspoon mace
1 cake, envelope or   1 cup chopped almonds
   tablespoon yeast   1 cup raisins, seedless
1 teaspoon salt   ½ cup candied cherries
½ cup sugar or ⅓ cup honey   ½ cup chopped citron
2 eggs beaten   ¼ cup candied orange peel
½ cup butter, softened   1 teaspoon grated lemon rind
5 to 6 cups flour, unbleached,   1 teaspoon orange rind
   sifted

Glaze:

1½ tablespoons hot milk   1½ cups confectioners' sugar

Soften yeast in milk, add sugar or honey, salt and softened butter, then beaten eggs. Sift 3 cups flour with spices and add to mixture, beat well, allow to rest 10-15 minutes. Add 2 cups flour along with fruits, rinds and nuts, mix well and add more flour if necessary to make fairly stiff dough. Cover and allow to rise till double in bulk. Punch down and knead 20 or 30 strokes. Cover and refrigerate overnight. Divide dough in two or leave as one, roll out in oblong form, butter well, fold over lengthwise, press together lightly. Brush top with 1 tablespoon water mixed with 1 egg white. Allow to rise until double in bulk. Bake 375° 30-40 minutes depending on size. Mix hot milk and confectioners' sugar together for glaze. Glaze while warm.

Mrs. Bernard Garfield
Haddonfield, New Jersey

Norma B. Tiekert
Sassamansville, Pennsylvania

STRAWBERRY NUT BREAD

Easy
Do ahead
Freeze

Preparing: 45 minutes
Baking: 50-70 minutes

1 cup butter
1½ cups sugar
1 teaspoon vanilla
¼ teaspoon lemon extract
4 eggs
3 cups sifted flour

1 teaspoon salt
1 teaspoon cream of tartar
½ teaspoon baking soda
1 cup strawberry preserves
½ cup sour cream
1 cup chopped walnuts

Cream butter, sugar, vanilla and lemon extract until fluffy. Add eggs, one at a time, beating well after each. Sift together flour, salt, cream of tartar and baking soda. Combine sour cream and strawberry preserves. Add preserve mixture alternately with dry ingredients to the creamed mixture, beaing until well combined. Stir in nuts. Divide mixture evenly into 5 small well-greased bread pans. Bake at 350° for 50 to 70 minutes. Cool 10 minutes in pans. Remove and cool completely on rack.

Mrs. James Heimarck
Bryn Mawr, Pennsylvania

WHOLE WHEAT BREAD

Easy
Freeze

Makes: Two 3½"x7½" loaves
Preparing: 2½ hours
Baking: 45 minutes

1 package dry yeast
¼ cup warm water
½ cup brown sugar, firmly
   packed
3 tablespoons butter
1 tablespoon salt

1 cup boiling water
¾ cup cold water
4 cups whole wheat flour
enough white bread flour to
   make a stiff dough, about 1½
   cups

Soften yeast in warm water. Combine sugar, butter, salt and boiling water in a large bowl. Add cold water and dissolved yeast. Add 4 cups whole wheat flour and the white bread flour to make a stiff dough. Knead on a lightly floured board until smooth and satiny. Let rise in a warm place until double in size, about 1½ hours. Punch down and let rise again about 30 minutes. Divide into 2 loaves; place in buttered pans and let rise until double. Bake in moderate 350° oven, 50 to 60 minutes, until loaves thump hollow and are done. Remove from pans immediately.

The Committee

Overtures

beverages and soups

GIN OR VODKA PUNCH

Easy   *Makes: 6 quarts*
                                          Preparing: 10 minutes

1½ cups lemon juice   **6 ounces Grenadine**
2 quarts orange juice   **2 quarts club soda**
2 fifths vodka

Mix all ingredients together. Serve over a block of ice.

Sally Wheat
Philadelphia, Pennsylvania

FISHHOUSE PUNCH (OLD PHILADELPHIA)

Easy   *Serves: 25*
                                          Preparing: 15 minutes

1 quart lemon juice   **⅝ pound sugar**
1 quart water   **noggin (shotglass) of peach**
2 quarts dark rum   **brandy**
1 quart brandy   **large cake of ice**

Place large cake of ice in punch bowl. Pour over it the combined ingredients, (more water may be added).

Mr. Fitz Eugene Dixon
Elkins Park, Pennsylvania

FOXY HOT AND SPICY CIDER

Easy   *Serves: 8*
Do ahead   *Preparing: 15 minutes*

8 cups cider—(7 cups if rum   **8 jiggers rum (optional)**
is used)   **nutmeg and ginger to taste**
3 sticks cinnamon (or 1
teaspoon ground
cinnamon)

Mix all ingredients and simmer for 5 minutes. Add rum if desired and serve hot.

Mrs. George S. Hundt, Jr.
Malvern, Pennsylvania

GLÖGG

Easy

Serves: 24
Preparing: 25 minutes

½ teaspoon cardamom seed
  (ground)
8 whole cloves
2 cinnamon sticks
½ cup grated orange rind
2 cups seedless raisins
1½ cups blanched, shredded
  almonds

1 quart water
2 fifths Bordeaux or Ruby Claret
  wine
2 fifths Port
1 cup lump sugar
1 cup brandy

Combine spices, orange rind, raisins, and nuts with water in pan. Bring to a
boil. Cover and simmer 10 minutes. Add wine; heat to simmering temperature. Remove from heat. Pour into metal serving container. Place sugar in
strainer over Glögg. Pour brandy over sugar. Ignite, being careful to turn
face away from flame. Ladle Glögg over sugar until sugar dissolves. Cover
to extinguish flame. Serve hot.

K. Carol Carlson, Vice President
ARA Services
Philadelphia, Pennsylvania

SPICED ICED TEA SYRUP

Easy
Do ahead

Makes: 5 quarts
Preparing: 20 minutes

2 cups sugar
2 cups water
4 rounded teaspoons black
  tea
5 mint leaves (optional)

1 teaspoon allspice
1½ cups strained orange
  juice
¾ cup strained lemon juice

Boil sugar and water five minutes. Add tea, mint and allspice. Cover and let
stand 10 minutes. Strain and add fruit juices. Jar and store in refrigerator for
future use. Use 1 tablespoon of syrup per glass of tea. Fill glass with ice and
water. In quantity, mix full recipe with four quarts of water.

Mrs. Walter Lamb
Chester Springs, Pennsylvania

WASSAIL

Easy

Serves: 20
Preparing: 15 minutes

"Wassailing," an ancient English custom for New Year's Eve or Day. The custom being to pass one bowl from friend to friend. The Saxon phrase "Wass hael" (be well) was repeated in turn.

1 cup sugar
4 cinnamon sticks
lemon slices
2 cups pineapple juice

2 cups orange juice
6 cups claret
½ cup lemon juice
1 cup dry sherry

Boil sugar, cinnamon stick, three lemon slices in ½ cup of water for five mintues and strain. Heat but *do not boil* remaining ingredients. Combine with syrup, garnish with more lemon slices. Serve hot, ladled from a bowl.

The Committee

FOURTH OF JULY SYLLABUB

Average
Do ahead

Serves: 12
Preparing: 30 minutes
Chilling: 3 hours

2 lemons
4 ounces brandy
6 ounces sugar

1 pint heavy cream
½ pint sweet white wine
rinds of 2 lemons

Peel the lemons thinly with a potato peeler. Squeeze out the juice and add enough brandy to make the liquid up to 5 or 5½ ounces. Pour the liquid into a small bowl, add the lemon peel and let stand for at least 6 hours. Strain the liquid through a fine sieve and stir in the sugar until it has dissolved completely. Whip the cream until it holds its shape. Mix the wine into the lemon and brandy, then add this liquid to the cream, a little at a time, whisking continuously. The cream should absorb all the liquid and still stand in soft peaks. Pile the mixture into individual glasses and chill for several hours. For the garnish, thinly peel the lemon rind and cut into narrow strips; blanch for 2-3 minutes in boiling water. Serve the syllabub with a cluster of drained lemon strips.

"County Lines"
West Chester, Pennsylvania

RICHMOND WHISKEY SOURS

Easy

Serves: 1
Preparing: 3 minutes

crushed ice
2 ounces bourbon
2 ounces limeade

1 ounce tonic
piece of lemon
optional: slice of orange, cherry

Fill a tall glass with crushed ice. Pour in bourbon, limeade and tonic. Stir. Squeeze piece of lemon and drop in. Add orange slice and cherry.

Mrs. D. B. Garst
Devon, Pennsylvania

SUPER LEMONADE

Easy
Do ahead

Preparing: 15 minutes
Resting: 1 hour

2 cups sugar
2½ cups water
juice of 6 lemons

juice of 2 oranges
grated rind of 1 orange
1 cup mint leaves

Cook sugar and water 5 minutes. Cool. Add juices and rind. Pour over mint leaves. Cover. Let stand 1 hour. Strain into jar and refrigerate. Use ⅓ cup syrup for each glass. Fill with crushed ice and water. Top with sprig of mint.

Mrs. George M. Ahrens
Rosemont, Pennsylvania

RUSSIAN TEA

Easy
Do ahead

Serves: 30
Preparing: 10 minutes

2 cups Tang
1 cup sugar
1 cup instant tea (100% tea)

½ cup Wylers lemonade mix
1 teaspoon cinnamon
½ teaspoon cloves

Mix together all ingredients. Store in a can or jar. Use 1 tablespoon per cup, add boiling water.

The Committee

PARTY TEA PUNCH

Easy

Serves: 8
Preparing: 15 minutes

3 cups water
3 spiced tea bags
⅓ cup sugar

1 12-ounce can apricot nectar
¼ cup lemon or lime juice
1 8-ounce bottle ginger ale

Boil water, remove from heat, add tea bags and sugar. Stir until sugar dissolves and let steep for four minutes. Strain into two quart pitcher. Cool. Stir in apricot nectar and lemon juice. Before serving add ginger ale. Serve over ice.

The Committee

WINTER ALFRESCO "BREW HA HA"

Easy
Do ahead

Serves: 20
Preparing: 10 minutes
Cooking: 20 minutes

1 gallon cider
2 cups sugar (or a bit less)
48 cloves, stuck in 2 apples
12 cinnamon sticks
6 tablespoons lemon juice

4 teaspoons allspice
1 cup orange juice
4 cups apple jack brandy
  (Laird's)

Boil all ingredients except brandy 10 minutes, then add brandy. Serve hot.

Mr. James Bodine
Rosemont, Pennsylvania

UNIVERSITY CITY HISTORICAL SOCIETY PUNCH

Easy

Serves: 30

1 large can grapefruit juice
1 large can pineapple juice
1 quart "Real Lemon" juice
1 pound sugar dissolved in
  ½ cup water

1 quart soda water
1 fifth of rum

Combine juices and sugar. Just before serving, add soda water and rum. Serve over a block of ice.

Mrs. Frederick L. Jones
Philadelphia, Pennsylvania

CHAMPAGNE PUNCH

Easy
Partial do ahead

Serves: 30 (½-cup punch cups)
Preparing: 10 minutes

1 quart plus 1 cup Sauterne
2½ cups brandy
5 pints Champagne

1 quart plus 1 cup soda water
large block of ice

Chill everything first. Pour Sauterne and brandy over ice in punch bowl. Add Champagne and soda water. Serve.

The Committee

CAFE BRULÔT

Serves: 10-12
Preparing: 10 minutes

1 stick cinnamon
12 whole cloves
peel of 1 orange and 1 lemon
6 sugar lumps

8 ounces brandy
8 ounces Curacao
1 quart strong black coffee

In a chafing dish put cinnamon, cloves, orange and lemon peels, and sugar. Add brandy and Curacao and stir together. Ignite brandy and gradually add coffee.

Mrs. Eugene R. Hook
Wynnewood, Pennsylvania

COFFEE LIQUEUR

Easy

Makes: 1 gallon
Preparing: 2 hours

6 cups sugar
6 cups water
½ cup instant coffee

½ cup vanilla
½ gallon vodka or gin

Bring sugar, water and coffee to boil. Lower heat and simmer two hours. Stir occasionally. Remove from heat, add vanilla. Allow to cool completely. Stir in gin or vodka. Bottle.

Mrs. William Lawson
Eastville, Virginia

MULLED WINE

Easy
Do ahead   *Serves: 6*

1 bottle red wine   **pinch of cinnamon**
½ bottle water   **lemon juice (small amount to**
1 tablespoon sugar   **taste)**

Pour into a large saucepan half a bottle of water for each bottle of wine. Heat the water and add a tablespoon of sugar, a pinch of cinnamon, and a little lemon juice. Then pour in the bottle of wine. Pour the mixture back into bottles, and stand in hot water to keep it warm.

Mrs. D. B. Garst
Devon, Pennsylvania

EGGNOG

Serves: 30
Preparing: 15 minutes

24 eggs separated   **1 quart heavy cream**
2 cups sugar   **2 quarts milk**
1 quart bourbon   **1 quart vanilla ice cream**
1 pint brandy

Beat the yolks and sugar until thick, add the bourbon and brandy and stir thoroughly. The liquor cooks the eggs. Add the cream and milk and continue whipping. Break up ice cream and add. Beat egg whites until stiff and fold in. Refrigerate if possible for 30 minutes before serving. Sprinkle with nutmeg.

Mr. Radford Beasley
Philadelphia, Pennsylvania

WHISKEY SOUR PUNCH

Easy
Do ahead   *Serves: 12*
Preparing: 10 minutes

⅓ cup frozen orange juice   **3 cups club soda, chilled**
  concentrate, thawed and   **3 cups whiskey (bourbon or**
  undiluted   **blend)**
⅓ cup frozen lemonade
  concentrate, thawed and
  undiluted

Combine all ingredients in large punch bowl and mix well. Add ice just before serving and garnish as desired, (lemon slices, mint, maraschino cherries, etc.).

The Committee

SNAPPER SOUP

Complicated

Serves: 24
Preparing: 5 hours

3 pounds cleaned snapper
¾ cup butter
1 cup diced celery
1 cup diced onions
1 cup sliced carrots
1 cup flour
1 tablespoon paprika
2¾ quarts beef stock
1½ cups tomato purée
1 teaspoon whole mixed
pickling spice

2 cloves garlic, crushed
1 teaspoon allspice
1 teaspoon salt
½ teaspoon pepper
⅓ cup cornstarch
⅔ cup water
1 hard-boiled egg, chopped
1 tablespoon Worcestershire
sauce
2 teaspoons chopped parsley
⅔ cup sherry

Wash snapper. Place in large stock pot with 1 gallon, 1 quart water. Bring to a boil. Skim during cooking. Simmer for 2 hours or until meat is tender. Separate stock from meat. Dice meat into ¼″ pieces. Set both aside. Cook vegetables in butter until onions are transparent. Add flour and paprika and blend well. Add snapper stock, beef stock, tomato purée and spices. Bring to a boil. Reduce heat and simmer 2 to 2½ hours. Strain soup and discard vegetables. Mix cornstarch with water and blend until smooth. Add to soup. Cook 15 minutes. Add remaining ingredients and cooked snapper meat. Remove from direct heat.

Snapper Soup is served very thick in Philadelphia to be thinned with a good lacing of sherry. You may want to cut the cornstarch in half to make spooning easier.

K. Carol Carlson
Vice-President, ARA Services
Philadelphia, Pennsylvania

UNION LEAGUE SPECIAL

Easy   *Serves: 1-20*
                                          Preparing: 15 minutes

Individual 6-ounce cocktail

1 ounce rye
½ ounce Myers Jamaican
  rum
½ ounce Triple Sec

1 ounce lemon juice
1 ounce orange juice
½ ounce sugar

Shake well with cracked ice and strain.

Gallon Recipe

1 bottle rye
16 ounces Myers Jamaican
  rum
36 ounces half lemon juice
  and half water

16 ounces Triple Sec
26 ounces orange juice
8 ounces sugar syrup

Stir with block ice or cubes until cold.

Union League
Philadelphia, Pennsylvania

PUNCH FOR A CROWD

Easy   *Serves: 30-40*
Must do ahead   *Preparing: 30 minutes*

4 cups sugar
2 cups water
2 cups strong tea (use 6 tea
  bags)
2 cups lemon juice
  (Realemon)

2½ cups orange juice, frozen or
  fresh
5 cups pineapple juice
2 quarts ginger-ale

Boil water and sugar together for 10 minutes. Combine tea, lemon juice, orange juice and pineapple juice. Mix with sugar water syrup. Put this mix in gallon jug and store in refrigerator two days before serving. When ready to serve pour in punch bowl and add ginger ale. Taste for strength and add water if necessary.

Mrs. Norman P. Robinson
Haverford, Pennsylvania

PHILADELPHIA PEPPER POT

Average
Do ahead

Makes: 1 gallon
Preparing: 3½ hours

¾ pound tripe, diced ¼″
3 cups water
⅓ cup chicken fat
1 cup chopped onion
1 cup chopped celery
½ cup chopped green pepper
1 quart chicken stock
1½ quarts beef stock

⅛ teaspoon pepper
1 tablespoon salt
¼ teaspoon thyme
1 bay leaf, crushed
1½ cups diced potatoes
1 cup flour
1 cup water
1 cup milk

Cook tripe in water over low heat until tender, about 2½ hours. In large stock pot melt fat and add vegetables. Cook until vegetables are very tender but not browned. Add tripe broth, chicken and beef stock to vegetables. Bring to a boil. Add seasonings, potatoes and tripe. Cook until potatoes are tender, about ½ hour. Combine flour and water into a smooth paste. Add to soup, stirring constantly. Cook for 10 minutes. Remove from direct heat and add milk.

K. Carol Carlson, Vice President
ARA Services
Philadelphia, Pennsylvania

THREE COLORS POTATO SOUP

Average
Do ahead

Serves: 6
Preparing: 15 minutes
Cooking: 40 minutes

5 medium potatoes, peeled
2 carrots, chopped
3 stalks celery, chopped
5 shallots, chopped
2 tablespoons parsley,
  chopped

2½ cups water or chicken stock
salt and pepper to taste
1 cup milk
1 cup chopped onions
2 tablespoons fresh sweet butter

Boil potatoes in salted water about 20 minutes. Drain and purée them in food processor. Save the water to use for the two cups. Melt butter and sauté the onions and shallots. Add carrots and celery and sauté a few minutes. Add potatoes, salt, pepper, water, milk and parsley. Bring to a boil and serve.

Esther Press, Chef
The Philadelphia Club

CZARNINA POLISH DUCK SOUP

Easy
Freeze

Serves: 6
Preparing: 2½ hours

The duck must be freshly killed and 3 to 4 ounces of blood must be saved and mixed with 3 tablespoons of vinegar immediately.

3 to 4 pound duck
1 small onion
5-6 peppercorns
9 prunes

1 bay leaf
1 pint light cream
1 tablespoon sugar
noodles or potatoes

Cut duck into small pieces. Place in large pot and cover with water. Add the onion, peppercorns, bay leaf, sugar and prunes. Cook until meat is soft, approximately 2 hours. Add duck's blood and vinegar to soup. Bring soup to boil. Take ½ cup of soup, mix with cream and add to soup. Bring soup to boil again. Soup can now be served with noodles or boiled potatoes. (The duck meat will be the main course after soup.)

Joseph R. Kaminski
Clementon, New Jersey

CORN CHOWDER

Easy
Do ahead

Serves: 6
Preparing: 30 minutes

4 slices bacon
4 medium green peppers,
  chopped
6 medium onions (yellow),
  chopped
1 14-ounce can cream style
  corn
2 cups chicken broth
1 cup whole milk

1 cup evaporated milk
1 tablespoon butter
1 teaspoon sugar
1½ tablespoons flour
1¼ teaspoons salt
2 shakes white pepper
2 shakes paprika
2 tablespoons parsley

Fry bacon, crumble and set aside. Fry chopped onions and peppers in bacon fat. Dissolve flour into ¼ cup chicken broth and add to rest of heated broth. Add corn, seasonings, bacon and heated milk. Top with butter, parsley and paprika just before serving.

Mrs. Donald Meads
Uwchland, Pennsylvania

CRÈME VICHYSSOISE I

Easy
Do ahead

Serves: 5-6
Preparing: 10 minutes
Cooking: 45 minutes

4 leeks, sliced
¼ cup butter
⅓ cup onion, sliced
2 cups potatoes, sliced or
  diced

3 cups chicken stock or 1 can
  chicken consommé diluted
  with 1½ cups water
½ cup heavy cream
salt and white pepper

Use only the inside white portion of leeks. Heat butter. Add sliced leeks and onion. Simmer 5 minutes or until soft but not browned. Add potatoes and chicken stock. Boil gently 30-40 minutes or until potatoes are tender. Press through sieve. Add cream and season to taste. Serve hot or cold. Beat until smooth before serving. Garnish with a dash of paprika or finely minced parsley.

Mrs. Chandler Gillespie
Haverford, Pennsylvania

SNOWDENS BEEF SOUP

Easy
Do ahead
Freeze

Makes: 3 quarts
Preparing: 30 minutes
Cooking: 50 minutes

1 pound ground chuck beef
1 1-quart 14-ounce can
  tomato juice
2 cans condensed beef
  bouillon
2 cups celery, chopped
2 cups onions, chopped

1 bunch carrots, chopped
4 medium potatoes, chopped
4 medium turnips, chopped
2 cans Veg-All (a mixed
  vegetable)
8 packets Herb-Ox instant broth
  seasoning, beef flavored

Sauté beef for five minutes in large pot. Add all other ingredients except Veg-All and broth seasoning. When all vegetables are tender and done, about 45 minutes, add Veg-All and beef flavored seasonings. Add salt and pepper to taste.

Elizabeth M. Ballinger
Moylan, Pennsylvania

CHINESE CONSOMMÉ

Easy
Do ahead

Serves: 6 or 8
Preparing: 10 minutes
Cooking: 20 minutes

6 cups chicken consommé,
  canned or homemade
2 bay leaves
1 cup clam bouillon
¼ cup dry white wine
1 carrot, peeled and
  shredded

1 celery stalk (with leaves) sliced
  thin on the diagonal ("Chinese
  cut")
1 red or green sweet pepper,
  seeded and slivered
2 scallions (tops too) sliced thin
  on the diagonal

In a covered saucepan, bring chicken consommé, bay leaves and clam bouillon to a boil. Lower heat and simmer 15 minutes. Remove bay leaves. Add dry white wine (if soup is made ahead, wine should be added when it is reheated, just before serving). Divide raw vegetables among soup bowls. Pour the broth over them, steaming hot, and serve.

Vegetables can be prepared and kept in a covered bowl in the refrigerator.

The Committee

EMILY'S CUCUMBER SOUP

Easy
Do ahead

Serves: 6
Preparing: 1 hour

4 tablespoons butter or
  margarine
1 cup finely diced celery
½ cup finely diced onion
3 tablespoons minced
  parsley
3 tablespoons flour

3 cups cream or half and half
2 cups consommé
2 cups finely diced, pared
  cucumber
seasonings of salt, pepper,
  Worcestershire and Tabasco

Let butter melt slowly. Add onion and celery and continue to cook over low heat until these are tender. *Do not* let them brown. Add cucumber and parsley and simmer 10 minutes more. Let cool slightly. Blend the flour in smoothly. Gradually stir in the cream. Then add the consommé. Return to heat, stirring carefully until thickened and smooth. Add seasonings. Serve with a sprinkling of minced parsley, chives or paprika for garnish. Delicious served either hot or cold.

The Committee

TOMATO SOUP

Average
Do ahead
Freeze

Makes: 3 quarts
Preparing: 3 hours

8 pounds fresh tomatoes
2 stalks celery
5 cloves
1 bay leaf
1 sprig parsley

4 tablespoons soft butter
4 tablespoons flour
3 teaspoons salt
3 teaspoons sugar
sour cream (garnish)

Bring to boil first five ingredients and simmer slowly about 2 hours. Strain. Blend thoroughly the last four ingredients. To this, slowly add a cup of hot strained tomatoes and mix until smooth. Gradually add to remaining juice. Bring to boil, stirring frequently. Sour cream may be added to each serving.

Mrs. William W. Lander
Villanova, Pennsylvania

FISH CHOWDER

Easy
Do ahead

Serves: 4-8
Preparing: 10 minutes
Cooking: 30 minutes

1 pound package white fillets
  (frozen ocean perch)
2 10-ounce cans chopped
  clams
1 large onion
1 minced clove of garlic
3 medium sized carrots
3 stalks of celery with leaves

2 large potatoes
3 tablespoons finely chopped
  parsley
lemon pepper
½ pint light cream
½ pint milk
butter
freshly ground black pepper

Put the fillets into a large saucepan and let them defrost, saving the liquid that melts off them. Dice onion, garlic, carrots, celery, potatoes, parsley. Put diced vegetables into the saucepan. Sprinkle lemon pepper over all, stir. Add clams with liquid. If there is not enough liquid to barely cover everything, then add a small amount of water. Cover the pot and simmer gently until the potatoes test done—20 or 25 minutes. Turn off the heat and stir in cream and milk. Stir, add more milk if you'd like it a bit thinner. Taste for salt. Heat just to boiling. Serve garnished with pats of butter and freshly ground black pepper.

Mrs. Harry Gorodetzer
Narberth, Pennsylvania

SPINACH CURRY SOUP

Easy

Serves: 6
Preparing: 10 minutes

½ pound fresh spinach
2 tablespoons flour
2 cups chicken stock or
  water

2 teaspoons curry powder
2 tall cans (3½ cups) evaporated
  milk
salt

Place above ingredients (except milk) in blender and blend until spinach is very fine. Turn into saucepan and add evaporated milk. Salt to taste. Cook until thickened, stirring to keep smooth. Serve hot or very cold.

Mrs. Dan Badal
Cleveland Heights, Ohio

CLAM-AVOCADO BISQUE

Easy
Do ahead

Serves: 4-6
Preparing: 15 minutes
Chilling: 30 minutes

2 diced avocados
1 7 or 8 ounce can minced
  clams with juice
1 cup cool chicken stock or
  broth

1 cup cream
½ teaspoon lemon juice
¼ teaspoon salt, to taste
⅛ teaspoon cayenne to taste

Blend all ingredients in order and chill. Serve in chilled soup dishes. Size of avocados controls consistency; add more stock for desired consistency.

Mrs. Richard L. Sperry
Bryn Mawr, Pennsylvania

ZUCCHINI CURRY SOUP

Easy
Do ahead
Freeze

Serves: 8
Preparing: 1½ hours

8 medium size zucchini
2 medium onions, chopped
½ to 1 tablespoon curry
  powder

4 cups chicken broth
1½ cups cream or half and half
salt and pepper to taste
parsley or chives, chopped

Wash the zucchini, trim the ends and cut into thick slices. Place in a saucepan with onion, curry and broth. Cover and simmer until vegetables are tender. Stir occasionally to make sure that the curry is thoroughly mixed in. Allow to cool slightly. Put the mixture into a blender or food processor to make it into a fine purée. This may have to be done in several batches. Put purée in a bowl and add cream or half and half. Season with salt and pepper. Chill thoroughly. Serve cold, garnished with parsley or chives. Or serve hot, without the cream. This may be garnished with a dollop of sour cream or whipping cream. Freeze only the purée before adding cream.

Mrs. Stevan Simich
Wayne, Pennsylvania

FRANNY'S SOUP

Easy   *Serves: 10*
Do ahead   *Preparing: 10 minutes*
                                Cooking: 30 minutes

2 cans mushroom soup
2 cans water
2 cans snapper soup
1 cup pre-cooked shrimp
1 cup pre-cooked
   mushrooms

1½ cups dry sherry
2 cups sour cream
1 to 3 teaspoons curry powder,
   to taste
1 teaspoon nutmeg

Blend ingredients except shrimp and simmer for 30 minutes. Add shrimp a few minutes before serving. Serve with French bread.

Mrs. Eric Fowler
Newtown Square, Pennsylvania

COLD CURRIED AVOCADO SOUP

Easy   *Serves: 4*
Do ahead   *Preparing: 10 minutes*

1 ripe avocado, peeled and
   pit removed
2 cups cold chicken broth
1 cup heavy cream
2 tablespoons white rum

1 teaspoon curry powder
pinch salt
coarsely ground white pepper
1 lemon

Into the blender jar put the avocado pulp, chicken broth, cream, rum, curry, salt, pepper. Blend till smooth and serve in bouillon cups. Garnish with slice of lemon.

Julie Dannenbaum
Philadelphia, Pennsylvania

COLD CUCUMBER SOUP

Easy
Do ahead

Serves: 6
Preparing: 20 minutes
Chilling: 2 hours

Better if done ahead so flavors marry. For very thick soup, use milk instead of water.

2 medium cucumbers, peeled, diced and cooked for 10 minutes, then drained
2½ cups water (use water leftover from cooking)

2 cans (10¾ ounce) cream of chicken soup
1 teaspoon lemon juice
½ teaspoon curry
drop green food coloring

Mix all ingredients in blender. Chill well. Garnish with lemon slices.

Mrs. Robert Alan Swift
Bryn Mawr, Pennsylvania

FAST GREEN CRAB SOUP

Easy

Preparing: 5 minutes
Cooking: 6 minutes

A microwave oven recipe!

1 10½-ounce can green pea soup
2 cups chicken broth
1 7-ounce can crabmeat, flaked

2 tablespoons light rum
salt and pepper to taste
1 cup heavy cream, whipped
1 tablespoon fresh chives, chopped

In a glass casserole, combine the pea soup and chicken broth. Cook in center of oven 4 minutes—or until boiling, stirring after 2 minutes. Stir in the crab meat, rum, salt and pepper. Cook 2 minutes, stirring after 1 minute. Stir in whipped cream. Taste for seasoning. Pour into hot bowls and garnish with chopped chives.

Mrs. B. P. Wadhams
Haverford, Pennsylvania

BLACK BEAN SOUP

Easy
Do ahead
Freeze

Serves: 12
Preparing: ½ hour
Cooking: 4 hours

Rice, chopped onions and sour cream are good accompaniments for this soup.

**2 cups black beans, soaked
  overnight
10 cups water
½ pound bacon, chopped
1 cup onions, chopped
½ cup celery, chopped
½ cup green pepper,
  chopped
3 cloves minced garlic**

**1 tablespoon minced parsley
1 cube beef bouillon
½ teaspoon thyme
1 teaspoon paprika
dash of cayenne
2 tablespoons olive oil
2 bay leaves
salt and pepper to taste
½ cup Chianti**

Bring beans and water to a boil; skim off scum, and then lower to simmer. Sauté bacon, onions, celery, green pepper and garlic lightly until golden and soft. Add this mixture plus parsley, bouillon, thyme, paprika, cayenne, olive oil, bay leaves, salt and pepper to the bean soup pot. Cover, simmer gently, stirring occasionally for 4 hours, reserving Chianti for the last half hour. Remove bay leaves before serving.

Barbara J. Sorlien
Philadelphia, Pennsylvania

INSTANT VICHYSSOISE

Easy
Do ahead

Serves: 6-8
Preparing: 15 minutes
Chilling: 4 hours

**1 package Knorr's leek soup
2 chicken bouillon cubes**

**1½ cups sour cream
chopped chives**

Prepare soup according to directions on package, adding bouillon cubes. Cool and chill thoroughly. Two hours before serving, stir in sour cream. Chill. Serve in chilled soup dishes. Sprinkle with chives.

Mrs. Baudrey Mays
Brussels, Belgium

OYSTER STEW

Average   *Serves: 8*
Partial do ahead   *Preparing: 45 minutes*

7 tablespoons butter	**4 celery stalks**
3-5 tablespoons flour	**3 dozen oysters**
2 cups milk	**1 pint table cream**
salt to taste	**1 teaspoon Worcestershire sauce**
pepper to taste	**few sprigs parsley**
4 small carrots	**¼ cup cooking sherry, if desired**
2 small turnips	

Make cream sauce with 3 tablespoons of butter, flour and milk. Season with salt. Stir until smooth and cook slowly until slightly thickened. Keep hot over boiling water. Cut all vegetables into little pieces, "about the size of the end of your little finger." Cook slowly in 2 tablespoons of the butter in the frying pan until glistening and almost soft. (Warning! Little pieces scorch easily!) Melt remaining 2 tablespoons of butter in a saucepan. Add oysters, oyster liquor and dash of salt and pepper. Cook only until edges of oysters curl, (they get tough if overcooked). Heat cream, making sure it doesn't boil. Assemble: Stir vegetables into cream sauce and combine with heated cream, oysters, oyster liquor and Worcestershire sauce. Add sherry. Pour into heated soup tureen or soup plates and sprinkle with chopped parsley.

Mrs. Theodore Widing, Jr.
Strafford, Pennsylvania

COLD CREAM OF TOMATO SOUP

Easy   *Serves: 6-8*
Do ahead   *Preparing: 5 minutes*
                                                                              Chilling: 3 hours

1 large can of tomato purée (Contadina)	**¼ teaspoon freshly grated pepper**
1 can Campbell's consommé, undiluted	**1¼ tablespoons onion juice**
1½ pints half and half	**2½ tablespoons sugar, or less**
½ teaspoon salt	**1 teaspoon curry powder, or to taste**

Blend all ingredients together. Chill well for several hours. Garnish with chopped chives or parsley.

Mrs. Geoffrey Stengel
Rosemont, Pennsylvania

CONSOMMÉ WITH AROMATIC SPICES

Easy
Do ahead

Serves: 8
Preparing: 5 minutes
Cooking: 30 minutes

4 cups beef consommé
  (homemade stock is best)
4 cups vegetable juices (V-8
  will do)
6 bay leaves
1 teaspoon crushed mint
1 tablespoon sugar
⅛ teaspoon cumin
⅛ teaspoon ginger

⅛ teaspoon chili powder
⅛ teaspoon cardamom
⅛ teaspoon lemon juice
generous pinch saffron
1 cup cooked rice
¼ cup Port wine
very thin slices of celery to
  garnish

Combine beef consommé, vegetable juices and bay leaves. Bring to a boil over high heat, covered. Uncover. Lower heat and simmer 10 minutes. Remove from heat. Cover and let steep about 15 minutes. Discard bay leaves. Return to low heat uncovered and add mint, sugar, spices, lemon juice and cooked rice. Simmer 10 minutes. Just before serving, add ¼ cup Port wine. Serve garnished with the celery slices.

The Committee

MEAT AND CABBAGE BORSCHT

Easy
Do ahead
Freeze

Serves: 4
Preparing: 30-45 minutes
Cooking: 2 hours

Meat, at least 3 pounds
  chuck or top rib (top rib
  preferable)
2 large cans of tomatoes (1
  can crushed and 1 can
  whole)
3 cups water (approximately)
salt to taste

pepper to taste
garlic to taste
1⅓ cups dark brown sugar (add
  little more if desired)
2 cups lemon juice, freshly
  squeezed
3 large onions, sliced
1 very large head cabbage, sliced

Braise meat with onions, until brown; add seasoning. Add tomatoes and water; cook for about ½ hour. Add sugar and lemon juice; cook additional ½ hour. Add cabbage last. Cook additional hour until meat is very tender.

Mrs. Leonard Mogill
Ardmore, Pennsylvania

GRANDMA DuPONT'S OKRA SOUP

Easy
Do ahead
Freeze

Serves: 6-8
Preparing: 45 minutes

1 quart okra
⅛ pound butter

1 quart chicken stock or veal
  stock

Slice a quart of okra into thin circles. Put butter into a frying pan. When hot, but not brown, add okra. Cook slowly for about 15 minutes, stirring all the time, until the "goo" runs. Do not brown. Heat to boiling, 1 quart of chicken or veal stock. Add the okra and boil over medium heat until the okra is soft and almost coming apart. Season with salt and pepper.

Mrs. Elwyn Evans
Wilmington, Delaware

ARMENIAN LEMON SOUP

Easy
Do ahead

Serves: 6
Preparing: 5 minutes
Cooking: 15 minutes

6 cups chicken broth
½ cup small noodles or
  vermicelli

1 egg, beaten
juice 1 lemon, strained
¼ cup finely chopped parsley

To six cups of boiling chicken broth add ½ cup small noodles or vermicelli and boil moderately until noodles are cooked. Just before serving, add into hot, but not boiling broth, the beaten egg, to which juice of lemon has been added. Dust with finely chopped parsley and serve immediately.

The Committee

WATERCRESS SOUP

Easy
Do ahead

Serves: 4-6
Preparing: 5 minutes
Cooking: 15 minutes

2 tablespoons butter or oil
3 or 4 bunches watercress,
  chopped
1 medium onion, chopped

1 can beef bouillon
½ pint sour cream
lemon juice

Sauté watercress and chopped onion in butter or oil until soft. Add bouillon and then purée in blender. Add sour cream and lemon juice to taste. Serve chilled or hot.

Mrs. Joseph H. Stein
Malibu, California

BUTTERNUT SQUASH SOUP

Easy   *Serves: 6*
Do ahead   *Preparing: 30 minutes*

4 cups chicken bouillon (4
  bouillon cubes)
3 medium onions, peeled and
  halved
3 cups butternut squash (2
  medium squash, peeled,
  seeded and cut up)

5 whole cloves
½ pint heavy cream
1 teaspoon curry powder
chopped parsley
salt and pepper to taste

Cook onions, squash and cloves in the bouillon until just soft. Pour entire mixture into blender. Add curry powder and cream. Blend for 2-3 minutes. Serve sprinkled with chopped parsley. May be prepared early in the day and reheated slowly just before serving; or serve cold.

Mrs. Stanley Clader
Rosemont, Pennsylvania

VIRGINIA'S VEGETABLE SOUP

Easy   *Serves: 16*
Do ahead   *Preparing: 10 minutes*
Freeze   *Cooking: 4 hours*

1 soup bone, with marrow
1½ pounds stewing beef
2 cans tomatoes (large size
  can)
1 pound onions, diced
5 white potatoes, diced

1 bunch carrots, diced
2 cups celery, diced
1 cup macaroni
1 cup spaghetti
salt to taste

Cook bone and beef for an hour in water to cover. Prepare vegetables and other ingredients. Put all together in large soup pot and add enough liquid to cover. Cook slowly for three hours. Add pastas last 15 minutes.

Mr. C. Wanton Balis, Jr.
Gladwyne, Pennsylvania

POTAGE DE LEGUMES

Easy
Do ahead

Serves: 4 to 8
Preparing: 15 minutes
Cooking: 1 hour

3 medium potatoes
3 small white turnips
2-3 leeks, or 2 medium
  onions
4 carrots, peeled
2 teaspoons parsley

1 tablespoon celery salt
½ teaspoon cracked peppercorns
1 pint milk
3 tablespoons butter
1 teaspoon allspice

Chop vegetables the size of walnuts. Place in pot and add enough water to come up to ¾ the volume of the vegetables. Add parsley and seasonings. Bring to a boil and simmer, covered, until vegetables are soft (¾ hour). Drain. Put through a food mill or blender. Add milk, butter, and allspice. Simmer until hot.

Mrs. Robert R. Masterton
Portland, Maine

OVEN FISH CHOWDER

Easy
Do ahead

Serves: 4-6
Preparing: 15 minutes
Baking: 1 hour

2 pounds cod or haddock
  fillets
4 potatoes, peeled and cubed
a few chopped celery leaves
1 bay leaf
2½ teaspoons salt
4 whole cloves

½ cup butter
¼ teaspoon dill seed or weed
¼ teaspoon white pepper
½ cup white wine or vermouth
2 cups boiling water
2 cups light cream

Place all ingredients in pot *except* cream. Cover and bake at 375° for 1 hour. Heat cream to scalding and add before serving with parsley or fresh dill garnish.

Mrs. William M. Dow
Haverford, Pennsylvania

VEGETABLE SOUP

Easy
Do ahead

Serves: 6-8
Preparing: 10-15 minutes
Cooking: 45 minutes

2 tablespoons olive oil
2 tablespoons butter or
  margarine
1 medium onion, chopped
1 pound lean ground beef
1 medium eggplant, diced
1 clove garlic, minced or
  mashed
½ cup diced carrots
½ cup sliced celery
1 (1 pound, 12 ounce) can
  pear-shaped Italian-style
  tomatoes

2 14-ounce cans beef broth
1 teaspoon salt
1 teaspoon sugar
½ teaspoon pepper
½ teaspoon ground nutmeg
½ cup small shell macaroni
2 tablespoons minced parsley
grated Parmesan cheese

Heat oil and butter in soup kettle. Add onion and sauté until limp. Add meat and stir until it loses all pinkness. Add eggplant, garlic, carrots, celery, tomatoes (broken up with fork), beef broth, salt, sugar, pepper and nutmeg. Cover and simmer about 30-40 minutes. Add macaroni and parsley, cook about 10 minutes more, or until macaroni is tender.

Mrs. William S. Cashel, Jr.
Gladwyne, Pennsylvania

GAZPACHO BLANCO

Easy
Do ahead

Serves: 6
Preparing: 20 minutes
Chilling: 2 hours

3 medium cucumbers, peeled
  and cut in chunks
3 cups chicken broth,
  homemade or canned
3 cups sour cream
3 tablespoons white vinegar

2 teaspoons garlic salt
2 tomatoes, chopped and peeled
¾ cup toasted almonds
½ cup sliced green onions
½ cup chopped parsley

Put ½ cup chicken broth in blender with cucumbers and blend quickly. Combine with remaining broth, sour cream, vinegar and garlic salt. Stir just enough to mix. Chill. Sprinkle rest of ingredients on top when serving.

The Committee

PURÉE OF CARROT SOUP

Easy
Do ahead

Serves: 6
Preparing: 10 minutes
Cooking: 30 minutes

3 cups sliced carrots
¾ cup sliced onions
1 quart chicken stock
2 teaspoons tomato paste
2 tablespoons butter

2 tablespoons plain white
  uncooked rice
salt, pepper
1 teaspoon (or less) cardamom

Combine all ingredients and cook in heavy saucepan until carrots are tender. Purée in blender. Serve hot or cold with carrot curls on top, or chopped parsley.

Mrs. Emory Eysmans
Bryn Mawr, Pennsylvania

Christopher D'Amanda, M.D.
Philadelphia, Pennsylvania

BROCCOLI CHOWDER

Easy

Serves: 6-8
Preparing: 30 minutes

2 pounds fresh broccoli
2 13½ ounce cans chicken
  broth
3 cups milk
1 cup chopped cooked ham
2 teaspoons salt, or to taste

¼ teaspoon pepper
1 cup half and half
2 cups (1 pound) shredded Swiss
  cheese
¼ cup butter or margarine

Combine broccoli and 1 can chicken broth in Dutch oven. Cover and cook 7 minutes or until broccoli is crisp-tender. Remove broccoli from broth; cool and chop coarsely. Add remaining can of chicken broth, milk, ham, salt and pepper to Dutch oven. Bring to a boil over medium heat, stirring occasionally. Stir in broccoli and remaining ingredients. Cook over low heat until thoroughly heated. Do not boil.

Mrs. Blair B. May
Wayne, Pennsylvania

Close Harmony

salads and dressings

CAULIFLOWER SALAD WITH ANCHOVY DRESSING

Average
Do ahead

Serves: 8
Preparing: 30 minutes plus chilling time

1 head cauliflower, rinsed and broken into flowerets
½ medium onion, finely minced
1 tablespoon chopped green pepper
8 tablespoons olive oil
1 teaspoon dried marjoram

1 teaspoon chopped pimiento
salt and pepper
6 anchovy filets, drained and finely chopped
½ cup white wine vinegar or cider vinegar
6 green pimiento stuffed olives, sliced

Parboil cauliflower 10 minutes in salted water. Drain and rinse in cold water. Sauté onion and green pepper in 2 tablespoons olive oil five minutes. Add remaining olive oil and everything except olives. Bring to boil and turn off heat. Pour mixture over cauliflower and chill. Garnish with green olive slices.

Mrs. Robert Bailey
Vail, Colorado

GREEK SALAD

Easy
Partial do ahead

Preparing: 30 minutes

1 cut clove garlic
2 quarts salad greens or spinach

½ cup sliced black olives (Greek or Italian)
4 ounces Feta cheese (cubed)

Dressing:

2 tablespoons lemon juice
6 tablespoons olive oil
salt and pepper to taste

pinch of oregano
pinch of mint

Rub salad bowl with cut garlic clove. Add washed greens, olives and cheese. Combine dressing ingredients and shake vigorously. Pour dressing over greens. Toss to coat every leaf.

Mrs. Emile C. Geyelin
Villanova, Pennsylvania

ASPARAGUS VINAIGRETTE SALAD

Serves: 25
Preparing: 20 minutes
Chilling: 4 hours

5 pounds asparagus
1½ cups salted water
½ teaspoon paprika
¼ teaspoon dry mustard
½ teaspoon salt
½ teaspoon sugar
½ garlic clove, crushed
½ cup vinegar
½ teaspoon Worcestershire

1½ cups salad oil
½ cup sweet relish, drained
1 cup finely chopped onion
¼ cup finely chopped
   fresh parsley
½ cup finely chopped green
   peppers
¼ cup finely chopped pimiento

Break off stalks as far down as they snap easily. Wash well. Cook asparagus in boiling salted water until tender; drain well. Place asparagus one layer deep in flat pan. Combine remaining ingredients. Stir to mix well. Pour over asparagus. Marinate 3 to 4 hours in refrigerator. Using a slotted spoon, arrange asparagus spears on large platter lined with lettuce leaves. Garnish with pimiento strips if desired.

K. Carol Carlson, vice president
ARA Services
Philadelphia, Pennsylvania

COLD PEA SALAD

Easy
Do ahead

Serves: 6
Preparing: 10 minutes plus chilling
time

1 17-ounce can English peas
2 tablespoons chopped
   celery
1 tablespoon chopped onion
2 tablespoons green pepper
1 teaspoon chopped pimiento

1 tablespoon pickle relish
2 tablespoons sharp cheddar
   cheese, diced
1 egg, hard boiled and chopped
1½ tablespoons mayonnaise

Drain peas. Combine next 6 ingredients and mix well. Add peas, eggs, and mayonnaise and mix gently. Chill thoroughly.

The Committee

SPAGHETTI-BEAN SPROUT SALAD

Average
Do ahead

Serves: 8-10
Preparing: 30 minutes
Chilling: 3 hours

This is to be served as a cold salad. But I have heated it and served it hot for a really great dish!

Sauce

¾ cup mayonnaise
1 tablespoon soy sauce
1 teaspoon salt

1 teaspoon garlic powder
dash black pepper

Ingredients

7 ounces vermicelli,
  cooked, drained
1 16-ounce can bean
  sprouts, drained
  (or fresh)
1 4-ounce can mushrooms,
  drained (or fresh)
½ cup chopped celery

⅓ cup chopped green
  pepper
¼ cup chopped onion
1 cup frozen peas (don't
  cook)
½ cup chopped cashews or
  peanuts

Mix sauce ingredients together. Mix all other ingredients together except nuts. Add to sauce. Refrigerate at least 3 hours. Add nuts before serving.

Mrs. J. Tant Priestley
Boulder, Colorado

ZINGY TOMATO ASPIC

Easy
Do ahead

Serves: 8
Preparing: 10 minutes
Chilling: 3 hours

2½ cups water
2 3-ounce packages lemon
  Jello
1 12-ounce jar chili sauce

¼ cup chopped stuffed olives
½ cup chopped celery
1 teaspoon lemon juice

Melt Jello in boiling water, then add the rest of the ingredients. Pour into mold and chill.

Mrs. John E. Krout
Rosemont, Pennsylvania

CHICKEN AND HAM SALAD VERONIQUE

Average   *Serves: 6-8*
Partial do ahead   *Preparing: 2 hours*

Chicken

4 pounds chicken, cut up
celery tops
1 onion, sliced
pinch of thyme
pinch of marjoram
salt, pepper
1 teaspoon curry powder

3 cups diced cooked ham
1 pound seedless grapes (2½ to 3
  cups)
lettuce, chicory or spinach
parsley
seasonal fruits (optional)

Dressing

1 cup Miracle Whip
½ cup sour cream
½ cup chutney, finely chopped

1 tablespoon lemon juice
1 teaspoon curry powder
½ teaspoon salt

Cook chicken with first seven ingredients in water to cover, 35 minutes or until tender. Cook chicken; cut into bite sized cubes. (Can be done day before.) Make dressing; combine chicken, dressing, ham and grapes. Serve on platter of greens. Garnish with parsley or seasonal fruits.

Mrs. K. S. East
Devon, Pennsylvania

CUCUMBER-GRAPEFRUIT ASPIC

Easy   *Serves: 6*
Do ahead   *Preparing: 15 minutes*
                                        Chilling: 2 hours

1½ tablespoons unflavored
  gelatine
¼ cup cold water
½ cup boiling water
1½ cups grapefruit juice
2 tablespoons lemon juice

1 tablespoon sugar
½ teaspoon salt
1 cup canned grapefruit sections
1 cup cucumber, seeded and
  finely chopped

Soften gelatine in cold water. Dissolve in hot water. Add grapefruit juice, lemon juice, sugar and salt. Chill until mixture begins to thicken. Fold in grapefruit sections and cucumber. Pour into mold and chill until firm. Serve with dressing: 2 parts mayonnaise dressing, 1 part sour cream.

Mrs. I. M. Scott
Meadowbrook, Pennsylvania

SPICED PEACH SALAD

Easy
Do ahead

Serves: 8
Preparing: 10 minutes

1 large box (6 ounce) peach
   Jello
6 ounce can apricot nectar
¼ cup vinegar
1 large can sliced peaches

½ cup sugar
¾ teaspoon ground cloves
¾ teaspoon ground cinnamon
2 cups liquid (juice from
   peaches, plus water)

Boil vinegar, sugar, spices and liquid until spices dissolve. Add Jello to hot mixture and dissolve. Then add sliced peaches and apricot nectar. Put in 8-cup ring mold or 8 individual molds.

The Committee

CRANBERRY SALAD

Easy
Do ahead

Serves: 6
Preparing: 15 minutes
Chilling: 2 hours

1 small box raspberry,
   strawberry or lemon Jello
½ cup water
1 can whole cranberry sauce

1 orange, ground in blender or
   food processor (use skin too)
chopped apple and nuts
   (optional)

Dissolve Jello in water in double boiler. Add cranberry sauce and orange. Mold. Can use plain gelatine if you prefer a less sweet salad. Fill center with chicken salad for luncheon, or serve with chicken or meat for dinner.

Mrs. George Riggs, Jr.
Gladwyne, Pennsylvania

BROCCOLI SALAD

Easy
Do ahead

Serves: 8
Preparing: 20 minutes
Chilling: 2 hours

2 packages chopped broccoli
2 hard-boiled eggs
1 can beef consommé
3 tablespoons lemon juice

1 teaspoon Worcestershire sauce
2 dashes Tabasco
¾ cup mayonnaise
1 package Knox gelatine

Cook broccoli until tender. Soak Knox gelatine in ¼ cup consommé. Boil rest of consommé and dissolve gelatine. Add lemon juice, Tabasco and mayonnaise. Fold in broccoli and chopped eggs. Chill until firm. Top with blue cheese dressing.

Mrs. Frank H. Phipps
Villanova, Pennsylvania

ASPARAGUS SALAD

Easy   *Serves: 4-6*
Do ahead   *Preparing: 15 minutes*
                                        Chilling: 30 minutes

2 pounds fresh asparagus   **¼ teaspoon salt**
¾ cup plain yogurt   **1 small head Boston lettuce**
1 to 2 garlic cloves, crushed   **2 hard-boiled egg yolks, sieved**
1½ tablespoons chopped
** parsley**

Cook asparagus 10 minutes until tender crisp. Drain, cool and refrigerate. Combine yogurt, garlic, parsley, salt; mix well and refrigerate. Place asparagus on bed of lettuce and top with dressing. Sprinkle egg yolk on top.

Mrs. Louis Hood
Wayne, Pennsylvania

AVOCADO SALAD MOLD

Easy   *Serves: 8*
Do ahead   *Preparing: 30 minutes*
                                           Chilling: 4 hours

1 3-ounce box lime Jello   **salt to taste**
1 cup boiling water   **paprika**
3 tablespoons lemon juice   **1 cup cottage cheese (or 1 cup**
1 teaspoon grated onion   ** whipped cream)**
1 cup mashed ripe avocado   **½ cup mayonnaise**

Dissolve Jello in hot water. Add lemon juice, avocado and onion to Jello. When this begins to set, add cottage cheese and mayonnaise. (If you are not calorie-counting, substitute whipped cream for cottage cheese.)

Mrs. William G. Foulke
Philadelphia, Pennsylvania

FOX POINT CRANBERRY SALAD

Average
Do ahead

Serves: 8 or 9
Preparing: ¾ hour
Chilling: 2 hours

3 cups cranberries
1 cup water
1¼ cups sugar
1 3-ounce package cherry
   Jello
1 envelope unflavored
   gelatine

1½ cups seedless or seeded half
   grapes
1 small can drained crushed
   pineapple
½ cup walnuts, cut in pieces

Dressing

1 4-ounce package
   marshmallows, cut up

1 3-ounce package cream cheese
½ pint heavy cream

Boil cranberries in sugar and water mix until cranberries snap (only a few seconds). Dissolve cherry Jello and gelatine in ½ cup cold water. Add boiled cranberries, sugar and water to gelatine. When cool, add the grapes, pineapple and walnuts. Pour into a 7″ or 8″ ring mold. Refrigerate. Mix dressing ingredients together and refrigerate overnight. Beat when ready to serve. Serve dressing on the side.

Mrs. Richard M. Linder
York, Pennsylvania

FIVE CUP SALAD

Easy
Do ahead

Serves: 10
Preparing: 5 minutes

Better if made the day before.

1 cup crushed pineapple
1 cup miniature
   marshmallows

1 cup Mandarin oranges
1 cup shredded coconut
1 cup sour cream

Combine all ingredients and mix well. Serve on a bed of lettuce.

Mrs. John M. Brownback
New Orleans, Louisiana

EDIE'S SALAD

Easy
Do ahead

Serves: 6-8
Preparing: 20 minutes
Chilling: 2 hours

1 large can pear halves,
   cubed in large pieces
1 package (8-ounce) cream
   cheese
¼ teaspoon ginger
1 8-ounce package lime Jello

1¼ cups water
pinch of salt
crème de menthe
mayonnaise
sour cream

Mix dissolved Jello, cream cheese and ginger together. Blend in mixer. Pour over pear halves in mold. Chill. Serve with crème de menthe dressing: crème de menthe mixed with mayonnaise and sour cream.

Mrs. Frank B. McKaig
Gulph Mills, Pennsylvania

SALAD JOSEPHINE

Easy
Partial do ahead

Preparing: 30 minutes

melon balls
cucumber balls
pre-fried bacon bits
small pieces cauliflower
   (smaller than florets)

corn niblets
broken pieces of lettuce
chopped walnuts (optional)
quail eggs (optional)

Dressing

½ clove garlic, mashed
juice of ½ lemon
salt and pepper to taste

olive oil, twice as much as lemon
   juice

Toss all together in glass salad bowl. Add dressing and chill.

L'Hotel Aigle Noir
Fontainebleau, France

CORN SALAD

Easy

Serves: Flexible
Preparing: 20 minutes

All ingredients in amounts to taste. Luncheon salad to be served with a good French bread, country sausage, wine and fruit.

canned "shoe peg" corn
  (drained)
coarsely chopped ham

slivered hearts of palm
cubed Gruyère cheese
slivered tiny sour pickles

Dressing:

1 part wine vinegar
3 parts olive oil
Dijon mustard (to taste)

minced garlic (to taste)
salt and pepper (to taste)

Assemble all salad ingredients in salad bowl. Whip dressing with electric beater and toss with salad.

Mrs. M. Todd Cooke
Newtown Square, Pennsylvania

CHINESE TUNA SALAD

Easy
Do ahead

Serves: 8
Preparing: 30 minutes
Chilling: overnight

¾ cup mayonnaise
1 tablespoon lemon juice
1 teaspoon soy sauce
⅛ teaspoon curry powder
⅛ teaspoon garlic powder
1 package (10½ ounce)
  frozen little peas, cooked
  and drained and cooled

2 large cans chunk tuna
2 hard-cooked eggs, chopped
  fine
4-5 stalks celery, chopped fine
4 large scallions
1 can chow mein noodles
½ cup slivered toasted almonds

Mix first five ingredients and chill overnight. Next day mix tuna, hard-cooked eggs, celery and scallions. Add peas. Chow mein noodles should be added at the last minute. Garnish salad with almonds. Serve with corn sticks or corn muffins and sliced tomatoes.

Mrs. Ralph B. Cole
Kennett Square, Pennsylvania

HUNGARIAN CUCUMBER SALAD

Easy
Do ahead

Serves: 6-8
Preparing: 1 hour 15 minutes
Chilling: 1-2 hours

**2 medium cucumbers (about
 1¼ pounds)**
2 teaspoons salt
3 tablespoons vinegar
3 tablespoons water

½ teaspoon sugar
¼ teaspoon paprika
¼ teaspoon pepper
**3 or 4 green onions or scallions
 (or 1 medium yellow onion)**

Wash and pare cucumbers; slice thinly into a bowl. Sprinkle the salt evenly on top. Mix lightly and set aside for 1 hour. Meanwhile, mix together vinegar, water, sugar, paprika and pepper. Slice the peeled onions and add to mixture. Squeeze cucumber slices, a few at a time, (discarding the liquid), and put into a bowl. Pour the vinegar mixture over the cucumbers and toss lightly. Sprinkle with more paprika, about ⅛ teaspoon. Chill for 1 to 2 hours.

Mrs. George S. Fabian
Bryn Mawr, Pennsylvania

JAVANESE VEGETABLE SALAD "GADO-GADO"

Easy

Serves: 24
Preparing: 30 minutes

1 pound green pepper
**2½ cups salted peanuts (12
 ounces)**
2 tablespoons brown sugar
½ cup lemon juice
2 pounds cabbage
**1 head iceberg lettuce (1½
 pounds)**

1 cup water chestnuts, sliced ⅛"
½ cup green onions, sliced ¼"
1¼ pounds cucumber
salt as needed
sliced hard-boiled eggs, garnish
tomato wedges, garnish

Wash and clean green pepper. Grind fine with peanuts. Add sugar and lemon juice. Blend well. Wash and shred cabbage. Wash and cut lettuce into ½" pieces. Peel and slice cucumber into ⅛" thick slices. Toss vegetables together. Add peanut-pepper mixture. Toss and add salt if needed. Garnish and serve immediately.

K. Carol Carlson, Vice President
ARA Services
Philadelphia, Pennsylvania

OUR CHICKEN SALAD

Easy
Do ahead

Serves: 32
Preparing: 60 minutes
Marinating: 2 hours
Chilling: 2 hours

10 pounds chicken breasts
1 tablespoon vinegar
¼ medium onion
1 peeled, sliced carrot
1 celery stalk with leaves
1 package of MBT seasoning
2 cloves

1 bay leaf
4 cups chopped celery
4 cups mayonnaise
4 packages MBT chicken broth
   mix
French dressing

French dressing:

1⅓ cups oil
1⅓ cups vinegar
8 tablespoons sugar
2 teaspoons salt
4 teaspoons Janes' Krazy
   Mixed-Up Salt

4 teaspoons dry mustard
4 tablespoons Worcestershire
sauce
1 small onion, chopped

Salt chicken on all sides and place in pan with water to cover. Add the next seven ingredients and cook until tender (about 35 to 45 minutes). Cool chicken and dice to make 16 cups. Blend ingredients for French dressing and pour over diced chicken and celery. Marinate for two hours. Partially drain and add mayonnaise mixed with MBT chicken broth mix. Chill one hour.

The Committee

COPPER PENNY CARROTS

Easy
Do ahead

Serves: 16
Preparing: 30 minutes
Marinating: overnight

2 pounds carrots, scraped
   and cut into circles (I use
   2-pound bag frozen sliced)
1 small green pepper,
   chopped
1 medium onion, cut into thin
   rings

1 can tomato soup
½ cup salad oil
1 cup sugar
¾ cup vinegar
1 teaspoon prepared mustard
1 teaspoon Worcestershire sauce
salt, to taste

Cook carrots in salted water until tender. Drain. Layer carrots, green pepper and onion in deep bowl. Blend soup, oil, sugar, vinegar, mustard, Worcestershire sauce and salt in saucepan and heat. Pour over vegetables while still warm. Cover dish tightly with foil. Refrigerate overnight or up to one week. Remove carrots with slotted spoon to serve.

Mrs. William Knorr
Springfield, Pennsylvania

NIPPY SALAD

Easy
Do ahead

Serves: 6-8
Preparing: 20 minutes
Chilling: 2 hours

1 package lime Jello
1¼ cups boiling water
1 cup cottage cheese
1 cup canned crushed
    pineapple

½ cup mayonnaise
1 to 1½ tablespoons horseradish

Dissolve lime Jello in boiling water and allow to almost set. Then add remaining ingredients. Place in mold in refrigerator to set.

Mrs. Horace W. Schwarz
Gladwyne, Pennsylvania

SALATA KUTHRA (Syrian Salad)

Easy

Serves: 8
Preparing: 20 minutes

6 tomatoes
2 green peppers
1 bunch green onions
1 avocado
½ bunch parsley
1 bunch radishes

1 firm cucumber
1 tablespoon fresh or dried mint
1 teaspoon garlic powder
juice of 3 lemons (no substitute)
⅓ cup olive oil (no substitute)
salt and pepper to taste

Chop all vegetables and combine them with seasonings, olive oil and lemon juice. Toss and serve.

Mrs. John A. Girvin
Gladwynne, Pennsylvania

GAZPACHO MOLD

Easy
Do ahead

Serves: 6
Preparing: 25-30 minutes
Chilling:3 hours

1 envelope unflavored
  gelatine
1⅔ cups tomato juice
2 tablespoons wine vinegar
2 large tomatoes, peeled,
  seeded and chopped
1 large or 2 small cucumbers,
  peeled, seeded and
  chopped

½ cup sliced scallions (⅛"
  slices)
1 clove garlic, minced
¾ teaspoon salt
⅛ teaspoon pepper
pinch of sugar

Soften gelatine in ¼ cup tomato juice. Heat remaining juices to simmer. Add softened gelatine and stir until thoroughly dissolved. Cool until syrupy. Add remaining ingredients and pour into one quart mold. Chill three hours or more. Unmold. Garnish as desired. Can make sauce of mayonnaise thinned with milk. Add sour cream and dill.

Mrs. Ralph S. Saul
Haverford, Pennsylvania

HAM SALAD JAMAICAN

Easy
Do ahead

Serves: 4
Preparing: 15 minutes

2 4½-ounce cans deviled
  ham spread
2 tablespoons orange
  marmalade
2 tablespoons prepared white
  horseradish

¼ cup minced peeled onion
2 tablespoons lemon juice
4 very large fresh peaches

In small bowl combine ham spread with marmalade, horseradish, onion, and lemon juice. Cut the top off each peach and save. With a teaspoon scoop out the pit and discard. Fill each peach with a fourth of the ham mixture. Replace peach top and serve on a bed of lettuce.

Mrs. Ruby Allen
Haverford, Pennsylvania

RICE SALAD WITH CHUTNEY DRESSING

Easy
Do ahead

Serves: 12
Preparing: 15 minutes
Chilling: overnight

1½ cups (one 18-ounce jar)
   chutney
½ cup vegetable oil
2 tablespoons lemon juice
½ teaspoon ground ginger
6 cups cold cooked rice (1¾
   cups uncooked rice)

2 cups chopped apples
2 cups chopped celery
½ cup golden raisins
¼ cup chopped toasted almonds

Combine chutney, oil, lemon juice and ginger in large bowl. Stir in remaining ingredients. Refrigerate, covered, overnight to blend flavors. Garnish with watercress.

Mrs. Ellis S. Rump, Jr.
West Chester, Pennsylvania

TOMATOES AND RIPE OLIVES WITH CUMIN DRESSING

Easy
Do ahead

Serves: 8-10
Preparing: 15 minutes
Chilling: 2 hours

6 average size or 8-9 small,
   ripe tomatoes
1 cup drained, pitted black
   olives

2 sweet onions, thinly sliced
¼ cup chopped parsley

Dressing:

1 teaspoon salt
2 teaspoons sugar
⅛ teaspoon tumeric
¾ teaspoon ground cumin

¼ teaspoon black pepper
6 tablespoons olive oil
4 tablespoons lemon juice

Slice or wedge tomatoes (peeling is optional). Mix with olives, onions and parsley. Marinate at least two hours in dressing. (Blend dressing ingredients with whisk or blender.) Serve very cold.

Barbara W. Trimmer
Hopetown Abaco, Bahamas

EASTERN SHORE CRAB SALAD

Easy   *Serves: 6*
Preparing: 30 minutes

1 1-pound can backfin lump
  crab meat
1 cup finely chopped celery
2 tablespoons chopped sweet
  red or green peppers
⅛ teaspoon paprika

½ teaspoon salt
3 tablespoons catsup
1 cup salad dressing
juice of ½ lemon
½ teaspoon prepared mustard
1½ tablespoons sugar

Remove all shell and sinew from crab meat, leaving lumps of the same size as much as possible. Place in bowl with celery and green pepper. In another bowl mix all the other ingredients to form the salad dressing mixture. Mix the dressing with the crab meat, being careful to keep the lumps of crab meat whole. Refrigerate until ready to use or serve at once on lettuce leaf. Garnish with sliced hard-cooked eggs or tomato wedges. Or, serve the salad in a hollowed-out ripe tomato.

Mrs. Neal D. Ivey, Jr.
Radnor, Pennsylvania

EGGS-TUNA TERRIFIC

Easy   *Serves: 4*
Preparing: 30 minutes

1 head iceberg lettuce,
  washed and drained
8 hard-boiled eggs, halved
  lengthwise
⅓ cup mayonnaise
1 tablespoon lemon juice
1 tablespoon milk

½ small onion, peeled
1 tablespoon drained capers
1 7-ounce can white tuna,
  drained
⅛ teaspoon salt
⅛ teaspoon pepper
10 ripe olives

Line a serving platter with lettuce leaves. Arrange eggs on lettuce leaves, cut side down. Place remaining ingredients, except olives, in an electric blender and blend at medium speed until smooth. Spoon the sauce over the eggs and garnish with olives.

Mrs. Ruby Allan
Haverford, Pennsylvania

MOLDED SPICED BEET SALAD

Easy   *Serves: 8-10*
Do ahead   *Preparing: 10-15 minutes*
                                                    Chilling: 45 minutes

2 cans, 1 pound each, sliced
  beets
3½ cups liquid (water and
  beet juice)
2 packages, 3 ounce each,
  lemon or orange Jello
¼ cup finely minced onion

½ teaspoon salt
¼ teaspoon allspice
1 teaspoon prepared horseradish
3 tablespoons lemon juice
½ cup sour cream
½ cup mayonnaise

Drain liquid from beets and measure. Add water to make 3½ cups liquid.
Set aside beets. Combine Jello, beet liquid, onion, salt, allspice and horseradish. Stir over medium heat until Jello dissolves. Remove from heat and
stir in lemon juice. Chill until syrupy. Dice beets and add to gelatine mixture.
Use 2 quart ring mold and chill. Serve with sour cream dressing: ½ cup sour
cream and ½ cup mayonnaise.

The Committee

MOLDED SPINACH SALAD

Easy   *Serves: 6*
Do ahead   *Preparing: 30 minutes*
                                                    Chilling: 6-8 hours

1 3-ounce package lemon
  Jello
1½ teaspoons vinegar
½ cup mayonnaise
1 cup creamed cottage
  cheese

1 package chopped spinach,
  cooked and drained well
½ cup finely chopped celery
½ cup finely chopped red onion

Dissolve lemon Jello in 1 cup hot water. Add vinegar and mayonnaise.
Blend with rotary beater. Pour in ice cube tray and put in freezer for about 12
minutes or until almost frozen. Then beat until fluffy. Fold in cottage cheese,
spinach, celery and onion. Put in mold and refrigerate 6-8 hours.

Mrs. Charles Vetterlein
Gladwyne, Pennsylvania

CANLIS' SPECIAL SALAD

Easy
Partial do ahead

Serves: 4-6
Preparing: 20 minutes

2 heads Romaine
2 peeled tomatoes
¼ cup chopped green onion
½ cup Romano cheese
  (freshly grated)

1 pound cooked bacon, finely
  chopped
1 cup croutons

Dressing:

1 cup olive oil
¼ cup lemon juice
½ teaspoon freshly ground
  pepper

¼ teaspoon chopped mint
¼ teaspoon oregano
1 coddled egg

Into a large bowl (wooden) pour approximately 2 tablespoons of good imported olive oil, sprinkle with salt, and rub firmly with a large clove of garlic. (The oil will act as a lubricant and the salt as an abrasive). Remove garlic and in the bottom of the bowl first place the tomatoes cut in eighths, add Romaine, sliced in 1 inch strips. You may add other salad vegetables if you choose, but remember to put heavy vegetables in first with Romaine on top. Add condiments. Dressing: Into a bowl pour the lemon juice and seasonings. Add coddled egg and whip vigorously. Then add olive oil, whipping constantly. When ready to serve, pour dressing over salad. Add croutons last. Toss generously.

Canlis' Restaurant
Honolulu, Hawaii

CREAMY BROCCOLI SALAD

Easy
Do ahead

Serves: 6-8
Preparing: 30 minutes

1 bunch fresh broccoli
1 medium head cauliflower
3 medium tomatoes, sliced
  (cut slices in half)
3 small red onions, sliced
  and separated into rings,
  (cut in half)

¼ teaspoon garlic salt
½ to ¾ cup mayonnaise
½ to ¾ cup sour cream
½ teaspoon lemon juice
  (optional)
8 to 10 cherry tomatoes

Remove large leaves and tough ends of lower stalks of broccoli. Wash thoroughly. Cut into bite sized pieces. Separate cauliflower flowerets into bite sized pieces. Combine broccoli, cauliflower, tomatoes and onions in large bowl. Combine garlic, salt, mayonnaise, sour cream and lemon juice. Add to vegetables. Toss gently. Garnish with cherry tomatoes.

The Committee

THREE GREEN SALAD

Easy
Do ahead

Serves: 6
Preparing: 15 minutes
Chilling: 2 hours

2 10-ounce packages frozen
 French-style green beans,
 or cut green beans
1 10-ounce package frozen
 chopped broccoli
1 8½-ounce can artichoke
 hearts, drained and
 quartered

½ cup chopped onion
1 cup buttermilk-style salad
 dressing
2 tablespoons anchovy paste, or
 chopped anchovies

Cook vegetables according to package directions and drain well. Combine vegetables and remaining ingredients. Toss lightly to mix. Refrigerate to chill and serve.

Mrs. Wolcott McM. Heyl
Philadelphia, Pennsylvania

FROZEN BANANA SALAD

Easy
Do ahead
Freeze

Serves: 9
Preparing: 10 minutes
Freezing: 3 hours

2 cups sour cream
1 8-ounce can crushed
 pineapple
1 tablespoon lemon juice
½ cup chopped nuts

¾ cup sugar
4 bananas, mashed
1 teaspoon salt
1 8-ounce jar maraschino
 cherries, quartered

Mix all above ingredients well. Pour into 9″x9″ pan. Freeze.

Mrs. Blair B. May
Wayne, Pennsylvania

TOMATO & CHEESE LAYERED SALAD

Easy
Do ahead

Serves: 8-10
Preparing: 15 minutes
Chilling: 2 hours

2 packages strawberry Jello
1 quart tomato juice
1 tablespoon grated
  horseradish
1 tablespoon grated onion
2 teaspoons salt

1 package lemon Jello
1 cup boiling water
1 cup cottage cheese
1 cup whipping cream, whipped
salt to taste

Heat tomato juice and seasonings to boiling, run them through sieve. Pour over strawberry Jello. Stir until dissolved. Mold and set aside to harden. Dissolve lemon Jello in boiling water. Set in pan of ice water and when thick, beat until stiff and frothy. Fold in cottage cheese and salt, and whipped cream. Blend well and pour on top of hardened red layer. Serve with mayonnaise mixed with a little heavy cream and two tablespoons horseradish. Can be made in a ring mold and the center filled with canned asparagus.

Mrs. John V. Calhoun, Jr.
Devon, Pennsylvania

GREEN SALAD

Easy
Do ahead

Serves: 8
Preparing: 15 minutes

1 clove garlic, minced
¼ cup salad oil
1 cup plain croutons
½ head lettuce
½ bunch curly endive
1 bunch watercress
¼ teaspoon dry mustard

¼ teaspoon black peppercorns,
  cracked
½ cup salad oil
¼ cup lemon juice
1 one-minute egg
½ teaspoon salt
¼ cup grated Parmesan cheese

Add garlic to ¼ cup salad oil. Let stand several hours. In skillet brown croutons in garlic flavored salad oil. Tear chilled and cleaned greens into salad bowl. Combine mustard, peppercorns, salt, Parmesan cheese, ½ cup salad oil, lemon juice and egg. Beat well. Pour over salad and toss (leaves should be coated). Add croutons, toss lightly. Serve immediately.

Mrs. Eugene R. Hook
Wynnewood, Pennsylvania

JELLIED TUNA OR CHICKEN SALAD

Easy
Do ahead

Serves: 6-8
Preparing: 1 hour
Chilling: 2 hours

2 6½-ounce cans chunk style
   tuna, drained (or equal
   amount of cubed chicken)
2 hard-boiled eggs, chopped
½ cup chopped stuffed green
   olives
1 tablespoon minced
   shallots, or onions

2 tablespoons capers
1 envelope Knox gelatine
¼ cup cold water
2 cups mayonnaise
watercress

Combine first five ingredients. Soften gelatine in cold water in measuring cup. Put cup in pan of boiling water, stirring until gelatin is dissolved. Stir into mayonnaise. Mix well with tuna mixture. Pour into 1¼ quart ring mold, or into individual molds. Chill. No salad dressing required. Serve with lots of watercress garnish.

Mrs. Charles Sheridan
Paoli, Pennsylvania

MOLDED MELON SALAD

Easy
Do ahead

Serves: 8-10
Preparing: 20 minutes
Chilling: 2 hours

1 tablespoon Knox gelatine
1 package (3 ounce) lime
   Jello
2 cups cantaloupe balls

2 cups honeydew melon balls
1 8-ounce package cream cheese
mint leaves

Dissolve Knox gelatine in ¼ cup water. Pour ¾ cup boiling water over lime Jello. Stir and add dissolved Knox gelatine. Add 1 cup cold water. Allow to partially thicken. Add slightly more than half the mixture to melon balls. Pour into mold. Allow remaining Jello to partially thicken. Add cream cheese and mix in blender or food processor. Pour on top of melon balls. Chill until set. Serve on bed of mint leaves.

Mrs. Norman P. Robinson
Haverford, Pennsylvania

PROVENCALE BEEF SALAD
WITH ANCHOVY VINAIGRETTE

Average
Partial do ahead

Serves: 12
Preparing: 30 minutes
Marinating: overnight

Dressing:

1½ cups corn oil
½ cup white vinegar
1 small can of flat anchovies
with oil
2 garlic cloves, peeled

1 teaspoon sugar
1 teaspoon black pepper
¼ cup minced parsley
1½ teaspoons salt

Salad:

3 pounds new potatoes in their
skins
4 cups ½" cubes of cooked
roast beef or filet
2 cups scallions, cut in ¼"
circles
1 small jar of capers, drained

1 basket cherry tomatoes,
stemmed
6 ounces Greek olives, pitted and
halved
⅓ cup minced parsley
Romaine lettuce

Combine dressing ingredients in a food processor or blender. Boil potatoes until tender in their skins. While still warm, cut potatoes in 1" cubes and toss with the anchovy vinaigrette. Allow the potatoes to marinate for 2-3 hours or overnight. At serving time, combine potatoes with all the other ingredients. Serve on bed of Romaine leaves.

The Commissary
Philadelphia, Pennsylvania

FROZEN STRAWBERRY SALAD

Easy
Do ahead
Freeze

Serves: 8-16
Preparing: 15 minutes
Freezing: overnight

1 8-ounce package cream
cheese
¾ cup sugar
1 10-ounce package frozen
strawberries, thawed and
undrained

1 13-ounce can crushed
pineapple, drained
1 8-ounce Cool Whip
1 cup finely chopped walnuts
1 diced banana

Beat cream cheese and sugar for 2 minutes, medium speed. Add, with a spoon, the strawberries, pineapple, Cool Whip, chopped walnuts and banana. Mix well by hand. Place in 13"x9"x2" glass pan and place in freezer overnight. Take out 1 hour before serving.

Roxanne Rewalt Hunt
Philadelphia, Pennsylvania

CHICKEN JEWEL RING SALAD

Easy
Do ahead

Serves: 8
Preparing: 1 hour
Chilling: 2 hours

Cranberry Layer

1 envelope unflavored
  gelatine
1 cup cranberry juice cocktail

1 can (1 pound) whole cranberry
  sauce
2 tablespoons lemon juice

Sprinkle gelatine on cranberry juice cocktail in saucepan to soften. Place over low heat, stirring constantly, until gelatine is dissolved. Break up whole cranberry sauce; stir into gelatine mixture and lemon juice. Turn into 6-cup mold. Chill until almost firm.

Chicken Layer

1 envelope unflavored gelatine
¾ cup cold water
1 tablespoon soy sauce
¼ cup coarsely chopped
  almonds, toasted

1 cup mayonnaise
1½ cups diced cooked chicken
½ cup diced celery

Sprinkle gelatine on cold water in saucepan to soften. Place over low heat, stirring constantly, until gelatin is dissolved. Remove from heat. Stir in soy sauce. Cool. Gradually stir into mayonnaise until blended. Mix in remaining ingredients. Spoon on top of almost firm cranberry layer. Chill until firm. Unmold on salad greens.

The White House
Washington, D.C.

GREEN BEANS COLONIAL PLANTATION

Easy   *Serves: 4-5*
Do ahead   *Preparing: 20 minutes*
                                          Chilling time

The Shakers, who conceived this excellent summer salad, toss in "six nasturtium leaves" and "12 nasturtium pods."

1 pound green beans
2 cups shredded lettuce
  and/or spinach
2 scallions (or shallots),
  chopped fine

2 sprigs summer savory or ¼
  teaspoon dried savory
French dressing (oil and white
  vinegar, pepper and salt,
  garden herbs)

Trim ends from whole green beans. Cook in a little boiling water until tender but still crisp. Drain thoroughly and cool. Shortly before serving, toss beans with all the remaining ingredients. Use only enough French dressing to lightly coat ingredients.

Colonial Plantation
Ridley Creek Park
Edgemont, Pennsylvania

GREEN BEAN SALAD

Easy   *Serves: 8*
Do ahead   *Preparing: 20 minutes*

3 cans whole green beans
4 spring onions (scallions),
  chopped
1 tablespoon salt
dash of pepper
1 can anchovy fillets, mashed

juice of 2 large lemons
1 tablespoon ice water
½ cup salad oil
1 hard boiled egg, chopped
1½ pimientos

Drain beans; chop onions and mix with beans. Make salad dressing with salt, pepper, lemon juice, ice water, anchovies and salad oil. Pour dressing over beans and onions. Chill. To serve, turn bean salad out on lettuce leaves and top with chopped egg and sliced pimientos. Can be made several days ahead.

Mrs. Frank B. McKaig
Gulph Mills, Pennsylvania

UNTOSSED LAYERED SALAD

Easy
Do ahead

Serves: 6-8
Preparing: 20 minutes
Chilling: 24 hours

½ 10-ounce bag of fresh
spinach
½ pound bacon, fried crisp
1 head of lettuce
6 hard-boiled eggs, chopped
fine
1 Bermuda onion, sliced thin

1 package (regular size) frozen
peas, defrosted
salt, pepper, sugar
1 pint mayonnaise
½ pint sour cream
1 cup grated Swiss cheese

Put layers of torn spinach in bottom of large glass bowl. Sprinkle with layers of crisp crumbled bacon, torn lettuce, chopped eggs, peas, and sliced onion. Sprinkle with salt, pepper and granulated sugar. Repeat procedure until all ingredients are used. Top with mayonnaise mixed with sour cream. Spread in layer over top of salad mixture. Top with layer of grated Swiss cheese. Refrigerate 24 hours and serve.

Peggy McCann
Philadelphia, Pennsylvania

CURRIED EGG MOLD

Easy
Do ahead

Serves: 20
Preparing: 15 minutes
Chilling: 3 hours

1 cup water
2 tablespoons dried chicken
bouillon
2 envelopes gelatine,
dissolved in ½ cup water
1¼ cups mayonnaise
2 tablespoons curry powder

2 tablespoons lemon juice
2 tablespoons Worcestershire
sauce
1 tablespoon Tabasco
2 tablespoons pepper
10 eggs, hard-boiled

Boil first two ingredients. Combine remaining ingredients in blender or food processor and add to boiled mixture. Pour into mold and chill. Serve with melba toast.

Mrs. Frank B. McKaig
Gulph Mills, Pennsylvania

CAULIFLOWER SALAD

Easy
Do ahead

Serves: 6-8
Preparing: 30 minutes
Marinating: 4 hours

1 package Good Seasons
  cheese garlic mix
1 cup sour cream
1 cup mayonnaise
1 cup radishes, sliced thin

1 tablespoon caraway seeds
3 small green onions, chopped
1 head cauliflower, cut into very
  small bits

Mix all ingredients together and let sit in refrigerator several hours to blend flavors.

Mrs. Robert Watson
Charlotte, North Carolina

MIXED VEGETABLE SALAD

Easy
Do ahead

Serves: 6-8
Preparing: 15 minutes
Chilling: 3 hours

1 bag large frozen mixed
  vegetables (or use 1 bag
  Italian vegetables)
1 green pepper, chopped
½ cup diced celery

one small head cauliflower cut
  into small pieces
½ cup mayonnaise
season to taste
½ pint sour half and half cream

Cook frozen vegetables for short period in very little water. Drain and rinse with cold water. Add remaining ingredients. Chill and serve on head of lettuce.

Mrs. Robert S. Blanton
Media, Pennsylvania

"WHAT IS IT" SALAD

Easy
Do ahead

Serves: 12-14
Preparing: 10 minutes
Chilling: 2 hours

3 3-ounce packages
  raspberry Jello
1½ cups boiling water

3 1-pound cans stewed tomatoes
3 to 4 dashes Tabasco sauce

Sour cream garnish

1 cup sour cream   **1 tablespoon horseradish**

Dissolve Jello in boiling water. Add tomatoes and Tabasco sauce. Pour into Bundt pan, or 2½ quart mold, which has been greased with mayonnaise. Chill until firm. Unmold and serve with sour cream sauce.

Mrs. Frank B. McKaig
Gulph Mills, Pennsylvania

DIAMOND F. FRENCH DRESSING

Easy   *Makes: 1½ cups*
Do ahead   *Preparing: 10 minutes*

½ teaspoon dry mustard   **1 cup Wesson oil**
½ teaspoon salt   **¼ cup lemon juice**
8 tablespoons sugar   **¼ cup vinegar**
½ cup catsup

Mix together catsup and dry ingredients. Add Wesson oil, one tablespoon at a time. Add lemon juice and vinegar and mix well.

Mrs. R. H. Pease
Tucson, Arizona

SALAD DRESSING BARLOW

Easy   *Serves: 14*
Do ahead   *Preparing: 5 minutes*

½ cup Wesson oil   **½ teaspoon sugar**
3 tablespoons white vinegar   **½ teaspoon chives**
1 tablespoon water   **½ teaspoon chopped garlic**
½ teaspoon paprika   **Pepperidge Farm seasoned**
½ teaspoon black pepper   **croutons**
½ teaspoon sweet basil

Put all ingredients except croutons in jar. Shake together. Pour over salad greens and sprinkle croutons on top.

Maryanne Barlow
Wynnewood, Pennsylvania

DILLED PEA SALAD

Easy
Do ahead

Serves: 12
Preparing: 15 minutes
Chilling: 15 minutes

2 packages frozen petit peas
1 10-ounce package frozen
  pea pods
½ cup sour cream
½ cup fresh dill, chopped, or
  1 teaspoon dried dill

½ to 1 teaspoon curry powder
salt and freshly ground pepper
Boston lettuce

Defrost peas and pea pods in refrigerator. Combine sour cream, dill, curry, salt and pepper. Add peas and pods, stirring gently with sour cream mixture, so as not to mash peas. Serve in glass bowl on Boston lettuce. Garnish with more chopped dill. Chill at least 15 minutes.

Mrs. A. Addison Roberts
Rosemont, Pennsylvania

DUTCH POTATO SALAD

Easy
Do ahead

Serves: 6
Preparing: 45 minutes

6 slices bacon
4 cups sliced, cooked
  potatoes
1 tablespoon minced onion
¼ cup diced green pepper
¼ cup bacon fat

½ cup vinegar
⅓ cup sugar
1 teaspoon salt
1 beaten egg
4 hard boiled eggs sliced

Cook potatoes, peel, and slice. Mince onion, slice eggs, and dice green pepper. Fry bacon until crisp; crumble. Reserve ¼ cup bacon fat for sauce. To make sauce, put bacon fat, vinegar, salt, and sugar in pan. Stir until sugar dissolves. Remove from heat and add beaten egg, stirring with wire whisk. Cook on *low* heat, stirring until sauce thickens. Pour over potatoes and mix. Serve hot or cold.

Mrs. James E. Halbkat
Newtown Square, Pennsylvania

POPPY SEED DRESSING

Easy   *Preparing: 15 minutes*
Do ahead

This dressing was "invented" to be used over fruit—particularly oranges and grapefruit.

1½ cups sugar
2 teaspoons dry mustard
2 teaspoons salt
⅔ cup white vinegar

3 tablespoons onion juice
2 cups salad oil (*not* olive oil)
3 tablespoons poppy seeds

Mix sugar, mustard, salt and vinegar. Add onion juice and stir in thoroughly. Add oil slowly, beating constantly until thick. Add poppy seeds and beat a few more minutes. (Can be made in food processor with steel blade.)

Mrs. Julius A. Mackie, Jr.
Bryn Mawr, Pennsylvania

SALAD DRESSING

Easy   *Preparing: 5-6 minutes*
Do ahead

1 teaspoon salt
1 teaspoon paprika
½ teaspoon pepper
¼ teaspoon dry mustard

2 cups olive oil
1 cup white vinegar
6 shakes tarragon vinegar

Mix dry ingredients. Add olive oil and stir. Add vinegar and stir. Store in closed bottle. Shake well before serving.

Mrs. D. Jacques Benoliel
Philadelphia, Pennsylvania

BLUE CHEESE DRESSING

Easy
Do ahead

Makes: 1 quart
Preparing: 15 minutes
Chilling: 24 hours

8 ounces blue cheese
1 pint mayonnaise
½ teaspoon Worcestershire
  sauce
1 tablespoon garlic powder
1 tablespoon chives

1 tablespoon coarsely ground
  pepper
1 cup sour cream
½ cup buttermilk (add more next
  day)

Crumble blue cheese with fork and mix with mayonnaise, Worcestershire sauce, garlic powder, chives, pepper. Add sour cream and buttermilk. Let stand in refrigerator overnight. Add buttermilk to preferred consistency. Will keep refrigerated one month.

Mrs. A. Addison Roberts
Rosemont, Pennsylvania

CREAMY SALAD DRESSING

Easy
Do ahead

Makes: ¾ cup
Preparing: 10 minutes

1 teaspoon egg yolk
2 to 3 teaspoons imported
  mustard (Dijon or
  Dusseldorf)
½ teaspoon finely chopped
  garlic
salt and freshly ground
  pepper

1 teaspoon vinegar
½ cup olive oil
2 teaspoons fresh lemon juice
1 teaspoon heavy cream
dash of Tabasco

Beat egg yolk and add 1 teaspoon of it to a mixing bowl. Add mustard. Add a dash or two of Tabasco sauce. Add the finely chopped garlic, then salt and pepper to taste, and vinegar. Blend by beating vigorously with a wire whisk. Continue beating, gradually adding the oil. Continue beating vigorously until thickened and well blended. Add fresh lemon juice. Beat in the heavy cream. At this point taste and add more salt, pepper or lemon juice to taste. Use sparingly over various lettuces with cucumbers, radishes, scallions, cherry tomatoes, vegetable wedges, sliced heart of celery.

The Committee

Sharps and Flats

cheese, eggs, and pasta

"AUNT CAROLYN'S ELEGANT PICNIC"

Easy
Do ahead
Freeze

Serves 6-8
Preparing: 30 minutes
Baking: 25 minutes

2 10-ounce packages puff
  pastry shells (cut shells in
  half for smaller
  sandwiches)
1 pound Feta cheese
1 teaspoon salt
3 tablespoons lemon juice

2 tablespoons grated onion
1 crushed garlic clove
2 teaspoons chopped dill
½ teaspoon oregano
¼ teaspoon pepper
2 eggs
1½ cups parsley leaves

Preheat oven to 450°. Thaw patty shells. Blend cheese with next 7 ingredients. Add 1 egg. Separate other egg; add yolk to mixture; set white aside. Roll out pastry patty shells on floured board to 7" rounds; place on cookie sheet. Fill centers with cheese mixture and parsley and fold into turnovers. Seal edges with egg white; press edges with fork; brush tops with egg white. Reset oven to 325° and bake turnovers for 20 minutes. May be served hot or cold. Baked sandwiches may be frozen and reheated.

Mrs. Worth D. Phillips
Rosemont, Pennsylvania

PASTA LORRAINE

Easy

Serves: 5-6
Preparing: 20 minutes
Cooking: 20 minutes

8 ounces noodles, uncooked
2 cups rice (Quick Minute
  rice)
1 bouillon cube
½ cup margarine

1 teaspoon salt
½ teaspoon pepper
½ teaspoon marjoram
½ teaspoon garlic powder
sesame seeds (optional)

Prepare rice according to directions. While rice is cooking, in a large fry pan mix margarine and seasonings, add noodles and brown till golden brown. When rice is completed, pour over noodles and simmer for about 10 to 20 minutes with water and bouillon cube to cover mixture half-way. Cook until noodles are tender.

Lorraine J. Fiorelli
Philadelphia, Pennsylvania

EGGS AURORE

Average
Partial do ahead

Serves: 4
Preparing: 30 minutes
Baking: 5-8 minutes

6 hard-boiled eggs
2 tablespoons flour
2 tablespoons melted butter
1¼ cups milk
¼ teaspoon salt

¼ teaspoon cayenne
¼ teaspoon nutmeg
4 to 6 triangles of bread
3 tablespoons Parmesan cheese
2 tablespoons melted butter

Cut eggs in half lengthwise and remove yolks. Cut the whites into thin strips. Make cream sauce by blending flour and butter, then gradually stirring in milk. Add salt, pepper and nutmeg. Fry triangles of bread in butter until crisp. Arrange upright around edge of shallow dish. Combine egg whites and cream sauce and pour half of this into center of dish. Sprinkle with grated Parmesan cheese. Rub half of the egg yolks over the cheese. Add remaining eggs and cream sauce, sprinkle again with Parmesan cheese and the rest of the egg yolks. Drizzle with melted butter and reheat dish briefly in 400° oven. Serve at once.

Mrs. Louis Hood
Wayne, Pennsylvania

EGG AND BACON CASSEROLE

Easy
Do ahead

Serves: 6-8
Preparing: 15 minutes
Baking: 15 minutes

8 hard cooked eggs, sliced
½ pound cooked bacon,
   crumbled

Sauce:

2 tablespoons butter
2 tablespoons flour
1½ cups milk

1 cup mild cheese, grated
½ teaspoon salt
⅛ teaspoon paprika

In flat casserole layer eggs and bacon until dish is filled. Prepare sauce: Melt butter, blend in flour and milk. Add grated cheese and seasonings. Stir until cheese has melted. Pour over eggs and bacon. Bake for 15 minutes in 325° oven.

Mrs. Pat Cain
High Point, North Carolina

NOODLES ITALIANO

Easy
Do ahead-Sauce

Serves: 6
Preparing: 20 minutes
Baking: 40 minutes

3 tablespoons olive oil
1 pound ground beef
2 medium onions, sliced
3½ cups Italian tomatoes
1 6-ounce can tomato paste
¾ cup dry red wine or water
1 teaspoon paprika
1 tablespoon salt

1 bay leaf
⅛ teaspoon thyme
½ teaspoon marjoram
1 clove garlic, minced
1 teaspoon Worcestershire sauce
⅛ teaspoon Tabasco sauce
8 ounces uncooked noodles

Heat oil; add meat and break it up. Cook until meat is brown over medium high heat. Add onion and garlic. Add tomato paste, tomatoes and wine, or water. Bring to a boil; add salt and spices. Put one half of sauce in 3-inch deep casserole, 8″ or 9″ square Add noodles, then remaining sauce. Bake covered (375°) for 20 minutes; uncover and bake 15-20 minutes longer. Sprinkle with Parmesan cheese and serve.

Norma B. Tiekert
Sassamansville, Pennsylvania

NOODLE PUDDING

Easy
Do ahead
Freeze

Serves: 12
Preparing: 20 minutes
Baking: 1 hour, 15 minutes

½ pound medium size egg
  noodles
½ pound butter or margarine,
  softened
1 cup sugar
2 teaspoons vanilla

1 pound sour cream
½ pound cream cheese, softened
6 large or 8 small eggs
1 large can (21 ounces) cherry
  pie filling

Cook noodles with salt. Grease baking dish, approximately 9″ by 13″. Line bottom of dish with noodles. Mix together all other ingredients except cherry pie filling and pour over noodles. Bake in 350° oven for 1 hour. Cool for 5 minutes. Pour cherries on top and bake again for 10 minutes. Must be served hot, as a side dish or dessert.

Mrs. John W. Hagen
Libertyville, Illinois

RAMEQUIN FORESTIÈRE

Easy
Do ahead

Serves: 6
Preparing: 15-20 minutes
Baking: 20-30 minutes

Ramequin Mixture

½ cup flour
4 eggs
2 cups cold milk
½ teaspoon salt
½ teaspoon nutmeg

1⅓ cups grated Swiss or
    Gruyère cheese
4½ tablespoons butter
⅛ teaspoon pepper

Filling Forestière

1½ cup minced mushrooms
1 tablespoon butter
1 tablespoon flour
1 tablespoon cooking oil

4 to 6 tablespoons sour cream
1 to 2 tablespoons minced shallots
salt and pepper to taste

Mixture

Place flour in 2½ quart saucepan and beat in milk with wire whisk. Stir slowly over heat and beat until thick. Remove from heat and beat in 3½ tablespoons butter, seasonings, and 1 cup cheese. Add eggs, one at a time. Turn half of the mixture into a buttered 9 x 11 x 2-inch baking dish. Spread filling mixture over it and cover with remaining flour and cheese mixture. Sauce is not thick but mushrooms will stay in place. Sprinkle remaining cheese and butter over top. Bake in upper third of oven, uncovered, at 325° to 350° for 20 to 30 minutes, until set. May be prepared the day before and refrigerated.

Filling

Sauté mushrooms in butter with shallots for 5 minutes. Sprinkle with flour and stir in 1 minute. Remove from heat and stir in sour cream and seasonings.

Variations for Fillings

chicken livers
shellfish
cooked asparagus
sliced baked ham

spinach cooked in oil with a little
    garlic
crabmeat mixed with mushroom
    filling

Mrs. John V. Calhoun, Jr.
Devon, Pennsylvania

SOUFFLÉ AU JAMBON (HAM SOUFFLÉ)

Easy   *Serves: 6*
                                   Preparing: 45 minutes

1 cup lean cooked ham   **2 cups Béchamel Sauce**
2 tablespoons unsalted butter **3 eggs, separated**
pinch paprika

Pound the ham in a mortar with the butter. Rub it through a very fine strainer. Stir the ham puree and the paprika into a very hot Béchamel sauce. Add the egg yolks, then the whites beaten stiff, being careful that they do not fall. Spoon the mixture into a buttered one-quart timbale mold or six buttered, three-inch porcelain soufflé dishes. Bake in a 300° oven until set. The mixture will double its volume above the mold. It must be served immediately. (You can grind the ham fine in a meat grinder or chop it in a blender or food processor.)

Leo Kessler, Executive Chef
Fairmont Hotel
Philadelphia, Pennsylvania

SPAGHETTI CARBONARA

Easy   *Serves: 4-6*
                                   Preparing: 30 minutes
                                   Cooking: 15 minutes

1 pound imported spaghetti   **8 black olives, pitted and finely**
6 to 8 slices thickly sliced   **chopped**
  bacon, diced   **3 or 4 eggs**
2 large cloves garlic, finely   **imported Parmesan**
  chopped   **salt**
1 small dried chili, crushed   **freshly ground pepper**
  (optional)

Start water boiling for spaghetti. Meanwhile fry bacon until crisp. Remove from pan; discard half of fat. Add ½ teaspoon salt to boiling water and add spaghetti. Cook 7 to 10 minutes. Beat eggs in bowl. When fat has cooled in pan add garlic and chili and drained spaghetti. Keep over low flame. Add eggs, bacon, olives and cheese. Stir thoroughly with wooden spoon until eggs appear scrambled. Put in warm serving dish and sprinkle generously with freshly ground pepper.

Richard Woodhams
Philadelphia, Pennsylvania

PASTA WITH SICILIAN SALAD SAUCE

Easy   *Serves: 4*
Partial do ahead   *Preparing: 30 minutes*

This sauce is not cooked.

2 pounds tomatoes, cut into
   small strips (or 1 large can
   whole Italian type
   tomatoes, drained)
20 black pitted olives, cut up
24 half-inch cubes Feta or
   Mozzarella cheese
6-8 anchovies cut into small
   pieces or 1 small can tuna
   (use both if desired)
2 teaspoons oil from
   anchovies and tuna

4 thin slices red onion, separated
   into rings and halved
½ cup imported olive oil
½ cup chopped Italian parsley
2 teaspoons mixed Italian
   seasoning
optional but tasty: 4 slices
   Genoa salami, slivered
salt and pepper to taste
½ pound thin spaghetti or short
   macaroni

An hour before serving, (or longer), combine the sauce ingredients in a bowl large enough to hold pasta when cooked. Let sauce sit at room temperature, stirring a few times. Cook ½ pound pasta until tender but still firm. Drain thoroughly and mix with sauce in bowl. All pasta should be lightly covered with oil. Serve immediately *without* grated cheese.

Mrs. John Dillworth
St. Davids, Pennsylvania

FETTUCCINE ALFREDO WITH A DIFFERENCE

Easy   *Serves: 6*
Partial do ahead   *Preparing: 30 minutes*

1 pound fettuccini, cooked
2 tablespoons butter
1 cup heavy cream
1 egg, beaten
1 cup grated Parmesan
   cheese

¼ pound pine nuts
⅛ pound golden raisins (puffed
   in boiling water 4 minutes)

Put cooked fettuccini in warm casserole. Add butter, heavy cream and egg, a little at a time. Toss after each addition. Add pine nuts and raisins. Season with freshly ground pepper and salt to taste. Serve with Parmesan cheese.

Mrs. Thomas V. Lefevre
Rosemont, Pennsylvania

FANCY EGG SCRAMBLE

Average
Do ahead
Freeze

Serves: 8-10
Preparing: 60 minutes
Chilling: overnight
Baking: 30 minutes

1 cup (4 ounces) diced
  Canadian bacon
¼ cup chopped scallions
3 tablespoons butter
12 beaten eggs
1 3-ounce can sliced
  mushrooms (or ¼ pound
  fresh)

1 recipe cheese sauce (see
  below)
4 tablespoons melted butter
2 cups soft bread crumbs, about
  3 slices
⅛ teaspoon paprika

Sauce: (Prepare first)

2 tablespoons butter
2 tablespoons flour
2 cups warm milk

½ teaspoon salt
⅛ teaspoon pepper
1 cup (4 ounces) cheddar cheese

In large skillet cook Canadian bacon and scallions in 3 tablespoons butter until scallions are limp (not brown). Add eggs and scramble just until set (slightly underdone). Fold eggs and mushrooms into warm cheese sauce (having made it first) and turn into 12"x7"x2" baking dish. Sprinkle bread crumbs over egg mixture. Dribble 4 tablespoons melted butter oven them and sprinkle paprika on top. Cover and chill (refrigerate overnight) until 30 minutes before baking. Bake uncovered at 350° for 30 minutes or a bit longer.

Cheese Sauce: Melt butter. Blend in flour. Add warm milk, salt and pepper. Cook and stir until bubbly and then stir in cheddar cheese until melted. If frozen, defrost in refrigerator night before.

Mrs. Leroy S. Heck
Mt. Kisco, New York

SCOTCH EGGS

Easy

Serves: 6
Preparing: 15 minutes
Baking: 20 minutes

1 pound bulk sausage
1 egg
¾ cup fine bread crumbs

6 hard-boiled eggs
English muffins

Mix pork sausage with egg and bread crumbs until a good consistency to coat thickly the hard-boiled eggs. Deep fry until sausage is brown. Drain on paper towels. Serve as is, or sliced in half on English muffins. Can be served cold.

Mrs. George S. Hundt, Jr.
Malvern, Pennsylvania

SEAFOOD SPAGHETTI

Average   *Serves: 10-12*
Partial do ahead   *Preparing: 20 minutes*

1 pound thin spaghetti   **3 cans minced clams**
1 stick butter   **1 cup sliced green onions**
.1 tablespoon bottled garlic   **2 tablespoons chopped fresh**
juice   **parsley**
1½ pounds raw shelled
shrimp, (or frozen)

Boil spaghetti according to package directions. Simmer shrimp. Sauté onion in butter and garlic juice. Add shrimp and heat. Add clams and juice. Pour everything over drained spaghetti and sprinkle tops of extra scallions on top. Serve with garlic bread, salad and fruit.

Mrs. Harry Gorodetzer
Narberth, Pennsylvania

CHILI AND CHEESE BAKE

Easy   *Serves: 12*
Do ahead   *Preparing: 15 minutes*
Freeze   *Baking: 50 minutes*

2 cans green chilies, seeded   **2 tablespoons flour**
and rinsed   **2 large cans evaporated milk**
1 pound Monterey Jack   **2 small cans (or 1 large) tomato**
cheese, grated   **paste**
4 eggs

Preheat oven to 400°. Butter an oblong pan and line with chilies. Cover with one half of cheese. In blender mix eggs, flour, milk, and pour over chilies and cheese. Bake for 30 minutes. Spread with tomato paste and top with remaining cheese. Bake 20 minutes longer.

David Coolidge
Naples, Florida

PASTA WITH BAY SCALLOPS

Average   *Serves: 6*
Partial do ahead   *Preparing: 30 minutes*

1 pound pasta
a little olive oil
6 egg yolks, lightly beaten
1 cup half and half
salt, pepper, and cayenne (or
   Tabasco) to taste
freshly chopped parsley
1½ pounds fresh bay
   scallops

2 medium zucchini, sliced into
   thin crescents
1 small eggplant, peeled and
   diced in ¼-inch cubes
3 medium red peppers in ¼-inch
   dice
½ pound freshly grated
   Parmesan cheese

Being careful not to overcook, boil the pasta to the "al dente" stage. Drain into a colander. Run cold water over the pasta and allow to drain again. Toss lightly with a little olive oil to prevent sticking. Lightly beat egg yolks. Add half and half, seasonings and parsley. Beat until blended and set aside in a large bowl. In a large frying bowl, sauté the pasta and scallops in some butter. When scallops turn opaque, add zucchini, eggplant and red peppers. Continue cooking, stirring constantly. When vegetables are hot, add the mixture to the bowl containing the eggs and cream. Stir vigorously. When the mixture begins to thicken, add the cheese to pasta-scallop mixture. Mix well and turn onto a warm plate.

FROG
Philadelphia, Pennsylvania

CRAB NOODLE CASSEROLE

Easy   *Serves: 6*
Do ahead   *Preparing: 15 minutes*
                                       Baking: 45 minutes

8-ounce bag fine noodles
1 pound crabmeat
¼ pound butter
½ pound pimiento cheese

½ pint cream
½ teaspoon grated onion
dash of paprika

Melt butter in double-boiler, add pimiento cheese, cream and onion. Stir until smooth. Cook noodles and add to sauce. Fold crabmeat into noodle mixture and pour into buttered casserole. Sprinkle with paprika and brown in 350° oven for 45 minutes.

Catherine Kuch
Chestnut Hill, Pennsylvania

TOP-OF-STOVE PUFFY OMELET

Average

Serves: 4
Preparing: 15 minutes
Cooking Time: 15 minutes

2 tablespoons quick cooking
  tapioca
¾ teaspoon salt
⅛ teaspoon pepper
¾ cup milk

1 tablespoon butter or margarine
4 eggs, separated
2 tablespoons butter or
  margarine

Combine tapioca, salt, pepper and milk in small saucepan. Cook over medium heat until mixture comes to a boil, stirring constantly. Add 1 tablespoon butter. Remove from heat. Beat egg whites until stiff. Beat egg yolks until thick and lemon colored. Gradually add tapioca mixture to egg yolks. Fold egg whites into yolk mixture. Melt 2 tablespoons butter in 10-inch skillet. Cook egg mixture in skillet over low heat 3 minutes. Cover and cook 10 minutes longer. Omelet is cooked when knife inserted in center comes out clean.

Mrs. George Embick
Villanova, Pennsylvania

CRÊPES FLORENTINE

Average

Serves: 3
Preparing: 15 minutes

3 small crêpes
1 cup finely chopped and
  cooked spinach, dry
salt, pepper and nutmeg to
  taste
2 teaspoons light cream

1 tablespoon butter
3 thin slices cooked ham
1 tablespoon hollandaise sauce
1 tablespoon whipped cream
1 teaspoon parmesan cheese

Place a slice of ham on each crêpe. Brown butter in saucepan. Add spinach, seasonings, and light cream. Heat up lightly and mix well. Divide the spinach filling and roll it in crêpes. Place in casserole and bake at 350° for 5 minutes. Mix together hollandaise sauce and whipped cream; spread over crêpes. Sprinkle Parmesan cheese on top and place under broiler until lightly brown. Serve in casserole.

Heinz Vollrath
Chef, Acorn Club
Philadelphia, Pennsylvania

CRAB QUICHE

Easy
Partial do ahead

Serves: 6-8
Preparing: 20 minutes
Baking: 50 minutes

1 9-inch pie shell baked 10 minutes at 425° (do not brown)
1 cup grated cheese
8 ounces crab meat
¼ cup minced onion
dash tarragon, basil, thyme, parsley

3 eggs, beaten
¾ cup sour cream
¾ cup half and half
¼ cup mayonnaise
½ teaspoon horseradish
1 teaspoon cornstarch
salt and pepper to taste

Sprinkle cheese over partially baked pie shell. Toss crabmeat with onion and herbs. Arrange over cheese in layer. Beat eggs. Add sour cream, half and half, mayonnaise, horseradish, cornstarch, salt and pepper to eggs. Pour slowly over crab mixture. Bake at 325° 50 minutes or until set. Let stand 5 minutes before cutting.

Patricia P. Davies
King of Prussia, Pennsylvania

EASY CHEESE QUICHE

Easy
Do ahead
Freeze

Serves: 15-30, depending on cut
Preparing: 10 minutes
Baking: 40 minutes

2 8-ounce packages shredded Cheddar or sharp cheese
2 eggs
2 cups milk
3 cups Bisquick

1 12-ounce package frozen onions (diced)
6 tablespoons butter or margarine
salt to taste
poppy seeds

Sauté onions in 2 tablespoons butter until the moisture is gone. Mix all ingredients in bowl, except one package of cheese, 4 tablespoons of butter and poppy seeds. Add onions to mixed ingredients; pour into ungreased 9½"x11" pan (I use Pam). Sprinkle 1 package cheese and poppy seeds over batter. Melt 4 tablespoons butter and drizzle over everything. Bake in preheated 400° oven for 40 minutes.

Carol Rieske
Upper Darby, Pennsylvania

SPAGHETTI ALLA PUTTANESCA CON VONGOLE

Average

Serves: 6
Preparing: 30 minutes
Cooking: 30 minutes

¼ cup olive oil
1 tablespoon finely minced garlic
4 cups peeled, chopped tomatoes, preferably fresh or use the imported Italian kind
⅓ cup finely chopped parsley
2 tablespoons finely chopped fresh basil or 1 teaspoon dried

1 teaspoon dried oregano
½ teaspoon red pepper flakes, or more to taste
2 tablespoons drained capers
18 pitted black olives (see note)
2 two-ounce cans flat anchovies
24 littleneck clams, the smaller the better (see note)
½ pound spaghetti, cooked to the desired degree of doneness

Heat the oil in a deep skillet and add the garlic. Cook, without browning, about 30 seconds, stirring. Add the tomatoes, half the parsley, basil, oregano, red pepper flakes, capers and olives. Cook over moderately high heat about 25 minutes. Stir frequently.

Meanwhile, drain the anchovies and chop them coarsely. Wash the clams under cold running water until clean.

When the sauce is ready, add the anchovies and remaining parsley. Cook, stirring, about one minute. Add the clams and cover the skillet closely. Cook about five minutes or until all the clams are opened. Serve piping hot with freshly cooked spaghetti.

Note: By all means use imported black olives for this dish, not the California version. Imported black olives are available in most specialty shops as well as in Italian, Greek and Spanish markets. We use a cherry pitter to remove the pits, but a paring knife will do. Pitted green olives would be a preferable substitute to California black ones.

Note, too, that canned clams may be substituted for the fresh clams and although the result will be palatable, the fresh are recommended. The clams may also be omitted, and it will still be an excellent dish.

Craig Claiborne
New York Times
New York, New York

Left-over cheese of all kinds may be put into a jar containing a little wine. When enough has been accumulated it will have a very interesting and delicious flavor.

SPINACH TART

Average
Do ahead
Freeze

Serves: 8
Preparing: 30 minutes
Baking: 25 minutes

1 baked 9-inch pie shell
3 tablespoons minced
  scallions
3 tablespoons butter
2 packages frozen spinach,
  cooked and well drained
¼ teaspoon nutmeg

¼ teaspoon salt
¼ teaspoon pepper
¼ pound cream cheese, softened
¼ pound Feta cheese, crumbled
4 eggs, separated
½ cup heavy cream
⅓ cup breadcrumbs

Sauté scallions in 2 tablespoons butter until soft. Add the cooked spinach, nutmeg, salt and pepper. Stir for five minutes. Transfer to a large bowl. Add the cream cheese, Feta cheese, egg yolks and heavy cream. Mix well. Beat the egg whites with a pinch of salt until stiff, fold into spinach mixture. Pour mixture into cooked pie shell, dot with 1 tablespoon butter and sprinkle with breadcrumbs. Bake at 375° in middle of oven, for 25 minutes. Let cool a few minutes before serving.

Mrs. Toba Schwaber Kerson
Bryn Mawr, Pennsylvania

FETTUCCINI-ZUCCHINI-MUSHROOM CASSEROLE

Average
Do ahead

Serves: 10
Preparing: 15-20 minutes
Cooking: 13 minutes

½ pound mushrooms, sliced
  thin
¼ cup butter
1¼ pounds zucchini, cut
  julienne
1 cup heavy cream

½ pound butter
1 pound fettuccini noodles
¾ cup Parmesan cheese
chopped parsley
2 tablespoons salt
1 tablespoon olive oil

In large skillet, sauté mushrooms in butter for 2 minutes over moderately high heat. Add zucchini, 1 cup heavy cream and butter, cut into bits; bring to boil; simmer 3 minutes. Boil noodles with 2 tablespoons salt and 1 tablespoon olive oil, for 7-10 minutes. Drain. Add to above and toss with cheese and add chopped parsley.

Mrs. Andrew Lewis, Jr.
Schwenksville, Pennsylvania

PAT GREEN'S LASAGNE

Easy
Do ahead
Freeze

Serves: 14
Preparing: 1 hour
Chilling: 24 hours
Baking: 45 minutes

1 pint tomato sauce
(Contadina)
2 pound jar spaghetti sauce
(Prince)
1 large can Contadina plum
tomatoes
1½ pounds sweet Italian
sausage
1 pound Bot-Boi noodles
3 pounds ground beef (lean
top of round)

2 pounds Ricotta or cottage
cheese (one egg added)
3 8-ounce packages sliced
Mozzarella
2 6-ounce packages sliced
Provolone
1 small container grated
Parmesan cheese

The following ingredients are optional:

2 bay leaves
basil

oregano
thyme

Prepare sauce the day before. In a *large* skillet brown the crumbled sausage after removing the casing. Stir it so it browns on all sides. Add the ground beef and brown it. Cut the plum tomatoes and add them with juice to meat. Add tomato and spaghetti sauces and stir. Cover and cook on very low heat for 1 hour. Add additional seasonings to meat sauce if desired. After simmering, cool and refrigerate overnight. The next day remove the hardened fat from top of bowl. Cook noodles according to package directions. Drain. In a large casserole assemble in layers as follows: ⅓ of meat sauce, ¼ of noodles, ½ Mozzarella (shredded), ¼ noodles, cheese-egg mixture, ⅓ meat sauce, ¼ noodles, ½ Mozzarella, Parmesan, ¼ noodles, ⅓ meat sauce and sliced Provolone. Heat in 375° oven for 45 minutes. If frozen, allow to defrost completely. If you have leftover fixings, make a small lasagne in a small bowl. When ready to serve, allow 45 minutes to heat in a 375° preheated oven.

Mrs. William Green
Philadelphia, Pennsylvania

BEEF AND MUSHROOM QUICHE

Easy
Do ahead
Freeze

Serves: 6
Preparing: 25 minutes
Cooking: 1 hour

1 unbaked 9-inch pie shell
½ pound lean ground beef
1 can cream of mushroom
  soup, condensed, undiluted
½ cup milk
2 eggs, slightly beaten
2 tablespoons chopped
  chives (or 1 teaspoon
  onion juice)

¼ teaspoon salt
pinch white pepper
dash of Tabasco, or sherry
  peppers from Bermuda
1 cup sliced, sautéed fresh
  mushrooms
1 cup shredded Cheddar cheese

Preheat oven to 450°. Prick bottom and sides of pie shell with fork. Bake 12 minutes. Remove from oven. Reduce oven temperature to 350°. In small skillet brown ground beef. Stir frequently and remove with slotted spoon. Set aside. In medium bowl, mix mushroom soup, milk, eggs, spices and Tabasco. Add ground beef, sautéed mushrooms and cheese. Pour into partially baked pie shell. Cover edges of pie shell with foil. Bake for 60 minutes or until knife inserted in middle comes out clean.

Mrs. Wolcott McM. Heyl
Philadelphia, Pennsylvania

SPINACH NOODLE BAKE

Easy
Do ahead

Serves: 10-12
Preparing: 30 minutes
Baking: 30 minutes

2 packages frozen, chopped
  spinach, thawed and
  squeezed dry
1 pound penne or ziti
  noodles, cooked and
  drained
1 pound Ricotta cheese
2 15½-ounce jars Ragu
  marinara sauce

3 eggs, lightly beaten
⅔ cup Parmesan cheese, freshly
  grated
⅓ cup chopped fresh parsley
2 teaspoons salt
½ teaspoon pepper

Preheat oven to 350°. Generously butter a 3-quart casserole. Combine all ingredients in a large mixing bowl and blend thoroughly. Turn into casserole and bake until golden brown and bubbly, (about 30 minutes).

Mrs. Edward L. Suddock
Portland, Oregon

SEAFOOD WITH PASTA

Average
Do ahead

Serves: 6
Preparing: 30 minutes
Baking: 20 minutes

3 cups maruzzelle no. 32
  (medium pasta shells)
½ cup butter or margarine
2 tablespoons flour
4 large cloves garlic, crushed
3 medium onions, grated
½ cup parsley, chopped
2 pimientos

½ to ¾ pounds raw cleaned
  shrimp, cut butterfly style
1 6½-ounce can minced clams
2 7-ounce packages king crab
  meat, defrosted
1 8-ounce bottle clam juice
½ cup grated Parmesan cheese

Cook shells in boiling water until tender, per package directions. Rinse with cold, then with hot water. Add ¼ cup butter, tossing until shells are coated. Cook in remaining butter the garlic, onions, flour, parsley, one chopped pimiento and all but a few of the shrimp, until shrimp turn pink, (about 5 minutes). Remove from heat. Cut each package of crab meat in six squares and add all but a few pieces. Add clams and bottled juice.

Alternate layers of pasta with cooked mixture in greased casserole, sprinkling each layer with cheese. Garnish with remaining shrimp, crab, pimiento. Bake uncovered at 300° until heated through, (about 20 minutes). This casserole may be refrigerated for several hours or overnight prior to baking.

Mrs. John C. Krell
Philadelphia, Pennsylvania

MACARONI AND SPINACH CASSEROLE

Easy

Serves: 6
Preparing: 10 minutes
Baking: 1 hour

5 small cans macaroni and
  cheese
1 package chopped spinach,
  thawed and drained

1 cup grated sharp cheese
1 small bunch scallions, chopped
  fine
½ teaspoon oregano

Mix all ingredients together in casserole and bake at 350° for 1 hour.

Mrs. John Folk
Devon, Pennsylvania

SHIRLEY VERRETT'S HAY AND STRAW

Average

Serves: 4-6
Preparing: 45 minutes
Cooking: 25 minutes

6 ounces green noodles
6 ounces yellow noodles or
spaghetti
boiling water, salt
3 tablespoons olive oil
1 clove garlic, halved
1 medium onion, chopped

¾ pound fresh mushrooms,
sliced
¼ pound sweet butter
black pepper to taste
¼ pound Parmesan cheese,
grated

Cook yellow and green noodles in boiling water in separate saucepans, each with ¾ teaspoon salt, half a tablespoon olive oil, for time specified on each package (usually 10-12 minutes). Drain; rinse in hot water, keep hot. Meanwhile, sauté garlic in 1 tablespoon oil for 3 minutes and remove. Add to the oil the chopped onion and sauté until tender, about 5 minutes. Remove. Add remaining oil and mushrooms. Sauté 5 minutes or longer, stirring constantly. Have ready a large earthenware, enamel or glass bowl containing the butter which has been cut into 6 or 8 chunks. Add noodles, onions, and mushrooms. Toss, as you would a salad, to mix. Add salt to taste, as well as black pepper, then add half the grated cheese. Toss again to distribute thoroughly. Pass remaining cheese to be added as desired.

Note:
Other additions may be chopped, drained anchovy fillets, halved pickled artichoke hearts, or olives (ripe, green or Greek style). If adding any of these, do not salt dish until they have been incorporated.

Shirley Verrett
New York, New York

TOP HAT CHEESE SOUFFLÉ

Average
Partial do ahead

Serves: 6-8
Preparing: 20 minutes
Baking: 60-90 minutes

½ cup butter
½ cup flour
½ teaspoon salt
¼ teaspoon black pepper
2 cups milk (half light cream
is better)

2 cups shredded extra sharp
cheddar cheese
6 egg yolks, well beaten
8 egg whites, beaten stiff
½ teaspoon cream of tartar

Prepare a 2-quart soufflé dish by placing ten inch wide foil around dish to extend five inches above rim. Secure with scotch tape. Melt butter over low heat in saucepan. Add flour gradually and stir. Allow to bubble a minute and add seasonings. Remove from heat. Add milk gradually, stirring until thick. Stir grated cheese into cream sauce, stirring constantly over low heat. Remove from heat; stir in egg yolks. (Recipe may be prepared ahead to this point.) Beat egg whites with cream of tartar until stiff. Fold egg whites into cheese-egg mixture. Pour into ungreased soufflé dish. With a table knife make a groove two inches from outer edge in a circle. Put dish in pan of hot water (1 to 2 inches deep). Bake at 350° for one to one and a half hours. Check in 60 minutes. Soufflé should be puffed and golden brown. Serve immediately.

Mrs. Andrew E. Schultz
Wynnewood, Pennsylvania

LINGUINI VONGOLE

Easy   *Serves: 4*
Do ahead   *Preparing: 30 minutes*
Cooking: 3½ hours including resting time

3 cans whole baby clams	**dash Angostura bitters (to kill**
½ pound sliced fresh	**the canned taste of the clams)**
mushrooms	**2 dashes soy sauce**
¼ cup olive oil	**1 cup white wine**
1 large onion	**1 pound linguini**
1 tablespoon oregano	
6 cloves garlic, or to taste,	
(always use 20% more of	
the good stuff)	

Heat oil in large skillet. Gently sauté, but do not brown, thinly sliced garlic, sliced onion, and mushrooms. Add clams, oregano, bitters and soy sauce. Slowly bring to boil, then simmer for 20 minutes. Cover and allow to sit without heat for 3 hours. Add wine and bring back to simmer for 30 minutes prior to serving. Meanwhile, cook linguini for 9 minutes in a large pot of salted boiling water with 1 tablespoon of oil. Pour linguini into colander and drain but do not wash. Put on serving plates and liberally lay sauce on top of each serving. Pour on remaining juice and serve with dry red wine and salad.

James Fawcett
Philadelphia, Pennsylvania

SOUTHERN CHICKEN TETRAZZINI

Average
Partial do ahead

Serves: 8
Preparing: 20 minutes
Cooking: 2½ hours

5 pounds chicken
1 small onion
2 one-pound cans stewed
  tomatoes
1 grated onion
2 tablespoons paprika
1 tablespoon Worcestershire
  sauce

1 tablespoon butter
1 pint light cream
1 small can mushrooms
½ pound grated New York State
  cheese
1 pound cooked spaghetti

Cook chicken with onion in water until tender. Simmer next 5 ingredients for 2 hours. Add chicken which has been minced. Slowly add cream, mushrooms, and cheese. Simmer slowly for 15 minutes. When ready to serve, add 1 pound cooked spaghetti, or enough to take up the liquid.

Mrs. J. Mahlon Buck, Jr.
Haverford, Pennsylvania

QUICHE FOR A CROWD

Easy
Do ahead

Serves: 10-15
Preparing: 45 minutes
Cooking: 30 minutes

8 eggs
3 cups whipping cream or
  half and half
12 ounces Gruyère or Swiss
  cheese, grated

½ pound smoked salmon or 1
  pound crisp bacon
1 teaspoon nutmeg
1 teaspoon cayenne pepper
½ teaspoon salt

Pastry:

2½ cups flour
pinch of salt
6 tablespoons butter

6 tablespoons Crisco
6 to 8 tablespoons ice water

Combine pastry ingredients and form into a ball. Chill for 20 minutes. Roll and fit into a jelly roll pan. Spread salmon or bacon and cheese on unbaked pastry. Combine remaining ingredients and pour over all. Bake at 375° until lightly browned. Cut into squares to serve.

Mrs. George Nesbitt
Chevy Chase, Maryland

CHICKEN MACARONI

Easy
Do ahead
Freeze

Serves: 8
Preparing: 30 minutes
Baking: 30 minutes

4 tablespoons butter
2 tablespoons flour
3-ounce package cream
  cheese
1 teaspoon salt
¼ teaspoon garlic salt
dash cayenne
dash nutmeg

1 cup milk
1 cup chicken bouillon
2 tablespoons chopped pimiento
1 cup sautéed mushrooms
2½ cups diced, cooked chicken
2 cups cooked macaroni
½ cup grated Swiss cheese

Melt butter over low heat and blend in flour, cream cheese and seasonings. Gradually add milk and bouillon, stirring constantly until slightly thickened. Combine with pimiento, mushrooms, chicken and macaroni. Turn into a greased 2-quart casserole. Top with grated cheese and bake in a 350° oven for 30 minutes or until slightly browned on top.

Olga Hyde
Gladwyne, Pennsylvania

CREAMED EGGS AND ASPARAGUS

Easy
Do ahead

Serves: 4 or 5
Preparing: 30 minutes

3 tablespoons butter
3 tablespoons flour
½ teaspoon salt
dash of pepper
1 to 1½ cups milk
1 cup grated sharp cheese
  (Cheddar)

6 hard-cooked eggs (deviled if
  desired)
2 10-ounce packages cut
  asparagus, cooked
hot toast points

Melt butter in skillet. Blend in flour, salt and pepper. Add milk. Stir constantly. Add cheese and asparagus. Cut 5 eggs in half and place in greased ovenproof dish. Cover with asparagus-cheese sauce.* Decorate top with remaining egg, sliced. Serve immediately on toast.

*Can be kept warm at this point in oven covered with foil.

Mrs. Frank H. Phipps
Villanova, Pennsylvania

STUFFED MACARONI SHELLS

Easy
Do ahead
Freeze

Serves: 8-10
Preparing: 30 minutes
Baking: 30 minutes

12 ounce box jumbo
  macaroni shells
2 15-ounce or 1 32-ounce
  carton Ricotta cheese
12 ounce package shredded
  Mozzarella
3 eggs
¾ cup grated Parmesan
  cheese

1½ teaspoons salt
¼ teaspoon pepper
¾ teaspoon oregano
⅓ cup chopped parsley
1 32-ounce jar spaghetti sauce
½ cup grated Parmesan

Cook shells in boiling, salted water, to which 1 teaspoon oil has been added, for 20-25 minutes. Drain well, and dry out singly on a layer of paper towels. Mix together Ricotta, Mozzarella, eggs, ¾ cup Parmesan cheese, salt, pepper, oregano and parsley. Stuff each shell with a rounded tablespoon or more of filling. (Stuffed shells may be frozen at this point). Spoon a little sauce in bottom of pan. Arrange shells on top, seam side down. Add more sauce. Sprinkle with Parmesan. Bake at 350° for 30 minutes.

Mrs. Norman P. Robinson
Haverford, Pennsylvania

NOODLES ROMANOFF

Easy

Preparing: 15-20 minutes
Baking: 30 minutes

½ to ¾ pound noodles,
  cooked according to
  package directions
1½ teaspoons butter
1 slice bread
½ cup Cheddar cheese,
  grated

½ cup sour cream
1 onion, diced
1 cup cottage cheese
salt and garlic salt to taste
dash of Tabasco

Cook noodles. Put bread and cheese in blender; blend together, then remove. Blend remaining ingredients except butter and mix with drained and buttered noodles in a casserole. Top with bread crumbs and grated cheese. Bake at 350° 30 minutes, or until bubbly and heated through.

Mrs. Eric A. Fowler
Newtown Square, Pennsylvania

VEGETABLE QUICHE
WITH WHOLE WHEAT DILL CRUST

Average

Serves: 10
Preparing: 1 hour
Chilling: 3 hours
Baking: 35 minutes

Crust:

2 cups whole wheat flour
1 teaspoon salt
1 tablespoon fresh dill or 1½
  teaspoon dried dill

¼ pound cold sweet butter cut
  into tiny pieces
½ to ¾ cup iced water

Filling:

1 cup finely chopped zucchini
1 cup finely chopped
  mushrooms
½ cup finely minced scallions
2 tablespoons olive oil
1 tablespoon butter
1 egg separated

5 whole eggs
½ cup milk
1 pinch thyme
salt and black pepper
1½ pounds Gruyère cheese,
  grated

Crust: Sift flour with salt into mixing bowl. Blend dill into flour, tossing in lightly with fork. Add butter and cut into flour, to make a fine meal. (May use a food processor.) Make well in mixture, pour in ice water, stirring with fork. Form dough into ball and knead 2 or 3 times. Chill 2 or 3 hours. Roll out dough to fit 2 9-inch quiche pans or 1 deep 10-inch pan. Prick bottom of dough with fork and bake 10 minutes at 400°.

Filling: Sauté vegetables in combined oil and butter for 6 or 7 minutes until vegetables wilt. Set aside to cool. Preheat oven to 400° degrees. Combine yolk of separated egg with 5 whole eggs. Beat milk into eggs until mixture is frothy. Add thyme, salt and pepper. Carefully stir in grated cheese. Alternate layers of vegetables and cheese mixture in crust ending with layer of cheese. Beat reserved egg white until frothy. Fold into top layer of cheese mixture. Bake 30-35 minutes or until golden brown. Let quiche cool for 15 or 20 minutes before cutting.

Mrs. Robert P. Tyson
West Chester, Pennsylvania

CHICKEN TETTRAZINI

Easy
Do ahead

Serves: 6-8
Preparing: 70 minutes
Baking: 10-12 minutes

4 whole chicken breasts
1 pound mushrooms, peeled
4 tablespoons butter
1 pound very thin spaghetti
3 tablespoons sweet butter
3 tablespoons flour

1¾ cups heavy sweet cream
⅓ cup dry sherry
½ cup grated Parmesan cheese
  (or a mixture of grated
  Parmesan and grated Swiss)
salt and pepper

Cover chicken with boiling water and simmer until tender, adding just a little salt to the water to season. Cool chicken in broth, then finely shred the chicken meat (or cut it into 2-inch chunks) and put the skin and bones back in the broth; cover, bring to a boil and simmer for 45 minutes. Remove cover from pan and let broth boil furiously for 10 to 15 minutes, or until reduced to about 2 cups. Strain. Meanwhile, thinly slice mushrooms and sauté them in 4 tablespoons of butter until tender and lightly browned, stirring frequently. Break the spaghetti into small pieces and cook in a large amount of boiling salted water until tender (about 15 minutes). Make cream sauce as follows: Melt 3 tablespoons of sweet butter; blend in flour and gradually stir in the hot, strained, reduced chicken broth, stirring constantly until perfectly smooth and absolutely free from lumps. Let it boil up 3 or 4 times, then stir in scalded cream, and sherry. Divide the sauce into 2 parts. Add the shredded chicken to one part; the cooked, well-drained spaghetti and mushrooms to the other part. Season both to taste with salt and pepper. Put the prepared spaghetti into a baking dish, making a cavity in the center and banking it around the side of the dish. Pour the chicken in the center; sprinkle with grated Parmesan cheese over the top and bake in a moderate oven until lightly browned (about 10 to 12 minutes). Serve from the baking dish.

Mrs. John J. Hosey, IV
Flourtown, Pennsylvania

HOT CHEESE SANDWICHES

Easy
Do ahead

Makes: 20 slices
Preparing: 20 minutes

1 pound of sharp cheese
¼ pound of bacon
3 eggs
2 tablespoons Worcestershire
  sauce

½ teaspoon dry mustard
½ teaspoon salt
½ teaspoon paprika

Grind bacon and cheese together; add and thoroughly mix the rest of the ingredients. Preferably using rye or pumpernickel bread, spread on each slice, making sure to cover entire surface of bread. Place under broiler until cheese melts and browns. Can be kept indefinitely in the refrigerator, but should be brought out ahead of time to insure easy spreading.

Mrs. Roger Scott
Lansdowne, Pennsylvania

LASAGNE

Average   *Serves: 12*
Partial do ahead   *Preparing: 1 hour*
Freeze   *Baking: 40 minutes*

4 tablespoons salad oil
1 tablespoon butter
12 ounces fresh mushrooms,
  sliced
½ pound Italian sausage, hot
  or mild to taste
1½ pounds hamburger
½ pound ground pork
1 cup grated Parmesan
  cheese
½ cup fresh bread crumbs
½ teaspoon pepper
4 dashes garlic salt

1½ tablespoons chopped fresh
  parsley
10 eggs
3 tablespoons olive oil
2 cups Ricotta cheese
2 pounds Mozzarella cheese,
  sliced
½ teaspoon oregano
1 pound lasagne
1 large jar Ragu mushroom
  sauce
1 large jar Ragu marinara sauce

Sauté mushrooms in 2 tablespoons salad oil and 1 tablespoon butter. Set aside in a bowl. Sauté Italian sausage (sliced or crumbled). Set aside in a bowl. Make meatballs: blend hamburger, pork, ½ cup Parmesan, bread crumbs, ¼ teaspoon pepper, two dashes garlic salt, two eggs and parsley. Mix well and shape into walnut-size balls. Brown in 2 tablespoons olive oil and 2 tablespoons salad oil. Dish can be prepared ahead to this stage. Mix Ricotta cheese, 8 eggs, ½ cup Parmesan, oregano and ½ teaspoon pepper. Set aside. Slice Mozzarella. Add 1 tablespoon olive oil and 1 teaspoon salt to six quarts of boiling water. Cook lasagne according to package directions. Drain. Mix two Ragu sauces in large bowl. Using 2 standard lasagne pans, layer ingredients in 3 layers ending with noodles as follows: noodles, mushrooms, sausage, meatballs, cheese mixture, Ragu sauce, ending with noodles. Cover with sliced Mozzarella cheese. Bake 40 minutes at 375°.

Lucy Smieler
St. Paul, Minnesota

FETTUCCINE ALFREDO

Easy

Serves: 3-4
Preparing: 20 minutes

1 stick sweet butter, at room
temperature
16 ounces sour cream, at
room temperature
2 crushed garlic cloves
1½ cups (8 ounces) packed
shredded Swiss cheese

⅔ cup Parmesan cheese
dash of Italian seasoning
1 package of spinach noodles,
prepared according to package
directions

Put heat on *low*, if heat is too high the mixture will separate. In a saucepan put the butter and the sour cream and cook until butter has melted and the mixture is combined. Stir occasionally. Add crushed garlic cloves to the mixture. Stir in the Swiss cheese a half cup at a time until it has melted. When all the Swiss cheese has been added and melted, add the Parmesan cheese to the mixture. Stir the mixture until the Parmesan cheese has been thoroughly blended. Add a dash of Italian seasoning and stir into the sauce until combined. While making the sauce, prepare the spinach noodles according to the package directions. When sauce and noodles are finished, toss together and serve.

Kathleen A. Frederick
Philadelphia, Pennsylvania

SPINACH LASAGNE

Average
Do ahead
Freeze

Serves: 8
Preparing: 30 minutes
Baking: 30 minutes

¼ pound hot sausage
¼ pound sweet sausage
2 teaspoons basil
1 pound Ricotta cheese
½ cup Parmesan cheese
1 (10-ounce) package noodles
garlic, salt, pepper, to taste

6 ounces tomato paste
2 pounds Italian tomatoes
½ pound cooked spinach (2
packages)
3 eggs, beaten
3 tablespoons spinach juice

Fry sausages; add paste and tomatoes. Cook noodles and drain. Mix Ricotta, Parmesan, spinach, eggs and juice. Alternate layers of noodles, sausage, and spinach. Bake 30 minutes at 350°.

Mrs. Roy Spreter
Bryn Mawr, Pennsylvania

Scales and Shells

seafood

CRAB APRÈS LA CHASSE

Average   *Serves: 12*
Do ahead   *Preparing: 30 minutes*
Freeze   *Baking 35-45 minutes*

1 small head of broccoli (or 2 packages frozen flowerets)
2 cups chopped onions
½ pound fresh mushrooms
2 cloves garlic, or shallots, minced or mashed
½ cup butter, melted
½ pound vermicelli, cooked
2 to 3 cups fresh crabmeat, picked
¼ cup stuffed green or black olives
½ pound shredded sharp cheese, (cheddar)
½ cup sour cream
1 1-pound, 12-ounce can tomatoes, drained and chopped
2 teaspoons salt
½ teaspoon basil

Break broccoli into smallest flowerets; discard all stems; boil 2 minutes and drain. In large frying pan, sauté onions, mushrooms and garlic in butter until tender. Combine with remaining ingredients, stirring until well mixed. Pour mixture into greased 3-quart casserole or baking dish. Sprinkle with seasoned bread crumbs and drizzle with butter. Bake, uncovered, in moderate oven (350°) for 35 to 45 minutes or until hot and bubbly. Can be doubled easily.

Mrs. George S. Hundt
Malvern, Pennsylvania

CRABMEAT DEWEY

Easy   *Makes: 1 quart*
         Preparing: 30 minutes

This is the original Union League recipe.

1 pound crabflakes
1 green pepper, diced
1 red sweet pepper, diced
6 fresh mushrooms, diced
1 pint cream
3 egg yolks
¼ pound butter
2 ounces sherry
caviar and truffles

Combine all ingredients except caviar and truffles. Cook in chafing dish and top with 3 slices of truffles and a dessert spoonful of caviar.

D. J. Redmond, Executive Chef
Union League
Philadelphia, Pennsylvania

MOUSSELINES DE SAUMON

Complicated   *Serves: 18*
Do ahead   *Preparing: 2 day process*

Serve with Sauce Vèrte as a beautiful first course.

2½ pounds fresh salmon   **⅓ cup boiling water**
1 onion   **1½ cups whipping cream**
6 mushrooms   **2 cans beef consommé (with**
1 cup or more white wine   **gelatin)**
salt and pepper   **8 or 10 slices smoked salmon**
2 envelopes clear gelatin   **truffles**

Use a pan large enough to place all the salmon with 1 sliced onion, 6 mushrooms, salt and pepper and enough white wine to cover the salmon. Cook in oven (low heat) for about ½ hour. Take out of oven and wait until it is cold. Then remove the skin and the bones. Mix in blender until very fine and pass through large strainer into a bowl. Add 2 envelopes of gelatin dissolved in boiling water; then slowly add 1½ cups whipping cream. Beat in blender, or by hand, with a whisk, until stiff. Dice 6 slices of smoked salmon and combine. Lightly oil 18 individual molds. In the bottom of each mold, put 2 teaspoons beef consommé (with gelatin). Place in center of each mold one slice of truffle. Fill the molds with the mousseline to the edge. Put in refrigerator on a tray until ready to serve. To remove, hold molds in hot water for a few seconds. To serve, decorate platter with the beef consommé gelatin, arranging slices of smoked salmon and cucumbers in center. Serve with Sauce Vèrte.

Cucumbers

5 cucumbers   **2 cups sugar**
2 tablespoons salt   **3 cups white vinegar**

Peel 5 cucumbers and slice rounds very fine. Sprinkle with salt and let stand 1 hour or overnight; then marinate with sugar, and white vinegar. Put in refrigerator. Squeeze out juice of marinade before serving.

Mrs. Walter H. Annenberg
Wynnewood, Pennsylvania

FILLET OF SALMON WITH CHAMPAGNE SAUCE

Average
Do ahead

Serves: 8 to 10
Preparing: 45 minutes
Cooking: 15 minutes

1 fresh salmon
1 onion
1 celery stalk
1 leek
salt and pepper

1 small can lobster bisque
16 ounces heavy cream
3 ounces flour
8 ounces champagne
parsley, chopped

Filet salmon, saving bones. To the bones add onion, celery, carrots and leek. Add half a gallon cold water, bring to boil and simmer half an hour. Skim the top of stock to remove impurities. Strain and save stock. Cut salmon in 8-ounce portions. Bring stock to light simmer and poach salmon 10-12 minutes. Heat heavy cream and add one small can lobster bisque. Salt and pepper to taste. Combine melted butter and flour. Cook over low heat 5-7 minutes. When cream mixture simmers, add roux until thickened. Add champagne. Place poached salmon portions in casserole dishes, ladle sauce over top, sprinkle with seasoned bread crumbs. Place under broiler until crumbs brown. Sprinkle with chopped parsley.

M. Pierre
The Riverfront Restaurant
Philadelphia, Pennsylvania

FILLETS DE SOLE CAPRICE

Easy

Serves: 4
Preparing: 30 minutes

16 fillets of Dover sole
melted butter
8 bananas

tomato sauce
fresh bread crumbs

Dip the fillets in melted butter first and then coat with fresh bread crumbs. Put them under the broiler to grill, adding melted butter. On each cooked fillet add a half a banana. Serve with a light, fresh tomato sauce.

Executive Chef Jean Jacques Cadiou
Sans Souci Restaurant
Washington, D. C.

SEAFOOD AU GRATIN

Easy
Do ahead
Freeze

Serves: 20
Preparing: 1 hour

9 pounds seafood, cooked and prepared (lobster, shrimp, crab)

Sauce:

½ pound butter
1 cup flour
7 cups milk
1 cup tomato purée
1 tablespoon plus 2
  teaspoons salt
½ teaspoon red pepper

1½ teaspoons paprika
2 cloves minced garlic
5 ounces Gruyère cheese, diced
¼ pound American cheese, diced
2 tablespoons MSG
½ cup sherry

Melt butter; blend in flour; cook one minute. Gradually add milk, tomato purée, and seasonings, until well blended. Add cheese and cook until thick and bubbly. Combine with fish when ready to serve. Heat thoroughly and add sherry. Serve with rice and a salad.

Mrs. Edwin Stiles
Haddonfield, New Jersey

DO AHEAD CRAB CASSEROLE

Easy
Do ahead

Serves: 6
Preparing: 10 minutes
Baking: 1 hour
Chilling: 8 hours

1 7-ounce can crabmeat
1 cup shell macaroni,
  uncooked
1½ ounces grated Parmesan
  or Cheddar cheese

2 hard-boiled eggs, chopped
1 can mushroom soup
1 cup milk
1 teaspoon chives or minced
  onion

Drain crabmeat. Combine all ingredients in a deep casserole. Refrigerate for at least 8 hours. (Put buttered crumbs on top if you wish). Bake, uncovered, 1 hour at 350°. Before serving, sprinkle with paprika. You can substitute shrimp, tuna, etc.

Mrs. Malissa Carter
Sedgwick, Maine

POACHED SCALLOPS

Easy
Do ahead

Serves: 6-8
Preparing: 5 minutes
Cooking: 6 minutes

A Microwave recipe

½ cup dry white wine
¼ cup water
1 medium white onion, sliced
3 sprigs of parsley
⅛ teaspoon dried tarragon
1½ pounds scallops

salt to taste
crisp Boston lettuce leaves
½ cup green mayonnaise
2 hard-boiled eggs, sliced
2 tablespoons chopped fresh
   parsley and watercress

In a glass casserole, combine wine, water, onion, parsley sprigs and tarragon. Cook (in center of microwave oven) for 2 minutes. Stir in the scallops and sprinkle lightly with salt. Cook 2 minutes; stir; and cook 2 minutes more. Stir again and let sit covered 5 minutes. Scallops should be firm but not hard. Let them cool in their liquid. Do not refrigerate. Drain and serve in individual dishes on lettuce leaves with a bit of green mayonnaise. Garnish with egg slices and chopped parsley. Green mayonnaise: blend ½ cup mayonnaise with 1½ tablespoons chopped fresh parsley and 1½ tablespoons chopped watercress.

Mrs. B. P. Wadhams
Haverford, Pennsylvania

SCALLOPED SCALLOPS

Easy
Do ahead

Serves: 4
Preparing: 15 minutes
Baking: 25 minutes

1 pound scallops (if large, cut
   in half)
1 cup Ritz-type cracker
   crumbs

½ cup soft bread crumbs
½ cup butter, melted
salt and pepper, to taste

Melt butter; add both crumbs. Butter a 1½-quart baking dish or individual serving dishes. Add alternate layers of scallops and crumbs, beginning with scallops and ending with crumbs. Bake in preheated oven at 400° for 25 minutes. Variation: A few shrimp added to the scallops makes a very special dish.

Barbara Jones
Bangor, Maine

BAKED SALMON

Average

Serves: 6
Preparing: 30 minutes
Baking: 50 minutes

1 3-pound fresh salmon
2 tablespoons butter
1 teaspoon salt
1 teaspoon pepper
3 carrots
3 medium size onions

1 pinch dried thyme
1 bay leaf
4 to 5 sprigs of parsley
1 stalk of celery
2 cups of California dry white
  wine

Sauce:

1 teaspoon flour
2 tablespoons butter
pan liquid
salt and freshly ground pepper
  (to taste)

small cooked mushrooms,
  for garnish

Clean a 3-pound salmon. Season with salt and pepper. Melt 2 tablespoons butter in pan (pan long enough to hold fish). Sauté finely chopped carrots and onions in the butter. Place salmon on these vegetables. Add thyme, bay leaf, parsley sprigs, celery, and wine. Cover fish with a piece of buttered wax paper or aluminum foil and bring wine to a boil. Cover pan and cook in hot (425°) oven for 45 to 50 minutes or until fish is done, basting from time to time. Place on warm serving dish, remove skin.

Sauce: Strain pan liquid into saucepan and cook over brisk flame until reduced by half. Stir in the flour, creamed with butter and cook until thickened. Add salt and pepper and pour over fish. Garnish with mushrooms.

Albert L. Borkow, Jr.
Philadelphia, Pennsylvania

CASCADES FRIED FLOUNDER AMANDINE

Easy
Partial do ahead

Serves: 6
Preparing: 15 minutes
Cooking: 10 minutes

2 pounds fresh flounder
  fillets
salt and pepper, to taste
2 tablespoons lemon juice
¾ pound saltine crackers
¾ cup almonds, slivered

3 eggs, beaten
⅔ cup milk
2 cups all-purpose flour
½ cup vegetable oil
½ cup butter

Cut flounder into 6 portions and season with salt, pepper and lemon juice. Coarsely crumble the crackers and mix with almonds. Beat the eggs and milk together to make an egg wash. Dredge the flounder in the flour and dip into the egg wash. Roll in cracker-almond mixture and pat down firmly so that the mixture will adhere. Heat the oil and butter. Fry the fish about five minutes on each side or until golden brown and flakes easily with a fork. Drain quickly on a paper towel and serve immediately.

Mrs. Robert Armistead
Williamsburg, Virginia

FISH AND BROCCOLI ROLLS

Easy
Do ahead

Serves: 4
Preparing: 30 minutes
Baking: 30 minutes

1 package frozen broccoli
1 package frozen or fresh
  fillet of flounder, sole, or
  perch
2 tablespoons milk
1 egg, slightly beaten

salt and pepper
½ cup dry, fine bread crumbs
¼ cup Parmesan cheese, grated
1 tablespoon butter
1 cup tomato juice

Cook broccoli until tender-crisp; drain. Dip fish fillets in seasoned milk and egg mixture. Roll in mixture of bread crumbs and cheese. Wrap each fillet around a piece of broccoli and secure with toothpick. Place in greased shallow baking dish and dot with butter. Pour tomato juice over fish rolls and bake in 400° oven for 30 minutes.

Mrs. John E. Krout
Rosemont, Pennsylvania

SEAFOOD BAKE

Easy

Serves: 6
Preparing: 20 minutes
Baking: 30 minutes

1 can cream of mushroom
  soup
⅓ cup salad dressing or
  mayonnaise
⅓ cup milk
1 6-ounce can drained shrimp
1 5-ounce can water
  chestnuts, drained and
  sliced

paprika
1 7-ounce can tuna, drained
1 cup celery, finely chopped
2 tablespoons chopped parsley
2 teaspoons grated onion
2 cups cooked Creamettes
  (macaroni) (½ of 1 pound
  package)

Blend ingredients and put in a 1½-quart ungreased casserole. Sprinkle paprika on top. Bake uncovered at 350° for 30 minutes. Can substitute crab for tuna!

Mrs. Harold E. Reinmiller
Norristown, Pennsylvania

Cider may be used when poaching fish to impart a nice flavor.

FISH DISH

Easy

Serves: 6
Preparing: 20 minutes
Baking: 15 minutes

3 packages frozen chopped
  spinach
2 cups sour cream
3 tablespoons flour
½ cup chopped green onions
  and tops

juice of 1 lemon
1½ teaspoons salt
1½ to 2 pounds thin fillets of
  sole, flounder or white fish
2 tablespoons butter
paprika

Cook spinach and drain. Blend sour cream with flour, green onions, lemon juice and salt. Combine half of mixture with spinach and spread evenly over bottom of a shallow baking dish. Arrange fish on top of spinach. Dot with butter. Spread remaining sour cream over sole. Dust with paprika. Bake at 350° for 15 minutes. Serve immediately.

Mrs. I. M. Scott
Meadowbrook, Pennsylvania

BETTY'S TUNA CASSEROLE

Easy
Do ahead

Serves: 4-6
Preparing: 15 minutes
Baking: 40 minutes

1 cup chopped celery
¼ cup chopped onion
1 can cream of mushroom
  soup
½ can water or chicken broth
1 7-ounce can tuna

1 can Chinese noodles, save
  some for the top
½ cup chopped cashews (can
  substitute sliced water
  chestnuts)

Combine all ingredients and top with one-third of the Chinese noodles. Bake at 325° for 40 minutes.

Mrs. Betty H. Heidler
Frazer, Pennsylvania

FLORENTINE TUNA AND NOODLE CASSEROLE

Average

Serves: 4-6
Preparing: 30 minutes
Baking: 20 minutes

1 tablespoon salt
3 quarts boiling water
8 ounces fine egg noodles
  (about 4 cups)
1 10-ounce package frozen
  chopped spinach, cooked
  and drained
1 13-ounce can tuna, drained
⅓ cup margarine
1 medium onion, chopped

⅓ cup flour
1 chicken bouillon cube
¾ teaspoon salt
¼ teaspoon pepper
⅛ teaspoon nutmeg
2 cups milk
1¼ cups water
2 ounces grated Swiss cheese
paprika

Cook noodles in boiling, salted water uncovered, until tender. Drain. In a saucepan sauté onion in margarine. Add flour, bouillon cube, salt, pepper and nutmeg. Gradually add milk and cook, stirring constantly. When sauce boils cook one more minute. Stir in 1¼ cups water. Layer noodles, spinach and tuna in 2½ quart casserole. Pour sauce on top. Sprinkle with cheese and paprika. Bake in 375° oven 20 minutes or until bubbling.

Kathy Dunlop
Villanova, Pennsylvania

SALMON LOAF WITH CANNED SALMON

Easy   *Serves: 6*
Do ahead   *Preparing: 1 hour*

1 level teaspoon Knox gelatine   **¾ cup milk**
¼ cup cold water   **2½ teaspoons vinegar or lemon**
2 egg yolks   **juice**
¼ teaspoon salt   **1 can salmon (1 pound)**
1 teaspoon dry mustard   **few grains cayenne or paprika**

Soak the gelatine in cold water 5 minutes. Mix egg yolks slightly beaten with salt, mustard and cayenne. If you like more seasonings, add more paprika or Worcestershire sauce. Add milk and vinegar. Cook in a double boiler, stirring constantly, until the mixture thickens. Add soaked gelatine and salmon (separated into flakes). Turn into a mold; chill. When ready to serve, remove to a bed of lettuce.

Mrs. S. Leonard Kent, Jr.
Bryn Mawr, Pennsylvania

SALMON STEAKS BAKED IN WINE

Easy   *Serves: 4*
                                       Preparing: 10 minutes
                                       Baking: 10-12 minutes

4 salmon steaks, one inch   **salt lightly, to taste**
  thick   **1 teaspoon finely chopped**
¾ cup dry, white wine   **tarragon or ½ teaspoon dried**

Preheat oven to 500°. Place salmon steaks in a shallow baking dish, pour on wine and sprinkle with tarragon. Bake 10 to 12 minutes or until fish flakes easily when tested with a fork.

Mrs. Thomas A. Bradshaw
Bryn Mawr, Pennsylvania

BROILED HERB FISH FILLETS

Easy

Serves: 2
Preparing: 10 minutes
Broiling: 10 minutes

2 fish fillets
2 to 3 teaspoons minced
fresh dillweed
½ to 1 teaspoon minced
fresh thyme
¾ teaspoon low sodium
seasoning

½ teaspoon grated ginger root
(optional)
¼ cup dry white wine (optional)
2 tablespoons margarine
1 teaspoon lemon juice

Place fillets skin side down in a lightly oiled 2-quart shallow baking dish. Sprinkle with dill, thyme, salt and ginger root. Pour wine over and around fish, if desired. Set aside. Combine margarine and lemon juice in a small saucepan. Cook over low heat until margarine melts. Pour over fillets. Broil 6 inches away from heat 7-10 minutes or until fish flakes easily when tested with a fork.

Mrs. Blair B. May
Wayne, Pennsylvania

MARINATED WHITE FISH

Easy
Do ahead

Serves: 6
Preparing: 10 minutes
Marinating: 36 hours

2 pounds or 3 or 4 fillets
(plaice, white fish, i.e. sole
or flounder)
8 limes, squeezed (or amount
needed to cover fish)

1 small glass jar pimiento
4 large tomatoes
oil cured olives
Romaine lettuce
salt to taste

Place fish fillets in glass baking dish so that fish lies flat and doesn't overlap. Cover with lime juice, and cover dish with poly-wrap. Store in refrigerator 24 to 36 hours, turning fish now and then. Fish will "cook" in the lime juice. Serve with sliced tomatoes, pimientos and olives on Romaine lettuce seasoned with salt and pepper and accompanied by toasted pita bread or some other crisp melba-like toast.

Mrs. Thomas V. LeFevre
Rosemont, Pennsylvania

SHRIMP AND CRABMEAT AU GRATIN

Average

Serves: 6
Preparing: 30 minutes
Baking: 30 minutes

1 pound shrimp shelled and deveined
1 9-ounce package frozen artichoke hearts
¼ cup butter or margarine
½ pound fresh mushrooms, sliced
1 clove garlic, crushed
2 tablespoons finely chopped shallots
¼ cup flour
½ teaspoon pepper

1 tablespoon snipped fresh dill or 2 tablespoons dill concentrate (optional)
¾ cup milk
1 8-ounce package sharp cheddar cheese, grated
⅔ cup dry white wine
2 7½-ounce cans king crabmeat
2 tablespoons seasoned cornflake crumbs
½ tablespoon butter or margarine

Cook shrimp in salted, boiling water, enough to cover, for three minutes or just until shrimp are pink. Drain. Cook artichoke hearts as package label directs. Drain. Preheat the oven to 375°. In 2 tablespoons hot butter in a skillet, sauté sliced mushrooms for five minutes. In 2 tablespoons butter in a saucepan, sauté the garlic and chopped shallots for five minutes. Remove from heat. Stir in the flour, pepper and dill. Stir in the milk. Bring to boiling, stirring; remove from heat. Add half of the cheese and stir until it is melted. Stir in the wine. Drain crabmeat; remove cartilage; flake. In a 2-quart casserole, combine the sauce, crabmeat, shrimp, artichokes, mushrooms and rest of cheese; mix lightly. Sprinkle with cornflake crumbs; dot with butter. Bake for 30 minutes or until the mixture is bubbly and the cornflake crumbs are browned.

Mrs. William T. Justice
Bryn Mawr, Pennsylvania

To help keep the shape of a whole boiled fish, insert a carrot before cooking.
Thread cocktail picks with slices of lemon, cucumber and green olives. Spear into salmon steaks or baked fish.
The coral inside a lobster is good to eat. It can be used to color and flavor mayonnaise that is served with the lobster.

FILLET OF FLOUNDER

Easy

Serves: 3 or 4
Preparing: 10 minutes
Baking: 20 minutes

**1 pound fillet of flounder or
  any firm white fish:
  haddock, sole, turbot, etc.**
**¼ cup melted butter or
  margarine (butter adds
  flavor)**

½ cup Parmesan cheese
1 cup sour cream

About 30 minutes before serving start heating oven to 400°. Lightly grease a flat baking dish. Divide flounder into 3 to 4 serving pieces. Mix together butter or margarine, cheese and sour cream and spoon over fish. Bake 20 minutes, uncovered, or until fish is tender and flakes easily. Serve immediately topped with a sprinkling of paprika and snipped parsley.

Mrs. Eugene R. Hook
Wynnewood, Pennsylvania

STUFFED FILLET OF SOLE

Average
Partial do ahead

Serves: 6
Preparing: 15 minutes
Cooking: 15-20 minutes

6 fillets of sole
**¾ pound crabmeat or lobster
  meat**
⅓ cup chopped celery
⅓ cup chopped parsley

½ cup chopped green onions
4 tablespoons butter
½ cup crushed Ritz crackers
⅓ cup dry vermouth
salt and pepper to taste

Butter inside of six custard cups and line with fillet of sole leaving middle open for stuffing. Sauté green onions in butter. Add celery and cook without letting onions brown. Add shellfish and stir for about 2 minutes. Add salt and pepper to taste. Add vermouth and boil rapidly for about one minute. Add parsley and Ritz cracker crumbs and stuff sole fillets in the custard cups. Recipe may be held at this point. When ready to bake put in preheated 350° oven and bake 15 to 20 minutes (until fish flakes easily). To serve, invert into plate or serving platter. Serve plain or with a dollop of hollandaise.

Toni Gal
Beverly Farms, Massachusetts

BLUEFISH WADHAMS

Average   *Serves: 4-6*
                                                Preparing: 10 minutes
                                                  Cooking: 12 minutes

Fish is one of the easiest dishes for microwave. This recipe could be used for sole, trout, or salmon.

1 whole bluefish, 3 to 3½   **4 tablespoons Herb Butter**
  pounds   **Wadhams***
Lawry's Seasoned Salt

Scale and clean fish, but leave it whole. Sprinkle inside with seasoned salt. Place on a large sheet of waxed paper or an inverted plate (or two saucers) to hold it above any liquid that may collect in bottom of dish. This, all in a shallow baking dish. Spread herb butter evenly over fish. Fold the edges of the waxed paper together, making the seam above the top of the fish. Cook in center of oven 4 minutes. Rotate dish ½ turn. Cook 3 minutes. Let set, still wrapped in paper, 5 minutes. Test. Ready when flakes easily with fork.

*Refer to index.

Mrs. B. P. Wadhams
Haverford, Pennsylvania

TUNA FLORENTINE

Easy   *Serves: 12*
Do ahead   *Preparing: 15-20 minutes*
Freeze   *Baking: 20 minutes*

3 large cans light tuna fish   **¾ teaspoon prepared mustard**
  (12½-ounce)   **3 tablespoons dry sherry**
4 10-ounce packages frozen   **1 tablespoon grated onion**
  chopped spinach   **½ cup Ritz crackers, crushed**
1½ cups mayonnaise   **½ cup Parmesan cheese, grated**
2 teaspoons lemon juice

Cook spinach briefly in salted water. Drain and place in 9"x13" casserole. Cover with drained tuna fish mixed with rest of ingredients. Mix Ritz crackers and Parmesan cheese and place on top. Bake for 20 minutes in 350° oven.

Mrs. J. Mahlon Buck, Jr.
Haverford, Pennsylvania

FISH FILLETS IN BEER BATTER

Easy
Partial do ahead

Serves: 4-6
Preparing: 20 minutes
Resting: 3 hours
Cooking: 10 minutes

The batter *must* be made ahead of time and allowed to stand.

1 pound fish fillets
juice of ½ lemon
2 tablespoons chopped
  parsley

2 tablespoons vegetable oil
salt and pepper to taste
oil for frying

Batter:

¾ cup flour
½ cup flat beer, at room
  temperature

1 teaspoon vegetable oil
1 egg, separated
salt and pepper, to taste

Prepare batter: place flour in bowl; stir in beer, salt, pepper and oil. Blend roughly, there should be a few lumps. Cover bowl with plastic. Let stand for 3 hours. Stir in egg yolk. Beat egg white until stiff and fold into mixture. Cut fillets into fingers. Place in shallow bowl. Add lemon juice, parsley, oil, salt and pepper. Heat oil for frying. Dip fish fingers in batter, one at a time, and fry in hot oil until golden brown. Drain on paper towels.

Mrs. John F. Lloyd
Ardmore, Pennsylvania

COQUILLES ST. JACQUES

Easy

Serves: 4
Preparing: 40 minutes
Cooking: 7 minutes

1 pound sea scallops
½ lime
1 cucumber
1 cup heavy whipping cream
1 tablespoon minced fresh
  tarragon (or 1 teaspoon
  dried)

Coulis de tomates:
3 tomatoes
2 tablespoons minced shallots
1 tablespoon sweet unsalted
  butter
salt, white pepper,
nutmeg
juice of ½ lime

Wash the scallops. Slice them in half crosswise. Sprinkle with juice of ½ lime. Peel the cucumber. Cut in half lengthwise and scoop out the seeds. Cut into strips ¼ inch thick and 1 inch long. Peel, juice and seed the tomatoes. Chop them finely. Cook the shallots in the butter until soft, about one minute. Add the tomatoes and seasonings. Simmer until thick, about ten minutes. Place the scallops and their juices in a large pan (each touching the bottom of the pan). Place the cucumbers on top. Cover tightly. Cook on medium-high heat about 2 minutes until milky opaque. Turn once. Add the tomato mixture. Add the cream and tarragon. Uncovered, bring to a boil and simmer until slightly thickened (about 3 minutes). Season with salt and white pepper as necessary. Garnish with fresh tarragon. Serve immediately over rice or noodles.

Mrs. Blaine L. Wicklein
Washington, D. C.

OYSTERS AND SPINACH BORDEN

Easy
Do ahead

Serves: 8
Preparing: 30 minutes
Baking: 30-40 minutes

2 packages frozen spinach,
  cooked and drained
2 small onions, chopped
6 tablespoons butter
6 tablespoons flour
1 cup evaporated milk
1 cup regular milk

3 egg yolks
1½ teaspoons Jane's Krazy
  Mixed-Up Salt
2 raw tomatoes, sliced ¼-inch
  thick
8 raw oysters
½ teaspoon salt

Cook frozen spinach; drain well. Sauté onions in butter. Stir in flour. Blend in evaporated and regular milk. Stir until smooth and thickened. Add salt, Krazy salt, and freshly ground pepper. Add spinach and egg yolks, simmer a bit to include them. Turn into pan about 9 x 11-inches. Alternate slices of tomato and raw oysters on top. Cover with Mornay Sauce, and bake at 350° for about ½ hour or until hot and bubbling.

Mornay sauce

5 tablespoons butter
5 tablespoons flour
½ cup Swiss cheese
2 cups milk

½ teaspoon salt
1½ teaspoons Worcestershire
  sauce

Melt butter over low heat. Add and blend flour. Slowly stir in milk, and season with salt. Cook and stir until smooth and boiling gently. Reduce heat and add cheese and Worcestershire sauce.

Mrs. J. Wilson Borden, Jr.
Bryn Mawr, Pennsylvania

SEAFOOD SOUFFLÉ

Easy

Serves: 4
Preparing: 10 minutes
Baking: 45 minutes

1 pound seafood chunks,
  (fish, shrimp, lobster, any
  or all)
2 tomatoes, chopped
½ cup mayonnaise
½ cup minced onion
½ cup grated Swiss cheese
2 teaspoons dried basil

bread crumbs and paprika for
  garnish
½ cup parsley
3 tablespoons chives, chopped
1 clove garlic, minced
1 cup mushrooms, chopped
2 eggs

Sauté onions, basil, garlic, parsley, chives and mushrooms. Mix eggs and mayonnaise in large bowl. Add cheese and tomato chunks to egg mixture. Add sautéed vegetables and seafood to mixture. Mix well. Put into 9-inch pie dish. Sprinkle with bread crumbs and paprika. Bake at 350° for 45 minutes.

Mrs. John F. Lloyd
Ardmore, Pennsylvania

FISHERMAN PIE

Easy

Serves: 6
Preparing: 20 minutes
Baking: 20 minutes

1 pound white fish fillets
1 pound peeled shrimp
2 large ripe tomatoes, peeled
  and chunked
1 medium onion, finely
  chopped

1 teaspoon fennel seed
salt and pepper
¼ cup white wine
½ cup bread crumbs
2 tablespoons butter

Butter a baking dish and layer it with half the fish fillets. Top with layer of shrimp. Add tomatoes, onion and fennel seed. Season with salt and pepper. Add another layer of fish fillets and white wine. Top with bread crumbs. Dot with butter. Bake 15 to 20 minutes at 400°.

Toba Schwaber Kerson
Bryn Mawr, Pennsylvania

CRABMEAT AND MUSHROOMS IN WINE SAUCE

Easy   Serves: 4
Do ahead   Preparing: 15 minutes
                                   Baking: 30 minutes

1 pound fresh crabmeat   ¾ cup white wine
¾ pound fresh mushrooms   ¾ teaspoon dry mustard
3 tablespoons butter or   ¼ teaspoon dry tarragon
  margarine   breadcrumbs
3 tablespoons flour   salt and pepper
¾ cup milk

Pull the crabmeat apart and remove the stiff membranes. Slice mushrooms and sauté in butter or margarine. Make cream sauce, melting the butter, blending the flour, and adding liquids and seasonings. Cook 2 or 3 minutes; add crabmeat and mushrooms. Sprinkle top with breadcrumbs and dot with butter. Bake in a medium oven 350° for 30 minutes, uncovered.

The Committee

Put lemon on fish after cooking, not before, to keep fish from getting mushy.

BROILED MARYLAND CRAB CAKES

Easy   Serves: 4
Do ahead   Preparing: 10 minutes
                                  Cooking: 10 minutes

1 pound crabmeat   3 to 4 tablespoons fine bread
1 cup mayonnaise   crumbs or cracker crumbs
1 egg white   1 tablespoon butter
½ teaspoon Old Bay seafood   1 cup melted butter
  seasoning

Preheat broiler to medium. Remove shell and cartilage from crabmeat. Blend mayonnaise, egg white, seasoning and cracker crumbs in bowl. Add crab and fold in gently. Divide mixture into 8 equal portions. Shape into patties. Coat them with crumbs and refrigerate. Heat butter and turn cakes in it to coat top and bottom. Broil about 4 inches from flame, about 5 minutes, turning once. Serve with additional melted butter with crackers or hamburger rolls. This makes 2 per person.

Mrs. Andrew C. Warren
Villanova, Pennsylvania

SHRIMP MANDARIN

Average

Serves: 8
Preparing: 30 minutes
Cooking: 15 minutes

¼ cup salad oil, heated
2 large onions, thinly sliced
3 cups sliced celery
(lengthwise into 1-inch
pieces)
2 cans (4 ounces each)
mushrooms, drained
2 pounds spinach, washed

2 pounds fresh shrimp, washed,
shelled, deveined
1 5-ounce can water chestnuts,
drained, sliced
1 11-ounce can Mandarin orange
sections, drained
2 tablespoons soy sauce
2 tablespoons sugar

In a deep heavy kettle, heat the salad oil. Add onion, celery, mushrooms, spinach, shrimp, sliced water chestnuts, orange sections, soy sauce and sugar. Bring to a boil; reduce heat and simmer, stirring frequently until the shrimp are cooked to a deep pink and vegetables crisp tender. Serve in a hot casserole with rice, soy sauce and toasted almonds.

Mrs. Adrian Siegel
Philadelphia, Pennsylvania

SHRIMP CURRY

Easy
Partial do ahead

Serves: 4-6
Preparing: 30 minutes
Cooking: 20 minutes

1½ pounds cooked shrimp,
cleaned
2 tablespoons butter
2 tablespoons flour
2 cups milk (use the coconut
milk, it's great!)
¼ teaspoon salt

dash of pepper
2 teaspoons curry powder
1 teaspoon ginger, powdered
1 tablespoon minced onion
2 teaspoons lemon juice
½ cup *fresh* coconut, grated

Melt butter. Add flour, salt, pepper, ginger and onion. Make a paste and add milk gradually. Cook until thickened. Add coconut, lemon juice, and shrimp. Simmer 20 minutes. Serve over white rice with condiments: mango chutney, white raisins, shredded coconut, chopped peanuts, chopped bacon, grated egg yolks and/or chopped green peppers.

Mrs. David W. Coolidge
Naples, Florida

SHRIMP LARIO

Easy
Do ahead

Serves: 6
Preparing: 30 minutes
Chilling: 8 hours
Baking: 45-50 minutes

2½ cups shrimp, cooked
1 3-ounce can sliced
  mushrooms
6 to 8 slices of day-old bread,
  trimmed, buttered and
  cubed
½ pound grated sharp
  cheese

3 eggs
½ teaspoon salt
½ teaspoon dry mustard
dash pepper
dash paprika
1½ cups milk

Grease a 2-quart casserole. Blend and place in casserole: shrimp, mushrooms, half of bread cubes, and half of cheese. Top with rest of cheese and bread cubes. Blend eggs and seasonings together. Add milk and pour over all. Cover and refrigerate, several hours or overnight. Bake at 325° for 45-50 minutes.

Grace Lario
Springfield, Pennsylvania

Canned shrimp loses its canned taste by soaking it in 2 tablespoons of vinegar and 1 teaspoon of sherry for 15 minutes.

BETTY'S CRAB

Easy
Do ahead

Serves: 6-8
Preparing: 20 minutes
Baking: 45 minutes

1 pound crabmeat
1 pint light cream
3 hard-boiled eggs
1 pint mayonnaise

2 tablespoons chopped parsley
½ cup sherry
⅔ package Pepperidge Farm
  stuffing (small bag)

Mix cream and mayonnaise together. Add all other ingredients, saving a little stuffing to sprinkle on top. Mix carefully. Put in buttered casserole and bake at 300° for 45 minutes.

May be made a day ahead and kept in refrigerator until baked.

Mrs. George Riggs
Gladwyne, Pennsylvania

CRABMEAT RUSKS

Easy
Do ahead

Serves: 6-8
Preparing: 10 minutes
Baking: 25-30 minutes

2 6-ounce cans of crabmeat
1 8-ounce package cream
  cheese, softened
3 tablespoons mayonnaise
2 tablespoons onion,
  chopped

lemon juice to taste
dash of Tabasco
8 Holland rusks
2 large ripe tomatoes, sliced
8 slices American cheese

The night before serving, mix together crabmeat, cheese, mayonnaise and seasonings. Refrigerate. To prepare for serving, butter rusks slightly. Place a slice of tomato on rusk and divide crab mixture evenly on top of tomato. Top with a slice of cheese. Bake in 350° oven until mixture is hot for 25-30 minutes.

The Committee

SHRIMP CASSEROLE

Very easy
Do ahead

Serves: 4
Preparing: 20-30 minutes
Baking: 10-15 minutes

1 pound shrimp, cooked,
  shelled and deveined
½ pound mushrooms, sliced
3 tablespoons butter
1 tablespoon flour
1 cup sour cream
5 tablespoons butter,
  softened

1 teaspoon imported soy sauce
salt and pepper, to taste
¼ cup freshly grated Parmesan
  cheese
1 teaspoon sweet Hungarian
  paprika

Put shrimp in a buttered shallow baking dish just large enough to hold them in one layer. Sprinkle with salt and pepper. Sauté mushrooms in three tablespoons of butter until browned. Transfer to bowl and toss with flour. Stir in sour cream, the five tablespoons of butter, well softened, soy sauce, salt, and pepper to taste. Pour sauce over shrimp and sprinkle with cheese and paprika. Bake, uncovered, in preheated hot oven (400°) for ten minutes.

Mrs. John T. Grisdale
Radnor, Pennsylvania

CRAB-ZUCCHINI BAKE

Easy

Serves: 2
Preparing: 20 minutes
Baking: 20 minutes

This recipe adapts for the microwave oven.

½ pound crabmeat
1 cup drained, shredded
  zucchini
1 cup shredded Swiss or
  Mozzarella cheese

2 eggs
¾ cup milk
2 tablespoons grated onion
salt and pepper to taste

Butter two 12-ounce casseroles. Press zucchini on bottom and sides. Sprinkle with grated onion and cheese. Spoon in crabmeat. Beat together eggs, milk and seasonings. Pour over crabmeat. Bake in preheated 400° oven for 15 minutes. Reduce heat to 350° and bake for 20 minutes. Microwave times: place in oven and cook for 5 minutes. Rotate and cook for 5 minutes or until set.

Mrs. John F. Lloyd
Ardmore, Pennsylvania

BAKED FLOUNDER AND CRAB

Easy
Do ahead

Serves: 8-10
Preparing: 20 minutes
Baking: 1 hour

2 pounds flounder, about 4
  fillets
1 pound lump crabmeat
5 tablespoons butter
½ cup flour
2 cups milk
1 teaspoon prepared mustard

juice of ½ lemon
⅛ teaspoon cayenne
1 teaspoon salt
1 tablespoon chopped parsley
½ cup dry sherry
bread crumbs

Cut flounder into bite-size pieces. Place in greased baking dish. Add crabmeat. Prepare a sauce with rest of ingredients (except bread crumbs). Pour sauce over fish in casserole. Top with bread crumbs and butter pieces. Bake at 350° for one hour.

Mrs. John B. Lukens
Lafayette Hill, Pennsylvania

BAKED STUFFED SHRIMP
WITH MINCED CLAM STUFFING

Average
Do ahead

Serves: 4
Preparing: 1 hour
Baking: 20 minutes

12 to 16 jumbo shrimp
2 tablespoons dry bread
  crumbs per shrimp
¼ pound melted margarine
2 cans minced clams, drained
garlic salt, to taste

½ teaspoon salt
¼ teaspoon pepper
½ teaspoon paprika
¼ cup parsley
1 tablespoon lemon juice

Shell and devein shrimp. Split the shrimp so it will fan out and lie flat. Place on buttered tin foil or large cookie sheet. For stuffing, mix all other ingredients together. If mixture is too dry add some juice from minced clams, a little water; melted butter or margarine. Place 2 tablespoons of stuffing on each shrimp and sprinkle paprika on top. Refrigerate until ready to bake. Bake at 350° for 20 minutes.

Mrs. David R. Walters
Keene, New Hampshire

BLUEFISH

Easy

Preparing: 20 minutes
Baking: 10 minutes

For each one pound of bluefish, prepare the following marinade:

2 tablespoons olive oil
½ tablespoon imported
  Italian dried oregano
1 tablespoon fresh chopped
  Italian parsley

fresh squeezed lemon juice
freshly ground pepper
salt to taste (very little or none
  needed)

Place fish skin side down on baking sheet. Mix marinade ingredients together and pour over fish. Allow to marinate 15 to 20 minutes. Place in upper third of preheated 425° oven. Bake 10 minutes. Finish under broiler for approximately three minutes. Serve with chopped parsley and lemon or lime wedges. (Use approximately one pound of bluefish for two persons.)

Richard and Darcy Lettieri
Weston, Massachusetts

SALMON QUICHE

Easy
Do ahead
Freeze

Serves: 4-6
Preparing: 15 minutes
Baking: 45 minutes

½ cup mayonnaise
½ cup milk
2 eggs
2 tablespoons flour

⅓ cup scallions, chopped
6 ounces Swiss cheese
1 7¾-ounce can red salmon

Mix together all ingredients except cheese. Cover bottom of 9" pastry shell with cheese. Add mixture. Bake at 350° for 45 minutes, or until golden brown. Can be served cold for a picnic.

Pearl Grika
Cherry Hill, New Jersey

SHRIMP AND ARTICHOKE CASSEROLE

Easy
Do ahead

Serves: 6
Preparing: 30 minutes
Baking: 30 minutes

6½ tablespoons butter
4½ tablespoons flour
¾ cup milk
¾ cup heavy cream
salt and pepper to taste
1 package frozen artichoke
    hearts, cooked
1 pound shrimp, cooked

½ pound fresh mushrooms,
    sliced
¼ cup sherry
1 tablespoon Worcestershire
    sauce
¼ cup grated Parmesan cheese
paprika

Preheat oven to 375°. Melt 4½ tablespoons butter and stir in flour. Gradually add milk and cream, stirring constantly. When mixture is thick and smooth, season to taste with salt and pepper. Arrange artichokes over bottom of buttered baking dish. Scatter shrimp over artichokes. Cook sliced mushrooms in remaining 2 tablespoons butter for 6 minutes. Spoon mushrooms over shrimp and artichokes. Add sherry and Worcestershire to cream sauce and pour it over all. Sprinkle with cheese. Bake 20-30 minutes.

Mrs. Richard Hopkins
Madison, New Jersey
Mrs. James P. Roberts
Haverford, Pennsylvania

PEASANT STEW

Easy
Do ahead

Serves: 6
Preparing: 20 minutes
Cooking: 30 minutes

2 pound halibut, bite-size
  pieces
¾ pound small or medium
  shrimp
1 6½-ounce can chopped
  clams
1 clove garlic
1 cup chopped onion
½ cup chopped green pepper

¾ cup chopped celery
¾ cup chopped carrots
2 tablespoons olive oil
1 28-ounce can tomatoes
1 cup tomato juice
1 cup white wine
¼ teaspoon sweet basil
¼ teaspoon oregano

Sauté garlic, onions, carrots, green pepper and celery in olive oil. Add tomatoes, juice, wine and herbs. Cover, simmer 20 minutes. Add halibut, clams and shrimp. Cover, simmer 5-10 minutes longer. Season with salt and pepper to taste. Sprinkle with chopped parsley.

Mrs. George W. Hager
Cherry Hill, New Jersey

GREEK SPINACH AND TUNA PIE

Easy
Do ahead

Serves: 6
Preparing: 10 minutes
Baking: 45 minutes

2 packages frozen chopped
  spinach, thawed and
  drained well
¼ cup chopped scallions
8 ounces Feta cheese,
  crumbled

1 7-ounce can tuna fish, drained
½ teaspoon dried dill
½ cup milk
4 eggs

Mix first five ingredients. Place in greased 10-inch pie plate. Mix eggs and milk and pour over other ingredients. Bake 45 minutes at 350°. Note: Mixture may be baked in a pre-baked pie shell if desired.

Mrs. William Brewster
Villanova, Pennsylvania

COLD DEVILED SHRIMP

Easy
Do ahead

Serves: 8
Preparing: 20 minutes
Chilling: 2 hours

2 pounds shrimp
1 lemon, very thinly sliced
1 red onion, thinly sliced
½ cup pitted black olives
2 tablespoons chopped
  pimiento
½ cup fresh lemon juice
¼ cup oil

1 tablespoon wine vinegar
1 garlic clove, pressed
½ bay leaf, broken up
1 tablespoon dry mustard
¼ teaspoon cayenne pepper
freshly ground black pepper
1 teaspoon salt

Bring a quart of water to a boil in a saucepan. Add cleaned shrimp and cook them a scant three minutes. Drain at once and put them in the bowl in which you wish to serve them. Add the lemon slices, onion, black olives (well drained) and pimiento. Toss together. In another bowl, combine the lemon juice, oil, vinegar, spices, herbs and mix together well. Stir this marinade into the shrimp mixture. Cover the dish and let it sit in the refrigerator for at least two hours, giving it a stir once or twice. At the table, spoon it onto small plates or serve as a salad.

Mrs. Louis Hood
Wayne, Pennsylvania

FISH LOAF

Easy
Do ahead

Serves: 8
Preparing: 20 minutes
Baking: 45 minutes

2 pounds ground raw
  haddock
6 Uneeda biscuits
1 cup milk

¼ pound melted butter
1 cup sour cream
3 eggs
salt and pepper to taste

Butter a 2-quart loaf pan. Soak Uneeda biscuits in milk and wring out tightly. Beat eggs until frothy. Melt butter. Combine all ingredients in a bowl, pack into greased pan and bake in a 350° oven for ¾ hour. Unmold and serve hot with a sauce made by combining melted cheese with cream of mushroom soup, or cold with a sauce of mayonnaise, horseradish and India relish.

James McCracken
New York, New York

SHRIMP MOBILE

Easy
Partial do ahead

Serves: 4
Preparing: 45 minutes

1 pound cooked shrimp
3 tablespoons white wine
1 medium onion, finely
   chopped
¼ teaspoon salt
¼ teaspoon garlic powder
juice of ½ lemon
1 can cream of celery soup
¼ teaspoon pepper

1½ teaspoons curry powder
1 3-ounce can seedless grapes
   (or ¼ cup fresh)
4 tablespoons sour cream
2 tablespoons butter
1 package frozen French green
   beans, cooked
1 cup rice, cooked

Sauté onion in butter, but don't brown. Add soup, curry powder, sour cream, salt, pepper, lemon juice and garlic powder. Add shrimp, grapes and wine and heat through. Serve over rice mixed with green beans.

Mrs. John W. Durr
Montgomery, Alabama

Try broiling fish spread with mayonnaise. Adds flavor and browns nicely.

SHRIMP AND FETA CHEESE

Average
Do ahead

Serves: 4
Preparing: 20 minutes
Cooking: 20 minutes

12 raw jumbo shrimp, shelled
   and deveined
2 tablespoons butter
1 egg
¼ cup heavy cream
1 cup Feta cheese, finely
   crumbled

dash of Tabasco
1 large tomato, peeled and sliced
juice of ½ lemon
1 tablespoon chopped fresh
   parsley
freshly ground black pepper

Preheat oven to 400°. Cook shrimp in butter until they turn pink. Combine egg and cream. Add cheese and Tabasco; blend thoroughly. Place shrimp in a baking dish and pour cheese mixture over them. Arrange tomato slices on top. Heat until mixture begins to bubble. Squeeze lemon juice on top of dish and sprinkle with pepper and parsley. Serve immediately.

Mrs. Anna Livanios
Piraeus, Greece

CRAB, VEGETABLE & CHEESE CASSEROLE

Easy

Serves: 4
Preparing: 15 minutes
Baking: 40 minutes

½ cup butter or margarine
1 small onion, chopped
3 small zucchini squash,
   unpeeled and sliced
½ medium clove crushed
   garlic
3 large tomatoes, sliced
½ pound shelled crab, cut up
   (canned is just as good)

1⅓ cups diced Swiss cheese
1 cup fine bread crumbs, Italian
   style
1 teaspoon salt
pepper to taste
1 teaspoon crushed basil

In large skillet, melt butter. Add onion, zucchini and garlic. Sauté until onion is transparent, stirring frequently. In large bowl, mix tomatoes, crab, 1 cup of cheese, ¾ cup bread crumbs, salt, pepper, and basil. Add zucchini mixture and mix thoroughly but lightly. Turn mixture into 2-quart casserole. Sprinkle with remaining cheese and bread crumbs. Dot with additional butter. Bake, uncovered at 375° for 30 to 40 minutes until crab and zucchini are cooked. Crab may be omitted and casserole served as a vegetable.

Maggie Lettieri
Brookline, Massachusetts

SHRIMP SCAMPI

Easy
Do ahead
Freeze

Serves: 8-10
Preparing: 1 hour

1 pound softened butter
⅓ cup white wine
¼ cup dry sherry
1 teaspoon black pepper
1 teaspoon tarragon

1 teaspoon rosemary
¼ teaspoon thyme
½ cup chopped garlic
4 pounds large shrimp

Clean and devein shrimp. Blend all other ingredients in blender or mixer until smooth and fluffy. Melt sauce in large frying pan and sauté shrimp until done. Serve over rice.

Le Bistro
Philadelphia, Pennsylvania

DANDY'S CRAWFISH

Easy   *Preparing: 30 minutes*

**2 5 to 6-inch crawfish tails (or
    frozen rock lobster tails)**
1 teaspoon salt
½ teaspoon pepper
1 tablespoon lemon juice
4 tablespoons flour
**1 egg, lightly beaten,
    combined with ½ cup milk**

2 tablespoons melted butter
2 tablespoons Parmesan cheese
¼ cup cooking oil
dash of paprika

Split crawfish tail on back only (butterfly) and loosen flesh from shell, but do not disconnect from end of tail. Season with salt, pepper and lemon juice. Let stand 15 minutes. Dip crawfish flesh and shell into milk and egg mixture. Roll in flour. Heat oil to 350°; place crawfish, shell side up and cook until flesh is light brown. Turn and cook until the shell is pink. Remove from oil and place in shallow baking dish, shell side down. Sprinkle with cheese, paprika and melted butter. Place in 350° oven for 3 minutes. Serve on heated plate with lemon butter, garnish with parsley and lemon slices.

Dandilea Hepburn
Hope Town Harbour Lodge
Abaco, Bahamas

SOLE VÉRONIQUE

Easy   *Serves: 4*
Do ahead   *Preparing: 20 minutes*
                                                  Baking: 15 minutes

4 sole fillets, one per person
1 cup fresh mushrooms
1 cup white seedless grapes
1 cup dry white wine
½ cup sour cream

½ cup mayonnaise
juice of one lemon
cherry tomatoes
parsley

Poach sliced mushrooms and grapes in wine. Mix sour cream, mayonnaise and lemon juice and spread over fillets. Pour mushroom mixture over top and bake for 15 minutes in a 350° oven. Garnish with tomatoes and parsley. Can be served either as a first course or an entrée.

Mrs. J. Mahlon Buck, Jr.
Haverford, Pennsylvania

TIPSY CRAB

Average
Do ahead

Serves: 6
Preparing: 25 minutes
Cooking: 20 minutes

1 pound picked backfin
  crabmeat
4 tablespoons butter
2 tablespoons flour
½ cup cream or evaporated
  milk
½ teaspoon dry mustard
½ teaspoon ground black
  pepper

½ teaspoon salt
2 tablespoons sherry
2 tablespoons bourbon whiskey
1 dash each: Tabasco sauce,
  Worcestershire sauce, red
  pepper
buttered bread cubes

Preheat oven to 350°. Blend in butter, flour and cream over low heat until thick. (To save time, use a flame-proof casserole.) Add seasonings, sherry, bourbon and crab. Cover with bread cubes, which have been stirred in melted butter. Bake at 350° until nicely browned, about 20 minutes.

Mrs. William Pollard
Devon, Pennsylvania
Mrs. Malcolm M. Remington
Cockeysville, Maryland

TIPSY STEAMED CRABS

Easy
Do ahead
Freeze

Preparing: 30 minutes

2 dozen hardshell Blue crabs
½ cup vinegar
1 teaspoon black pepper
1 teaspoon salt

1 can beer (12-ounces)
hot pepper seeds (optional if you
  like it very spicy)

Boil crabs in vinegar, beer, salt and pepper about 25 minutes or until red. If crabs are extra large, add 1 cup of water and another can of beer. Cool and refrigerate. Clean and eat with your favorite sauce.

Mrs. Wesley Connors
Philadelphia, Pennsylvania

SOLE MOUSSE

Easy

Serves: 6
Preparing: 10 minutes
Baking: 30 minutes

Place in blender in following order:

5 fresh fillets of sole, cut into pieces
1 cup light cream
5 eggs

4 egg whites
2 tablespoons melted butter
salt and pepper
hollandaise sauce

Blend mixture 3 minutes or until smooth. Transfer to casserole. Put casserole in pan of hot water and bake at 350° for 30 minutes, or until knife inserted in center comes out dry. Serve hot with hollandaise sauce.

Mrs. Danilo M. DeDominicis
Wayne, Pennsylvania

Thaw frozen fish in milk to give it a fresh caught flavor. Drain before cooking.
Always use bread crumbs for frying fish. Cracker crumbs absorb grease.

LOBSTER NEWBURG

Easy
Do ahead

Serves: 24
Preparing: 30 minutes

1 cup butter
1 cup flour
1½ teaspoons salt
½ teaspoon white pepper
1 tablespoon paprika

3 quarts hot milk
1 cup dry sherry
¼ cup lemon juice
4 pounds cooked lobster, cut into 1-inch pieces

Melt butter in saucepan. Blend in flour and seasonings. Cook over low heat 10 minutes, stirring constantly. Do not brown. Add hot milk. Stir with wire whip until smooth. Bring to a boil; lower heat and simmer for 5 minutes. Remove from heat. Stir in sherry and lemon juice. Add lobster meat. Taste for salt. Serve with steamed rice or steamed white and wild rice.

K. Carol Carlson, Vice President
ARA Services
Philadelphia, Pennsylvania

Kettles and Drumsticks

poultry

CHICKEN WITH CHARACTER

Easy
Do ahead
Freeze

Serves: 6-8
Preparing: 2 hours
Broiling: 45 minutes

Marinade

⅔ cup sesame oil
⅓ cup soy sauce
3 large cloves garlic, crushed

1 teaspoon ginger, fresh, minced
½ teaspoon dry mustard
⅛ teaspoon Tabasco sauce

12 chicken thighs
onion powder
garlic powder

paprika
cayenne

Mix together ingredients in marinade. Brush the marinade on chicken very heavily. Use remainder of marinade by pouring it over the chicken in tray. Marinate chicken for two hours, turning often. Sprinkle onion powder, garlic powder, paprika and cayenne, *in that order*, on chicken, to taste. Cook under broiler, or on outside grill, until well done, approximately 20 minutes each side.

Robert S. Harper
Voorhees Township, New Jersey

CHICKEN GEORGE MURPHY

Average

Serves: 6
Preparing: 30 minutes
Cooking: 1½-2 hours

1 whole roasting chicken
salt, pepper and paprika
1 clove garlic, minced
2 slices bacon, cut up
1 green pepper, seeded and
  sliced

1 cup sliced mushrooms
1 10-ounce package frozen peas
1 10-ounce package frozen
  French-style green beans

Wash chicken and put in large Dutch oven. Salt, pepper and paprika chicken generously. Place remaining ingredients on top of chicken. Cover and cook at 325° for 1½-2 hours. Do not add water (frozen vegetables provide enough.)

Mrs. Robert Alan Swift
Bryn Mawr, Pennsylvania

PARSLEY PARMESAN CHICKEN

Easy
Do ahead

Serves: 4-5
Preparing: 15 minutes
Chilling: 4 hours
Baking: 1 hour

¼ cup Italian salad dressing
1 2 to 3 pound fryer, cut up
1 egg, slightly beaten
2 tablespoons water
½ cup grated Parmesan

½ cup dry bread crumbs
2 tablespoons chopped parsley
½ teaspoon paprika
½ teaspoon salt
½ teaspoon pepper

Marinate chicken in salad dressing, coating well. Cover and chill about four hours, basting occasionally.

Drain chicken and reserve salad dressing. Combine egg and water; mix well and set aside. Combine cheese, bread crumbs, parsley, paprika, salt and pepper. Stir well. Dip chicken in egg and coat with crumb mixture. Place in greased 13" x 9" x 2" baking dish. Spoon reserved salad dressing over top. Bake at 350° for one hour.

The Committee

CHICKEN LIVERS SUPREME

Easy

Serves: 4
Preparing: 15 minutes
Cooking: 35 minutes

1 pound chicken livers
flour
½ pound sliced bacon
½ cup chopped onions
1 4-ounce can mushrooms
   (stems and pieces)

⅛ teaspoon salt
¼ cup butter or margarine
½ cup red table wine

Wash and dry chicken livers thoroughly. Sprinkle with salt and roll in flour. Shake off excess flour. Place butter in skillet and sauté livers until half cooked. Remove livers from skillet. Cut up bacon in strips (crossways, about ½" strips) and fry until lightly brown. Remove bacon. Remove all but 3 tablespoons bacon fat and add chopped onions and mushrooms. Cook until onions are soft. Add livers, bacon and wine. Stir well and place cover on skillet. Cook slowly for about 20 minutes.

Marie E. Winstanley
Glenside, Pennsylvania

CHICKEN PUFF

Average
Partial do ahead

Serves: 4-6
Preparing: 30 minutes
Cooking: 1 hour

2 cups diced chicken (or more)
1 can cream of mushroom soup
½ cup milk
1 3-ounce can sliced mushrooms, drained
1 cup cooked noodles
½ cup chopped celery
½ cup chopped green pepper
½ cup slivered almonds
2 tablespoons diced pimiento

½ cup chopped onions
1 tablespoon butter
1 teaspoon Worcestershire sauce
½ teaspoon salt
dash pepper
⅛ teaspoon marjoram
⅛ teaspoon thyme
6 dashes Tabasco sauce
4 eggs
½ cup grated sharp cheddar cheese

Combine chicken, soup and milk. Add mushrooms, noodles, celery, almonds, peppers, pimientos, and onions (which have been sautéed in butter). Season with Worcestershire sauce, salt, pepper, thyme, marjoram and Tabasco sauce. Mix together well and cook ½ hour until hot and bubbly. Pour into greased 2-quart casserole. Beat egg yolks and combine with cheese. Fold in beaten egg whites. Place on top of hot chicken mixture. Bake at 350° until top is puffy and brown (about ½ hour).

Mrs. John K. Montgomery
Radnor, Pennsylvania

CHICKEN PORTUGAISE

Average

Serves: 6
Preparing: 30 minutes
Cooking: 45 minutes

8 pieces of chicken
½ stick butter
2 tablespoons brandy
salt and pepper
6 mushrooms
1 tablespoon lemon juice
2 teaspoons tomato paste
2 teaspoons potato flour
½ cup Madeira
1½ cups light stock

¼ teaspoon chopped fresh tarragon
1 bay leaf
1 teaspoon chopped garlic
1 green or red pepper, diced
rind of 1 orange, shredded
3 tomatoes
sections of 2 oranges
chopped parsley

Brown chicken in butter. Flame with brandy. Salt and pepper the chicken. Remove chicken from pan and sauté mushrooms, sliced, in the same pan with butter and lemon juice. Remove mushrooms and set aside. Stir in, off the fire, tomato paste and potato flour. Add Madeira and light stock. Bring to boil. Put chicken back and add fresh tarragon and bay leaf. Cover with wax paper and lid; cook approximately 35 minutes. (Cooking time depends upon size and age of chicken pieces.) While chicken is cooking, sauté garlic in a little pan. Add green or red pepper and the shredded rind of an orange. Cook 2 minutes. Add tomatoes, skinned, pipped and sliced, and add also the sections of oranges. Mix with mushrooms and combine with chicken. Serve garnished with chopped parsley.

Julie Dannenbaum
Philadelphia, Pennsylvania

COQ AU VIN

Average　　　　　　　　　　　　　　　　　　　　　　　　*Serves: 6*
Freeze　　　　　　　　　　　　　　　　　　*Preparing: 20 minutes*
　　　　　　　　　　　　　　　　　　　　　　Cooking: 1½ hours

Adapted from a French cookbook with the help of my French sister-in-law. The proportions are flexible. The dish can wait for hours before serving if necessary, and is even better the second day.

**6 pieces of chicken (I use 6
　legs or 12 thighs)
4 slices of bacon, cut up
4 carrots in ¾" slices
2 large onions, sliced
1 clove garlic, crushed
3 tablespoons flour
2 tablespoons minced
　parsley
1 teaspoon dried marjoram**

**½ teaspoon thyme
1 teaspoon salt
¼ teaspoon pepper
1½ cups Tokay red wine (this
　type of wine makes all the
　difference)
1 bay leaf
½ pound mushrooms, sliced
2 tablespoons butter**

In large heavy skillet or electric fry pan, sauté bacon, carrots, onion, garlic. Remove vegetables from pan and brown chicken in the bacon fat remaining. Add flour and spices to vegetables and spoon them over the chicken in the frying pan. Pour wine over vegetables and chicken and add bay leaf. Simmer 1½ hours covered. Sauté mushrooms in butter; add to chicken for last 10 minutes.

Mrs. David P. Eastburn
Doylestown, Pennsylvania

CHICKEN AND HAM LOAF CHADDS FORD

Average
Do ahead

Serves: 6-8
Preparing: 30 minutes
Baking: 1 hour

8 ounces cooked, skinned
and diced chicken
1 crusty sandwich loaf
3 ounces butter
2 finely chopped onions
½ pound thinly sliced
mushrooms
1 tablespoon chopped
parsley
salt and black pepper

½ pound sausage meat, partially
cooked
6 ounces lean bacon, diced
8 ounces cooked, diced ham
2 tablespoons sherry
¼ teaspoon sage
¼ teaspoon thyme
2 heaping tablespoons bread
crumbs

Cut a ½-inch slice off the top of the loaf and carefully pull out the soft bread inside. Leave ½" inner lining of bread to preserve the shape. Melt 2 ounces butter and brush this onto the loaf, inside and out. Replace the lid and put the loaf on a baking tray in the center of the oven, preheated to 400°. Bake for 10 minutes or until crisp and golden. Leave to cool. Cook the onions in the remaining butter until soft; add the mushrooms and cook for 2 minutes. Stir in the parsley and season with salt and pepper. Mix together the sausage meat, bacon, ham and 2 heaped tablespoons of breadcrumbs. Stir in the sherry and herbs and season to taste. Press half of the sausage mixture well down into the loaf case; cover with half the onion and mushroom mixture. Arrange the chicken on top and cover with the onion and final layer of sausage meat. Replace the lid. Wrap it in foil and bake in the center of the oven at 375° for 1 hour. Serve the loaf hot or cold, cut into thick slices. Very nice for picnics.

"County Lines"
West Chester, Pennsylvania

CHICKEN JUBILEE CASSEROLE

Easy
Do ahead

Serves: 4
Preparing: 1 hour
Baking: 1 hour

1 3½-pound frying chicken
1 cup French dressing
1 can (6-ounce) frozen
orange juice

1 cup pitted black cherries
½ cup currant jelly
2 tablespoons brandy

Have butcher cut chicken in eighths and place in large bowl. Marinate with French dressing for 1 hour. Turn chicken once or twice so that marinade will touch all of chicken. Preheat oven to 400°. Melt orange juice in a saucepan. Add cherries and jelly. Heat until well-blended. Drain the chicken and place in a casserole. Pour cherry mixture over it. Cover and cook for 1 hour. If sauce seems too watery, uncover casserole for the last ½ hour. Just before serving, heat the brandy in a ladle; flame it and pour over chicken.

Sam di Lorenzo
Delaware Market House
Gladwyne, Pennsylvania

Another summer favorite! Fill a green or red pepper with chicken salad and slice ½ inch thick. Serve on watercress or lettuce.

CHICKEN YORKSHIRE

Easy   *Serves: 4*
Partial do ahead   *Preparing: 30 minutes*
                                        Baking: 45 minutes

Rather like Yorkshire pudding.

1 broiler-fryer, cut in serving   **¼ teaspoon pepper**
   pieces   **¼ cup oil**
⅓ cup flour   **2 teaspoons salt**
1½ teaspoons poultry
   seasoning

Mix together flour and seasonings. Dip chicken pieces to coat in mixture. Brown chicken well on all sides in oil. Drain on paper towel. Place in lightly greased 13″ x 9″ x 2″ baking dish.

For Puff:

1 cup flour   **2 tablespoons minced**
1 teaspoon salt   **parsley**
¼ teaspoon poultry   **1 teaspoon baking powder**
   seasoning   **1 tablespoon melted butter**
1½ cups milk   **3 eggs, slightly beaten**

Mix together dry ingredients, set aside. Beat eggs, milk and melted butter together. Add to flour mixture. Beat until smooth. Pour over chicken. Bake at 400° for 45 minutes or until puffed and golden.

Mrs. John F. Lloyd
Ardmore, Pennsylvania

CHICKEN SUPREME

Easy
Do ahead

Serves: 12 or 78
Preparing: 45 minutes
Chilling: 24 hours
Baking: 45 minutes

The Anchorage Concert Association has used this recipe to serve such guest artists as Andre Watts, pianist and the Norman Luboff Choir.

Chicken Supreme for 12

6 large chicken breasts, cooked, cut into bite size pieces
2 10-ounce packages frozen chopped broccoli
2 10-ounce cans cream of chicken soup
1 cup mayonnaise
¾ to 1 teaspoon curry powder, to taste
3 tablespoons lemon juice
8 ounces grated Cheddar cheese
bread crumbs
2 2½-ounce jars mushrooms

Chicken Supreme for 78

39 chicken breasts (14-16 pounds)
13 10-ounce packages frozen chopped broccoli
13 cans cream of chicken soup
6½ cups mayonnaise
6½ teaspoons curry powder, more or less
19½ tablespoons lemon juice
(1½ cups Chablis or white wine)
3¼ pounds cheddar cheese, grated
32½ ounces canned mushrooms
bread crumbs

Mix first six ingredients until thoroughly blended. Place in a greased 9" x 13" pan. Sprinkle cheese on top and spread with mushrooms and sprinkle with bread crumbs. Refrigerate overnight or up to 2 days. Bake in 350° oven for 45 minutes.

Mrs. Richard E. Anglemyer
Anchorage, Alaska

ROAST DUCK NORMANDIE

Average

Serves: 2
Preparing: 30 minutes
Baking: 2 hours

1 4 pound duck, dressed
salt and pepper
1½ cups bread cubes
2 apples, peeled, cored, large dice

1 tablespoon minced shallots, sautéed and cooked
1 orange, peeled, seeded, large dice
½ cup pitted prunes, quartered

Wash duck and dry. Season cavity with salt and pepper. Combine all ingredients for stuffing and mix well. Stuff duck with mixture and pack fairly tight. Truss duck and roast in preheated 350° oven for 1½ to 2 hours until tender. Duck will self baste. When finished, remove duck from pan and cut in two, removing back bone. Serve ½ of duck with stuffing in each side.

Brian Dodge, Chef
Black Bass Hotel
Lumberville, Pennsylvania

STUFFED CHICKEN BREASTS WITH TOMATO SAUCE

Average
Do ahead

Serves: 8
Preparing: 1 hour
Cooking: 1 hour

Tomato sauce:

¼ cup olive oil
¾ cup chopped onion
1 clove garlic
6 cups imported tomatoes, in thick sauce
¼ cup white wine
½ teaspoon basil

¼ teaspoon thyme
½ teaspoon oregano
1 piece orange rind
salt and pepper, to taste
1 teaspoon sugar
2 tablespoons sour cream

Combine all ingredients but sour cream. Simmer for 40 minutes.

4 large large whole chicken breasts
salt and freshly ground pepper, to taste
9 tablespoons butter
¼ cup finely chopped onion
1 10-ounce package spinach
1 cup ground, cooked ham
1 cup Ricotta cheese

1 egg yolk
½ cup freshly grated Parmesan cheese
¼ teaspoon grated nutmeg
¼ pound ground sausage
clove garlic, minced
⅛ teaspoon dried basil
¼ cup dry sherry

Preheat oven to 350°. Skin and bone chicken and split in half. Make a pocket on the underside of chicken. Salt and pepper the breasts. Heat 3 tablespoons butter and cook onion. Cook spinach and drain thoroughly. Chop and add to skillet. Add ham, Ricotta, egg yolk, Parmesan, nutmeg, sausage, garlic and basil. Blend thoroughly. Stuff the breasts with 2 or 3 tablespoons of stuffing. Arrange in baking dish, stuffed side down. Melt rest of butter and dribble it over chicken. Sprinkle with wine. Bake 1 hour, basting often. Serve with hot tomato sauce.

Mrs. Andrew C. Warren
Villanova, Pennsylvania

CHICKEN AND HOT ITALIAN SAUSAGE CASSEROLE

Easy
Do ahead

Serves: 4-6
Preparing: 30 minutes
Baking: 30-45 minutes

1 box frozen Birdseye Italian
   rice
1 can cream of mushroom
   soup
⅓ can of water
4 to 6 boned chicken breasts
Herb-Ox chicken stock
1 pound Italian sausage, cut
   in small pieces and cooked

½ pound mushrooms, sliced
10 green olives, chopped
10 black olives, chopped
1 onion, chopped
1 green pepper, chopped
grated Parmesan cheese

Precook chicken in chicken stock for one-half hour. Precook sausage. Remove chicken from stock. Prepare rice according to directions on package. Combine all ingredients except cheese. Sprinkle cheese on top. Casserole can be refrigerated the day before, if desired. Bake in 350° oven 30 to 45 minutes.

Mrs. William I. Kent
Gladwyne, Pennsylvania

PENNSYLVANIA DUTCH BARBECUED CHICKEN

Easy
Do ahead
Freeze

Serves: 6-8
Preparing: 1 hour
Cooking: 1½ hours

2 chickens, cut up,
   approximately 2½ pounds
   each
1 pound can crushed
   pineapple, with juice

⅓ bottle (6 ounces) barbecue
   sauce (preferably "Open Pit")
sliced sweet potatoes (optional)
   may use canned or partially
   cooked potatoes

Place 2 cut-up chickens in two oblong pyrex oven dishes. Cover with crushed pineapple and barbecue sauce. Cover with aluminum foil. Place in 375° oven for 45 minutes. Remove foil; reduce oven to 350°. Bake 45 minutes more. Sweet potato slices can be cooked in casserole the last 15 minutes until tender. At this point casserole may be frozen. Cook 45 minutes or until brown.

Mrs. Newton Burrison
Philadelphia, Pennsylvania

SOUTHERN FRIED CHICKEN

Easy
Do ahead
Freeze

Serves: depends on number of chicken parts
Preparing: 30 minutes
Cooking: 1-1½ hours

1¼ to 2 cups flour (add more
  as needed)
3 to 4 eggs, use more as
  needed
salt and pepper, to taste
chicken parts of your choice
  (I use breasts, and thighs
  and legs, separated)

shortening, enough to half-fill
  large frying pan (cast iron
  preferred)
½ stick butter per pan

Beat eggs thoroughly. Put flour, salt and pepper into paper bag. Roll chicken pieces in beaten egg to coat well. Place two or three pieces at a time into paper bag. Shake vigorously. Fry coated chicken in hot shortening and butter, turning frequently until golden. Turn down heat to moderate and cook for approximately 1 to 1½ hours. Turn every 15 to 20 minutes. Drain on paper towels. Serve hot or cold.

Mr. & Mrs. Emilio Gravagno
Lansdale, Pennsylvania

CURRIED CHICKEN LIVERS

Easy
Do ahead
Freeze

Serves: 4-6
Preparing: 15-20 minutes

2 to 3 teaspoons unsalted
  butter
1½ pounds fresh chicken
  livers
1 large (or 2 small) shallots,
  finely chopped

½ pint heavy cream
2½ to 3 teaspoons curry powder,
  or to taste
½ teaspoon salt
freshly ground pepper

Melt butter in large skillet. Add chopped shallots and sauté for one minute. Add livers and sauté until almost done and still quite pink. Sprinkle with salt and pepper. Remove from pan to keep warm. Add curry powder and cream to pan. Deglaze pan and cook down until sauce thickens a little. Return livers to pan and cook a few minutes longer. Place on heated dish and serve immediately with rice, or without, as part of a brunch buffet.

Maude de Schauensee
Devon, Pennsylvania

SUPREME DE VOLAILLE SAUTÉ A L'ORANGE

Average

Serves: 4
Preparing: 20 minutes
Cooking: 20 minutes

4 8-ounce boneless chicken
   breasts, cut in half and
   flattened
flour
2 leeks (white part only); cut
   in julienne strips and
   washed in cold water
2 carrots, peeled and cut into
   thin strips (leeks and
   carrots should be thin
   strips about 1" long)

1 quart heavy cream, hot,
   scalded*
salt and pepper, to taste
finely grated rind of 2 oranges
   and juice of both oranges
pinch of tarragon (leaf)
5 ounces of clarified butter or
   any suitable cooking oil

Heat cooking oil in sauté pan and add lightly floured chicken breasts. Cook 4 minutes on each side. Remove from pan and put on warm platter in a warm place. Pour off excess cooking fat and add leeks, carrots, orange juice and rind. Cook for several minutes and add hot cream, tarragon and 2 turns of fresh black pepper. Cook for 4 minutes on high flame. When sauce begins to thicken put breasts in pan to warm. Lower flame. Cook for 2 minutes more and serve with curried rice or fresh green vegetables.
*Cream may be boiled and allowed to simmer for 30 minutes prior to making chicken dish.

A. Mark Kaplan
Chef de Cuisine
Pump House Inn
Canadensis, Pennsylvania

CHICKEN BREAST STUFFED WITH SAUSAGE

Average

Serves: 6
Preparing: 30-40 minutes
Baking: 1 hour

6 chicken breasts
3 tablespoons chopped
   onions
2 tablespoons chopped
   celery
1 tablespoon chopped
   parsley

2 tablespoons butter
1 pound lean country sausage
salt and pepper, to taste
½ teaspoon poultry seasoning
2 eggs
1½ slices bread

Remove bones from chicken breasts and separate breasts into two equal pieces. In small pan, sauté onion, celery and parsley in butter. Add sausage and cook thoroughly, crumbling sausage with a fork. Season with salt, pepper and poultry seasoning. Add eggs, then bread that has been crumbled into large crumbs. Form sausage meat mixture into balls and roll each chicken breast piece around the stuffing mixture. Tie with string. Place in an ovenproof dish and bake, covered, at 325° for 30 minutes. Remove cover and bake an additional 30 minutes. Serve whole or sliced.

Sam Di Lorenzo
Delaware Market House
Gladwyne, Pennsylvania

CHICKEN BREASTS ALFREDO

Average
Freeze

Serves: 4-6
Preparing: 30 minutes
Baking: 30 minutes

3 whole chicken breasts, split, boned (about 1½ pounds)
½ cup all-purpose flour
3 eggs, beaten
3 tablespoons water
½ cup grated Romano cheese

¼ cup snipped parsley
½ teaspoon salt
1 cup fine bread crumbs
3 tablespoons butter
2 tablespoons vegetable oil
6 slices Mozzarella cheese

Cheese sauce

1 cup whipping cream
¼ cup water
¼ cup butter

½ cup grated Romano cheese
¼ cup snipped parsley

Coat chicken with flour. Mix eggs, water, Romano cheese, parsley and salt. Dip chicken pieces in egg mixture, then into bread crumbs. Heat butter and oil in large skillet. Cook chicken breasts over medium heat until brown, about 15 minutes. Remove chicken to baking dish, 11¾" x 7½". Heat oven to 425°. Make cheese sauce. Pour cheese sauce over chicken. Top each piece with a slice of cheese. Bake until cheese melts and chicken is tender, about 8 minutes.

Cheese Sauce: Heat cream, water and butter in 1-quart saucepan until butter melts. Add cheese; cook and stir over medium heat 5 minutes. Stir in parsley.

E. Jane Thiry
Jenkintown, Pennsylvania

CHICKEN-TERRY

Easy
Do ahead

Serves: 6-8
Preparing: 40 minutes
Baking: 25 minutes

1 4-pound stewing chicken or
  breasts
2 10-ounce packages frozen
  asparagus
2 cups milk
2 8-ounce packages cream
  cheese

1 teaspoon salt
1½ cups shredded Parmesan
  (pizza cheese)
¾ to 1 teaspoon garlic salt

Early in day simmer chicken in seasoned boiling water until tender. Bone chicken, slice thinly or in chunks.

Cook asparagus as directed on package. Cut asparagus into bite-size pieces. Place in lightly greased 2-quart casserole. In double boiler blend milk, cream cheese, salt and garlic salt until smooth and hot. Stir in ¾ cup shredded cheese until smooth. Pour 1 cup of sauce over asparagus. Then top with chicken. Cover with remaining sauce and sprinkle ¼ cup cheese on top. Bake 25 minutes in 350° oven. Let stand 5 to 10 minutes before serving.

Mrs. Frederick Lind
Villanova, Pennsylvania

SESAME BAKED CHICKEN

Easy
Do ahead

Serves: 3-4
Preparing: 30 minutes
Baking: 1 hour

1 egg, lightly beaten
½ cup milk
½ cup whole wheat flour
1 tablespoon baking powder
1 tablespoon sea salt
2 tablespoons sweet paprika

2 tablespoons sesame seeds
1 frying chicken (2½ to 3
  pounds) cut into serving
  pieces
½ cup melted butter

Preheat oven to 350°. Beat the egg and milk together. Combine the flour, baking powder, salt, paprika and sesame seeds in a paper bag. Dip the chicken pieces in the egg mixture and then shake in the paper bag. Place the chicken pieces skin side up in a baking dish so that they do not touch each other. Pour melted butter over top and bake until done, about one hour.

Ms. Amy Stewart
Haddonfield, New Jersey

CHICKEN AND HAM CASSEROLE

Average
Do ahead

Serves: 6-8
Preparing: 45 minutes
Baking: 1 hour and 15 minutes

1 cup flour
1 tablespoon salt
1 teaspoon pepper
1¼ teaspoons powdered savory
6 whole chicken breasts (preferably boned)
¼ pound butter
8 slices precooked ham
1 pound mushrooms (choose several of the nicest and save for slicing; chop the rest)
2 onions, peeled and chopped

1 clove garlic, peeled and crushed
1 tablespoon minced parsley
⅛ teaspoon mace
1 cup chicken broth (or ½ cup each chicken broth and dry sherry)
2 teaspoons light brown sugar
½ cup orange juice
2 heads Belgian endive, quartered
1 package frozen peas

Place flour, 2 teaspoons salt, 1 teaspoon pepper and 1 teaspoon savory in a paper bag and shake to blend. Lightly dredge the chicken breasts by shaking them in the seasoned flour. Brown chicken in ¼ cup melted butter, adding more butter as needed. When golden brown, remove chicken breasts and drain on paper toweling. Trim slices of ham of extra fat; cut in half lengthwise and roll up, securing with a toothpick. Brown ham lightly and drain on paper toweling. To the same skillet add remaining butter (if any), the chopped mushrooms, onions, garlic, parsley, ¼ teaspoon savory, 1 teaspoon salt, pinch pepper, mace and sauté until mushrooms and onions are tender. Add chicken broth (and, if you like, the sherry), brown sugar and orange juice. Cook, stirring for about 5 minutes. As artistically as possible, arrange chicken breasts and ham rolls (remove toothpicks) in a large round shallow baking dish. Pour mushroom-onion mixture over all. Sauté the sliced mushrooms in a little butter and place these around the pieces of chicken and ham along with the quartered endive. Cover casserole tightly with aluminum foil and bake in a moderately slow oven, 325° for 1 hour. Remove foil, baste well with juices. Break frozen peas into clusters and place them in the casserole. Bake for about 15 minutes more, basting frequently, until peas are just done. Serve at once.

Mrs. Robert Bellamy
St. Davids, Pennsylvania

MANDARIN WALNUT CHICKEN

Easy
Do ahead

Serves: 24
Preparing: 20 minutes
Cooking: 30 minutes

If fresh ginger root is not available, substitute 1 ounce dried ginger for 2 ounces fresh ginger.

6¾ cups walnut meats (1½ pounds)
2 cloves garlic, crushed
1 cup chicken fat or margarine
2 ounces fresh ginger root, peeled and sliced thin
3 cups bamboo shoots, diced ¼"
2 quarts hot chicken stock

½ cup dry sherry
1 tablespoon salt
¼ teaspoon white pepper
1⅓ cups cornstarch
2 cups cold water
3½ quarts cooked chicken meat, diced or cut into ½" x ½" x 1½" pieces
scallions, sliced into 1" pieces

Sauté walnuts and garlic in melted fat for one minute. Combine ginger, bamboo shoots, chicken stock, sherry, salt and pepper. Add to walnut mixture. Heat to boiling. Dissolve cornstarch in cold water. Stir into hot mixture. Cook until thick, stirring constantly. Add cooked chicken. Bring to boil. Garnish with scallions just before serving.

NOTE: Serve with steamed rice or fine egg noodles.

K. Carol Carlson, Vice President
ARA Services
Philadelphia, Pennsylvania

TARRAGON CHICKEN WITH SOUR CREAM

Easy
Partial do ahead

Serves: 4
Preparing: 30 minutes
Cooking: 55 minutes

2 small frying chickens, quartered
4 tablespoons butter
½ cup chopped onion
1 chopped garlic clove
4 tablespoons tomato paste
4 tablespoons flour
3 cups chicken stock

2 teaspoons salt
1 teaspoon pepper
1 tablespoon dried tarragon
1½ cups sour cream
4 tablespoons grated Parmesan cheese
rice

Brown chicken in butter. Remove from pan and keep warm. To skillet, add onion and garlic. Cook until tender. Stir in tomato paste, flour, then chicken stock. Stir until boiling; continue stirring until it thickens. Return chicken to skillet and add salt, pepper and tarragon. Cover, simmer gently 45 minutes. Remove chicken to warm platter. Gradually add sour cream to sauce. Heat gently. Pour sauce over chicken. Sprinkle with cheese. Serve with rice.

Toba Schwaber Kerson
Bryn Mawr, Pennsylvania

CHICKEN BREAST ROYALE

Average

Serves: 4-8
Preparing: 30 minutes
Baking: 90 minutes

¼ cup flour
½ teaspoon salt
¼ teaspoon paprika

dash pepper
4 chicken breasts

Stuffing

2 cups dry bread crumbs
1 tablespoon chopped onion
½ teaspoon salt
¼ teaspoon poultry seasoning
pepper

2 tablespoons melted butter
¼ cup hot water
⅛ pound melted butter
parsley

Mushroom sauce

2 tablespoons butter
½ pound chopped
  mushrooms
¼ cup chopped onions
2 tablespoons flour

½ cup heavy cream
½ cup sour cream
½ teaspoon salt
¼ teaspoon pepper

Combine first four ingredients in paper bag. Place and shake chicken breasts, one at a time, in bag. Set aside. Mix together stuffing ingredients except ⅛ pound melted butter and parsley. Stuff breasts and dip in melted butter. Bake, uncovered, 45 minutes in 325° oven. Turn and bake 45 minutes more. Sprinkle with chopped parsley. Serve with mushroom sauce. Mushroom sauce: Sauté mushrooms and onions in butter. Add flour, cream, sour cream and seasonings. Cook over low heat ten minutes. Do not boil.

Marion W. Yarbro

GINGER CHICKEN

Easy

Serves: 4-6
Preparing: 10 minutes
Marinating: 2 hours
Baking: 1 hour

½ cup red currant jelly
1 teaspoon ground ginger·
1 teaspoon dry mustard
1 cup orange juice
½ cup butter

2 tablespoons Worcestershire
  sauce
2 cloves garlic, crushed
2 drops hot pepper sauce
4 or 6 small chicken breasts

Make a smooth paste of jelly, ginger and mustard. Add remaining ingredients except chicken. Heat until butter is melted and sauce is blended. Cool sauce. Marinate chicken breasts in sauce in refrigerator for 2 or 3 hours. Place chicken and sauce in covered baking dish. Bake at 350° one hour, turning once. Baste once or twice. During last 10 minutes of cooking time, remove cover and increase heat to 400°. Serve with rice.

Mrs. William G. Kay Jr.
Bryn Mawr, Pennsylvania

HOT CHICKEN SALAD

Average
Do ahead

Serves: 8-10
Preparing: 40 minutes
Baking: 30 minutes

4 large chicken breasts
  poached in water to which
  carrot, onion, salt, pepper
  and tarragon have been
  added, to taste
2½ cups diced celery
1 cup slivered almonds

1 teaspoon Accent
4 teaspoons grated onion
2 cups Hellman's mayonnaise
1½ packages artichoke hearts
1 cup Chinese noodles
2 cups grated sharp cheese
  (about 6 ounces brick cheese)

Combine and mix the first six ingredients. Add artichoke hearts. Mix and place in buttered casserole dish. Top with grated cheese and noodles. Bake 10 minutes at 400°, then turn oven to 300° and bake for 20 minutes.

Mrs. Henry H. Bitler
Bryn Mawr, Pennsylvania
Mrs. Peter Zambelli
Haverford, Pennsylvania

CHICKEN IN ROSÉ SAUCE

Easy
Do ahead

Serves: 8
Preparing: 40 minutes
Baking: 30 minutes

Only 230 calories and very good for low-cholesterol diets.

4 chicken breasts, split and
  skinned
4 tablespoons margarine
2 tablespoons flour
¾ cup chicken broth
½ cup rosé wine

¼ cup thinly sliced onion
½ cup sliced mushrooms
1 10-ounce package frozen
  artichoke hearts; cook
  according to package
  instructions

Preheat oven to 350°. Melt 2 tablespoons margarine in baking pan. Add chicken breasts. Bake 30 minutes. Melt remaining margarine in a saucepan; add flour and cook briefly, stirring. Add chicken broth and wine, stirring constantly until sauce is thick and smooth. Remove chicken breasts from oven. Turn and cover each with sliced mushrooms, onion and artichokes. Pour sauce over all, bake 30 minutes or until tender.

Nelson J. Leidner
Huntingdon Valley, Pennsylvania

ANOTHER CHICKEN RECIPE

Average
Do ahead

Serves: 4-6
Preparing: 30 minutes
Cooking: 30-45 minutes

2 cups cooked chicken,
  cubed
3 sliced hard-boiled eggs
½ cup Pepperidge stuffing
  crumbs
1 tablespoon chopped
  parsley

salt and pepper
1 cup milk
¾ cup mayonnaise
grated rind from 1 orange

Mix chicken, eggs, stuffing and parsley. Combine milk, mayonnaise and orange rind and add to chicken mixture. Put in greased casserole; sprinkle with more stuffing crumbs. Bake at 350° for 30-45 minutes. Good served with orange, Mandarin, or fruit salad.

Mrs. Richard B. Anthony
Wayne, Pennsylvania

CHICKEN BREASTS HARPIN

Average
Do ahead
Freeze

Serves: 6-8
Preparing: 1 hour
Chilling: 1 hour
Baking: 45 minutes

3 to 5 whole chicken breasts
1 can (9-ounce) pitted ripe
  olives, sliced
½ cup margarine or butter
¾ pound mushrooms, sliced
  (or 1 large can sliced
  mushrooms)
6 tablespoons flour

1½ teaspoons salt
¼ teaspoon pepper
½ teaspoon curry powder, more
  if desired
3 cups chicken broth, from water
  used to cook chicken
1 cup heavy cream (or
  evaporated milk)

Simmer chicken breasts in water to cover 30 minutes. (May be done day before.) Drain. Reserve 3 cups broth. Bone chicken; arrange in 12" x 8" x 2" baking dish. Top with olives. In skillet sauté mushrooms in margarine or butter about 5 minutes. Remove from heat. Stir in flour, salt, pepper and curry. Gradually add broth and cream, stirring constantly. Cook until thickened. Pour over chicken. Refrigerate until about 1 hour before serving. Bake 45 minutes at 325°. This may be made day before serving and should be served with noodles or rice.

Mrs. Roger D. Blackburn
Haddonfield, New Jersey

BAKED CHICKEN BREAST SUPREME

Easy
Do ahead
Freeze

Serves: 6
Preparing: 30 minutes
Baking: 1 hour and 20 minutes

2 tablespoons butter or
  margarine
2 tablespoons salad oil
6 large chicken breasts, split
  and boned
1 can (10½-ounce)
  condensed cream of
  chicken soup or mushroom
  soup
½ cup light cream

½ cup dry sherry (or, if desired,
  ½ cup apple juice plus 3
  tablespoons sherry flavoring)
1 teaspoon tarragon leaves
1 teaspoon Worcestershire sauce
¼ teaspoon chervil leaves
¼ teaspoon garlic powder
1 can (6-ounces) sliced
  mushrooms, drained

Heat oven to 350°. In oven heat butter and oil in baking dish, 13½" x 9" x 2", until butter is melted. Place chicken in baking dish, turning to coat with butter. Arrange chicken with skin side up (I remove skin). Bake *uncovered* one hour. Heat other ingredients in pan on stove, adding one ingredient at a time. After chicken has baked 1 hour, remove and drain off fat. Pour soup mixture over chicken. Cover tightly and cook 15 to 20 minutes longer.

Priscilla Carr
Huntingdon Valley, Pennsylvania

CHICKEN ALAMOS

Average   *Serves: 6-8*
Do ahead   *Preparing: 25 minutes*
                                      Cooking: 40 minutes

4½ pound roasting chicken,   ¼ teaspoon ground cloves
  cut into serving pieces   ¼ teaspoon ground coriander
1 teaspoon salt   ½ cup golden raisins
½ teaspoon pepper   ¼ cup green pitted olives
1 teaspoon paprika   1½ cups orange juice
1 tablespoon garlic powder   1 orange
¼ teaspoon ground   1 avocado
  cinnamon

In heavy waterless cooker, sprinkle cut-up chicken with salt and pepper, paprika and garlic powder. Sauté in butter until brown on both sides. Now sprinkle browned chicken with cinnamon, cloves and coriander. Add raisins, olives and orange juice. Simmer, covered, 40 minutes or until tender. Place on serving platter with slices of orange and avocado as decoration.

Myrna J. Panitz
Cherry Hill, New Jersey

CHICKEN BREASTS IN ASPIC

Average
Do ahead

Serves: 10-12
Preparing: 1 hour
Chilling: 4 hours

6 chicken breasts
2 cups of water
1 onion
1 teaspoon salt
celery stalk and leaves

parsley, bay leaf,
peppercorns and marjoram
2 tablespoons plain gelatine (1
  packet)
1 cup sour cream

Boil chicken breasts 20 to 30 minutes until tender. Drain and strain stock. Boil and reduce to 1 cup. Skin and bone chicken breasts. Split. Place in dish for serving. Dissolve gelatine in stock and dissolve over hot water. Stir cool stock and gelatine into sour cream. Stir this mixture to heavy cream stage. Pour over breasts and refrigerate. For better results: Do one light coat. Refrigerate. Then do second coat. Refrigerate for several hours before serving. Suggested garnishes: thin strips of pimiento or thin slices of olives, black caviar, slices of avocado dipped in lemon juice, slices of lemon and lime, watercress or parsley.

Mrs. H. Ober Hess
Gladwyne, Pennsylvania

CHICKEN LIVERS IN WHITE WINE

Easy
Do ahead

Serves: 4-6
Preparing: 15 minutes
Cooking: 20 minutes

½ cup butter
1 medium onion, chopped
2 tablespoons chopped
  parsley
2 pounds chicken livers, cut
  in half

1 teaspoon tarragon
1 teaspoon salt
¼ teaspoon pepper
½ cup Chablis wine

Melt butter in skillet; add onion and parsley. Sauté for 5 minutes. Add livers. Cook over medium heat for 10 minutes or until cooked through, stirring with wooden spoon. Remove to covered casserole; set in warm oven. Add tarragon, salt, pepper and wine to drippings. Bring to boiling point; stir well. Pour sauce over livers. May be kept in 150°-175° oven until ready to serve.

Mrs. George M. Ahrens
Rosemont, Pennsylvania

MUSTARD CHICKEN

Easy
Do ahead

Serves: 4
Preparing: 10 minutes
Cooking: 45 minutes

2½ to 3 pounds chicken
  (quartered)
1 3½-ounce jar Dijon mustard
1½ cups chicken broth

1 cup sour cream
1 cup orzo (small pasta available
  in all supermarkets)
salt and pepper

Coat chicken pieces on all sides with mustard. Let stand several hours in refrigerator. Sprinkle with pepper only. Put in heavy casserole. Add ½ cup of broth. Bake, covered, at 350° for 45 minutes. With baster, use broth at bottom of pot to wash mustard off chicken. Prepare orzo by boiling 5 minutes in boiling salted water. Finish cooking orzo in the 1 cup of broth left. When ready to serve, mix orzo and sour cream in juice from chicken. Salt if necessary.

Mrs. T. J. Kaiser
Berwyn, Pennsylvania

CHICKEN PECAN

Average
Do ahead
Freeze

Serves: 6-8
Preparing: 30 minutes
Cooking: 1 hour

1 4 to 5 pound chicken
2 cups pecans
3 slices bread (no crusts)
1 medium onion
1 bunch celery tops

1 bay leaf
1 to 2 tablespoons paprika
  (according to taste)
dash cayenne
dash Tabasco

Simmer (do not boil) chicken with onions, celery tops, and bay leaf in enough water to cover chicken. Cook until chicken is tender. Cool in stock. Remove chicken and reduce stock by half. Cut chicken, with scissors, into bite-sized pieces. *Sauce:* Grind pecans twice. Soak bread in a little chicken stock and squeeze dry. Add bread to pecans. Add paprika and cayenne; put mixture in grinder (blender) again. Place in bowl, beating well with whisk, and add the lukewarm stock gradually. Add 2 cups or more until consistency of thin mayonnaise. Mix a little sauce with the cut-up chicken. Place in serving casserole and cover evenly with remaining sauce. Sprinkle with paprika. Heat in oven and serve.

Mrs. George S. Fabian
Bryn Mawr, Pennsylvania

CURRIED CHICKEN WITH VEGETABLES

Average

Serves: 4
Preparing: 30 minutes
Cooking: 15 minutes

2 whole chicken breasts
1 cup flour
1 teaspoon Accent
1 teaspoon salt
½ teaspoon pepper
½ cup oil
1 medium onion
1 green pepper

1 tablespoon flour
1 teaspoon salt
¼ teaspoon pepper
1 14-ounce can whole tomatoes
1 cup water
2 teaspoons curry powder
1 chicken bouillon cube

Bone and skin chicken breasts. Cut into 2" x 2" chunks. Dredge in flour with Accent, salt, pepper. Heat oil in large skillet. Brown chicken and drain on plate with paper towel. Chop onion and green pepper and sauté in chicken oil until tender. Add remaining flour, salt, pepper and curry powder. Stir in. Add whole tomatoes, 1 cup water and bouillon cube. Simmer covered for 15 minutes. Add chicken to mixture and simmer until thickened. Serve over rice.

Anne Welch
Malvern, Pennsylvania

CHICKEN TERIYAKI: YUMI'S VARIATION ON A THEME

Easy
Do ahead

Serves: 6
Preparing: 40 minutes
Baking: 1 hour

Chicken

2 breasts, halved
4 thighs

4 legs

Sauce to marinate

½ green pepper, finely
   chopped
¼ medium-sized onion, finely
   chopped
⅔ cup soy sauce
¼ teaspoon black pepper
¼ teaspoon salt

½ rounded teaspoon ground
   ginger or 1 teaspoon of grated
   fresh ginger
1 teaspoon sugar
¼ teaspoon garlic powder
1 teaspoon sesame oil

Marinate chicken in above sauce ½ hour or longer. Bake the chicken in this same sauce for 1 hour at 375°. Turn pieces 3 or 4 times during baking. If needed, broil each side 2 or 3 minutes until golden brown before removing from oven.

Mrs. Henry G. Scott
Narberth, Pennsylvania

DUCK WITH ORANGE SAUCE

Average

Serves: 8
Preparing: 30 minutes
Cooking: 2 hours

4 wild ducks
celery
onion
apple slices

salt and pepper
bacon
Worcestershire sauce

Orange sauce

⅔ cup brown sugar
⅔ cup white sugar
2 tablespoons flour

2 cups orange juice
dash salt
grated orange peel

Wash and dry the ducks. Stuff each duck with equal amounts of celery, onions, and apples. Salt and pepper all over and place bacon strips over the top of each. Place in baking pan. Add about ½ inch of water to the pan and sprinkle with enough Worcestershire sauce to slightly color the water. Cook ducks at 325° for about 2 hours, basting every 30 to 45 minutes. When done, remove stuffing from ducks and discard. Reserve bacon and place around duck when serving. Serve with orange sauce. For orange sauce, combine all ingredients and simmer until thickened.

The Committee

CHINESE CHICKEN

Easy
Do ahead
Freeze

Serves: 6-8
Preparing: 30 minutes
Baking: 40 minutes

1 can Durkee onion rings
1 can cream of mushroom
　soup
½ soup can of milk
¼ cup chopped onions
1 package frozen Chinese
　vegetables (defrost but do
　not cook)

1 package blunt cut string beans
　(defrost but do not cook)
1 can mushroom caps
¼ pound shredded sharp cheese
2 cups diced chicken or turkey

Blend all ingredients but onion rings, bake at 375° for 30 minutes. Crush onion rings and sprinkle on top of casserole. Return to bake for 10 minutes. If you double or triple the recipe, a turkey breast is easier to deal with than all of those chicken breasts. Cooking time may be a little longer for large batch.

Mrs. Richard Hopkins
Jenkintown, Pennsylvania

CURRIED CHICKEN

Easy
Do ahead

Serves: 6
Preparing: 30 minutes
Baking: 30 minutes

¾ cup fine cornflake crumbs
1 teaspoon salt
¾ to 1 teaspoon curry
　powder
3 large chicken breasts,
　halved, boned, skinned

½ cup mayonnaise
¼ cup sherry
½ cup seedless raisins
1 package (6-ounce) long grain
　and wild rice

Combine crumbs, salt and curry. Coat chicken with mayonnaise; roll in crumbs, coat evenly. Place on lightly greased shallow baking pan, tucking edges of chicken under. Bake at 350° until tender, about ½ hour. Combine sherry and raisins; let stand while chicken cooks. Drain raisins, reserve sherry. Prepare rice according to directions, using sherry as part of cooking liquid. Stir raisins into cooked rice before serving.

Mrs. Robert J. McKain
Rosemont, Pennsylvania

PICNIC CHICKEN

Easy

Serves: 6
Preparing: 20 minutes
Cooking: 50 minutes

2 2½ to 3 pound fryers or
  broilers
½ cup white wine
3 cups Italian seasoned
  bread crumbs

½ cup finely chopped pecans
1 cup grated Parmesan cheese

Moisten chicken pieces with wine. Shake off excess moisture. Place rest of ingredients in plastic bag and toss a few pieces of chicken in the mixture at a time. Arrange coated chicken, skin side up, in a single layer in ungreased, shallow baking pan. Bake at 400° for 50 minutes, or until chicken is tender and coating is crisp. Can be served hot or cold.

Mrs. Malissa Carter
Sedgwick, Maine

CHICKEN IN A POT

Easy

Serves: 4
Preparing: 10 minutes
Baking: 1½ hours

3½ to 4 pound broiling
  chicken or small roaster
1 cup chicken broth
1 clove garlic, minced
1 small eggplant
1 large onion

6 stalks celery
4 carrots
1 can (16-ounce) stewed
  tomatoes
1 teaspoon salt
¼ teaspoon pepper

Into a 4 or 6-quart Dutch oven or casserole place a whole drawn chicken. Add chicken broth, garlic, eggplant, which has been sliced into ½" or ¾" slices and then cut into quarters, ½" slices of carrots, ½" slices of celery, wedges of onion. Add salt and pepper. Over all these ingredients pour the tomatoes. Cover and cook in 325° oven for 1½ hours or until chicken is tender. Any fresh or frozen vegetables can be substituted or added.

Dr. Sol Schoenbach
Executive Director
Settlement Music School
Philadelphia, Pennsylvania

PEACH STUFFED CHICKEN BREASTS

Serves: 6
Preparing: 30 minutes
Baking: 45 minutes

6 whole chicken breasts, boned and skinned
1 teaspoon salt
1/8 teaspoon pepper
3 fresh peaches, peeled and diced (or frozen)
1/2 cup onion
1/2 cup coarsely chopped cashews
1/8 teaspoon ground ginger

1/2 cup butter
Creamy Peach Sauce:

2 fresh peaches, peeled and sliced
1 8-ounce sour cream
1/2 cup firmly packed brown sugar
2 teaspoons Dijon mustard
1 tablespoon brandy
1/4 teaspoon salt

Place each breast on a sheet of waxed paper. Flatten to 1/4" thickness with mallet. Sprinkle salt and pepper over inside of breasts. Set aside. Combine peaches, onion, cashews and ginger, stirring well. Place 1/2 cup filling in center of each breast, fold side of chicken over filling and secure with toothpick. Melt butter in 13" x 9" x 2" baking pan. Place breasts, top side down, in butter. Bake at 375° for 25 minutes. Turn chicken and bake additional 20 minutes. Serve with Creamy Peach Sauce, gently warmed.

Mrs. Revere G. Counselman
Wayne, Pennsylvania

CHICKEN WITH 40 GARLIC CLOVES

Easy
Do ahead

Serves: 6-8
Preparing: 20 minutes
Baking: 1 1/2 hours

Garlic cloves, when cooked whole in any liquid, are not strong in taste, but do impart a definite flavor.

8 chicken legs and thighs
40 cloves garlic
4 stalks celery
1/2 cup olive oil
6 sprigs parsley
1 tablespoon tarragon

1/2 cup dry vermouth
2 1/2 teaspoons salt
1/4 teaspoon pepper
dash nutmeg
1 stalk fennel

Rinse chicken in cold water and pat dry. Peel garlic, leaving cloves whole. Cut celery in thin slices. Put oil in a shallow dish and turn chicken pieces in oil to coat on all sides. Lay celery slices in bottom of a heavy casserole with tight-fitting cover. Add parsley and tarragon. Put chicken pieces on top and sprinkle with vermouth, one teaspoon salt, pepper and nutmeg. Toss in all the garlic; sprinkle with remaining salt. Add fennel before putting on casserole lid. Cover with aluminum foil to make a tight seal. Bake at 375° for 1½ hours without removing lid.

May be done a day or two in advance, refrigerated and rewarmed before serving. Flavor becomes enhanced.

Irvin Rosen
Philadelphia, Pennsylvania

SPARKLING CHICKEN

Easy
Do ahead

Serves: 6-8
Preparing: 30 minutes
Cooking: 45 minutes

4 chicken breasts, boned, skinned, cut in half
½ teaspoon salt
½ teaspoon pepper
½ cup sliced almonds
2 tablespoons finely chopped shallots

2 tablespoons flour
1 cup dry Champagne
½ cup heavy cream
¼ pound sliced mushrooms
1 cup butter

Melt ½ cup butter in shallow baking pan. Place chicken in pan and brush with melted butter; sprinkle with salt and pepper. Bake 375°, 30 to 40 minutes. Melt remaining ½ cup butter in saucepan. Add shallots and mushrooms; sauté until shallots are tender, about 10 minutes. Sprinkle with flour. Add cream, stirring constantly. Simmer until thickened. Add Champagne and heat; do not boil. Add more salt and pepper to taste. Place chicken on heated platter; pour sauce over all. Sprinkle almonds on top. Garnish with parsley.

To prepare ahead: bake chicken, refrigerate. Store sauce. Before serving, cover chicken with foil, heat. Heat sauce, serve.

Agnes Harris
Cape Cod, Massachusetts

Serve chicken salad on a ring of honeydew melon for a cool summer dish.

SIMPLY GREAT PHEASANT

Easy

Serves: 4
Preparing: 30 minutes
Baking: 3 hours

1 cup flour
1 teaspoon salt
½ teaspoon pepper
1 pheasant, cut into serving
   pieces

½ cup butter
1 pint heavy cream

Combine the flour, salt and pepper in a paper bag. Shake the pheasant pieces in this until well coated. In a heavy roaster melt the butter and slowly brown the pheasant pieces on all sides. Add more butter if necessary. Cover and bake in 300° oven for 2 hours. Remove and cool for a while. Add the cream slowly to the pheasant, cover and bake for 1 more hour. Serve with wild rice.

Mrs. Thomas G. Williams
Great Falls, Montana

TURKEY AND STUFFING

Average
Do ahead

Preparing: 30 minutes
Cooking: 25 minutes per pound

turkey, medium size
6 slices bacon, diced
1 large chopped onion
1 cup chopped celery
2 to 3 slices ham, diced
1 pound ground meat
   (mixture beef, veal, pork)
½ pound mushrooms,
   chopped and sautéed

4 cups bread crumbs
3 to 4 eggs, beaten
poultry seasoning
parsley
oregano
salt and pepper

Combine ingredients in large bowl, seasoning to taste. Stuff turkey. Place turkey in 375° oven in open roasting pan, brown all sides. Then place breast down, having rubbed it with butter. Cover with foil and roast at 325° for 25 minutes per pound.

Mrs. D. B. Garst
Devon, Pennsylvania

"TEX-MEX" CHICKEN CASSEROLE

Easy
Do ahead
Freeze

Serves: 8
Preparing: 20 minutes
Baking: 1 hour

4 whole chicken breasts,
  cooked, skinned, boned
  and cut into 1" pieces
⅔ pound shredded cheddar
  cheese
1 dozen *corn* tortillas, cut
  into 1" squares

1 can cream of mushroom soup
1 can cream of chicken soup
1 cup milk
1 onion, grated
1½ cans green chilies, chopped

Grease a large shallow casserole. Mix together soups, chilies, onion and milk. Pour a little of this mixture into casserole. Add a layer of tortillas, then chicken, then soup mixture. Continue until all is used, ending with soup mixture. Top with cheese and bake at 350° for one hour.

Mrs. Robert L. Kress
Bryn Mawr, Pennsylvania

CHICKEN WITH ROQUEFORT CHEESE

Easy

Serves: 4 to 6
Preparing: 15 minutes
Baking: 45 minutes

Blue cheese or Danish Bolina may be used in this recipe, but you might want to use a little more than ¼ pound.

1 whole chicken cut up or 3
  whole chicken breasts
½ pint sour cream

¼ pound Roquefort cheese
salt and pepper or
garlic salt to taste

Salt and pepper chicken. Use a little garlic salt if desired. Broil chicken in a baking pan until brown on both sides. Cover and bake at 350° for ½ hour or until tender. Blend sour cream and Roquefort cheese. Uncover chicken and pour mixture over chicken and bake 10 minutes longer uncovered.

Betts McCoy
The Villanova Cheese Shop
Villanova, Pennsylvania

SAMMY'S CHICKEN CHOW MEIN

Easy
Do ahead
Freeze

Serves: 10-12
Preparing: 30 minutes
Cooking: 1¼ hours

1 4 or 5 pound stewing
  chicken, stewed and cut up
  in bite-size pieces
½ cup onion, chopped fine
½ cup celery, chopped fine
½ cup butter

4 cups chicken stock, (liquid
  used in cooking chicken)
1 can water chestnuts, sliced
1 can bamboo shoots
1 tablespoon soy sauce
salt and pepper, to taste

Fry onion and celery in butter for five minutes. Add chicken stock, water chestnuts and bamboo shoots. Cook slowly for ¾ hour. Add the chicken and cook for ½ hour more. Season with soy sauce, salt and pepper. Sprinkle with Chinese noodles and serve over rice.

Mrs. Dion S. Birney
Washington, D. C.

If you wish a crisp, brown crust on a roasted or broiled chicken, rub with mayonnaise before baking.

CHICKEN CASSEROLE

Easy
Do ahead

Serves: 6-8
Preparing: 20 minutes
Cooking: 1½ hours

4 chicken breasts, boned and
  split
salt and pepper, to taste
6 slices Swiss cheese
½ cup water or white wine

¼ pound melted butter
1 can cream of chicken soup
2 cups Pepperidge Farm stuffing
  mix

Place chicken in 9″ x 13″ baking dish and top with cheese. Thin soup with water or white wine. Mix until smooth and pour over chicken. Mix stuffing with melted butter and sprinkle over top. Bake at 300° for 1½ hours.

Mrs. William M. Dow
Haverford, Pennsylvania

Main Themes

meats

ESCALOPES OF VEAL CALVADOS

Easy
Partial do ahead

Serves: 5
Preparing: 30 minutes

5 thin slices of veal (leg, if possible)
¼ pound butter
1 pound mushrooms, sliced
½ apple, peeled and sliced

½ cup white wine
¼ cup Calvados (apple brandy)
4 tablespoons heavy cream
salt and pepper, to taste

Melt 3 tablespoons butter; put in veal slices, salt and freshly ground pepper. Sauté, but do not brown. When finished, remove to heated platter and cover. In same pan, melt 2 tablespoons butter, sliced apple and mushrooms. After liquid has evaporated, add Calvados. Add white wine and reduce. Lower flame, stir in cream and continue cooking until sauce has thickened. Put mushrooms and apples over veal. Strain sauce and add seasonings, if necessary. Pour over veal and serve.

The Greenhouse
Radnor, Pennsylvania

AUSTRIAN VEAL GOULASH

Easy
Do ahead
Freeze

Serves: 6-8
Preparing: 30 minutes
Cooking: 1 hour

2 pounds veal, cut into 1" cubes
2 large onions, minced
1 tablespoon fat (or 2 strips finely chopped bacon)
1 tablespoon paprika
1 teaspoon salt

1 tablespoon vinegar
1 large tomato, peeled, seeded and chopped
¼ cup water
1 tablespoon flour
½ cup sour cream

Brown minced onions in fat; or, for better flavor, use two strips of finely chopped bacon. Add veal, cut into cubes, paprika, salt and vinegar. Cook until meat browns, stirring occasionally to prevent scorching. Add tomato and ¼ cup water. Cover and cook slowly for 45 minutes or until meat is tender, adding a little water from time to time. Taste for seasoning. Mix flour with ½ cup sour cream and add to the goulash. Cook for a few more minutes. Serve with buttered noodles or rice.

Mrs. Eugene Ormandy
Philadelphia, Pennsylvania

MONTEREY VEAL À LA PARMA

Easy

Serves: 4
Preparing: 20 minutes

**8 veal scallops (tenders), or 8
  chicken cutlets**
4 slices prosciutto
**4 Monterey Jack cheese
  slices**
½ fresh lemon

¼ cup butter
1 tablespoon olive oil
**2 tablespoons white wine
  (optional)**
seasoned salt and pepper

Sauté veal lightly in oil and butter. Add lemon and wine to pan juices and reduce. Return 4 scallops to the pan. Cover with prosciutto and cheese in layers. Top with the remaining scallops and heat until the cheese has melted. Spoon pan juices over veal.

Mrs. C. Wilbur Ufford
Haverford, Pennsylvania

SWEETBREADS ROSEMONT

Easy
Partial do ahead

Serves: 2
Preparing: 30 minutes

1 pair sweetbreads
½ cup dry white wine
salt
¼ cup flour
2 tablespoons butter
**2 slices Canadian bacon or
  ham**

2 large mushroom caps
¼ cup dry sherry
2 slices toast
chopped parsley
seasoned salt and pepper

Plunge sweetbreads in boiling water to which wine and generous pinch of salt have been added. Simmer 20 minutes. Drain and plunge into ice water. This may be done a day ahead. Carve sweetbreads into ½" slices. Dredge lightly with flour. Sprinkle with seasoned salt and pepper. Brown in butter. Brown Canadian bacon. Place on top of sweetbreads. Add mushroom caps and sherry. Cover and simmer 10-15 minutes. Top with chopped parsley and serve on slices of toast.

Dr. Stanley C. Clader
Rosemont, Pennsylvania

VEAL ROLLATINI

Easy
Partial do ahead

Serves: 4
Preparing: 30 minutes
Broiling: 10 minutes

6 ounces boneless veal
  shoulder, cubed
½ cup snipped chives
1 tablespoon olive oil
1 tablespoon dry white wine
1 teaspoon rosemary
¼ teaspoon basil

¼ teaspoon sage
salt and pepper to taste
½ cup Ricotta cheese
1½ cups tomato sauce
12 veal scallops (each about 2
  ounces)
3 tablespoons olive oil

In food processor (using steel blade), place veal cubes, chives, oil, wine, rosemary, basil, sage, salt and pepper. Process about 30 seconds or until mixture forms a paste. Transfer to a bowl and mix in the Ricotta. In a saucepan (over high heat) reduce tomato sauce to one cup. Keep warm. Flatten veal scallops between wax paper. Divide mixture and spread over scallops. Roll these, tucking in ends. Thread three rolls on each of four 6-inch skewers. Brush baking sheet and rolls with oil. Salt and pepper rolls and broil (4 inches from heat) for five minutes on each side. Arrange on heated platter and cover with tomato sauce.

Sam Di Lorenzo
Delaware Market House
Gladwyne, Pennsylvania

VEAL MARENGO

Easy
Do ahead
Freeze

Serves: 6
Preparing: 40 minutes
Cooking: 1 hour 45 minutes

4 tablespoons vegetable oil
2 pounds veal, cubed
2 tablespoons flour
10½ ounces chicken broth
salt and pepper, to taste
2 sprigs parsley, celery
  leaves, 1 teaspoon crushed
  thyme, 1 bay leaf, tied in
  cheese cloth

2 medium onions, diced
1 large tomato, cut in eighths
1 garlic clove, minced
1 cup dry white wine
2 tablespoons tomato paste
1 package dry onion-mushroom
  soup mix
½ pound mushrooms, sliced
1 tablespoon parsley

In heavy skillet brown veal cubes and onions. Do not crowd in pan. When all cubes are browned, sprinkle with the flour, salt and pepper. Add garlic, tomato paste, wine, broth, dry soup mix and bag of spices. Bring to boil and simmer for 1 hour and 15 minutes. Add tomato and sliced mushrooms. Cook for 30 minutes longer. Remove bag of spices. Serve over rice. Sprinkle with parsley.

To freeze: Put in freezer after 1 hour 15 minutes of cooking, before adding the tomatoes and mushrooms. Thaw. Add tomatoes and mushrooms and cook for 30 minutes to serve.

Mrs. John F. Lloyd
Ardmore, Pennsylvania

Dry wine serves as a tenderizer for meat.
Frozen meats can be defrosted in a 175° oven. Leave in store wrapping.

VEAL SCALOPPINI WITH CHEESE

Average
Do ahead

Serves: 6
Preparing: 20-25 minutes
Cooking: 20 minutes

2 pounds veal, cut into thin, even slices
½ cup butter
3 tablespoons Marsala or sherry wine
1 tablespoon flour
½ cup milk

½ cup water
1 bouillon cube
dash of nutmeg
freshly ground black pepper, to taste
½ pound Swiss cheese, sliced very thin

Pound veal until very thin. Heat six tablespoons of the butter in skillet. Add veal and cook until brown on both sides. Add Marsala and cook a few seconds longer. Remove from the heat. To make sauce, melt remaining butter in a saucepan. Add the flour and stir with a wire whisk until blended. Meanwhile bring water and milk to a boil and dissolve bouillon cube in the mixture. Add all at once to the butter-flour mixture, stirring vigorously until sauce is thick and smooth. Season with nutmeg and pepper. Arrange veal in a single layer in a shallow baking dish. Scrape loose brown particles from the skillet and pour the drippings over the meat. Top with sauce and arrange cheese over all. If desired, this can be refrigerated several hours. Before serving, heat in a 425° oven until cheese melts and is brown, about 20 minutes.

Mrs. R. T. McSherry
Wayne, Pennsylvania

JARRET DE VEAU GRATINÉ

Average

Serves: 6
Preparing: 30 minutes
Cooking: 1½ to 1¾ hours

6 slices leg of veal
2 pieces of fat (veal)
2 carrots
1 cup dry white wine
1 egg yolk
2 onions

1 bouquet garni
2 tablespoons Cognac
5 tablespoons Gruyère cheese,
 grated
7 ounces heavy cream
salt and pepper

In bottom of a large pot, put one piece of fat. Cover with carrots and onions, finely minced. Lay veal slices on top. Add salt and pepper. Bury the bouquet garni. Add Cognac and wine. Put other piece of fat on top. Cover pot and cook slowly 1¼ hours. Take out pieces of fat and put meat and carrots in ovenproof dish. Put juice through sieve. Remove grease. Add cream into which the egg yolk has been stirred. Correct seasoning. Pour into the dish and sprinkle with grated cheese. Brown at 250°. Don't let it boil. Serve with pasta, green vegetables or rice.

Mrs. Danilo M. DeDominicis
Wayne, Pennsylvania

VEAL VEROUCHKA

Average
Do ahead
Freeze

Serves: 6
Preparing: 30 minutes
Cooking: 2 hours
Baking: 1 hour

¼ pound butter
2 pounds veal, in bite-size
 pieces
½ pound mushrooms, sliced
2 onions, chopped

1 pint sour cream
1 cup dry white wine
1 cup raw rice
6 slices crumbled, cooked bacon

Brown veal on all sides in heavy skillet. Sauté onions and mushrooms in butter. Combine veal, onions and mushrooms with sour cream and wine. Cover and cook slowly on top of stove for 2 hours, stirring occasionally. Cook and drain rice; then layer veal and rice in casserole. At this point it may be refrigerated or frozen until ready to bake. Crumble bacon on top and bake uncovered at 300° for 1 hour.

Mrs. William M. Dow
Haverford, Pennsylvania

GOLD GREEN VEAL LOAF

Do ahead

Serves: 6-8
Preparing: 30 minutes
Baking: 1½ hours

1½ pounds ground veal
½ pound ground pork
2 eggs
½ cup fine bread crumbs
¾ cup chopped parsley
½ cup chopped chives
1 cup chopped basil (fresh)
¼ cup coarsely chopped
  green pepper

1 teaspoon dry mustard
1½ teaspoons salt
2 dashes Tabasco
2 teaspoons grated lemon peel
2 lemons, finely sliced
½ pound bacon, sliced
½ teaspoon pepper
1 teaspoon Worcestershire

Combine all ingredients except lemon slices and bacon. Knead and shape into a loaf. Cover completely with lemon slices and wrap with bacon. Bake, covered, 1½ hours at 350°. Put under broiler to brown. Drain off fat and chill. (Place in 8" x 8" pyrex dish to allow room for fat to drain, then cover loaf with foil.)

Mrs. Robert P. Tyson
West Chester, Pennsylvania

VEAL FRICASSÉE

Easy
Do ahead

Serves: 10
Preparing: 30 minutes
Cooking: 1 hour

3 pounds veal steak, cut
  thick
salt and pepper
flour
4 tablespoons butter

1½ cups sour cream
2 teaspoons Worcestershire
  sauce
1 teaspoon celery salt
4 tablespoons chopped parsley

Cut veal into serving pieces; sprinkle with salt and pepper and roll in flour. Brown in hot butter or other fat. Mix sour cream, Worcestershire sauce and celery salt. Pour over meat. Cover and simmer 1 hour or until tender. Remove cover and reduce liquid if necessary. Sprinkle with parsley just before serving.

Mrs. Randall E. Copeland
Haverford, Pennsylvania

VITELLO TONNATO

Easy
Do ahead

Serves: 6-8
Preparing: 2 hours
Baking: 2 hours

**2 pound piece, boned leg of
    veal or filet**
1 cup water
2 egg yolks

4 ounces olive oil
lemon juice
salt to taste
2 ounces canned tuna fish in oil

Season and roast veal as you would any other meat. Leave it to cool. Having poured the fat from the pan, make a little stock from the juices in the pan with a cup of water. Don't use flour.

Make tuna sauce by making a stiff mayonnaise and thinning it to the consistency of thick cream with the stock. Pour the sauce over the sliced veal. Cover, refrigerate and serve the next day.

Maionese Tonnato

2 egg yolks
4 ounces olive oil
salt

lemon juice
2 ounces canned tuna fish in oil

Make a stiff mayonnaise with egg yolks, salt and oil, adding oil to beaten egg yolks very slowly. Season with lemon juice. Sieve tuna with oil. Incorporate the purée into the mayonnaise gradually.

Mrs. H. John Heinz, III
Pittsburgh, Pennsylvania

ROAST SHOULDER OF LAMB WITH APRICOTS

Easy   *Serves: 6*
Preparing: 15 minutes
Baking: 1 hour 45 minutes

6 lb. shoulder of lamb, bones   **6 dried apricots**
cracked and tied in place   **1 cup peach nectar**
salt and pepper   **½ cup ginger ale**
2 medium onions, (quartered)   **½ teaspoon ginger**

Preheat oven to 350°. Have lamb at room temperature and rub with salt and pepper. Place lamb on rack in roasting pan and surround with onions. Place apricots on top of lamb and cook for 10 minutes. Combine peach nectar, ginger ale and ginger. Reduce oven heat to 325° and pour ¼ cup peach nectar mixture over roast. Cook for 1½ hours, pouring the peach nectar mixture (¼ cup) over roast three times during cooking time. When roast is done, turn off heat and allow to remain in oven 10 minutes more. Baste with pan drippings before serving.

Sam Di Lorenzo
Delaware Market House
Gladwyne, Pennsylvania

RACK OF LAMB

Easy   *Serves: 6*
Partial do ahead   *Preparing: 15 minutes*
Roasting: 35-45 minutes

2 racks of lamb, well-trimmed   **1 tablespoon chopped shallots**
salt, pepper   **2 or more tablespoons finely**
2 cups fresh soft   **chopped parsley**
breadcrumbs   **melted butter—lamb drippings**
½ teaspoon chopped garlic

Preheat oven to 450°. Salt and pepper lamb. Place fat side down and roast 15 minutes. Turn and roast another 10 minutes. Remove from oven. Combine bread crumbs, garlic, shallots, and parsley. Bind together with melted butter and lamb drippings. Coat meat with breadcrumb mixture to form a crust. (This can be done in the morning and set aside.) Return to 450° oven for 20-30 minutes before serving. Test for pinkness.

Mrs. Frank L. Newburger, Jr.
Rydal, Pennsylvania

MOROCCAN LAMB

Average
Do ahead

Serves: 6
Preparing: 30 minutes
Cooking: 1¼ hours

¼ cup vegetable oil (olive oil
   optional)
2½ pounds lamb cubes (no
   fat or gristle)
1 clove garlic (minced)
1 large onion (chopped)
2½ teaspoons salt
¾ teaspoon pepper
2 bay leaves
2 cups water

2 whole cloves
½ teaspoon ginger (ground)
½ teaspoon saffron (optional)
4 large tomatoes, ripe (or
   1 large can of whole tomatoes
   and juice)
2 large yellow onions
1 cup golden raisins
⅓ cup almonds (whole)

In a heavy pan heat the oil. Brown lamb, then add onions and garlic, cooking until wilted. Add salt, pepper, bay leaves, cloves, ginger and saffron. Add chopped tomatoes. Cook a few minutes; add two cups water. Cover and simmer 1¼ hours, stirring occasionally. Sauté onions (cut in 8ths) in oil until golden. Add onions to stew, plus 1 cup raisins which were soaked in warm water for ½ hour. Add almonds which have been browned in butter. Serve over rice.

Margaret Feary Walsh
Rosemont, Pennsylvania

OVEN BARBECUE LAMB RIBLETS

Easy

Serves: 8
Preparing: 15-30 minutes
Cooking: 1¾ hours

Country ribs may be substituted for the lamb riblets.

2 rib sections breast of lamb,
   cut in 2-rib portions
1 cup catsup
1 cup water
¼ cup vinegar
2 tablespoons sugar
4 teaspoons Worcestershire
   sauce

2 teaspoons dry mustard
clove of garlic, mashed or
   minced with 2 teaspoons salt
4 medium onions
1 lemon

Brown rib portions on both sides. Drain off the fat. Arrange lamb in a roaster with tight-fitting cover. Tuck in between the lamb pieces, onions and lemon, thinly sliced. Sprinkle with salt, pepper and smoked salt, if desired. Combine ingredients for sauce and pour over lamb. Cover tightly. Bake in 325° oven for 1½ hours or until fork tender. Spoon sauce over ribs two or three times, adding a bit of water if necessary to keep sauce from sticking to pan. Uncover and bake 15-20 minutes more.

Betty A. Jennings
Philadelphia, Pennsylvania

To keep fats in the frying pan from spattering, sprinkle salt in the bottom of the pan.

BUTTERFLIED LEG OF LAMB
WITH HERBAL MUSTARD COATING

Easy

Serves: 8
Preparing: 20 minutes
Marinating: 4 hours
Cooking: 40 minutes

6-7 pound leg of lamb, boned and butterflied (about 5 pounds boneless meat)
½ cup mustard, prepared
2 tablespoons soy sauce

1 clove mashed garlic
1 teaspoon ground rosemary or thyme
¼ teaspoon powdered ginger
2 tablespoons olive oil

Blend with electric mixer or whisk mustard, soy sauce, mashed garlic, rosemary or thyme, and ginger. Add oil slowly, beating with mixer until thick and creamy. Coat lamb on both sides with this mixture. This can be done right on the broiling pan. Cover, refrigerate for several hours (up to half a day.)

Prior to broiling, remove meat from refrigerator and let sit at room temperature for 1½ hours. Broil lamb, *fat side down*, on broiler rack 6 inches from *preheated broiler* for 18 minutes. Turn lamb and broil fat side up 20 minutes (for medium rare). (Note: This can become smokey, but the meat is not burning—it's the fat). Let sit on warm platter or carving board for about 5 minutes before slicing thinly across grain. Serve with mint jelly or mint sauce. (In summer, it is lovely garnished with mint and lemon slices, or cherry tomatoes). Serves 8.

Mrs. Geoffrey P. Mynott
Devon, Pennsylvania

LAMB SHANKS EN PAPILLOTE

Easy
Do ahead
Freeze

Serves: 1
Preparing: 10 minutes
Baking: 1 hour

1 lamb shank
½ small green zucchini
equal size piece raw eggplant
  with skin on
½ medium onion
½ medium fresh tomato

¼ teaspoon dried thyme
¼ teaspoon salt
¼ teaspoon pepper
2 leaves fresh basil (when in
  season)

Preheat oven to 375°. Using a piece of aluminum foil big enough to accomodate all ingredients, place shank in middle of square and add all other ingredients. Fold foil to form a package with an opening at top to allow steam to escape. Place package on cookie pan and bake one hour or until done. Each papillote is placed on a plate and everyone opens it himself. This can also be done in a casserole. Arrange ingredients above, according to number being served, in a large shallow casserole. Cover securely with foil and bake as above.

Mrs. William W. Bodine, Jr.
Villanova, Pennsylvania

SHOULDER LAMB CHOPS WITH MANDARIN ORANGES

Easy

Serves: 4
Preparing: 15 minutes
Baking: 1¼-1½ hours

4 thick shoulder lamb chops
1 #1 can Mandarin oranges
1 cup raw rice
3 cups beef bouillon (or part
  bouillon combined with
  juice from oranges to equal
  3 cups liquid)

½ teaspoon dried mint
salt and pepper to taste

Sear the lamb chops briefly. Place uncooked rice in the bottom of greased casserole dish. Arrange chops on top of rice and cover with drained oranges. Pour in the bouillon. Sprinkle mint, salt and pepper on top. Bake covered in a 350° oven for 1¼ to 1½ hours.

Mrs. Sophie Farmer
Duluth, Minnesota

LAMB SHANKS IN RED WINE

Easy
Do ahead
Freeze

Serves: 4
Preparing: 20 minutes
Cooking: 2 hours

**4 lamb shanks, salted and
  peppered with fresh ground
  pepper**
¼ cup brandy
**½ cup onions, finely chopped
  (green onions are best)**

½ cup celery, finely chopped
1 cup or more red wine
1 tablespoon butter
1 cup water

Brown lamb shanks on all sides in butter. Heat brandy. Pour warm brandy over shanks. Ignite. When flame is out remove shanks.

Brown onions and celery in pan, add red wine. Place shanks in deep baking dish. Pour wine, onions and celery over shanks. Add one cup water. Shanks should be covered with liquid.

Bake covered at 325° for two hours, turning several times. Best served with wild rice. Very good done the day before and reheated.

Mrs. Frank H. Reichel, Jr.
Villanova, Pennsylvania

LAMB ROAST

Easy

Serves: 12
Preparing: 20-30 minutes
Baking: 2-3 hours

7 pound leg of lamb
1 cup water
1 garlic clove (optional)

Milani 1890 French dressing
1 cup burgundy or sherry

Sear lamb in 325° oven on all sides, in roasting pan. Pour water in pan and place lamb on rack on roasting pan. Pour ½ cup of the wine over lamb. Cover and cook for 1 hour in 325° oven, basting frequently with Milani dressing. After 1 hour, turn down oven to 300°, and uncover roast. Continue baking and basting for 2 more hours. 30 minutes before meat is done, pour over remaining wine. Test with meat thermometer (170° for rare, 180° for well done). Let rest 15 minutes before carving.

Mrs. John F. Lloyd
Ardmore, Pennsylvania

COLD STUFFED BELL PEPPER ROUNDS

Easy
Do ahead

Serves: 6
Preparing: 1 hour
Chilling: overnight
Baking: 45 minutes

½ **pound ground beef**
½ **pound ground veal**
½ **pound ground pork**
parsley
1 medium onion, minced
salt and pepper

1 egg
6 bell peppers, red and green,
  (medium size)
1 head Romaine lettuce
pimiento

Mix together meats, parsley, onion, salt and pepper. Mix in 1 whole egg. Cut top off peppers. Clean out seeds and dividing tissue. Stuff meat loaf into peppers. Set in baking pan with small amount of water. Bake 45 minutes at 350°. Cool, chill in refrigerator overnight. When ready to serve slice crosswise and arrange on head of Romaine lettuce. Garnish with pimiento. Serve with horseradish or mustard sauce.

Mrs. Thomas V. LeFevre
Rosemont, Pennsylvania

SAVORY LAMB STEW

Easy
Do ahead

Serves: 6
Preparing: 20 minutes
Cooking: 2 hours 15 minutes

4 pound boneless lamb
  shoulder
½ **cup flour**
salt and pepper to taste
3 tablespoons oil
1 cup bouillon
1 cup celery (chopped)

2 medium onions (chopped)
1 green pepper (chopped)
1 orange, (peeled and sliced)
1 apple (peeled, cored and
  quartered)
½ **cup apricot brandy**

Have meat cut into 2" cubes. Mix flour with salt and pepper and coat the lamb cubes. Heat oil in a Dutch oven and brown meat on all sides. Add bouillon and bring to a boil. Reduce heat and add all other ingredients except brandy. Simmer covered for 1¾ hours, stirring occasionally. One half hour before stew is done, add brandy. (If too juicy, increase heat slightly).

Sam Di Lorenzo
Delaware Market House
Gladwyne, Pennsylvania

LAMB CURRY

Do ahead

Serves: 24
Preparing: 30 minutes
Cooking: 2 hours

**12 pounds lamb, boned and
  cut into bite size pieces**
2 cups butter or oil
16 large onions, chopped
24 cloves garlic, crushed
8 tablespoons curry powder

8 lemons, sliced
16 apples, peeled and chopped
6 cups chicken broth
2 tablespoons salt
**1 teaspoon coarsely ground
  black pepper**

Brown lamb in butter or oil; remove from pans and set aside. Add onions and garlic to fat remaining in pans and sauté, stirring constantly, until onions are soft but not brown. Add curry powder and cook, still stirring, for about 5 minutes. Put meat back into pans. Stir in lemon slices, apples, chicken broth, salt and pepper. Bring to a boil, reduce heat, cover and simmer 1½ to 2 hours or until meat is tender and apples and onions have cooked down into sauce. Stir curry occasionally and check seasoning, adding more if necessary. If sauce seems thin, cook uncovered.

Serve with rice. (8 cups of uncooked rice for 24 people.)

Garnishes to personal taste, for example:

scallions, chopped
watermelon pickle
coconut, shredded
sweet relish
crystalized ginger, chopped
green pepper, chopped
bacon, cooked and chopped
capers

chutney
Mandarin oranges
pimiento, chopped
peanuts, chopped
chives, chopped
sour cream
olives, chopped
plum jam

Diantha Stolz
"Cherchie"
Devon, Pennsylvania

RELINI

Easy
Do ahead

Serves: 4
Preparing: 20 minutes
Baking: 1 hour

flank steak
1 package frozen chopped
  spinach (thawed) for each
  steak
1 onion (preferably Bermuda)

12 to 15 fresh mushrooms, sliced
  (or 1 small can)
butter
salt and pepper to taste
cream sherry wine

Pound the steak well on both sides with cleaver, or have the butcher put it through the tenderizer on *one* side only.

Sauté mushrooms and onion in butter, add the spinach, salt and pepper. Spread as much of this mixture on steak as will fit, then roll steak, jelly-roll style, and tie in 2 or 3 places with string. Brown the meat on all sides in skillet, pile remaining spinach mixture on top of meat, pour in some sherry, enough to cover bottom of pan. Cover with loose-fitting lid, turn heat low and simmer for one hour. Add more sherry as needed.

Dorothy Charlebois
N. Massapequa, New York

SWEET AND SOUR MEAT LOAF

Easy
Do ahead

Serves: 4
Preparing: 15 minutes
Baking: 1 hour

1½ pounds ground beef
salt
pepper
½ cup bread crumbs
1 onion, grated

1 8-ounce can tomato sauce
1 cup water
2 tablespoons vinegar
2 tablespoons prepared mustard
2 tablespoons brown sugar

Mix together the first five ingredients plus one half of the 8-ounce can tomato sauce. Form into a loaf. In a separate bowl mix together the remaining tomato sauce and the rest of the ingredients. Pour over meat. Bake at 350° for 1 hour, basting often with sauce.

Mrs. John M. Brownback
New Orleans, Louisiana

STUFFED BEEF TENDERLOIN

Easy
Do ahead

Serves: 8
Preparing: 20 minutes
Baking: 1 hour

¼ cup butter or margarine
1 medium chopped onion
½ cup diced celery
1 4-ounce can sliced
    mushrooms, drained
2 cups soft bread crumbs

1 teaspoon salt
1 teaspoon pepper
½ teaspoon basil leaves
⅛ teaspoon parsley flakes
3 pounds beef tenderloin
4 slices bacon

Melt butter over low heat. Sauté onions, celery and mushrooms about 10 minutes, until soft. Put bread crumbs in 1 quart bowl. Mix lightly seasonings, butter, and onion mixture. Make lengthwise cut ¾ way through beef along the side. Stuff and fasten with toothpicks. Place bacon across top. Bake uncovered in 350° oven for about an hour. Test for desired rareness.

The Committee

AUNT MARTHA'S CASSEROLE

Easy
Do ahead
Freeze

Serves: 8-10
Preparing: 30 minutes
Chilling: 4 hours
Baking: 35 minutes

½ pound egg noodles
1 tablespoon butter
1 pound ground lean beef
2 8-ounce cans tomato sauce
½ pound cottage cheese

8-ounce package cream cheese
¼ cup sour cream
⅓ cup minced onion
¼ cup chopped green pepper
2 tablespoons melted butter

Cook noodles and drain. Sauté beef in butter. Stir in tomato sauce. Remove from stove. Salt to taste. Combine cheeses, sour cream, onion, green pepper. Layer in one large or two 2-quart casseroles as follows: layer of half noodles, cheese combination, remainder of noodles. Dribble with melted butter. Top with layer of beef-tomato mixture. Chill at least four hours or day before. Bake 350° for 35 minutes.

Mrs. A. Addison Roberts
Rosemont, Pennsylvania

KOULIBIAC

Average
Do ahead

Serves: 6
Preparing: 30 minutes
Chilling: 24 hours (pastry)
Baking: 35 minutes

Koulibiac pastry

1 egg yolk
½ pound butter
approximately ⅓ cup water

2½ cups flour
salt
pinch of sugar

Work ingredients together until smooth and pliable. Let pastry rest refrigerated 24 hours.

Koulibiac stuffing

1 pound ground beef
½ cup finely sliced
  mushrooms
⅛ pound butter

2 tablespoons chopped parsley
2 hard-boiled eggs, chopped
1 raw egg
salt and pepper to taste

Sauté the meat and mushrooms separately in butter. Pass the meat through chopper for finer texture. Mix all ingredients; bind with raw egg. Roll pastry into rectangle. Place on towel for easy folding. Arrange stuffing in middle; wrap and seal pastry. Turn sealed side down on oiled baking tray. Bake at 350° 30-35 minutes.

Mrs. A. Addison Roberts
Rosemont, Pennsylvania

DUTCH POTATO MEAT ROLL

Easy
Partial do ahead

Serves: 6
Preparing: 30 minutes
Baking: 50 minutes

¾ cup fresh breadcrumbs
½ cup milk
3 tablespoons dry bread
  crumbs
2 cups dry hot mashed
  potatoes
2 tablespoons chopped
  parsley

3 tablespoons butter
1 cup chopped onion
1 clove garlic, mashed
1 teaspoon salt
1 cup mayonnaise
1 pound best hamburger meat

Soak the ¾ cup fresh breadcrumbs in the ½ cup milk for 10 minutes. Mix and keep warm: 3 tablespoons dry breadcrumbs, 2 cups dry hot mashed potatoes and chopped parsley. Preheat oven to 375°. Heat butter in skillet. Cook onions and garlic for 10 minutes or until soft. Mix in beef, soaked breadcrumbs, salt, pepper and mayonnaise. Add onion mixture, combine well. Take a strip of waxed paper and spread with 3 tablespoons dry breadcrumbs. Spread beef mixture over crumbs, about ½" thick. Cover with hot mashed potatoes. Roll up like jelly roll. Pour a little melted butter on top and bake for 50 minutes. Baste occasionally throughout baking time.

Flora Senecal
Pottstown, Pennsylvania

BEEF BRISKET

Easy   *Serves: 6-8*
Partial do ahead   *Preparing: 15 minutes*
                                              Cooking: 1½ to 2 hours

3 to 4 pounds beef brisket, first cut
6 tablespoons butter
6 tablespoons flour
2 garlic cloves
2 teaspoons Worcestershire sauce
2 cups stock or 2 bouillon cubes

1 cup red wine
½ cup Marsala wine or rye whiskey
6 tablespoons sherry
6 tablespoons brandy
salt and pepper
1 teaspoon thyme

Heat butter in skillet; when melted add flour. Gradually add stock. When sauce is thick, add other ingredients. Place into pan with meat and cook, covered, at 325° for 50 minutes per pound. Sauce may be prepared in advance.

Mrs. James Bradbeer
Gulph Mills, Pennsylvania

PEPPER STEAK

Easy

Serves: 4
Preparing: 20 minutes
Cooking: 40 minutes

3 cups cooked rice
1 pound thin sliced beef
   round
1 tablespoon paprika
2 tablespoons butter or
   margarine
2 cloves garlic (or equivalent
   of garlic powder), crushed
1½ cups beef broth
1 large onion, cut in 8ths

1 green pepper, cut in strips
2 tablespoons cornstarch
¼ cup water
¼ cup soy sauce
2 ripe tomatoes, cut in 8ths
1 box frozen pea pods (optional)

Cut beef into thin strips and sprinkle with paprika; let stand while cutting up other ingredients. Brown meat in butter. Add garlic and broth. Cover and simmer 20-30 minutes. Stir in onions and green peppers. Cook 5 minutes more. Blend cornstarch, water and soy sauce. Stir into meat mixture. Cook, stirring until thickened. Add pea pods; cook 2 minutes and add tomatoes. Stir gently to heat through. Serve over rice.

Carole and Kenneth Scutt
Rosemont, Pennsylvania

CARPET BAG STEAK

Easy

Serves: 4
Preparing: 15 minutes
Cooking: 20 minutes

8 oysters
very fine cracker crumbs
1 egg, beaten with one
   teaspoon water

4 teaspoons clarified butter
4 tenderloin steaks (8 ounce)
herbed hollandaise sauce

Cut oysters in half, dip in egg wash, and coat by rolling in cracker crumbs. Fry to a golden brown in clarified butter and set in a warm spot until steaks are done. Cut a deep pocket in each steak and broil to desired degree of doneness. Stuff each steak with four pieces of oysters and top with herbed hollandaise sauce. Serve.

The Committee

MOUSSAKA

Average
Do ahead
Freeze

Serves: 10
Preparing: 1½ hours
Baking: 45 minutes

Meat sauce

1½ pounds ground beef or
lamb
2 tablespoons butter
1 cup chopped onion
1 clove garlic, crushed
½ teaspoon oregano
½ teaspoon nutmeg
1 teaspoon basil

3 tablespoons chopped parsley
¼ teaspoon pepper
1 teaspoon salt
1 8-ounce can tomato sauce
1 cup wine, red or white
2 medium eggplants
salt
½ cup vegetable oil

Cream sauce

2 tablespoons butter
½ cup flour
½ teaspoon salt
dash pepper
2 cups milk

2 eggs, beaten
½ cup grated cheddar cheese
¼ cup dry bread crumbs
½ cup grated Parmesan cheese
2 tablespoons melted butter

Meat Sauce—Brown onions in butter and add meat. Cook until meat is crumbly and has lost red color. Add spices, tomato sauce and wine. Simmer 1 hour, covered. Turn heat up and reduce sauce by one-half, stirring frequently. Make meat sauce a day ahead and refrigerate. Peel and cut eggplants in ½" slices. Sprinkle with salt and drain in a colander. Brush eggplant with oil and place on a cookie sheet in a single layer. Place under broiler until golden brown; turn slices and broil on other side.

Cream Sauce—Prepare cream sauce by melting butter in saucepan and adding flour. Gradually stir in milk, salt and pepper. Cook and stir until thickened and gradually add beaten eggs and grated cheese.

Sprinkle bread crumbs in bottom of a 2½-quart shallow casserole. Layer half of eggplant, meat sauce and remaining eggplant. Pour cream sauce over top and sprinkle with Parmesan cheese. Drizzle 2 tablespoons melted butter over top. Bake at 350° for about 45 minutes (until golden brown) and cool for about 15 minutes on a warming tray. Cut into squares to serve. Serve with a Greek salad, crusty bread and wine. Note: Casserole may be frozen or made early in the day and refrigerated. In either case, add Parmesan cheese and melted butter just before baking.

Mrs. Robert Hedges
Huntingdon Valley, Pennsylvania

"SUPER BOWL" CHILI

Easy
Do ahead
Freeze

Serves: 30
Soaking: overnight
Preparing: 1 hour
Cooking: 2 hours

6 pounds ground beef
2 packages brown gravy mix
1 1½-ounce bottle Gravy
  Master
3 pounds onions, chopped
5 giant size cans tomatoes,
  blended
2 medium size cans tomato
  sauce
1 5½-ounce can hot chili
  purée

½ cup dry red wine
2 pounds dried pinto beans
1 teaspoon oregano
1 teaspoon cumin
2 teaspoons chili powder
1 teaspoon cayenne pepper
1 teaspoon paprika
1 teaspoon Accent
1 teaspoon salt

Soak beans 8 hours. Cook until tender. Sauté ground beef and chopped onions. Add remaining ingredients and drained pinto beans. Simmer 2 hours, stirring occasionally. Cool. Reheat for party. Serve in soup bowls.

Garnishes: shredded sharp cheese, chopped Bermuda onion, tortilla chips and chopped ripe olives.

Flavor improves with reheating.

Boyd A. Gilmour
Libertyville, Illinois

"SOMETHING ELSE"

Easy
Partial do ahead

Serves: 18
Preparing: 20 minutes
Cooking: 40 minutes

1 cup raisins
4 tablespoons olive oil (or
  vegetable oil)
3 cups finely chopped onions
  (frozen are fine)
4 large garlic cloves, minced
  fine
3 cups chopped green
  pepper

½ cup vinegar (cider or wine)
¾ teaspoon cinnamon
1 teaspoon ground cloves
2 or 3 bay leaves
Tabasco to taste
12 cups chopped tomatoes
6 pounds lean ground steak
1 10-ounce jar green olives

Plump raisins in warm water to cover for 20 minutes. In large casserole, place oil and sauté the onions, peppers, garlic. Stir. Add vinegar, other seasonings. Stir thoroughly. Cook slowly about 10 minutes, stirring now and then. Brown ground meat in oil. Add olives then raisins, drained dry. Add chopped tomatoes, stirring frequently. Skim. Serve with brown rice. (If you prefer, raisins can be added to the rice rather than to the meat.)

Mrs. Boris Sokoloff
Philadelphia, Pennsylvania

Put water in the bottom of the broiler pan to prevent grease from spattering and catching fire. The drippings will make excellent gravy.

TAMALE PIE

Average
Do ahead
Freeze

Serves: 6
Preparing: 30-40 minutes
Baking: 20 minutes

Chicken or leftover meat can be used instead of chuck.

1½ pounds ground chuck
1 onion, chopped
1 or 2 cloves garlic, chopped
1 green pepper, chopped
1 28-ounce can tomatoes, drained
1 teaspoon salt
1 tablespoon chili powder
¼ teaspoon oregano

¾ cup cornmeal
½ cup water
salt
1½ cups water, boiling
½ cup or more ripe olives, pitted and chopped
1 cup cheese, Monterey Jack or cheddar, shredded

In a large skillet, crumble beef and cook over medium heat until no longer red. Add onion, garlic, pepper and stir. Add seasonings and cook 5 minutes. Add tomatoes and olives and stir until tomatoes break apart, then cover and cook 15 minutes.

Mix ½ cup water with cornmeal and stir gradually into 1½ cups boiling water. Keep stirring until thickened over low heat.

Line a casserole with the cornmeal and fill the shell with the meat mixture. Sprinkle with the cheese and bake in a 350° oven for 20 minutes or until cheese bubbles.

Mrs. Robert McCloskey
Little Deer Isle, Maine

KAREWAI TENDERLOIN STEAK (FILET)

Easy

Serves: 4
Preparing: 25 minutes

4 slices filet mignon 1½"
 thick
salt and pepper
2 tablespoons clarified butter
1 clove garlic, mashed
2 tablespoons butter

¼ pound mushrooms, sliced
¾ cup catsup
¾ cup dry white wine
1 tablespoon chopped parsley
2 tablespoons butter
4 slices French bread 1" thick

Sprinkle filets with salt and pepper. Place clarified butter in skillet, heat and add garlic. Sauté 1 minute. Remove garlic pieces to a saucepan. Sauté steaks 5 minutes on each side for medium rare. While steaks are cooking, add butter to garlic in saucepan and fry for 1 minute. Add mushrooms, stir and then stir in catsup. Simmer 2 minutes, stir in wine and parsley, simmer 5 minutes. Remove steaks from skillet and keep warm. Add butter to pan drippings and fry bread until brown on both sides and top with steaks. Spoon hot sauce over steaks, garnish with finely chopped parsley and serve with broiled tomatoes.

Colleen Danko
Philadelphia, Pennsylvania

DAUBE

Average
Do ahead

Serves: 4
Preparing: 45 minutes
Cooking: 3-3½ hours

2 pounds beef, top rump or
 chuck, cut into chunks
½ pound unsmoked bacon or
 salt pork, cut into small
 cubes
3 to 4 ounces pork rinds, cut
 into small squares
2 medium onions, sliced
2 to 3 carrots, sliced
2 to 3 tomatoes, sliced
3 to 4 cloves garlic, flattened
 with a knife

a bouquet of thyme, bay leaf and
 parsley
5 to 6 thinly sliced strips of
 orange peel
4 tablespoons olive oil
1 cup red wine, brought to a boil
 and set aflame to get rid of the
 alcohol
Greek or Italian olives to be
 added 1 hour before end of
 cooking time

In bottom of heavy ovenproof pot put olive oil, bacon, then vegetables and ½ the pork rinds. Arrange the meat evenly on top of this. Bury the garlic and the bouquet of herbs among the chunks of beef. Put the remaining pork rinds on top. Start cooking on top of the stove on moderate heat. After 20 minutes or so, pour the bubbling wine over all and cover tightly (put a piece of foil between pan and lid for extra tight fit). Put into a 200° oven for about 3 hours. To serve, put meat with bacon and rinds on platter, pour sauce over all. If desired, sprinkle chopped garlic, parsley and a few capers over top. Serve with noodles or rice.

Richard Stilwell, New York, New York

ROUND STEAK SAUERBRATEN

Easy
Freeze
Do ahead

Serves: 5-6
Preparing: 30 minutes
Cooking: 1½ hours

1½ to 2 pounds round steak, ½ inch thick (or leftover round roast cut the same way)
1 tablespoon butter
1 large clove garlic, minced
1 envelope brown gravy mix
1¾ cups water
¼ cup Port wine
1 tablespoon instant minced onion

2 tablespoons white wine vinegar
2 tablespoons brown sugar
½ teaspoon Jane's Krazy Mixed-Up Salt
¼ teaspoon pepper
½ teaspoon ground ginger
1 teaspoon Worcestershire sauce
1 bay leaf
hot buttered noodles

Cut meat in 1" squares. In large skillet brown meat and garlic on all sides in hot fat. Sprinkle with Jane's Krazy Mixed-Up Salt. Remove meat from skillet. Add gravy mix and water. Bring to boil, stirring constantly. Stir in remaining ingredients except noodles. Return meat to skillet; cover and simmer 1½ hours or until tender, stirring occasionally. Remove bay leaf. Serve over hot buttered noodles. Meat may be frozen but not the noodles.

Bert and Toby Phillips
Wallingford, Pennsylvania

BEEF IN BLACK SAUCE

Easy
Do ahead
Freeze

Serves: 6-8
Preparing: 2½ to 3 hours

3 pounds beef cut in 3" x ½"
strips (eye round, cross rib,
etc.)
⅓ cup olive oil
1½ cups sliced onions
1 tablespoon salt
¼ teaspoon freshly ground
pepper

4 tablespoons lemon juice
½ cup currants
4 cups water
4 potatoes, peeled and cubed
½ cup sliced olives
2 teaspoons capers
parsley sprigs

Heat the oil in a flameproof casserole; brown the meat and onions in it until very dark. Add salt, pepper, lemon juice, currants, and water. Cover and cook over low heat for 1½ hours. Add the potatoes, olives, and capers. Cook covered 45 minutes longer. Taste for seasoning. Garnish with parsley sprigs for color.

Mrs. D. B. Garst
Devon, Pennsylvania

MEATLOAF SURPRISE

Easy
Do ahead

Serves: 4-6
Preparing: 20 minutes
Cooking: 30 minutes

1 loaf Italian bread (short, fat
loaf)
1 6-ounce can evaporated
milk
1 pound ground chuck

1 onion, chopped fine
1 egg
1 teaspoon salt
¼ teaspoon pepper
catsup to taste

Cut top of bread horizontally, reserving top. Scrape out inside of loaf. Soak a portion of crumbs in milk for 5 minutes (use own judgment for proper amount). Add meat, onion, egg and seasonings to crumb mixture. Pack into bread shell. Set top in place. Bake on cookie sheet at 350° for 30 minutes. If loaf browns too much, cover with foil.

Mrs. John E. Krout
Rosemont, Pennsylvania

"DINNER PARTY" STEW

Easy
Do ahead
Freeze

Serves: 6
Preparing: 30 minutes
Cooking: 2 hours

1 pound lean beef, cut into cubes
½ teaspoon salt
dash pepper
3 medium onions, sliced
3 tablespoons fat
½ cup tomato juice
1¾ cups meat stock or 1¾ cups hot water with 3 bouillon cubes, dissolved

1 teaspoon sugar
½ cup sour cream
1 small can mushrooms (save juice)
3 tablespoons flour
1 bay leaf

Brown meat and onions in hot fat 10 to 15 minutes with salt and pepper. Add tomato juice, meat stock, sugar and bay leaf. Bring to boil, then reduce heat. Cover pan and simmer gently for 2 hours. Blend in sour cream and mushrooms. Make a paste of flour and mushroom juice to thicken gravy; stir in gently. Serve over rice.

Mrs. Malcolm Jones
Bangor, Maine

TEXAS HASH

Easy
Do ahead
Freeze

Serves: 4-6
Preparing: 15 minutes
Baking: 45 minutes

2 onions, chopped
1 pound ground beef
1 can tomatoes, chopped (14 or 15-ounce can)
2 cans tomato sauce (14 or 15-ounce can)

1 cup rice
1 teaspoon chili powder
2 teaspoons salt
¼ teaspoon pepper

Brown onions and ground beef. Pour off fat. Add all other ingredients to beef and onion mixture. Place in covered casserole and bake 45 minutes in a 375° oven.

Corinne A. Bibby
Villanova, Pennsylvania

MAIÁLE UBRIACCO
(Drunken Pig)

Easy

Serves: 6-8
Preparing: 10 minutes
Cooking: 2-3 hours

1 boned pork loin, 3 to 4
    pounds
2 tablespoons olive oil
3 to 4 cloves garlic, finely
    chopped

4 to 5 sprigs fresh chopped
    parsley
salt and pepper
1 to 2 quarts Burgundy or
    Chianti

Slightly brown garlic in oil in large Dutch oven. Remove garlic with slotted spoon. Salt and pepper pork and brown in oil on all sides. Remove pork; add three cups wine to oil still in pan. Replace pork on rack in pan. Steam lightly covered for two or three hours, until pork is well done. It will be necessary to add wine to pan every fifteen to twenty minutes during cooking. Watch closely, as pan must not go dry. Remove pork and boil down remaining wine sauce until thickened, or add gravy thickener. Serve meat on hot platter and pour sauce over it. Serve with wild rice or buttered, parsleyed noodles.

Donald R. Clauser
Philadelphia, Pennsylvania

TOAD IN THE HOLE

Easy

Serves: 4
Preparing: 20 minutes
Baking: 30 minutes

about 1 pound link sausages
1 cup flour
2 eggs

1 cup milk
½ teaspoon salt

Arrange the sausage in a shallow baking dish and bake in a hot oven (425°) for about 10 minutes, or until lightly browned. Mix flour with salt; stir in eggs and milk. Beat well with rotary beater. Pour off some of the sausage fat. Pour the batter over the sausages. Bake about 30 minutes until puffed up and brown.

Leonard Bogdanoff
Philadelphia, Pennsylvania

POLYNESIAN PORK

Easy

Serves: 12-14
Preparing: 20-30 minutes
Cooking: 3 hours

whole loin of pork, boned
salt

pepper
rosemary

Sauce

½ cup soy sauce
½ cup catsup
¼ cup honey (or orange
marmalade, if you prefer)

½ cup molasses (or brown sugar,
if you prefer)
2 large cloves of garlic, crushed

Garnish

Mandarin oranges
white grapes

watercress

Have butcher bone and tie whole loin of pork. Sprinkle with salt, pepper, rosemary. Roast at 300° for 3 hours (or a bit longer if necessary). During last two hours, baste frequently with sauce. Make sauce by combining above ingredients. Before serving, cut strings with kitchen scissors. Garnish roast with watercress, Mandarin oranges and white grapes.

Mrs. Lynn Kippax
Swarthmore, Pennsylvania

SAUSAGE AND MUSHROOM CASSEROLE

Easy
Do ahead

Serves: 4
Preparing: 10-15 minutes

1 pound spicy pork sausage
links
1 pound sliced mushrooms
3 tablespoons butter
2 tablespoons flour

2 cups milk
1 heaping tablespoon Major Grey
Chutney, chopped fine
salt and pepper

Cook, drain and cut the sausage into small pieces. Sauté mushrooms in butter for about 3 minutes. Add flour and milk, stirring until mixture thickens. Add the sausage and chutney to the creamed mushrooms. Serve over toast or in party shells.

Mrs. Robert P. Tyson
West Chester, Pennsylvania

PORK CHOPS WITH BRANDIED PEACHES

Average

Serves: 4
Preparing: 60 minutes

4 8-ounce loin pork chops
  (about 1 inch thick)
2 ripe, fresh peaches, peeled
  and sliced
2 teaspoons fresh ginger
  peeled and chopped
1 tablespoon fresh shallots
  (or scallions), peeled and
  chopped

½ cup peach brandy
3 cups chicken stock (reduced
  ahead of time to ½ cup)
1½ cups heavy cream
1 tablespoon peanut oil

Brown pork chops thoroughly in heavy skillet in peanut oil. Transfer chops to baking dish and place in 400° oven for 20 minutes. Pour oil from skillet and deglaze with peach brandy. Add shallots, ginger and reduced stock. Reduce by half. Add peach slices and heavy cream. Continue reducing process until sauce coats spoon. Take pork chops from oven; place on warm serving dish. Pour sauce over chops. Serve.
Note: The best sauces are made by reduction process. Please be careful not to over-cook pork chops.

H. Royer Smith, Chef
Philadelphia Art Alliance
Philadelphia, Pennsylvania

SAUERKRAUT WITH PORK

Easy
Do ahead

Serves: 6
Preparing: 20 minutes
Baking: 90 minutes

2½ pounds fresh pork
  shoulder, cut in 1½ inch
  cubes
3 teaspoons salt
¼ teaspoon pepper
flour
3 tablespoons shortening or
  salad oil

3 or 4 onions, sliced
2 tablespoons paprika
1½ cups water
2 1-pound cans sauerkraut
1 green pepper, chopped
1 cup sour cream

Season pork with one teaspoon salt and ⅛ teaspoon pepper and dredge with flour. Brown meat in shortening or oil. Remove meat to casserole. Brown onions in drippings; add paprika, ⅛ teaspoon pepper and water. Simmer until brown bits in pan are loosened. Add sauerkraut, green pepper and 2 teaspoons salt. Mix well and pour mixture over meat in casserole. Bake in moderate oven (350°) for 1½ hours. Just before serving, stir in sour cream.

Mary L. Winstanley
Abington, Pennsylvania

HAM LOAF

Easy

Serves: 24
Preparing: 20 minutes
Baking: 1½ hours

**4 pounds ham and 1 pound
  pork ground together**
8 eggs
3 cups soft bread crumbs
3 cups milk
1 teaspoon pepper

Topping:

**8 teaspoons horseradish
  mustard**
1 cup brown sugar
1½ cups pineapple juice

Soften crumbs in milk, add to meat. Add eggs and pepper; mix lightly until well blended. Place in flat 12" x 20" pan.

Blend mustard and brown sugar. Spread over meat surface just before placing in 350° oven. Pour pineapple juice over all. Bake for 1½ hours.

Barbara M. Alder
Havertown, Pennsylvania

ALSATIAN CASSEROLE

Easy

Serves: 4
Preparing: 30 minutes
Cooking: 2½ hours

6 slices bacon
4 medium potatoes, thinly
   sliced
2 onions, thinly sliced
¼ teaspoon pepper
¾ cup dry white wine

1 tablespoon chopped parsley
4 loin pork chops
1 tsp. salt
1 tsp. caraway seeds
2 cloves garlic, crushed

Fry 2 slices bacon. Brown pork chops in bacon fat. Arrange ½ potatoes in bottom of large casserole. Top with ½ onions and ½ salt and pepper. Place chops over onions. Add remaining potatoes, onions, salt and pepper. Crush caraway seeds, add wine and garlic. Place remaining bacon on top. Cover with double foil and lid. Roast at 300° until meat and potatoes are tender. Discard bacon and skim off fat. Top with parsley and crumbled bacon.

L'Epicure
Shelly Hippler-Conway
Haverford, Pennsylvania

APPLE PORK ROAST

Easy

Serves: 6
Preparing: 10 minutes
Roasting: 3 hours

6 pounds pork roast
8 ounce jar of honey
3 ounce frozen concentrated
   orange juice, defrosted

2 cooking apples, cut in ¾"
   slices
2 teaspoons cinnamon

Saw back bottom bone and re-tie to roast. Make 6 evenly spaced pockets (or more if thinner slices are to be cut) large enough for a ½" to ¾" slice of apple. Insert the slices of apple into each pocket. Sprinkle cinnamon across the top of the roast. Blend honey and defrosted orange juice, pour over roast. Wrap the roast in foil, covering the entire piece of meat. Cook for 2 hours at 325°. Unwrap foil and cook for 1 hour more. Serve in 6 or more slices.

Sam Di Lorenzo
Delaware Market House
Gladwyne, Pennsylvania

FILET OF PORK

Easy
Partial do ahead

Serves: 8-10
Preparing: 20 minutes
Cooking: 1 hour, 50 minutes

1 3 to 5 pound pork filet
1 cup minced onions
4 shallots
½ cup celery, finely chopped
3 cloves garlic, put through
   garlic press
1 teaspoon thyme

1 teaspoon basil
2 cups black olives ("Greek"
   preferred), chopped
2 fresh tomatoes, cubed
½ pound Roquefort cheese
pepper

Sauté pork in butter on all sides over medium heat for one hour, turning frequently. Place pork and juices in roasting pan. Add vegetables and herbs. Cover and cook in 350° oven for 30 minutes. Remove from oven. Partially slice pork in serving pieces. Place thin slices of cheese between slices of meat. Baste with juices in pan. Return to oven for 20 minutes.

Peter Orth
Guilford, Connecticut

HOMEMADE SCRAPPLE

Easy
Do ahead
Freeze

Serves: 4-6
Preparing: 5 minutes
Cooking: 45 minutes
Chilling: 3 hours

1 pound bulk sausage
1 quart water
1 cup yellow cornmeal

1 teaspoon salt
½ teaspoon sage
¼ cup water

In large saucepan break up sausage into small pieces. Add 1 quart water; bring to boil and then simmer 30 minutes, stirring occasionally. Add ¼ cup more water, cornmeal, salt and sage. Simmer 15 minutes more, stirring frequently. Meanwhile, chill large loaf pan with ice cubes. Empty and fill with sausage mixture. Cover with foil and chill. May be sliced and frozen with wax paper sheets between slices.

Mr. John Folk
Merion, Pennsylvania

RAKOTT KRUMPLI
(Hungarian Layered Casserole)

Easy
Do ahead

Serves: 6
Preparing: 45 minutes
Baking: 30 minutes

3 pounds medium potatoes
1½ tablespoons salt
6 eggs, hard-boiled
¼ pound butter
1 cup sour cream

6 ounces boiled ham, sliced
julienne style
6 ounces sliced sausage
(Kielbasa)
1 tablespoon paprika

Preheat oven to 350°. Drop potatoes in their skins in water to cover with 1 tablespoon salt. Cook until fork tender. Peel and slice potatoes. Cook, peel and slice eggs. Butter an ovenproof deep dish. Arrange a layer of potatoes on bottom. Season with salt. Melt butter and sprinkle a little on top of potatoes. Cover with ham strips, repeat potatoes, salt and butter. Arrange egg slices, then sausage slices on top, finishing with layer of potatoes. Pour over remaining butter and spread the sour cream on top. Sprinkle with paprika. Bake, uncovered, for 30 minutes. Lengthen cooking time to 1 hour if casserole was refrigerated.

Mrs. George S. Fabian
Bryn Mawr, Pennsylvania

SUSIE'S HAM LOAF

Easy
Do ahead
Freeze

Serves: 8-10
Preparing: 15 minutes

1 pound ground smoked ham
1 pound ground pork
3 cups Wheaties
2 eggs
1 cup milk

salt and pepper
¼ cup brown sugar
6 slices canned pineapple
juice from pineapple

Mix all ingredients together (easier by hand). Put three slices of pineapple on bottom of loaf pan. Put in mixed ingredients. Put three slices of pineapple on top. Mix enough pineapple juice with brown sugar to spread easily over the top of loaf. Bake 350° for 1½ hours.

Mrs. Norman P. Robinson
Haverford, Pennsylvania

Medleys

vegetables

EGGPLANT CANNELONI

Do ahead
Freeze

Serves: 6
Preparing: 1 hour
Baking: 15 minutes

Filling
1 cup grated Mozzarella
½ cup grated Parmesan
½ cup Ricotta
1 egg
1 tablespoon finely chopped
    parsley
2 tablespoons finely chopped
    fresh raw spinach
salt
pepper
2 large eggplants
flour
¼ cup olive oil
2 teaspoons sweet butter
garlic salt

Sauce
2 tablespoons butter
2 tablespoons flour
1 cup stewed tomatoes
1 can tomato paste
pinch salt
pepper
1 teaspoon sugar
1 clove garlic

Combine the three cheeses, egg, parsley, spinach, salt and pepper in mixing bowl or blender and work to a fine paste. Put on a flat plate and place in the refrigerator to chill.

Peel the 2 eggplants and cut in half lengthwise. Starting from the cut surfaces, shave three thin slices from each of the four halves so you will have 12 thin slices. Dredge in flour and sauté in oil and butter until tender. Drain on paper towels and sprinkle with garlic salt.

Divide the filling into 12 even pieces and place on the broad end of each eggplant slice and roll up. Arrange with the seam down in a buttered ovenproof dish. Blend all ingredients for tomato sauce in blender or Cuisinart and blend to a smooth paste. Put into a saucepan and stir over a medium flame until the mixture thickens and boils. Cover with tomato sauce and sprinkle with more Parmesan cheese. Bake in 425° oven for 10-15 minutes or until sauce is bubbly.

Mrs. David Acton,
Haverford, Pennsylvania

While cooking cauliflower, avoid odors by adding a slice of bread. Pour off with water.

SHERRIED MUSHROOMS IN CREAM

Average   *Serves: 4*
Partial do ahead   *Preparing: 25 minutes*
Freeze

1 pound sliced mushrooms
2 tablespoons butter
2 tablespoons flour
1 cup milk or cream, or
   combination of both

salt and pepper to taste
2 tablespoons sherry
½ cup Pepperidge Farm stuffing
2 teaspoons melted butter
paprika

Sauté mushrooms in small amount of butter. Do not overcook. Remove from pan and make sauce with 2 tablespoons butter and 2 tablespoons flour. When cooked, add 1 cup milk or cream. Add sherry, salt and pepper and enough paprika to give a bit of "pinkness" to the sauce. Add mushrooms and any juice that has collected from them. Pour into greased 1-quart baking dish. Top with stuffing which has been mixed with melted butter. Bake at 375° until brown and hot.

Mrs. James E. Halbkat
Newtown Square, Pennsylvania

FLEMISH CARROTS

Average   *Serves: 6*
                                         Preparing: 45 minutes

12 long carrots, or 24 baby
   carrots
4 tablespoons butter
¼ cup hot water
1 teaspoon sugar

salt and pepper, to taste
2 egg yolks
¼ cup heavy cream
1 tablespoon minced parsley

Wash and scrape carrots and cut them into ¾" lengths. Melt butter in a heavy saucepan; add carrots, water, salt and pepper and sugar. Cover closely and simmer for 20 to 25 minutes, stirring often and adding a few drops of water if necessary to keep carrots from sticking. When they are tender, there should be no water left, only a buttery sauce. Beat together egg yolks, heavy cream and parsley. Stir into carrots and reheat until hot. Do not boil. Serve at once.

Mrs. Louis Hood
Wayne, Pennsylvania

BAKED CHEESE-STUFFED TOMATOES

Easy

Serves: 8
Preparing: 20 minutes
Baking: 25 minutes

4 large tomatoes (2½
  pounds)
2 cups grated cheese
½ cup light cream
2 egg yolks, slightly beaten
2 tablespoons snipped chives
3 tablespoons grated onion

½ teaspoon dried marjoram
  leaves
1 teaspoon dry mustard
1½ teaspoons salt
⅓ cup packed dry bread crumbs
2 tablespoons butter or
  margarine melted

Preheat oven to 350°. Lightly grease a 12" x 8" x 2" baking dish. Halve tomatoes crosswise. Scoop out pulp, leaving shells intact. Chop pulp coarsely. Combine tomato pulp with cheese, cream, egg yolks, chives, onion, marjoram, mustard and salt. Mix well. Spoon cheese mixture into tomato shells. Toss bread crumbs with melted butter; sprinkle over cheese mixture. Arrange tomato halves in prepared dish. Bake 25 minutes or until tomatoes are tender.

Janet Wilson
Philadelphia, Pennsylvania

LITTLE SLIPPER SQUASH

Easy

Serves: 4
Preparing: 15 minutes
Baking: 30 minutes

4 small, tender summer
  squash (one per person)
¼ pound sharp cheddar
  cheese, grated
1 small onion, chopped

½ tablespoon flour
½ cup milk
1 egg
salt and pepper to taste
¼ cup bread crumbs

Parboil whole squash for 5 minutes in salted water. Cut in two lengthwise. Scoop out center seeds. Sauté onion in butter, then add flour, stirring well. Reduce heat and add milk, stirring to make a thick cream sauce. Stir in 1 egg, salt and pepper and grated cheese. Fill squash cavities with this stuffing, sprinkle fine bread crumbs over top. Place in a shallow pan with ½ inch water and bake in 350° oven until stuffing is brown, about 30 minutes.

Mrs. Louis Hood
Wayne, Pennsylvania

EGGPLANT MOUSSE

Average
Partial do ahead

Serves: 6
Preparing: 45 minutes
Baking: 45 minutes

3 large eggplants, peeled, cubed, and liberally salted
5 tablespoons cooking oil
3 onions, peeled and diced
1 bunch parsley, washed and chopped
3 cloves garlic, peeled and crushed
½ teaspoon nutmeg
1 teaspoon thyme
½ cup chopped fresh basil (optional but recommended)
salt and pepper to taste
6 eggs, beaten lightly
hollandaise or tomato sauce or Parmesan

The day before, put salted eggplant into colander and weigh it to press out bitter juices. The next day, squeeze out as much juice as possible with hands. In large skillet, heat oil and cook eggplant, onion and garlic until soft and translucent, about 25 minutes over low heat. Purée this mixture in blender or food processor with nutmeg, thyme, parsley, optional basil and eggs. Season with salt and pepper to taste. Pour into oiled soufflé dish and bake for 45 minutes at 350° or until knife inserted comes out clean. Serve with hollandaise or tomato sauce or grated Parmesan cheese.

H. Royer Smith, Chef
Philadelphia Art Alliance
Philadelphia, Pennsylvania

CARROTS WITH BUTTER-PECAN SAUCE

Easy

Serves: 6-8
Preparing: 35 minutes

24 small carrots or 2 packages frozen carrots
¼ cup butter, melted
2 tablespoons sliced pecans
2 tablespoons lemon juice
1 tablespoon chopped chives
¼ teaspoon salt
⅛ teaspoon pepper
⅛ teaspoon marjoram

Wash and peel fresh carrots. Cook, covered, in small amount of boiling, salted water for 20 to 30 minutes, or until tender. (Or, cook frozen carrots according to package directions.) Drain. In another pan combine remaining ingredients and heat through. Serve over hot carrots.

Miss Josie Miller
Washington, D. C.

FRESH CORN PUDDING

Easy

Serves: 4-6
Preparing: 15 minutes
Baking: 1 hour

4-5 ears fresh corn
3 eggs, beaten
3 tablespoons flour
2 tablespoons sugar

1 teaspoon salt
1 tablespoon melted butter
1 cup light cream

Score kernels by running point of knife down each row of corn. Cut kernels from cob and scrape cob with back of knife to release milky residue. You should have 2 cups corn. Beat eggs until thick. Add corn plus rest of ingredients and stir well. Turn into lightly greased 1½-quart baking dish. Bake at 325° about 1 hour, or until knife inserted near center comes out clean.

Mrs. James E. Halbkat
Newtown Square, Pennsylvania

Sauté green beans in a small amount of oil before adding liquid to cook them. Improves flavor and shortens cooking time.

MARTINI SAUERKRAUT

Easy
Do ahead

Serves: 6
Preparing: 20 minutes
Baking: 3 to 4 hours

2 pounds fresh sauerkraut
½ pound bacon
½ cup thinly sliced carrots
1 cup thinly sliced onions

1 cup dry vermouth
¼ cup gin
2 to 3 cups chicken or beef stock
salt to taste

Rinse sauerkraut well. You may soak it in a large quantity of water for 15 minutes if you wish. Squeeze dry.
Cut bacon into pieces and cook with onions and carrots 10 minutes, without browning. Stir in sauerkraut, vermouth, gin and then the stock to cover. Add salt to taste. Place in covered casserole and bake in 350° oven 3 to 4 hours or until all liquid is absorbed.

Mrs. David Acton
Haverford, Pennsylvania

CORN-BROCCOLI CASSEROLE

Easy
Do ahead

Serves: 4
Preparing: 5-10 minutes
Baking: 35-40 minutes

1 10-ounce package chopped
  broccoli, thawed and
  drained
1 8½-ounce can creamed
  corn
1 tablespoon grated onion

½ teaspoon salt
dash pepper
1 beaten egg
1 cup cheese croutons,
  (Pepperidge Farm)
3 tablespoons butter

Combine first six ingredients. Put ¾ of croutons into the mixture and top with remaining croutons. Dot with butter. Bake 35 to 40 minutes at 350°.

Mrs. Gerald Rickert
Des Moines, Iowa

SHREDDED ZUCCHINI WITH WALNUTS

Easy
Do ahead

Serves: 6
Preparing: 20 minutes
Cooking: 10 minutes

6 small zucchini squash
½ stick butter

salt and pepper, to taste
½ cup chopped walnuts

Wash 6 small zucchini squash and grate on medium cut grater. Sauté in butter lightly adding salt and pepper to taste. Serve in individual dishes. Sprinkle top with chopped walnuts.

Can be done ahead and "held" in a double boiler until serving time.

Charles and Helen Wilson's
L'Auberge
Strafford, Pennsylvania

CASHEW CASSEROLE

Easy
Do ahead

Serves: 6-8
Preparing: 10 minutes
Baking: 20 minutes

2 tablespoons corn oil
1 cup celery, finely chopped
1 2-ounce can mushrooms
1 can mushroom soup
1 small onion
½ soup can milk

liquid from mushrooms
1 cup cashew nuts, coarsely
  chopped
1 3-ounce can chow mein
  noodles

Sauté celery, onion, and mushrooms in oil for a few minutes. Do not brown. Add milk and mushroom liquid to the cream of mushroom soup; stir until smooth. Combine with mushroom mixture and add nuts and noodles. Pour into a greased casserole and bake at 350° for 20 minutes.

Mrs. James B. Palmer
Newfane, Vermont

French fry carrots instead of potatoes for a change.

DIANE'S ONIONS

Average
Do ahead

Serves: 2
Preparing: 10 minutes
Cooking: 30 minutes

1 pint small white onions, ,
  peeled
2 tablespoons brown sugar
1 tablespoon butter
1 tablespoon liquid from
  cooking onions

4 strips bacon, diced and fried
  crisp
chopped parsley
Parmesan cheese

Boil onions in salted water until half cooked. Drain and save 1 tablespoon cooking liquid. Add to onions in pan, brown sugar, butter and cooking liquid. Cook for a few minutes, but be sure onions remain slightly crisp. Top with grated cheese, bacon and parsley, when ready to serve.

Mrs. Charles W. Young
Bryn Mawr, Pennsylvania

BROCCOLI OR ASPARAGUS BAKED IN CREAM SAUCE

Easy　　　　　　　　　　　　　　　　　　*Serves: 8-10*
Do ahead　　　　　　　　　　　*Preparing: 30 minutes*
　　　　　　　　　　　　　　　　　Baking: 50 minutes

1 can cream of mushroom
　soup, undiluted
1 cup sour cream
2 eggs, well-beaten
1 cup grated sharp cheddar
　cheese
1 jar (2 ounce) pimientos,
　chopped
1 jar (4 ounce) mushroom
　pieces, with liquid
¼ cup minced onion

¼ cup diced green pepper
1½ cups slightly crushed corn
　flakes
½ cup broken pecans
6 tablespoons melted butter
3 packages frozen broccoli
　(asparagus) spears, cooked
　and drained
½ teaspoon salt
¼ teaspoon pepper

Line a buttered pan (13" x 9" x2") with vegetable spears. Mix all ingredients except corn flakes, pecans and butter. Pour over vegetables. Sprinkle corn flakes and pecans over all. Dribble butter on top. Bake at 300° for 50 minutes, or until custard-like sauce is partially set.

Mrs. Donald O. Bailey
Wayne, Pennsylvania

PEAS ORIENTAL

Easy　　　　　　　　　　　　　　　　　*Serves: 12-14*
Do ahead　　　　　　　　　　　*Preparing: 15 minutes*
　　　　　　　　　　　　　　　　　Baking: 50 minutes

3 10-ounce packages frozen
　peas, cooked
2 small cans water chestnuts,
　thinly sliced, drained
2 large cans bean sprouts,
　drained

1 pound small mushrooms,
　sautéed in butter
2 10½-ounce cans cream of
　mushroom soup
2 3½-ounce cans French fried
　onion rings

Beat soup with fork. Mix all vegetables except onion rings with soup and place in large buttered casserole. Bake at 350° for approximately 30 minutes. Top with French fried onion rings and continue baking another 15-20 minutes.

Mrs. Stanley E. Johnson
Philadelphia, Pennsylvania

WILD RICE CASSEROLE

Average
Do ahead
Freeze

Serves: 8-10
Preparing: 1 hour
Cooking: ½ hour

Excellent as a casserole with boned chicken breasts, or as a filling for squab, cornish hens, chicken or turkey.

1 cup wild rice	**¼ cup dry sherry**
¼ cup olive oil	**½ cup sliced fresh mushrooms**
½ cup diced celery	**¼ cup chopped green pepper**
½ cup chopped onion	**½ teaspoon chopped parsley**
½ can condensed beef	**1 teaspoon salt**
consommé	**½ teaspoon Angostura bitters**

Prepare rice by method given below. Heat the olive oil in a heavy skillet. Stirring constantly, add the drained wild rice, the finely diced celery and chopped onion. When blended, add the condensed beef consommé and dry sherry. Then stir in the sliced mushrooms, chopped green pepper, chopped parsley, salt and Angostura bitters. Cover tightly and simmer for ½ hour or until rice is done. Add more consommé if necessary.

Wild Rice: Wash wild rice in cold water and then soak one hour in tepid water. Or, "Quickly Soak"—wash wild rice in cold water. Then stir rice into three times amount of boiling water (1 cup rice requires 3 cups boiling water). Parboil for 5 minutes only. Remove from heat—let stand in same water, covered for one hour. Drain, wash and cook according to recipe.

Mrs. H. Ober Hess
Gladwyne, Pennsylvania

SPINACH, BROCCOLI AND ARTICHOKE COMBO

Easy
Do ahead

Serves: 6-8
Preparing: 15 minutes

1 box frozen chopped spinach	**butter or hollandaise**
	salt and pepper
1 box frozen chopped broccoli	**dash lemon**
	chopped onion (optional)
1 large can artichoke hearts	

Do not overcook spinach and broccoli. Cook them together in a large skillet, covered. Add a dash of salt, *and no water*. Loosen and separate them as much as possible. Cook about 6 minutes altogether. Add quite a bit of butter (melted), a dash of lemon, fresh pepper and salt and the artichoke hearts, drained and cut up. A little chopped onion adds flavor. You may use hollandaise instead of butter if you want a richer dish.

Mrs. J. Harrison Worrall
Philadelphia, Pennsylvania

Broccoli stems will cook as rapidly as flowerets if you make an X incision at base of stem. Also use this method for pearl onions and Brussels sprouts.

SPINACH STUFFED MUSHROOMS WITH CRAB SAUCE

Average

Serves: 6-8
Preparing: 20 minutes
Cooking: 20 minutes

1 pound large, fresh
  mushrooms
1 12-ounce package frozen
  spinach soufflé, thawed

butter
Parmesan cheese

Creamy crabmeat sauce

2 tablespoons butter
1 tablespoon flour
1 cup half and half
salt and pepper

1 6-ounce package frozen
  crab, thawed and drained
2 tablespoons sherry
½ cup shredded cheddar cheese,
  divided

Wash, dry and remove stems from mushrooms. Set aside. Place caps on greased baking sheet. Fill with spinach soufflé. Dot with butter and sprinkle with Parmesan. Bake at 350° for 20 minutes or until brown. Spoon crabmeat sauce on top.

To make sauce: Melt butter; blend in flour. Cook until bubbly, stirring constantly. Gradually add half and half. Stir until thickened. Add salt and pepper to taste. Remove from heat. Stir in crabmeat, sherry and one-half of the cheese. Add remaining cheese and cook over low heat until heated through.

Mrs. R. G. Counselman
Wayne, Pennsylvania

TOMATOES ALBERT

Easy
Do ahead

Serves: 6
Preparing: 10 minutes
Cooking: 5 minutes

6 medium-sized tomatoes
2 tablespoons mayonnaise
2-4 teaspoons curry powder
2 tablespoons capers

3 tablespoons fine bread crumbs
dash of cayenne pepper
 (optional)

Topping:

coarse bread crumbs
finely grated Romano cheese

unsalted butter

Cut tops off tomatoes at level permitting access to side pulp and seed compartments; these are to be cleaned of pulp and seeds, (use little finger). Mix mayonnaise, curry powder, capers and fine bread crumbs. Add dash of cayenne pepper. Stuff each emptied side compartment with mayonnaise mixture. Top each tomato with coarse bread crumbs, layer on Romano cheese. Top with slab of unsalted butter. Store in cool place until ready to use. Place under broiler for 5 minutes, or until tops are nicely browned and tomatoes slightly warmed.

Christopher D'Amanda, M. D.
Philadelphia, Pennsylvania

ZUCCHINI PANCAKES

Easy
Partial do ahead

Serves: 4
Preparing: 30 minutes
Cooking: 10 minutes

2 cups grated zucchini
2 large eggs, beaten
¼ cup minced onion
½ cup flour

½ teaspoon baking powder
½ teaspoon salt
¼ teaspoon oregano

Place zucchini in strainer. Press out as much moisture as possible. Mix with eggs and onion in small bowl. Combine dry ingredients and stir into zucchini mixture. Heat oil in skillet over medium heat. Drop mixture by tablespoons and brown lightly on both sides. Serve with lemon wedge and a dot of butter, or a dollop of sour cream.

Mrs. John F. Lloyd
Ardmore, Pennsylvania

FRUITED BULGUR

Easy

Serves: 8
Preparing: 15 minutes
Baking: 45 minutes

1 large onion, minced
¾ cup slivered, blanched
  almonds
¼ cup butter
1 pound bulgur

4½ cups chicken stock
¾ cup dried apricots, coarsely
  chopped
4 tablespoons dried currants

Sauté minced onion and ¾ cup of slivered almonds in ¼ cup butter until golden. Add 1 pound of bulgur and cook until well mixed. Add the chicken stock, apricots, and currants. Place in casserole and bake, covered, in preheated 350° oven for 45 minutes or until all the liquid is absorbed.

Mrs. Toba Schwaber Kerson
Bryn Mawr, Pennsylvania

EASY, QUICK CORN PUDDING

Easy
Do ahead

Serves: 6-8
Preparing: 10 minutes
Baking: 1 hour

1 16-ounce can cream-style
  corn
1 large can evaporated milk
2 eggs

⅓ cup sugar
¼ teaspoon salt
¼ cup flour
4 tablespoons butter

Beat the eggs into corn. Add sugar, salt and flour. Stir in milk. Put butter in center of pudding. Bake in 350° oven for 1 hour. Stir pudding three or four times during the first 20 minutes of cooking so that the butter is mixed throughout the pudding.

Mrs. Anthony Cucchi
King of Prussia, Pennsylvania

BROCCOLI STRATA

Easy
Do ahead

Serves: 6-8
Preparing: 30 minutes
Chilling: 1 hour
Baking: 1 hour

1 10-ounce package frozen
   chopped broccoli
6 slices rye bread
4 slices American cheese
4 slices Swiss cheese,
   shredded
4 eggs

2 cups milk
1 tablespoon chopped onion
1 teaspoon salt
1 2-ounce jar pimientos, drained
   and chopped
½ teaspoon prepared mustard
2 tablespoons melted butter

Cook broccoli, covered, in boiling salted water for 3 minutes. Drain well. Toast 4 slices bread. Arrange in 9" x 9" x 2" baking dish. Top with American cheese, broccoli, pimiento. Beat eggs; blend in milk, onion, salt, mustard, dash pepper. Pour over casserole. Cover. Refrigerate at least one hour. Tear 2 slices bread into blender and make crumbs. Combine with melted butter. Sprinkle on Swiss cheese. Top with crumbs and bake uncovered at 350° for 60-65 minutes.

Mary G. Brennan
Winchester, Massachusetts

ZUCCHINI

Easy

Serves: 3-4 as main dish
6 as vegetable
Preparing: 20 minutes
Baking: 30-45 minutes

3 cups thinly sliced zucchini
   (unpared)
4 eggs, slightly beaten
½ teaspoon salt
½ teaspoon seasoned salt
½ teaspoon dried oregano

dash pepper
½ cup vegetable oil
½ cup chopped onion
½ cup grated Parmesan cheese
2 tablespoons snipped parsley
1 cup Bisquick

Beat eggs with seasonings; stir in oil. Mix with all other ingredients, adding zucchini last. Bake in greased 9"x13" pan, 350° for 30-45 minutes, until golden brown.

Mrs. Marvin D. Heaps
Swarthmore, Pennsylvania

MARIE'S BAKED BEANS

Average
Do ahead

Serves: 4 to 6
Preparing: 15 minutes
Soaking: overnight
Baking: 4 to 5 hours

¾ pound California small
  white beans
½ teaspoon baking soda
¼ pound lean salt pork
1 teaspoon dry mustard

⅓ cup dark molasses
1 teaspoon salt
2 tablespoons brown sugar
½ teaspoon black pepper
1 medium onion, chopped

Sort beans and rinse. Soak overnight in cold water. Par-boil in the morning with soda. Rinse beans in a colander. Mix all seasonings and put in a bean pot. Add pork and chopped onion. Add beans on top and cover all with boiling water. Bake covered, 4 to 5 hours in a 275° oven. The last hour, uncover and bring pork to top of pot and let brown. Add water if needed.

Mrs. Raymond Elliott
Framingham, Massachusetts

BROCCOLI AND RICE CASSEROLE

Easy

Serves: 10-12
Preparing: 20 minutes
Baking: 45 minutes

3 tablespoons butter
1 8-ounce jar Cheeze-Whiz,
  room temperature
1 can cream of chicken soup,
  undiluted
½ cup milk

1 8-ounce can water chestnuts,
  sliced thin
¼ cup chopped onions
1 cup instant rice, uncooked
1 package frozen broccoli,
  thawed

Place butter in bottom of casserole dish in 3 chunks. Stir in Cheeze-Whiz. Add and mix one at a time: chicken soup, milk, water chestnuts, onions, rice and broccoli. Bake for 45 minutes at 350°.

Roxane Rewalt Hunt
Philadelphia, Pennsylvania
Anne Fagan
Broomall, Pennsylvania

TWICE BAKED YAMS

Easy
Do ahead

Serves: 6
Preparing: 15 minutes
Cooking: 1 hour and 20 minutes

6 medium yams
1 teaspoon salt
ground nutmeg

½ cup apricot preserves
¼ cup butter or margarine
orange juice

Bake yams until done, about one hour. Cut slice off top of each yam and scoop out the inside, being careful not to break skin. In mixing bowl mash the potatoes and add the preserves, butter, salt and enough orange juice to moisten; beat until fluffy. Pile lightly into shells and sprinkle with nutmeg. Bake at 350° until heated through for 15-20 minutes.

Mrs. Malissa Carter
Sedgwick, Maine

"Quick Soak Method for Wild Rice." Wash rice in cold water before stirring it into 3 times the amount of boiling water. Parboil for 5 minutes only. Remove from heat. Let stand in the same water covered for 1 hour. Drain, wash and cook as directed.

BAKED WILD RICE

Easy
Do ahead
Freeze

Serves: 10-12
Preparing: 10 minutes
Cooking: 1 hour, 20 minutes

1 box Uncle Ben's Rice with
Seasonings
¼ cup wild rice
1 medium onion
½ pound mushrooms

1 can water chestnuts
¼ cup butter
1 can Campbell's consommé
1 cup Chablis or Burgundy

Pour contents of Uncle Ben's rice with seasonings into slightly greased casserole. Wash and drain wild rice and add to casserole. Sauté chopped onion and mushrooms that are sliced and slice can of water chestnuts. Add to rice mixture, stir in consommé and wine. Cover with foil tightly and bake at 325° for one hour 20 minutes. Make early in day and pop in oven when desired.

Mrs. Victor H. Johnson
Madison, Wisconsin

CELERIAC WITH CREAMED SPINACH

Average
Do ahead

Serves: 6
Preparing: 30 minutes
Baking: 15 minutes

2 knobs celeriac (or 1 #2 can artichoke bottoms)
chicken stock to cover
2 packages frozen spinach
2 tablespoons butter
1 tablespoon flour

½ cup milk
salt
garlic powder
nutmeg
lemon juice

Scrub celeriac; peel and shape it with a vegetable peeler. Cut crosswise to form discs the size of artichoke bottoms. Cook in chicken stock until tender. Cook spinach according to the directions on the package. Make a cream sauce with the butter, flour, and milk. Add the salt, garlic powder and nutmeg. Combine with the spinach and mound on the 6 celeriac rounds. Squeeze lemon juice on each one and heat in 375° oven for 15 minutes.

Mrs. David Acton
Haverford, Pennsylvania

BAKED ONIONS AND RICE

Easy
Do ahead

Serves: 6
Preparing: 15 minutes
Baking: 20 minutes

2 cups cooked rice
8 onions
2 tablespoons butter
2 tablespoons flour
1 cup milk

¾ cup grated sharp cheddar cheese
cayenne pepper
1 teaspoon salt

Pare the onions under water and parboil them until tender, changing the water once. Slice. Make a sauce by melting the butter, adding the flour, salt, a pinch of pepper and the milk. Cook mixture until it is smooth. Let it cool and add grated cheese. Bring sauce to boiling point, stirring constantly. Place in a baking dish in alternate layers of rice and sliced onions. Pour on the cheese sauce. Bake in 350° oven for 20 minutes.

Mrs. John F. Daley, Jr.
West Chester, Pennsylvania

STIR FRIED VEGETABLES

Easy
Partial do ahead

Serves: 6-8
Preparing: 15 minutes
Cooking: 20 minutes

1 bunch fresh broccoli
  (stems cut into ¼" slices,
  flowerets broken)
1 medium onion or bunch of
  scallions, chopped
2 medium carrots, sliced ¼"
  thick

mushrooms (optional)
1 to 2 cloves garlic, minced
1 teaspoon fresh grated ginger
3 tablespoons peanut, safflower
  or corn oil
¼ cup (scant) soy sauce

Heat oil and garlic in wok, or large fry pan. Add sliced broccoli stems and carrots. Stir fry on high heat until slightly tender (about 10 minutes). Add chopped onions and soy sauce. Then add zucchini and grated ginger and other vegetables, stirring all the time to coat vegetables with soy sauce and oil. The whole cooking time should take 15-20 minutes. This is one of those recipes where amounts and times aren't crucial. You just want the vegetables to be a little crisp. Serve on brown rice or plain.

Julie and Neil Courtney
Springfield, Pennsylvania

MARINATED CARROTS

Easy
Do ahead

Serves: 8
Preparing: 20 minutes
Marinating: 24 hours

1 pound carrots
3 tablespoons salad oil
3 cloves garlic, minced
1 tablespoon coarsely
  chopped onion

¼ cup vinegar
1½ teaspoons salt
½ teaspoon dry mustard
1 tablespoon pickling spices
⅛ teaspoon pepper

Pare carrots and cut into ¼" strips and then into 3" pieces. Heat in a large skillet and sauté garlic and onion for five minutes; then add vinegar and salt. Wrap mustard, pickling spice and pepper in cheesecloth. Place carrots in the skillet with the spice bag. Simmer, covered, 5 minutes until crisp. Remove spice bag. Pour remaining contents into a jar and refrigerate 24 hours. Drain to serve.

Mrs. J. Wilson Borden, Jr.
Bryn Mawr, Pennsylvania

POTATOES LOUIS

Average

Serves: 6
Preparing: 15 minutes
Cooking: 20-30 minutes

6 medium sized potatoes
2 tablespoons butter
¼ pound lean bacon
2 tablespoons flour

1 cup stock or water
salt and pepper to taste
bouquet garni

Wash, peel and cube the potatoes. Melt butter in a heavy saucepan. Dice the bacon and fry lightly in the butter until golden brown. Stir in flour, and when it begins to darken, add stock, bouquet garni and then potatoes. Cover and simmer 20-30 minutes.

Mrs. Louis Hood
Wayne, Pennsylvania

CREAMED ONIONS

Easy
Do ahead

Serves: 10
Preparing: 20 minutes
Baking: 45 minutes

3 Bermuda onions, sliced in
  ¼" rings
3 tablespoons butter
¾ pound grated Swiss
  cheese

1 can cream of chicken soup
½ cup milk
2 slices white bread, cubed
10 slices party rye, buttered

Slice onions in ¼" rings and glaze in butter until golden, not brown. Put in 2½-quart casserole. Combine cheese, chicken soup and milk. Stir until smooth. Add bread cubes to onions and pour sauce over all. Place buttered party rye on top and bake in 350° oven for 40-45 minutes.

Mrs. Frank McKaig
Gulph Mills, Pennsylvania

MUSHROOMS PROVENÇALE

Easy

Serves: 6
Preparing: 10 minutes
Cooking: 15 minutes

2 cups sliced mushrooms*
1 cup finely chopped
    mushrooms*
2 tablespoons oil
1 tablespoon chopped
    shallots

1 tablespoon white bread crumbs
1 clove garlic, chopped
1 tablespoon chopped parsley
lemon juice to taste
salt and pepper to taste

*The *combined* total of mushrooms required for this recipe is about 1 pound.

Warm oil in saucepan until very hot. Add 2 cups mushrooms, salt, pepper. Sauté until lightly brown. Add remaining cup of mushrooms, chopped fine. Add shallots and garlic and sauté for 3 minutes more. Add bread crumbs and lemon juice. Simmer 1 minute. Add parsley and serve at once.

Heinz Vollrath
Acorn Club Chef
Philadelphia, Pennsylvania

STUFFED MUSHROOMS

Easy

Serves: 8
Preparing: 10 minutes
Baking: 30 minutes

16 large mushrooms and
    stems
2 tablespoons butter
1 tablespoon green onion,
    chopped very fine
1 cup fine bread crumbs (2½
    slices)

1 teaspoon salt
¼ teaspoon black pepper
1 tablespoon lemon juice
1 cup cream
parsley

Wash mushrooms in cold salted water. Remove stems and chop fine. Sauté stems and onions in butter. Add bread crumbs, seasoning and juice. Cook 2 minutes. Stuff mushrooms with sautéed mixture. Place in shallow baking dish and pour in cream, (small amount over top, the rest in bottom of pan). Bake 30 minutes in 350° oven. Garnish with chopped parsley.

Mrs. Harold S. Strickland
Greenwich, Connecticut

TOMATO SOUFFLÉ

Easy

Serves: 24
Preparing: 30 minutes
Cooking: 1 hour, 15 minutes

1 cup butter
1½ cups flour
1 quart hot milk
3 cups condensed tomato
   soup
1 cup tomato purée

1¼ cups egg yolks
2 cups grated Parmesan cheese
½ teaspoon salt
2½ cups egg whites
½ teaspoon cream of tartar
¼ teaspoon salt

Melt butter. Blend in flour. Cook over low heat 10 minutes, stirring occasionally. Combine milk, soup and purée. Add to roux. Cook, stirring constantly, until thick and smooth. Beat yolks until thick. Add an equal amount of hot tomato sauce and mix. Beat whites with salt and cream of tartar until stiff but not dry. Fold into hot sauce. Mix gently until thoroughly combined. Pour 3 inches deep into greased baking dish. Place in ¼" deep hot water bath. Bake in 350° oven until set and browned, about 1¼ hours. Serve immediately.

K. Carol Carlson, Vice-President
ARA Services
Philadelphia, Pennsylvania

POTATOES SUPREME

Easy
Do ahead
Freeze

Serves: 12-14
Preparing: 15-20 minutes
Baking: 1 hour

2 pounds frozen hash brown
   potatoes
½ cup melted butter
1 teaspoon salt
½ teaspoon pepper
½ cup chopped onions

2 cups grated sharp cheese
1 pint sour cream
1 can cream of chicken soup,
   undiluted
2 cups fresh buttered
   bread crumbs

Defrost potatoes and combine in large bowl with butter. Add rest of ingredients, except crumbs. Put in 3-quart buttered casserole. Top with crumbs. Bake at 350° for one hour.

Mrs. Herbert Blades
St. Davids, Pennsylvania

SESAME POTATOES

Average

Serves: 6
Preparing: 20 minutes
Baking: 15-20 minutes

**2 pounds large, fresh boiling
  potatoes, peeled
3 ounces butter, melted
salt**

**white pepper
paprika
½ cup sesame seeds**

Slice potatoes ⅛" thick. Drop in boiling salted water. Boil approximately 5 minutes until potatoes' consistency is firm when pierced with fork. Drain immediately. Pour melted butter into roasting pan then put sliced potatoes into pan. Season with salt, white pepper and paprika. Add sesame seeds. Mix thoroughly in roasting pan. Incorporate all ingredients. Bake in 400° oven until potatoes are fully cooked and crunchy (similar to potato chips).

PAGE'S SWEET CORN

Easy
Do ahead

Serves: 6
Preparing: 20 minutes
Cooking: 1 hour

**14 ears fresh corn
½ cup butter**

**salt and pepper to taste
¾ cup brown sugar**

Scrape kernels off corn, preferably with corn scraper (to break kernels and make corn creamy). Add butter broken into pieces. Salt and pepper. Top with brown sugar. Bake in 325° oven 1 hour or longer, until top is golden brown and corn is not runny.

Mrs. L. Rodman Page, Jr.
Radnor, Pennsylvania

CHAMPAGNE-KRAUT

Easy
Do ahead

Serves: 6
Preparing: 10 minutes
Cooking: 45 minutes

**1 pound sauerkraut
½ fresh pineapple
1 tablespoon honey**

**1 piccolo champagne (split or ½
  bottle)
cayenne pepper**

Drain kraut before putting it in an open pot with water to barely cover. Simmer 15 minutes. Add pineapple which has been diced, and bring to a boil. After 3 minutes reduce heat and simmer for 20 minutes; stir occasionally. Add champagne, stir lightly and keep at low simmer for 15 minutes.

Mrs. Lille Eckholdt
Liederback, Taunus
West Germany

ASPARAGUS SUPREME

Easy
Do ahead
Freeze

Serves: 4-6
Preparing: 15 minutes
Baking: 30-35 minutes

4 cups fresh asparagus, or 2 8-ounce packages frozen cut asparagus
1 can cream of shrimp soup
2 tablespoons coarsely shredded carrot

½ cup sour cream
1 teaspoon grated onion
⅛ teaspoon pepper
½ cup herb seasoned stuffing

Cook asparagus in water. Drain. Combine soup, sour cream, carrot, onion and pepper. Fold in asparagus. Bake uncovered in 350° oven for 30 to 35 minutes. For microwave, bake uncovered for 8 minutes on "high".

Mrs. George Phillips
Nashua, New Hampshire

BROILED TOMATO CUPS

Easy
Partial do ahead

Serves: 10 to 12
Preparing: 10 minutes
Broiling: 5 minutes

5 to 6 tomatoes
½ cup sour cream
½ cup mayonnaise
¼ cup grated Parmesan cheese

1 teaspoon garlic salt
juice of 1 lemon
1 teaspoon chopped parsley
3 green onions, chopped

Cut tomatoes in half crosswise. Combine remaining ingredients, blending well. Top each tomato half with small amount of mixture. Broil until bubbly.

Mrs. William G. Kay, Jr.
Bryn Mawr, Pennsylvania

MUSHROOMS AND SOUR CREAM CASSEROLE

Easy

Serves: 8-10
Preparing: 20 minutes
Baking: 1 hour

6 tablespoons butter
3 tablespoons flour
1 16-ounce carton sour
   cream
¼ cup minced onion
¼ cup minced parsley
2 teaspoons salt

2 teaspoons prepared mustard
½ teaspoon lemon juice
¼ teaspoon ground nutmeg
¼ teaspoon pepper
2 pounds fresh mushrooms,
   sliced

Melt butter in saucepan over low heat. Blend in flour. Cook 1 to 2 minutes, stirring constantly. Stir in sour cream. Add remaining ingredients, except mushrooms and cook until heated through. Remove from heat.

Combine sauce and mushrooms; pour into a greased 2½-quart casserole and bake at 350° for 1 hour, stirring occasionally.

Mrs. R. G. Counselman
Wayne, Pennsylvania

CALIFORNIA BEAN CASSEROLE

Average
Do ahead
Freeze

Serves: 10
Preparing: 20 minutes
Baking: 30 minutes

2 packages frozen French
   green beans
2 tablespoons butter
2 tablespoons minced onion
8 ounces bean sprouts

1 cup mushroom soup
1 12-ounce can water chestnuts
½ soup can milk
½ cup shredded cheddar cheese
1 3⅓-ounce can onion rings

Cook beans; drain; set aside. Melt butter in pan. Add onion, sprouts, and water chestnuts. Cover pan; cook 3 minutes. Arrange ½ beans in buttered 2½-quart casserole. Spread ½ sprout mixture over this. Combine soup and milk. Spoon ½ over vegetables. Repeat layers. Sprinkle cheese over this. Bake at 400° for 25 minutes. Remove from oven; cover with onion rings. Return to oven and bake 5 minutes more.

Mrs. James B. DuHamel
Los Altos, California

RICE AND CHEESE CASSEROLE

Easy

Serves: 8
Preparing: 20 minutes
Baking: 30 minutes

1 cup onions
¼ cup butter
4 cups cooked rice
2 bay leaves
2 cups sour cream
1 cup cream-style cottage
  cheese

½ teaspoon salt
¼ teaspoon pepper
3 4-ounce cans green chilies,
  drained
2 cups cheddar cheese, grated

Grease 12" x 8" x 2" casserole. Sauté onions in butter. Mix with rice and bay leaves. Add sour cream, cottage cheese, salt and pepper. Layer rice mixture, chilies, grated cheese. Do this twice. Bake in 350° oven for 30 minutes until bubbly around edges.

Mrs. Robert O. Bach
Gladwyne, Pennsylvania

Rice will be fluffier and drier if a slice of dry bread is put on top of it after cooking and draining.

TOMATOES FLORENTINE

Easy

Serves: 6
Preparing: 10 minutes
Baking: 15 minutes

½ cup milk
1½ tablespoons flour
1½ tablespoons butter
¾ teaspoon dried basil, or ½
  teaspoon fresh

salt and pepper to taste
bread crumbs
1 package frozen, chopped
  spinach
6-8 ripe medium-sized tomatoes

Melt butter in saucepan. Stir in flour, then milk to make a thick cream sauce. Add basil, well-drained spinach, salt and pepper. Cut tops from tomatoes and hollow. Mix some of tomato pulp with spinach. Stuff mixture into tomato shells. Sprinkle with bread crumbs and bake at 350° for 15 minutes.

Sally Hood
Amherst, Massachusetts

STUFFED TOMATOES A LA DUCHESSE

Easy
Partial do ahead

Serves: 6-12
Preparing: 20 minutes
Baking: 15 minutes

**12 medium sized firm
  tomatoes
1 pound white potatoes**

**¼ pound butter
3 egg yolks
1 ounce grated cheddar cheese**

Wash and dry the tomatoes. Slice off the top of each and carefully remove core and seeds. Turn tomatoes upside down to drain while preparing the stuffing. Boil the peeled potatoes in salted water for 20 minutes. Drain well and dry potatoes in the pan over a low heat. Using a potato masher or a fork, mash the potatoes in the pan until free of lumps. Add the butter and a few drops of milk and put the pan over a gentle heat. Beat until dry, light and fluffy. Season and add the egg yolks. Season the inside of the drained tomatoes with salt and pepper and fill with the potato stuffing. Sprinkle with grated cheese, spoon over with a little melted butter and arrange in a well-buttered ovenproof dish. Bake in a preheated oven 425° for approximately 15 minutes, or until the tomatoes are tender but still retaining their shape.

Hofgut-Neuhof
Frankfurt Am Main, West Germany

BEETS WITH MANDARIN ORANGES

Easy
Do ahead

Serves: 6
Preparing: 15 minutes

**2 #1 cans of small, whole
  beets, drained
1 11-ounce can of Mandarin
  oranges, drained
½ cup sugar**

**1½ teaspoons cornstarch
2 tablespoons lemon juice
½ cup dry wine (white or red)
2 tablespoons butter**

Drain and set aside beets and Mandarin oranges.

In saucepan combine sugar, cornstarch, lemon juice, wine, butter. Cook over moderate heat, stirring constantly. When sauce is clear, add beets and oranges; then pour complete contents into casserole and store uncovered in moderate oven to keep warm. If preparing ahead, heat in moderate oven prior to serving.

Mary L. Winstanley
Abington, Pennsylvania

VEGETABLE GUMBO CRÊOLE

Average

Serves: 8-10
Preparing: ½ hour
Baking: 1 hour

2 packages frozen okra (or 1 pound of fresh okra) cut crosswise
2 packages frozen lima beans
2 green peppers, chopped
4 medium tomatoes, sliced crosswise

2 packages frozen corn (or 8 ears of fresh corn, cut off cob)
1 small bunch of celery, coarsely chopped
bread crumbs
butter

Partially cook lima beans in salted water and then add corn. Add green peppers, okra and celery and cook until just done. Drain. Place a layer of the vegetable mixture (reserve part of okra for top layer) in a buttered and crumbed baking dish. Then add a layer of tomatoes. Season with salt and pepper; dot with butter and bread crumbs. Repeat until casserole is filled. On top, place a layer of okra that has been dipped in bread crumbs and sautéed in a little butter. Cover with bread crumbs and dot with butter. Bake in 300° oven for about 1 hour. It can be cooked in the morning and reheated slowly before serving. It's even better the second day.

Dinah Shore
With permission of Doubleday & Company
publishers of *Someone's In The Kitchen with Dinah*

FLUFFY TURNIPS

Easy

Serves: 6
Preparing: 30 minutes
Baking: 20 minutes

6 medium turnips
2 egg yolks
1 teaspoon salt
dash of cayenne

⅛ teaspoon basil
1 teaspoon grated lemon rind
2 egg whites
2 tablespoons brown sugar

Cook cubed turnips until tender, about 20 minutes; drain and mash. Beat egg yolks and add to turnips along with salt, pepper, basil and lemon rind. Beat egg whites and fold gently into turnip mixture. Pour into casserole, sprinkle with brown sugar and bake 20 minutes.

The White House
Washington, District of Columbia

PECAN TOPPED SWEET POTATOES

Easy
Do ahead

Serves: 10-12
Preparing: 20 minutes
Baking: 30 minutes

3 pounds sweet potatoes or
  yams, cooked and peeled
2 eggs
¾ cup brown sugar
¼ pound melted butter
1 teaspoon salt

1 teaspoon cinnamon
1 teaspoon vanilla
½ teaspoon nutmeg
½ cup orange juice
1 cup pecan halves, chopped

Mash sweet potatoes (you should have about 6 cups). Beat in eggs, ¼ cup of the brown sugar, 12 tablespoons butter, salt, cinnamon, vanilla and nutmeg. If potatoes seem dry, beat in orange juice until light and fluffy. Put in a 2-quart casserole. (Refrigerate if you wish). Before baking, sprinkle on pecans and remaining ½ cup brown sugar. Drizzle with remaining butter. Bake uncovered in 375° oven for 30 minutes or until heated through.

Mrs. Walter C. Bass, Jr.
Radnor, Pennsylvania

GREEN BEAN CASSEROLE

Easy

Serves: 6
Preparing: 30 minutes
Baking: 40 minutes

2 pounds green beans
dash of sugar
salt and pepper, to taste
2 sliced onions
3 sliced tomatoes
8 strips bacon, cooked

6 tablespoons butter
2 teaspoons prepared mustard
1 teaspoon horseradish
6 tablespoons brown sugar
1½ teaspoons salt
dash of pepper

Boil green beans in water with salt, pepper and sugar for 10 minutes. Drain and put into casserole. Add and layer: sliced onions, sliced tomatoes, 8 strips bacon, cooked. Mix in saucepan over low heat; butter, prepared mustard, horseradish, brown sugar, salt and pepper. Heat, stir, pour over beans. Bake at 400° for 40 to 50 minutes for canned or frozen beans. Bake 40-45 minutes for fresh beans.

Mrs. Glenn Krieder
West Chester, Pennsylvania

OKRA FRITTERS

Serves: 6
Preparing: 15 minutes
Cooking: 15 minutes

1 cup thinly sliced okra	**½ teaspoon salt**
½ cup chopped onion	**½ teaspoon curry powder**
½ cup chopped tomato	**¼ teaspoon pepper**
¼ cup all-purpose flour	**1 egg, beaten**
¼ cup corn meal	**hot peanut oil**

Combine first nine ingredients, stirring well. Drop by tablespoonfuls into hot oil. Cook until golden brown, turning once.

Mrs. John M. Brownback
New Orleans, Louisiana

MUENSTER POTATOES IN GLASS

Easy

Serves: 6
Preparing: 45 minutes

6 medium potatoes	**salt and pepper to taste**
2 tablespoons butter	**½ cup heavy cream**
1 medium onion, chopped	**1 cup grated Muenster cheese**
2 large tomatoes	**¼ cup chopped parsley**

Cook potatoes until tender in salted water. Drain and peel. Sauté the onion in butter until tender. Peel and chop the tomatoes and add to the onions, cooking for five minutes and stirring frequently. Season and stir in cream and cheese, cooking over low heat until cheese is partially melted. Pour sauce over hot potatoes and serve in glass casserole.

Mrs. John W. Hagen
Libertyville, Illinois

SQUASH YUMMY

Easy
Do ahead
Freeze

Serves: 8
Preparing: 30 minutes
Cooking: 45 minutes

1½ pounds yellow squash
1 carrot
1 onion
2½ sticks margarine
2 cups (1 8-ounce bag)
  Pepperidge Farm stuffing
  mix

½ cup sour cream
1 small jar sliced pimiento
1 can cream of chicken soup

Slice squash, carrot, onion and cook in slightly salted water. Mix stuffing mix with melted margarine and place one cup in bottom of casserole. Place squash mixture on top. Pour mixture of sour cream, pimiento and soup on top. Cover with remainder of crumbs. Bake at 350° for 45 minutes.

Mrs. Alfred Rauch, Jr.
Haverford, Pennsylvania

For festive occasions, barely heat ½ cup of cherry tomatoes and toss over a green vegetable.

SPINACH ARTICHOKE CASSEROLE

Easy
Do ahead

Serves: 8-10
Preparing: 20 minutes
Baking: 30 minutes

3 packages frozen chopped
  spinach
2 jars marinated artichoke
  hearts
8 ounces sour cream

3 tablespoons butter
⅔ package Knorr Leek Soup Mix
salt and pepper to taste
½ package Pepperidge Farm
  seasoned stuffing

Cook spinach, drain well, removing as much water as possible. Add butter to spinach. Mix sour cream and soup mix together and add to spinach. Drain artichoke hearts, cut into pieces and place in bottom of flat casserole. Spread spinach mixture over artichokes. Top with stuffing crumbs. Bake at 350° for 30 minutes.

Mrs. Benjamin Quigg, Jr.
Jenkintown, Pennsylvania

CAULIFLOWER AND TOMATO AU GRATIN

Easy
Do ahead

Serves: 6
Preparing: 20 minutes
Baking: 30 minutes

1 head cauliflower
1 cup grated American
cheese
2 medium onions
5 sprigs parsley
3 tablespoons butter

3 tablespoons bread crumbs
1 16-ounce can tomatoes
1 bouillon cube
1 tablespoon sugar
1 teaspoon salt
dash pepper

Cook cauliflower as usual. Drain and toss sections with ¾ cup cheese. Chop onions and parsley and cook in butter until limp. To this, add tomatoes, bouillon cube, sugar, salt and pepper and crumbs. Cook slowly five minutes. Put ½ tomato mixture in bottom of buttered casserole. Add cauliflower and top with remaining sauce. Sprinkle remaining cheese on top. Bake 30 minutes in 350° oven.

Radford Beasley
Philadelphia, Pennsylvania

BAKED POTATOES IN CREAM

Easy
Do ahead
Freeze

Serves: 6
Preparing: 15-20 minutes
Baking: 2 hours

5 large baking potatoes
1 large garlic clove
2 pints of heavy cream (1½
might do, depending on
shallowness of baking
dish)

½ cup Gruyère or Swiss cheese,
grated
salt
freshly ground pepper

Peel potatoes and place in cold water. Preheat oven to 300°. Mince garlic. Butter casserole. Dry and thinly slice one potato at a time. Place a layer of potatoes in casserole. Sprinkle with garlic, salt and plenty of pepper. Pour cream over to just about cover. Repeat procedure. Bake for 1½ hours. Sprinkle with cheese and bake 30 minutes more.

E. Jane Thiry
Jenkintown, Pennsylvania

POTATOES CRISTINA

Easy
Do ahead

Serves: 4-6
Baking: 20-25 minutes

2 pounds potatoes
2 eggs
½ cup Parmesan cheese
1 pinch nutmeg
4 ounces Mozzarella cheese

2 thick slices of Mortadella,
  (Italian cold cut), cut in cubes
1 handful breadcrumbs
2 tablespoons pure olive oil
salt and pepper to taste

Boil the potatoes. Peel them and make a purée. Add to this purée: salt, pepper and nutmeg to taste. Add Parmesan, milk and two eggs. Mix these ingredients well and put one layer (one inch) in a well-oiled casserole. On the first layer, put some slices of Mozzarella, slightly salted, and a sprinkling of Parmesan cheese. Add a second layer of purée, then some pieces of Mortadella with another sprinkling of cheese. Add a third layer of purée. Continue as before until all ingredients are used. On top put a layer of bread crumbs. Sprinkle with oil. Bake at 350° for 20-25 minutes. Cool slightly before serving, so that it is not too soft.

Mrs. Riccardo Muti
Ravenna, Italy

GREEN TOMATO CASSEROLE

Easy
Partial do ahead

Serves: 8
Preparing: 15 minutes
Baking: 30 minutes

8 green tomatoes, sliced
2 onions, sliced
½ stick margarine
1 teaspoon curry powder

1 cup sour cream
½ cup bread crumbs
¼ cup Parmesan cheese, grated
salt and pepper to taste

Sauté tomatoes and onions in margarine until tender. Add curry powder, salt and pepper. After mixture has cooled, stir in sour cream. Pour in shallow 2-quart casserole. Top with bread crumbs and cheese. Bake 30 minutes at 350°.

Mrs. William Lander
Villanova, Pennsylvania

BRUSSELS SPROUTS TRIMMER

Easy
Partial do ahead

Serves: 1 pint serves 3-5
' 1 quart serves 4-8
Preparing: 40 minutes
Cooking: 10 minutes

1 pint or 1 quart Brussels
  sprouts
Spice Islands chicken stock
2 bay leaves
6 whole cloves

1 small onion
4 tablespoons butter
garlic powder
salt to taste

Remove any spotted or dried outside leaves from sprouts. Cut off excess stem. Soak for minimum of 30 minutes in warm salted water. To one quart water for 1 pint sprouts, (1½ quarts water for 1 quart sprouts), add 2-3 teaspoons Spice Islands chicken stock, bay leaves, cloves, and onion. Add drained sprouts and cook until tender. Drain well. Melt butter in large frying pan, add sprouts. Sprinkle with powdered garlic and sauté until delicately browned.

Allen Trimmer
Hopetown, Abaco, Bahamas

HERBED SPINACH BAKE

Average
Do ahead

Serves: 6
Preparing: 30 minutes
Baking: 20 minutes

1 package frozen chopped
  spinach, cooked and
  drained
1 cup cooked rice
1 cup shredded sharp
  cheddar cheese
2 eggs, slightly beaten
⅓ cup milk

2 tablespoons margarine,
  softened
2 tablespoons chopped onion
½ teaspoon Worcestershire
  sauce
1 teaspoon salt
¼ teaspoon rosemary or thyme

Combine all ingredients and blend well. Pour into 10" x 6" x 1½" baking dish and bake for 20 minutes at 350° or until knife inserted in center comes out clean.

Betty Dexter
Philadelphia, Pennsylvania

JOAN'S MUSHROOM CASSEROLE

Easy
Do ahead
Freeze

Serves: 8
Preparing: 15 minutes
Chilling: 1 hour
Baking: 1 hour

1 pound mushrooms
8 slices white bread
salt
1 teaspoon celery salt
a little grated onion
¼ pound butter
½ cup mayonnaise

2 eggs, lightly beaten
1 cup milk
½ cup sherry
1 can condensed mushroom
  soup
½ cup sharp grated cheese

Sauté mushrooms. Butter three slices of bread. Cut into 1" squares and put in casserole. Combine mushrooms with salt, seasonings, mayonnaise, onion and spread over bread. Put three more slices of cubed and buttered bread on top. Beat eggs, add milk and pour over all. Refrigerate at least one hour or overnight. One hour before planning to serve spoon on mushroom soup, mixed with sherry and two more slices cubed buttered bread. Bake at 325° for 1 hour. Sprinkle grated cheese on top for last 10 minutes.

Mrs. John V. Calhoun, Jr.
Devon, Pennsylvania

EGGPLANT ANATOLIAN

Average
Do ahead
Freeze

Serves: 6
Preparing: 30 minutes
Cooking: 15 minutes

1 eggplant, peeled and cubed
1 onion, finely chopped
salt and pepper to taste
½ cup salad oil
1 small can tomato paste

½ green pepper, chopped
2 tomatoes, peeled and chopped
juice of 1 lemon
2 cloves garlic, crushed

Brown eggplant in onion and salad oil for 10 minutes. Simmer remaining ingredients for 15 minutes. Combine and serve over fluffy white rice with lemon wedges.

Mrs. T. Wistar Brown
Bryn Mawr, Pennsylvania

VEGETABLES AU GRATIN

Easy
Do ahead

Serves: 6
Preparing: 30 minutes
Baking: 50 minutes

1 12-ounce can shoe peg
  corn
1 pound can Italian tomatoes
  (drained)
2 8-ounce jars onions,
  drained
¼ cup butter
¾ cup green pepper, diced
1 clove garlic, crushed

¼ cup flour
⅔ cup milk
¾ teaspoon salt
⅛ teaspoon basil
⅛ teaspoon oregano
⅛ teaspoon pepper
1 cup grated sharp cheddar
  cheese

Cook pepper and garlic in butter until soft. Stir in flour. Add milk and seasonings. Cook, stirring until thickened. Add ½ cup of grated cheese. Add drained, chopped tomatoes, corn and onions. Place in baking dish. Top with remaining cheese. Bake, uncovered, 50 minutes in a 325° oven.

Mrs. William F. Black
Montgomery, Alabama

RED CABBAGE

Average
Partial do ahead

Serves: 6-8
Preparing: 3 hours

1 medium head red cabbage
2 tablespoons finely chopped
  onion
3 tablespoons butter
2 tart apples, pared, cored
  and sliced

1 teaspoon salt
¼ cup boiling water
4 to 6 tablespoons red wine
2 tablespoons brown sugar (or to
  taste)

Remove core and hard veins from cabbage. Shred and soak in cold water for one hour. Sauté onion in butter few minutes. Add cabbage and simmer for 15 minutes, covered. Add apples, salt and boiling water to cabbage. Stir, cover and simmer one hour or more. Add boiling water, if necessary, as it absorbs. When cabbage is tender and water dissipated, add red wine and brown sugar. Simmer, covered, for additional ½ hour, until all ingredients are well blended and piping hot.

Mrs. Nicholas H. Luderssen
Bryn Mawr, Pennsylvania

BAKED GRITS

Easy

Serves: 6-8
Preparing: 40 minutes
Baking: 1 hour

1 cup grits
4 cups water
2 teaspoons salt
1 16-ounce jar Cheez Whiz or
   2 cups grated sharp cheese

4 eggs
½ cup margarine or butter
1 tablespoon Worcestershire
   sauce
cayenne, to taste

Bring the water to a boil and add salt. Gradually add the grits, stirring continuously with a wire whisk or wooden spoon. Stir well, until mixture returns to a boil or mixture may become lumpy. Cover and cook over low heat thirty to forty minutes, stirring frequently. (If instant grits are used, use the same amount of grits, but cook according to package directions.) Preheat the oven to 325°. Beat 4 eggs. Add eggs, butter and Cheez Whiz to cooked grits. Stir until cheese and butter are melted. Pour into two-quart casserole. Place casserole in a pan of hot water. Bake one hour at 325°.

Mrs. D. W. Gregg
Bryn Mawr, Pennsylvania
Heyward M. Pepper
Flourtown, Pennsylvania

ZUCCHINI AND TOMATO CASSEROLE

Easy
Do ahead
Freeze

Serves: 6
Preparing: 15 minutes
Baking: 10-15 minutes

3 medium zucchini, unpeeled,
   cut in small pieces
¼ cup sour cream
1 tablespoon butter
1 tablespoon Parmesan
   cheese, grated

1 8-ounce can stewed tomatoes,
   drained
½ teaspoon salt
⅛ teaspoon paprika
1 tablespoon chopped chives
1 egg yolk, beaten

Simmer zucchini covered until tender, 6 to 8 minutes. Combine sour cream, butter, Parmesan cheese, salt, paprika and chives. Stir over low flame until cheese is melted. Add egg yolk. Add zucchini and drained stewed tomatoes. Place all in baking dish. Brown in 375° oven for 10-15 minutes.

Mrs. C. Willis Edgerton
Haverford, Pennsylvania

Accompaniments

sauces, relishes, etc.

BREAD STUFFING
WITH APPLES, APRICOTS AND ALMONDS

Average　　　　　　　　　　　　　　　　　　*Serves: 12*
Partial do ahead　　　　　　　　　　　*Preparing: 30 minutes*

Use to stuff a roasting chicken or serve as a side dish after heating in oven.

**2 loaves firm white bread,
cubed, toasted (350° oven
25 minutes)
2 cups chicken broth
1 cup butter
½ bunch celery with leaves
3 large Spanish onions,
chopped**

**3 Winesap apples, cored and
coarsely chopped
1 cup dried apricots
½ cup sliced almonds
1 tablespoon sage
1 tablespoon thyme
2 teaspoons rosemary
salt and pepper, to taste**

Sauté the onions and celery in butter. Then add and sauté the apples, apricots and almonds. Season with sage, thyme and rosemary. Cook 2 minutes. Heat together chicken broth and butter. Pour over bread cubes and toss until evenly coated. Combine with other ingredients. Add salt and pepper to taste.

FROG
Philadelphia, Pennsylvania

FRESH FRUIT COMPOTE

Easy　　　　　　　　　　　　　　　　　　*Serves: 10*
Do ahead　　　　　　　　　　　*Preparing: 20 minutes*
　　　　　　　　　　　　　　　　　Marinating: 24 hours

**3 peaches, peeled and sliced
1 medium cantaloupe, cut in
bite-sized pieces
2 cups blueberries
1½ cups sour cream (or Poly
King Sour)**

**2½ tablespoons minced
crystallized ginger
slivered toasted almonds**

The day before serving, mix together the sour cream and minced ginger. At least 6 hours before serving, mix together the cut up fruit and the sour cream mixture. When serving, sprinkle with almonds.

Mrs. John F. Lloyd
Ardmore, Pennsylvania

HERB BUTTER WADHAMS

Easy   *Makes: ½ pound*
Do ahead   *Preparing: 10 minutes*
Freeze   *Microwave: 10 seconds*

Especially for Bluefish Wadhams but can be used on other kinds of fish as well as steaks and chicken.

½ pound chilled unsalted   **1 teaspoon Dijon mustard**
  butter   **1 tablespoon chopped fresh**
1 teaspoon lemon juice   **parsley**
½ teaspoon soy sauce   **½ teaspoon pepper**
½ teaspoon Worcestershire   **¼ teaspoon dried tarragon**
  sauce   **¼ teaspoon dried thyme**

Place butter in glass measuring cup. Heat in microwave oven 10 seconds. Should be just slightly softened. Blend in remaining ingredients, working into a smooth mixture. Shape into two sticks. Wrap in plastic wrap, then aluminum foil. Freeze. To use, take direct from freezer and slice off pieces as you need them. Let come to room temperature before using.

Mrs. B. P. Wadhams
Haverford, Pennsylvania

GOLDEN MARMALADE

Easy   *Makes: about 12-15 glasses*
                                         Preparing: 2 hours
                                       Standing: overnight

Use firm oranges, Valencia, Navel, etc.

6 whole oranges, medium to   **sugar**
  large   **1 cup of lemon juice**
3 whole lemons

Either slice oranges very thin or cut in small pieces to use in blender. Cut in blender to small pieces, not too fine but also not too big. Discard seeds and excessive membrane. Cover fruit with water and let stand all night. In morning, cook and boil mixture 45 minutes.

Measure and add 1½ times as much sugar as fruit. Boil 45 minutes. Just before removing from stove add 1 cup lemon juice. Seal in glasses.

The Committee

RHUBARB CONSERVE

Easy
Do ahead

Preparing: 1 hour
Cooking: 45 minutes

5 or 6 bunches rhubarb,
    about 30 stalks
1 medium size can crushed
    pineapple
3 medium oranges (all the
    juice, no pulp)

1 lime (all the juice, no pulp)
1 package seedless raisins
4 parts sugar

Cut rhubarb into 1-inch pieces. Mix all ingredients together. Measure and add four cups sugar per 1 cup mixture. Cook 45 minutes, stirring constantly. Seal in jars.

Mrs. Andrew L. Lewis
Lederach, Pennsylvania

PINEAPPLE PUDDING

Easy

Serves: 6-8
Preparing: 15 minutes
Baking: 1 hour

¼ pound margarine or butter
1 cup sugar
4 eggs
5 slices white bread with
    crusts removed, cubed

1 20-ounce can crushed
    pineapple, minus 2
    tablespoons juice

Cream butter and sugar. Beat well. Add eggs. Beat until the mixture looks light in color. Stir in bread and pineapple. Bake at 350° for 1 hour. Good accompaniment with ham in place of potatoes.

Mrs. R. S. Auchincloss, Jr.
St. Davids, Pennsylvania

PEPPER RELISH

Easy

Preparing: 1 hour
Cooking: ½ hour

1 dozen red peppers
1 dozen green peppers
1 dozen medium onions
1 quart vinegar

3½ cups sugar
3 ounces mustard seed
2½ tablespoons salt

Clean peppers and grind them up together with onions. Put into large saucepan and pour boiling water over to cover. Let stand 5 minutes. Drain. Mixture should be as dry as possible. Place in a kettle with vinegar, sugar, mustard seed and salt. Bring to a rolling boil over high heat. Reduce to medium heat and cook ½ hour. Taste for sugar. Seal in Mason jars.

Mrs. D. B. Garst
Devon, Pennsylvania

PURPLE PLUM BASTE

Easy   *Makes: 2 cups*
Do ahead   *Preparing: 15 minutes*
Freeze

Delicious with chicken or pork on the grill or in the oven.

1 pound can plums, pitted   **2 tablespoons chopped onion**
  and puréed   **2 tablespoons brown sugar**
¼ cup lemon juice, or wine   **2 tablespoons salad oil or butter**
  vinegar   **½ teaspoon salt**

Combine all ingredients, simmer 10-15 minutes.

Mrs. John A. Girvin
Gladwyne, Pennsylvania

FABULOUS FRUIT COMPOTE

Easy   *Serves: 10*
Do ahead   *Preparing: 10 minutes*
Baking: 1½ hours
Chilling: overnight

This could be served warm as accompaniment to meat or cold as dessert.

1 can pitted dark cherries   **¼ cup lemon juice**
  and juice (large can)   **½ teaspoon grated lemon rind**
1 12-ounce can diced   **½ teaspoon grated orange rind**
  peaches, drained   **¾ cup brown sugar**
1 package dried apricots   **½ pint sour cream**
1 cup orange juice

Place in covered casserole and bake at 350° for 1½ hours. Cool overnight. Serve with sour cream.

Mrs. T. Edson Jewell, Jr.
Wellesley Hills, Massachusetts

OYSTER CORNBREAD DRESSING

Easy

Serves: 24
Preparing: 30 minutes
Baking: 30 minutes

¾ cup butter
1 cup chopped onions
2 cups diced celery
1½ cups oysters, cut into ½"
   pieces
1½ quarts dry stale
   cornbread, crumbled

3 cups dry white bread, crumbled
2 teaspoons salt
2 teaspoons celery seed
½ teaspoon pepper
2 tablespoons sage
2 cups chicken stock

Cook oysters and vegetables in butter until tender. Mix seasonings with bread. Add cooked vegetables, oysters and butter. Mix gently. Add stock slowly. Amount needed will vary with moisture content of bread. Dressing should be moist. Place dressing in greased baking pan no deeper than 2 inches. Bake in 375° oven until thoroughly heated and lightly browned, about ½ hour.

K. Carol Carlson, Vice President
ARA Services
Philadelphia, Pennsylvania

HOLLANDAISE SAUCE

Easy
Do ahead
Freeze

Makes: 1¼ cups
Preparing: 10 minutes

Blender method—it's a cinch!

4 egg yolks
2 tablespoons cream
1 tablespoon lemon juice

⅛ teaspoon salt
pinch cayenne
1 cup butter (2 sticks)

Into container of blender put in egg yolks, cream, lemon juice, salt and cayenne. Heat butter until very hot, do *not* let it brown. Turn blender on low speed. Remove cover and pour in hot butter in a heavy stream. Empty into freezer container, leaving ½" headspace, cool, seal and freeze. (It can, of course, be used and not frozen). Stir into sauces to thicken, without defrosting, using small pieces at a time. For eggs Benedict, defrost over hot, but not boiling water, stirring frequently.

Mrs. George S. Fabian
Bryn Mawr, Pennsylvania

MICROWAVE HOLLANDAISE

Easy   *Makes: ½ cup*
Do ahead   *Preparing: 5 minutes*

⅓ cup butter or margarine   ¼ teaspoon dry mustard
1-2 tablespoons lemon juice   dash Tabasco sauce
2 egg yolks   (add ½ teaspoon tarragon to
¼ teaspoon salt   make Bearnaise sauce)

Place butter in 1-quart casserole. Heat in microwave oven (full power) for 45-60 seconds or until melted. Beat with wire whisk into remaining ingredients which have been placed in 1-quart casserole. Cook in microwave on cookmatic level 8 (medium high) for 1 to 1⅓ minutes until thickness desired. Be sure to stop microwave every 12 seconds to beat with wire whisk during the 1 to 1½ minutes cooking time. Can be doubled.

Can be made earlier in the day. Do not complete the cooking time, or sauce, when reheated will be too thick. To reheat, cook on level 8 (medium high) at 12-second intervals until heated, stirring with wire whisk between each 12-second interval.

The Committee

SPICED FRUIT MIX

Easy   *Serves: 40 plus*
Do ahead   *Preparing: allow three days*
Freeze

½ gallon watermelon rind,   4 gallons water
   canned   1 cup vinegar
½ gallon kumquats, canned   1 tablespoon cinnamon, or three
½ gallon pineapple chunks,   sticks
   canned   1 tablespoon nutmeg
½ gallon canned cherries,   1 teaspoon cloves
   sliced and pitted   2 pounds sugar
1 jar tiny gherkins

Mix together water, vinegar, sugar and spices. Add all fruit and let stand 24 hours. Stir occasionally. Drain and discard liquid. Repeat water, vinegar, sugar and spice mixture; pour over fruit and allow to stand another 24 hours. Drain to serve as accompaniment for meat.

Dan Meyers, Chef
Mushroom Fortside Restaurant
Fort Washington, Pennsylvania

CHILI SAUCE

Average
Do ahead

Preparing: 30 minutes
Cooking: 4 hours

1 peck tomatoes (8 quarts)
6 peppers, chopped (3 red, 3
  green)
6 medium-sized onions,
  chopped
1 pound brown sugar
salt, to taste

2 tablespoons mustard seed
2 tablespoons celery seed
½ teaspoon cinnamon
½ teaspoon cloves
dark red pepper
4 cups vinegar

Peel and cut up tomatoes. Add all other ingredients except vinegar. Bring to a boil and simmer 3½ hours. Add vinegar and boil 30 minutes longer. This sauce mixed with mayonnaise makes an excellent Russian dressing or shrimp sauce.

Mrs. Walter Lamb
Chester Springs, Pennsylvania

BAKED CRANBERRIES

Easy
Do ahead

Serves: 8
Preparing: 5 minutes
Baking: 45 minutes

2 cups raw cranberries

1½ cups sugar

Butter casserole. Add raw cranberries. Sprinkle with sugar. Cover tightly. Bake at 375°. Stir once. Bake until sugar has dissolved, about 45 minutes.

The Committee

BRANDIED PEACH PRESERVES

Easy
Do ahead

Preparing: 1 hour

10 or 12 peaches
1 cup cold water
4½ cups granulated sugar
6 whole cloves

½ cup brandy
¾ cup chopped pecans
chopped candied ginger
  (optional)

Pare peaches; cut in half and remove pits. Simmer fruit in water about 20-25 minutes. Add ½ of sugar. Stir occasionally. When peaches are translucent remove from syrup and put fruit in bowl. Add sugar and cloves to syrup. Cook until syrup is thick. (Add chopped candied ginger if you like.) Cool and then add brandy. Pour over peaches. Add chopped nut meats. Ladle into sterilized jars or ramekins. Cover with hot syrup. Seal tightly.

Mrs. Boris Sokoloff
Philadelphia, Pennsylvania

MOCK MINCE MEAT

Easy   *Makes: 6 pints*
Do ahead   *Preparing: 30 minutes*
                                        Cooking: 20 minutes

6 cups chopped green   **2 teaspoons salt**
  tomatoes   **1 cup ground suet**
6 cups chopped apples   **1 cup vinegar**
2 pounds raisins   **2 tablespoons cinnamon**
3 pounds brown sugar   **1 teaspoon nutmeg**
2 tablespoons cloves

Pour boiling water over chopped green tomatoes, drain; repeat, drain well. Mix other ingredients into drained tomatoes, bring to boil, boil 20 minutes. Seal in pint jars, or put in freezer containers. (For pie, bake in hot oven 400° to 500° about 30 or 35 minutes, until golden brown.)

Mrs. Lib Dewey
Green Lane, Pennsylvania

HOT CARAMEL SAUCE

Easy   *Serves: 2 cups*
Do ahead   *Preparing: 5 minutes*
                                        Cooking: 15 minutes

⅔ of ¼ pound butter   **½ cup milk**
1 cup light brown sugar   **1 teaspoon vanilla**
1 rounded tablespoon flour

Blend the first 3 ingredients thoroughly and add about ½ cup milk until the desired thickness. Add vanilla. Double recipe for plenty of sauce.

Diantha Stolz
"Cherchie"
Devon, Pennsylvania

WATERMELON PICKLES

Easy
Do ahead

Makes: 3 pints
Preparing: 10 minutes
Soaking: overnight
Cooking: 30 minutes

2 pounds watermelon rind
4 cups sugar
2 cups white vinegar
1 tablespoon whole cloves

2 cups water
1 lemon, thinly sliced
2 tablespoons cinnamon bark

Trim dark green and pink parts of rind. Cut rind into 1 inch cubes. Soak overnight in salt water (¼ cup salt to 1 quart water). Cook until just tender. Drain. Combine sugar, vinegar, water, lemon and spices, (tied in bag). Simmer 10 minutes. Remove spice bag. Add rind. Simmer until clear. Fill hot sterilized jars to ½ inch from top. Seal. Yield 3 pints.

Mrs. M. Welliver
Albany, Oregon

Before sealing jars and jellies with wax, insert a string to hang over the lip of the glass for easy removal of hardened sealer.

MUSTARD SAUCE

Easy
Do ahead

Makes: 3-4 cups
Preparing: ½ hour

1 pint cream
½ cup sugar
4 scant tablespoons dry
  mustard

4 egg yolks
½ cup vinegar
½ cup water

Dissolve mustard in 4 tablespoons cream. Bring rest of cream to boil. Add sugar and mustard. Mustard will be lumpy, but it doesn't matter. Heat again to just below boil and then pour over well beaten egg yolks stirring constantly till thickened (2 minutes). Add vinegar and water. Boil, stirring, a few minutes.

Keeps in refrigerator at least a month; separates, but just stir.

Mrs. William W. Bodine, Jr.
Villanova, Pennsylvania

MARINADE FOR LONDON BROIL

Easy
Do ahead

Preparing: 5 minutes
Marinating: 2 hours

9 tablespoons red wine
2 tablespoons soy sauce
2 tablespoons vinegar
1 clove garlic, cut up
2 tablespoons olive oil

½ teaspoon salt
½ teaspoon oregano
½ teaspoon Accent
½ teaspoon pepper

Mix all ingredients well. Marinate steak, turning often for two or more hours.

Mrs. Eugene R. Hook
Wynnewood, Pennsylvania

MUSTARD BUTTER

Easy
Do ahead

Preparing: 10 minutes

1 cup softened butter
2 tablespoons Dijon mustard
  (I use more to taste)

1 tablespoon lemon juice
⅛ tablespoon crushed garlic
salt and pepper to taste

Blend all ingredients; store in refrigerator. Serve at room temperature.

James M. Ballengee
Bryn Mawr, Pennsylvania

BLUEBERRY SAUCE

Easy
Do ahead
Freeze

Preparing: 15 minutes
Cooking: 5 minutes

4 cups blueberries
1 cup sugar

½ lemon, quartered
1 small stick cinnamon

Using just a tablespoon or so of water to freshly washed berries, add sugar, lemon and stick cinnamon. Cover, and let cook slowly over low heat. Stir as needed. Will only take about 5 minutes or so after bubbling. Will be thickened. To be used with Blueberry Cake Pudding. Serve cool or lukewarm. Any sauce remaining can be kept for ice cream or other uses.

The Committee

EMILY'S MAYONNAISE

Easy
Do ahead

Makes: 2 cups
Preparing: about ¾ hour

1 pint of Mazola oil
4 egg yolks
1 teaspoon salt

dash Tabasco sauce
½ teaspoon onion juice
2 tablespoons lemon juice

Chill small mixing bowl. Have all ingredients cold. Beat the yolks until thick. Add ½ of oil fairly slowly. Stop beating and scrape sides of bowl. Add lemon juice, salt, onion juice, and Tabasco. Add rest of oil slowly. Scrape sides of bowl and beat again.

Mrs. Elwyn Evans
Wilmington, Delaware

CANDIED APPLES

Easy
Do ahead

Serves: 6
Preparing: 10 minutes
Cooking: 1 hour

6 medium cooking apples,
   peeled, cored and
   quartered
1 cup sugar

¼ cup cinnamon candies
½ cup syrup from a can of
   peaches
1½ cups water

Combine sugar, candies, syrup and water. Cook until dissolved. Drop apples into syrup. Cook on low to medium heat for one hour, turning frequently. May be served warm, at room temperature or cold.

Mrs. Hubert T. Holman
Fayetteville, Tennessee

KATHY'S MUSTARD SAUCE

Easy
Do ahead

Preparing: 20 minutes

1 4-ounce can Colman's dry
   mustard
3 cups flour
1 cup sugar

5 tablespoons salt
½ cup cider vinegar
boiling water

Mix all ingredients together, adding sufficient boiling water to reach proper consistency (like heavy cream). Mix until smooth. If using blender, mix one or two cups at a time. Excellent on steaks and fish.

Mrs. John K. Armstrong
Bryn Mawr, Pennsylvania

SPICY SAUCE FOR BARBECUE

Easy   *Serves: 4*
Do ahead   *Preparing: 10 minutes*
Cooking: 15 minutes

2 tablespoons butter or   1 medium onion (chopped)
  margarine   ½ cup catsup
1 clove garlic (minced)   ½ teaspoon Tabasco
2 tablespoons cider vinegar   1 tablespoon brown sugar
1 teaspoon salt   ¼ cup water
1 teaspoon dry mustard

Combine all ingredients in a saucepan and heat slowly. Simmer for about 15 minutes. Brush on meat while meat is cooking. Use as baste for chicken, spareribs, hamburgers, hotdogs on outdoor grill.

Mrs. David B. Walters
Keene, New Hampshire

MUSTARD MOUSSE

Easy   *Preparing: 15 minutes*
Do ahead   *Chilling: 3 hours*

4 eggs   ½ cup water
¾ cup sugar   ½ teaspoon salt
1 tablespoon strong dry   1 envelope gelatine
  mustard   1 cup heavy cream, whipped
½ cup cider vinegar

Soak gelatine in ¼ cup cold water. Beat eggs; add mustard and sugar. Stir well with whisk to get all lumps out. Add ¼ cup cold water and vinegar to gelatine. Stir. Add to egg mixture and cook in double boiler until custard-like consistency. Cool. Fold in whipped cream. Pour into mold. Chill until firm. Unmold and serve.

Mrs. Walter W. Suppes
Johnstown, Pennsylvania

PICKLED GREEN TOMATOES

Easy
Do ahead

Preparing: 1 hour or 2 depending on
how many you make

2 cups white distilled vinegar
1 cup water
3 tablespoons salt
garlic cloves (peeled, 1 or 2 per jar)

pickling spices (½ teaspoon per jar)
quartered green tomatoes
sterilized Mason jars

Combine vinegar, water and salt for pickling solution. Place 1 or 2 cloves of garlic in sterilized jars. Add ½ teaspoon pickling spices. Fill jar with quartered green tomatoes. Add solution of vinegar to cover tomatoes. Seal tops and let sit. Tomatoes will be ready in about 2 weeks.

Janet Pensiero
Wyndmoor, Pennsylvania

Core shiny red apples for candlesticks for a summer dinner party.

Grind frozen cranberries for relish to avoid juice from squirting.

PEACH CHUTNEY

Easy
Do ahead

Serves: 8-10
Cooking: 1½ hours

1 29-ounce can yellow cling sliced peaches
1 cup sugar
¾ cup vinegar
1 cup pitted prunes
⅓ cup chopped candied or crystalized ginger

1 clove garlic, minced
⅓ teaspoon curry powder
¼ teaspoon cinnamon
¼ teaspoon ground cloves
⅓ cup chopped blanched almonds

Drain peaches, reserving syrup. In large saucepan, combine reserved syrup, sugar, vinegar, prunes, ginger, garlic, curry powder, cinnamon and cloves. Add peaches and bring to boil. Reduce heat and simmer uncovered for 1 hour and 15 minutes. Stir frequently and then stir in nuts.

Mrs. G. G. Amsterdam,
Philadelphia, Pennsylvania

CRÈME FRAICHE

Easy

Preparing: 5 minutes
Chilling: 1 hour

1 cup sour cream
1 teaspoon vanilla extract

confectioners' sugar to taste

Mix and keep in refrigerator. Let sit out ½ hour before serving. Serve with fresh fruit or any dessert calling for crème fraiche.

James M. Ballengee
Bryn Mawr, Pennsylvania

SAUCE VERTE

Easy
Do ahead

Preparing: 10 minutes
plus chilling time

Serve with Mousselines de Saumon.

1 bunch of watercress
1 bunch of spinach
1 bunch of tarragon

½ cup of mayonnaise
salt and pepper

Boil for 10 minutes: watercress, spinach and tarragon. Let cool. Squeeze and mix in blender. Combine with mayonnaise, salt and pepper.

Mrs. Walter H. Annenberg
Wynnewood, Pennsylvania

MINT SAUCE

Easy
Do ahead

Serves: 10
Preparing: 5 minutes

⅓ cup Cross and Blackwell
  Mint Sauce

⅓ cup chili sauce
⅓ cup currant jelly

Melt jelly. Mix in other ingredients. Store in jar in refrigerator. Keeps for a long time. Delicious with lamb.

Mrs. William H. McCoy, 2nd
Wilmington, Delaware

BAKED APRICOTS

Easy
Do ahead

Serves: 10-12
Preparing: 10 minutes
Baking: 1 hour

2 large cans peeled apricots,
halves preferred
1 pound box light brown
sugar

1 large box Ritz crackers
½ pound butter

In a greased baking dish put a layer of drained and peeled apricot halves. Cover with brown sugar, then a layer of Ritz crackers and dot thickly with lumps of butter. Repeat this to top of dish. Bake slowly in 300° oven, approximately 1 hour. It should be thick and crusty on top.

Mrs. Stanley E. Johnson
Philadelphia, Pennsylvania

CHOCOLATE SAUCE

Easy
Do ahead
Refrigerate

Serves: 12
Preparing: 5 minutes
Cooking: 10 minutes

3 squares Bakers
unsweetened chocolate
1 can Eagle Brand
condensed milk

⅛ teaspoon salt
½ to 1 cup hot water
1 teaspoon vanilla, if desired

Melt chocolate in double boiler and add condensed milk. Stir five minutes. Add salt and water for desired consistency. Add vanilla last. Heat before serving.

Mrs. Henry H. Bitler
Bryn Mawr, Pennsylvania

HORSERADISH MOUSSE KRAMER

Easy
Do ahead

Serves: 8-10
Preparing: 20 minutes
Chilling: 4 hours

1 package lemon Jello
1 bottle horseradish

1 cup sour cream

Dissolve Jello in 1 cup hot water and let set until consistency of egg white. Add horseradish and sour cream. Place in mold and chill until firm. Delicious with ham or beef.

Bernard Kramer ("Uncle Ben")
Main Line Times
Wynnewood, Pennsylvania

EASY FISH OR CHICKEN SAUCE

Easy

Serves: 4
Preparing: 5 minutes
Cooking: 5 minutes

1 stick butter or margarine
2 tablespoons Old Bay
  seasoning
1 to 2 tablespoons Dijon
  mustard

salt and pepper, to taste
4 cups vermouth or white wine

Mix and heat. Pour half over fish fillets while broiling. Serve remainder with the fish while serving. Garnish with lemon slices or parsley.

Fish or chicken can also be broiled with vermouth as a moistener.

Susan Schiffer Stautberg
Philadelphia, Pennsylvania

TOMATO AND MUSHROOM SAUCE

Easy
Do ahead

Serves: 8
Preparing: 15 minutes
Cooking: 1½ to 2 hours

1 large can tomatoes (1
  pound, 12 ounce)
1 pound mushrooms, sliced
½ green pepper, chopped
1 red pimiento, chopped

2 onions, chopped
4 tablespoons sugar
salt and pepper to taste
½ teaspoon soy sauce

Cook all ingredients (except mushrooms) uncovered for 1½ to 2 hours. Sauté the mushrooms in butter for 10 minutes. Add them at the end of the cooking time and heat through. Can be served with meats as an accompaniment or simply as a vegetable.

Mrs. Ellis S. Rump, Jr.
West Chester, Pennsylvania

PICKLED BLACK-EYED PEAS

Easy
Do ahead

Preparing: 15 minutes
Resting: 2 days

**2 No. 2 cans cooked
  black-eyed peas
1 scant cup salad oil
¼ cup wine vinegar
1 clove garlic (remove after
  one day)**

**½ cup thinly sliced onion
½ teaspoon salt
cracked or freshly ground black
  pepper**

Drain liquid and place black-eyed peas in a bowl. Add remaining ingredients, mix thoroughly. Store in jar in refrigerator at least two days before eating and up to two weeks. Serve any time of year but, of course, always serve on New Year's Day to insure prosperity for the coming year.

Nancy Hanks
Washington, D. C.

HOT FRUIT COMPOTE

Easy
Do ahead

Serves: 8-10
Preparing: 20 minutes
Baking: 30 minutes

**2 #2 cans fruits for salad,
  drained and cut into
  chunks
2 bananas, just ripe, sliced
6 to 8 coconut macaroons,
  the chewy kind**

**butter
½ cup Cointreau, Triple Sec or
  Grand Marnier**

Layer fruits and bananas in a 2-quart pyrex dish. Break up macaroons and spread over fruit. Dot with butter and pour orange liqueur over all. Bake 25 to 30 minutes at 350° degrees.

Mrs. Jeremiah Sawyer
New Orleans, Louisiana

SWEET TOMATO CHUTNEY

Average
Do ahead

Makes: about 2½ cups
Preparing: 20 minutes
Cooking: 2½ hours

1 whole head garlic, peeled
and coarsely chopped
1 piece fresh ginger about 2"
long, 1" thick, and 1" wide,
peeled and coarsely
chopped
1½ cups wine vinegar
1 pound (12 ounce) can
whole tomatoes

1½ cups granulated sugar
1½ teaspoon salt
⅛ to ½ teaspoon cayenne
pepper
2 tablespoons golden raisins
2 tablespoons blanched, slivered
almonds

Put prepared garlic and ginger in ½ cup vinegar in blender or food processor until smooth. In a 4-quart heavy bottomed pot with non-metallic finish, place tomatoes, juice from can, rest of vinegar, sugar, salt and cayenne. Bring to boil. Add purée from blender. Lower heat and simmer gently, uncovered for 1½ to 2 hours until chutney becomes thick, (a film should cling to spoon). Stir occasionally at first and more frequently later, as it thickens. Makes about 2½ cups and should be as thick as honey when cooked. Add almonds and raisins; simmer, stirring another 5 minutes. Cool and bottle. Refrigerate. Keeps for months.

Mrs. Donald B. Aspinall
Villanova, Pennsylvania

HORSERADISH MOUSSE

Easy
Do ahead

Serves: 6-8
Preparing: 20-30 minutes

2 cups low-cal cottage
cheese
1 tablespoon grated onion
4 tablespoons horseradish
sauce

¼ cup skimmed milk
1 tablespoon gelatine dissolved
in ¼ cup cold water
3 drops Tabasco
salt and pepper, to taste

Put horseradish, cheese and onion in blender until smooth. Heat milk and add to softened gelatine. When dissolved, add cheese, onion, horseradish mixture, Tabasco, salt and pepper. Refrigerate in a mold. Garnish with pimiento.

Mrs. E. Dyson Herting
Wayne, Pennsylvania

SANGRIA JELLY

Easy
Do ahead

Makes: 4 half-pints
Preparing: 10 minutes
Cooking: 5 minutes

½ bottle liquid pectin
1½ cups red Burgundy wine
1 tablespoon grated orange
  rind
¼ cup fresh orange juice

2 tablespoons fresh lemon juice
2 tablespoons Triple Sec,
  Cointreau or Grand Marnier
3 cups sugar

Combine all ingredients except pectin in top of double boiler. Stir over boiling water three to four minutes until sugar is dissolved. Remove from heat, add pectin and stir for one minute. Fill glasses to within one-fourth inch of top and seal with paraffin or cool and cover tightly with plastic wrap. If sealed with paraffin it will keep on the pantry shelf for two months; if sealed with plastic wrap it will keep longer in the refrigerator. This recipe makes four half-pint containers.

Mrs. F. Homer Hagaman
Wynnewood, Pennsylvania

BLENDER MAYONNAISE

Easy

Serves: 1¼ cups
Preparing: 5 minutes

¼ cup olive oil
2 tablespoons lemon juice
½ teaspoon dry mustard

½ teaspoon salt
1 egg
1 cup salad oil

Combine all ingredients but salad oil in blender or processor. Blend a few seconds. Remove top and slowly pour in salad oil, blending until thick.

Mrs. Henry Wendt
Devon, Pennsylvania

BUTTERNUT SAUCE

Easy

Preparing: 10 minutes
Cooking: 10 minutes

1 12-ounce bag Nestle's
  chocolate morsels

½ pound salt butter
½ cup walnuts, finely chopped

Melt butter in a saucepan. Add chopped walnuts and roast for a few minutes in butter over low heat. Add the morsels and mix until melted. Remove from fire; keep warm. Spoon over hard ice cream.

Charles and Helen Wilson's
L'Auberge
Wayne, Pennsylvania

ENRICO CARUSO'S SPAGHETTI SAUCE

Easy   *Serves: 8*
Do ahead   *Preparing: 30 minutes*
                                                       Cooking: 1 hour

1 cup olive oil	**½ pound lean bacon**
1 large bunch parsley	**1 large can of Italian tomatoes**
6 large onions, sliced thin	**1 large can tomato purée**
6 cloves of garlic, chopped	**salt, to taste**

Sauté onions, garlic and parsley slowly in olive oil. Add bacon cut in small pieces. Add tomatoes and purée and cook covered, slowly one hour.

Mrs. Walter Lamb
Chester Springs, Pennsylvania

HOT PEPPER JELLY

Easy   *Preparing: 45 minutes*
Do ahead
Freeze

Serve with cream cheese on stoned wheat thins.

6½ cups sugar	**1 bottle Certo**
1½ cups vinegar	**5-6 drops green food coloring**
1½ cups hot peppers,	**(optional)**
blended fine in blender	
1½ cups bell peppers,	
blended well in blender	

Boil peppers, vinegar, and sugar five minutes. Add Certo, bring to boil and boil one minute. Add green coloring. Pour into jelly jars, cover with paraffin (or freeze).

Mary Jane Kuehn
North Salem, New York

LEMON JELLY

Easy   *Preparing: 45 minutes to*
                                                                      1 hour

6 lemons, peeled and sliced   **¾ cup sugar for each cup of**
  thin   **juice**
2 cups apples, peeled, cored
  and cubed

Place lemon slices and apples in bottom of glass baking dish. Press down with spoon to release juices. If juices do not cover fruit add a little water. Cook in microwave oven for 10-15 minutes or until fruit is soft. Put into cloth jelly bag and let juice drip into bowl. Measure juice and add sugar accordingly. Discard pulp. Place juice and sugar in saucepan; stir until dissolved, then cook uncovered over medium heat until jelly sheets on spoon. It may be somewhat runny but will jell as it cools. Pour into sterilized jars: cover with melted paraffin.

May be served on toast or spooned over chicken before baking.

Mrs. John F. Lloyd
Ardmore, Pennsylvania

Warm a glass of currant jelly with about one half as much Port wine for a game sauce.

CITRUS MARMALADE

Easy   *Preparing: 3 day process*
Do ahead

Make this only when the best citrus crops are available.

1 orange   **water (1½ times measured fruit)**
1 grapefruit   **sugar (¾ cup per each cup**
1 lemon   **measured fruit)**

Wash fruit. Put fruit through coarse food chopper. Measure quantity. Add 1½ times water and let stand overnight. Boil hard for ten minutes. Let stand overnight again. Add ¾ cup sugar for each cup fruit. Boil lightly until jellied, which may take a couple of hours. It thickens further in the jar. Pour into hot sterilized jars. Seal.

Mrs. Thor S. Johnson
Berwyn, Pennsylvania

Rhapsodies

cakes, pies and desserts

MANDARIN ORANGE CAKE

Easy   *Serves: 10*
Do ahead   *Preparing: 10 minutes*
Freeze   *Baking: 20 minutes or until done*

Cake

1 box butter golden cake mix   1 11-ounce can Mandarin
½ cup oil   oranges with juice
4 eggs

Frosting

1 3-ounce package vanilla   1 No. 2 can crushed pineapple,
   instant pudding mix   drained
1 9-ounce carton Cool Whip

Mix cake ingredients together with electric mixer. Pour into well greased and floured round layer cake pans. Bake in 325° oven.

Mix frosting ingredients together with a spoon. Spread between layers, and on top and sides of cake. Store in refrigerator and serve cold.

Mrs. Betty H. Heidler
Frazer, Pennsylvania

CHOCOLATE CAKE SURPRISE
(Microwave)

Easy   *Serves: 15-20*
Do ahead   *Preparing: 5 minutes*
Freeze   *Cooking: 10 minutes*
                                        Setting: 10 minutes

2 cups unsifted all-purpose   ¼ cup unsweetened cocoa
   flour   ⅛ teaspoon salt
1 cup sugar   1 cup mayonnaise
1 teaspoon baking soda   1 cup water

In mixing bowl blend flour, sugar, soda, cocoa and salt. Stir in the mayonnaise and water. With electric beater, beat on low speed until all ingredients are mixed and moistened. Then beat at high speed 1½ minutes. Grease bottom only of a glass baking dish, deep enough so batter will only fill it halfway. Cook in center of oven 10 minutes, rotating dish a quarter turn every 2 minutes. Let cake set 10 minutes to finish carry-over cooking. Cake is done if toothpick stuck in center comes out clean. Let cool completely before frosting.

Mrs. Barbara P. Wadhams
Haverford, Pennsylvania

CHOCOLATE BOURBON CAKE

Easy
Do ahead
Freeze

Serves: 16-18
Preparing: 30 minutes, plus chilling
time

2 cups butter
1 cup sugar
1 cup powdered sugar
1 dozen eggs, separated
4 ounces unsweetened
  chocolate, melted

1 teaspoon vanilla
1 cup chopped pecans
1 dozen double lady fingers
4 dozen macaroons, broken and
  soaked in ½ cup bourbon
1½ cups heavy cream, whipped

Cream butter and sugars until light and fluffy. Beat egg yolks until light and blend into butter mixture. Beat in chocolate; add vanilla and pecans. Beat egg whites until stiff, but not dry. Fold into chocolate mixture. Line a 10" springform pan around sides and bottom with split lady fingers. Alternate layers of soaked macaroons and chocolate mixture over lady fingers. Chill overnight. Remove sides of springform pan and cover top with whipped cream. If frozen, add whipped cream after defrosting.

Mrs. Stephen L. Davenport
Gladwyne, Pennsylvania

FRESH PEACH CAKE

Easy
Do ahead

Serves: 12
Preparing: 30 minutes
Baking: 30-35 minutes

½ cup butter
1½ cups brown sugar, firmly
  packed
1 egg
2 cups flour
1 teaspoon soda
dash of salt

1 cup buttermilk
2 full cups of diced fresh ripe
  peaches, or 2 1-pound cans
  sliced peaches
¼ cup sugar
1 teaspoon cinnamon

Cream butter with brown sugar until light and fluffy. Beat in egg. Sift together flour, soda and salt; add to creamed mixture alternately with buttermilk, beating until smooth after each addition. Gently fold in peaches. Pour batter into greased 13" x 9" pan. Sprinkle sugar and cinnamon, mixed together, over top. Bake at 350° for 30-35 minutes, or until done. Serve with whipped cream.

Mrs. Geoffrey Stengel
Rosemont, Pennsylvania

CARAMEL PINEAPPLE CAKE ROLL

Easy
Do ahead
Freeze

Serves: 6-8
Preparing: 15 minutes
Baking: 18 to 20 minutes

1 #2 can crushed pineapple,
  drained
½ cup dark brown sugar
¾ cup cake flour
1 teaspoon baking powder

½ teaspoon salt
4 large eggs, separated
¾ cup sugar
2 teaspoons vanilla
1 teaspoon grated lemon rind

Icing:

1 cup heavy cream

3 tablespoons confectioners'
  sugar

Butter well a 10" x 15" jelly roll pan. Spread drained fruit evenly over pan and sprinkle with brown sugar. Sift flour with baking powder and salt. Beat egg whites until foamy and add ¾ cup of white sugar gradually, beating until stiff. Beat yolks into stiffened whites, and add vanilla and lemon rind. Sprinkle flour over all and gently fold in. Spread batter evenly over the pineapple and brown sugar. Bake in preheated oven at 375° for 18 to 20 minutes. Turn upside down on damp towel and sprinkle lightly with confectioners' sugar. Roll up in towel and cool. Remove towel when cool, place cake on platter and ice. For icing: beat heavy cream with sugar until stiff.

Joan Specter
Philadelphia, Pennsylvania

SWISS CHERRY TORTE

Easy
Do ahead

Serves: 8
Preparing: 30 minutes
Baking: 40 minutes

Do ahead 2 days but *do not* refrigerate!

1 cup flour
5 tablespoons confectioners'
  sugar
¼ pound sweet butter
2 eggs
1 cup sugar
pinch salt

¼ cup flour
¼ tablespoon baking powder
1 tablespoon vanilla
¾ cup chopped nuts
1 16-ounce can pitted tart
  cherries, well drained
9" or 10" pie plate

Combine confectioners' sugar, flour and butter. Mix well and pat into lightly greased pie plate. Bake at 350° for 15 minutes. Cool. Do not start next step until cool.

Combine eggs and sugar and beat until thick and fluffy. Add salt, flour, baking powder and vanilla; beat thoroughly. Fold in nuts and well-drained cherries. Pour into crust and bake 40 minutes at 325°. Can be served with whipped cream.

Mrs. Robert S. Kress
Bryn Mawr, Pennsylvania

If you need confectioners' sugar, put ½ cup of granulated sugar and 1 teaspoon cornstarch in blender and blend for 2 minutes.

CHEESE CAKE

Average   *Serves: 8-10*
Do ahead   *Preparing: 20 minutes*
                                           Baking: 30 minutes

Crust

¾ package Zwieback crumbs,   ¼ cup sugar
  (save ¼ package crumbs   ½ cup melted butter
  for topping)   1 teaspoon cinnamon

Cheese Filling

2 pounds cream cheese   1 tablespoon lemon juice
⅛ teaspoon salt   1 pint sour cream
1 cup sugar   4 tablespoons sugar
4 eggs, well beaten   1 teaspoon vanilla

Crust: Mix ingredients. Press ¾ of mixture on bottom and sides of a 10″ springform pan. Pour in cheese filling.

Cheese Filling: Cream the cheese. Beat eggs and one cup sugar until thick and lemon colored. Add to the cheese with lemon juice and salt. Beat well. Pour into lined springform; bake 20 minutes at 375°. Blend sour cream, vanilla and four tablespoons sugar and spread over partially baked cake. Sprinkle with remaining crumbs. Spread sour cream over cake and bake at 475° for ten minutes. Cool.

Mrs. Irwin Stein
Philadelphia, Pennsylvania

CHOCOLATE SWIRL CHEESECAKE

Average
Do ahead

Serves: 12
Preparing: 25 minutes
Baking: 50 minutes

1 6-ounce package chocolate
   chips
½ cup sugar
1¼ cups graham cracker
   crumbs
2 tablespoons sugar
¼ cup butter, melted

2 8-ounce packages cream
   cheese, softened
¾ cup sugar
½ cup sour cream
1 teaspoon vanilla
4 eggs

Preheat oven to 325°. Combine over hot (not boiling) water chocolate chips and sugar. Heat until melted and smooth. Set aside. In small bowl combine graham cracker crumbs, 2 tablespoons sugar and melted butter. Mix well. Pat firmly into 9″ springform pan, covering bottom and 1½″ up sides. Set aside. In large bowl, beat cream cheese until light and creamy. Gradually beat in ¾ cup sugar. Mix in sour cream and vanilla. Add eggs, one at a time, beating well after each addition. Divide batter in half. Stir melted chocolate mixture into first half. Pour into crumb-lined pan. Cover with plain batter. With a knife, swirl plain batter with chocolate batter to marbleize. Bake at 325° 50 minutes, or until only a 2 to 3 inch circle in center will shake. Cool at room temperature. Refrigerate until ready to serve.

Mrs. Randy Gardner
Cherry Hill, New Jersey

DUMP CAKE

Easy
Do ahead

Serves: 12
Preparing: 10 minutes
Baking: 1 hour

1 large can crushed
   pineapple and juice
   (unsweetened)
1 package yellow cake mix

1 cup butter
½ cup chopped pecans
1 cup grated coconut

Preheat oven to 325°. Place the pineapple and juice in bottom of a 13″ x 9″ x 2″ cake pan. Add yellow cake mix sprinkled on top. Cut thin slices of butter over top and sprinkle with chopped pecans and coconut. Bake for one hour. Cut in squares. May be served with ice cream or whipped cream. Serve warm or cold.

The Committee

WONDER CAKE

Easy
Do ahead

Serves: 12
Preparing: 20 minutes
Chilling: 12 hours

30 marshmallows
1 cup milk
1 pint whipping cream,
whipped

½ pound vanilla wafers
1 cup chopped pecans
pinch salt

Put marshmallows and milk in double boiler until dissolved. When cold, add whipped cream. Grind ½ pound vanilla wafers and 1 cup pecans. Add pinch salt. Mix well. Divide and spread ¾ mixture in springform pan. Add marshmallow mixture and remaining crumbs on top. Chill in refrigerator for 12 hours.

Mrs. E. Dyson Herting
Wayne, Pennsylvania

VICTORY CAKE

Easy
Do ahead
Freeze

Serves: 10-12
Preparing: 20 minutes
Baking: 50-60 minutes

1 cup Sun Maid raisins
1 cup brown sugar, packed
1 cup water
½ cup shortening
1 teaspoon cinnamon
1 teaspoon nutmeg
1 teaspoon cloves, ground
1½ cups sifted all-purpose
flour

1 teaspoon baking soda
½ teaspoon salt
½ cup chopped walnuts
¼ cup Bacardi, dark rum
5 tablespoons applesauce
1 large apple, peeled and cut into
small pieces
confectioners' sugar

Combine raisins, sugar, water, shortening, spices and apples. Heat to boiling and simmer 2 minutes. Cool 5 to 10 minutes. Stir flour, soda and salt into raisin mixture, along with walnuts, rum and applesauce. Mix well. Turn into greased 9" or 10" tube pan. Bake in 350° oven 50 to 60 minutes, just until cake tests done. Cool in pan. Dust with confectioners' sugar.

Mrs. Raoul Querze
Bala Cynwyd, Pennsylvania

PRALINE CHEESE CAKE

Easy
Do ahead
Freeze

S∂rves: 12
Preparing: 30 minutes
Baking: 50-55 minutes
Chilling: 2 hours

1 cup graham cracker
  crumbs
3 tablespoons sugar
3 tablespoons margarine or
  butter, melted
3 8-ounce packages
  Philadelphia cream cheese

1¼ cups dark brown sugar
2 tablespoons flour
3 eggs
1½ teaspoons vanilla
½ cup finely chopped pecans
pecan halves for garnish
maple syrup for garnish

Heat oven to 350°. Combine crumbs, sugar, margarine (butter); press into bottom of 9″ springform pan. Bake at 350° for 10 minutes. Remove from oven. Combine softened cream cheese, sugar, flour, mixing at medium speed until well blended. Add eggs one at a time, mixing well after each addition. Blend in vanilla and chopped nuts. Pour mixture over crumb crust in springform pan. Bake at 350° for 50 to 55 minutes. Loosen cake from rim of pan. Cool before removing rim. Chill for several hours. Brush with maple syrup and garnish with pecan halves. Freeze without garnish.

Mrs. Arlin Adams
Philadelphia, Pennsylvania

CARROT CAKE

Easy
Do ahead
Freeze

Serves: 12
Preparing: 30 minutes
Baking: 45 minutes to 1 hour

4 eggs
1½ cups Wesson oil
2 cups sugar
3 cups shredded carrots
2 cups flour

2 teaspoons cinnamon
1 teaspoon soda
1 teaspoon salt
dash each of nutmeg and cloves

Icing:

8 ounces cream cheese
1 stick butter
1 box confectioners' sugar
  (2 cups)

2 cups chopped nuts (optional)
2 teaspoons vanilla

Beat eggs slightly and blend in all other ingredients. Bake in two round pans (greased and floured) at 350° for 45 minutes or in 1 9″ x 13″ pyrex dish at 350° for one hour. Mix icing ingredients and ice cooled cake. Keep in cool place.

Mrs. William C. Buck
Villanova, Pennsylvania

PINEAPPLE YUMMY CAKE

Easy
Do ahead

Serves: 8-10
Preparing: 5 minutes
Baking: 30 minutes

Cake

2 cups flour
2 cups sugar
1 16-ounce can crushed
  pineapple, with juice

2 eggs
2 teaspoons baking soda
1 teaspoon vanilla
½ cup chopped nuts, optional

Frosting

¼ pound butter
1 8-ounce package cream
  cheese

1 teaspoon vanilla
1½ cups confectioners' sugar

Cake
Put all ingredients in bowl and mix well. Pour into 8″ x 13″ pan. When finished baking at 350° for 30-35 minutes, frost. Can frost while warm.

Mrs. Drew Lewis
Schwenksville, Pennsylvania

ZUCCHINI CAKE

Easy
Do ahead
Freeze

Preparing: 45 minutes
Baking: 35-40 minutes

Cake

2½ cups flour
2 teaspoons baking powder
1 teaspoon baking soda
1 teaspoon salt
2 teaspoons cinnamon
½ teaspoon cloves
3 eggs

½ cup oil
1⅓ cups sugar
½ cup orange juice
1 teaspoon almond extract
1½ cups shredded zucchini
 (about 2 medium size)

Orange icing

2 tablespoons softened butter
or margarine
3 cups confectioners' sugar

¼ cup orange juice
2 teaspoons lemon juice

Cake: In large bowl mix flour, baking powder, soda, salt, cinnamon and cloves; set aside. With whisk, beat eggs. Stir in oil, sugar, juice, extract and zucchini; mix well. Add to flour mixture, stirring just to moisten. Pour into greased pan 13" x 9" x 2". Bake in preheated 350° oven, 35 to 40 minutes or until toothpick inserted in center comes out clean.

Icing: In small bowl beat together until well blended softened butter or margarine, confectioners' sugar, orange juice and lemon juice.

Mrs. J. P. Hayden
Cincinnati, Ohio
Mrs. Donald Hayes
West Chester, Pennsylvania

CHOCOLATE SPONGE CAKE

Average
Do ahead

Serves: 8-10
Preparing: 30 minutes
Baking: 50 minutes
Cooling: 2 hours

5 eggs, separated
1 cup sugar
1 1-pound can Hershey
 chocolate syrup

¾ cup sifted flour
1 teaspoon salt
1 teaspoon vanilla
½ pint heavy cream

Beat egg yolks thoroughly. Add sugar and ½ of the Hershey syrup. Fold in flour and vanilla. Fold in stiffly beaten egg whites. Pour into ungreased 9" springform pan and bake at 325° for about 50 minutes. Invert on a rack and cool for two hours before removing from pan. Cut crosswise into two layers. Fill and frost with icing made by whipping cream and beating in remaining half can of chocolate syrup.

Muriel E. Gilman
Wilmington, Delaware

Dissolve 1 teaspoon plain gelatine in whipping cream and the cream will stand indefinitely.

TEXAS SHEET CAKE

Easy   *Serves: 24-36*
Do ahead   *Preparing: 30 minutes*
Freeze   *Baking: 30 minutes*

Cake

2 cups flour   **½ cup buttermilk**
2 cups sugar   **2 eggs, beaten**
1 cup margarine   **½ teaspoon cinnamon**
4 tablespoons cocoa   **1 teaspoon soda**
1 cup water   **1 teaspoon vanilla**

Frosting

4 tablespoons cocoa   **1 box confectioners' sugar**
½ cup margarine   **1 teaspoon vanilla**
6 tablespoons milk   **1 cup walnuts**

Cake: Mix flour and sugar. Put margarine, cocoa and water in a saucepan and bring to rapid boil. Mix into flour and sugar immediately. Add buttermilk, eggs, cinnamon, soda and vanilla. Mix well and spread into greased and floured sheet pan (11" x 17"). Bake at 350° for 30 minutes. Frost immediately.

Frosting: In a saucepan bring to boil cocoa, margarine and milk; mix with remaining ingredients and frost cake.

Mrs. J. P. Hayden
Cincinnati, Ohio

PENNSYLVANIA GERMAN CHOCOLATE CAKE
WITH CARAMEL ICING

Easy

Preparing: 25 minutes
Baking: 45 minutes

2 cups brown sugar
½ cup butter
¾ cup buttermilk
2 eggs
½ cup cocoa
½ cup boiling-hot strong
  coffee

1 teaspoon baking soda
1 teaspoon salt
1 teaspoon vanilla
2½ cups sifted all-purpose flour
1 teaspoon cider vinegar

Caramel Icing

½ cup butter
1 cup brown sugar
¼ cup evaporated milk
pinch of salt

1¾ to 2 cups confectioners' sugar
(enough for a spreading
  consistency)

Cream sugar, butter and eggs until fluffy. Mix in the buttermilk. Combine cocoa and coffee in a saucepan, adding the liquid slowly to prevent lumping. Then mix with creamed mixture. Moisten the baking soda with the vinegar and stir in with the salt and vanilla. Gradually beat in the flour, beating until smooth. Pour into a greased and floured 13" x 9" pan. Bake at 350° for 45 minutes. Cool. Ice with caramel icing.

Caramel Icing

Melt butter in a saucepan, add the brown sugar and boil over low heat for 2 minutes, stirring constantly. Add milk and salt and stir until it comes to a full boil. Remove from heat and cool until lukewarm. Gradually beat in the confectioners' sugar, beating until the icing is thick enough to spread.

Mrs. Glenn Kreider
West Chester, Pennsylvania

HUNGARIAN CHOCOLATE CAKE

Average

Serves: 8-10
Preparing: 30 minutes
Baking: 30 minutes

2 eggs
2 cups buttermilk
2 cups flour
2½ cups sugar
12 teaspoons cocoa
2 teaspoons baking soda

½ cup melted butter
2 cups whipped cream, flavored
with brandy
2 cups chocolate buttercream
frosting
sliced almonds, grated chocolate

In large bowl of electric mixer, blend eggs and buttermilk; add flour and sugar and blend well. Blend in cocoa and baking soda; add butter. Pour into three 9″ layer cake pans which have been greased, floured, lined with wax paper and greased and floured again. Bake in a 350° oven 25-30 minutes or until done. Cool on wire racks about 10 minutes before removing from pans. Allow to cool completely before assembling cake as follows: Top one layer with half the whipped cream. Place the other layer on top and spread frosting evenly on sides. Spread remaining whipped cream on top. Press almonds onto sides and sprinkle top with grated chocolate.

Morgan's
Philadelphia, Pennsylvania

FORGOTTEN DESSERT

Easy

Serves: 9
Preparing: 30 minutes
Rest in oven overnight

5 egg whites
¼ teaspoon salt
½ teaspoon cream of tartar
1½ cups sugar

1 teaspoon vanilla
½ pint heavy cream, whipped
strawberries or raspberries

Beat egg whites and salt until foamy. Add cream of tartar and continue beating until stiff peaks form. Add sugar, 1 tablespoon at a time. Beat 15 to 20 minutes until sugar is dissolved. Add vanilla. Grease 8″ x 8″ pan well; place in 450° oven. Turn off heat immediately. Let stay in oven overnight. Remove and frost with ½ pint heavy cream, whipped. Serve topped with crushed strawberries or raspberries.

Dorothy Baker
Rosemont, Pennsylvania

GATEAU CHOCOLATE

Average
Do ahead

Serves: 16-20
Preparing: 30 minutes
Baking: 3 hours

14 ounces of semi-sweet
  chocolate
7 ounces unsalted butter
  (2 quarter pound sticks minus
  2 tablespoons)
1½ cups granulated sugar
10 large eggs, separated
1 teaspoon pure vanila
2 tablespoons Grand Marnier

1 teaspoon lemon juice
butter and flour for preparing
  pan
confectioners' sugar (for
  sprinkling)
2 cups whipped cream, lightly
  flavored with sugar and vanilla
  (optional)

Preheat oven to 250°. Place rack in lower third of oven. Melt chocolate and butter together; stir to blend. Lightly mix egg yolks and add all but 2 tablespoons of sugar. Stir in melted chocolate and butter. Add vanilla and Grand Marnier. Add lemon juice to egg whites; beat until thickened. Slowly add 2 tablespoons of sugar and beat until stiff and glossy. Fold whites into chocolate mixture, gently but thoroughly. Turn mixture into prepared (butter and flour bottom and sides) 12″ springform pan. Bake for about 3 hours or until a thin knife blade inserted into the center comes out clean. Cool in pan. It is easier to serve cake on the baking pan bottom. Sprinkle with confectioners' sugar when cool. Whipped cream may be spooned onto each portion after the cake has been cut.

Mrs. Robert B. Shellenberg
Wayne, Pennsylvania

POLYNESIAN CAKE

Easy
Do ahead
Freeze

Serves: 8
Preparing: 20 minutes
Baking: 50 minutes

Cake

1 cup oil (Mazola)
2 cups flour
3 eggs
2 cups sugar
2 teaspoons baking soda
2 teaspoons cinnamon

2 teaspoons vanilla
2 jars of baby food carrots
1 cup chopped nuts
1 8-ounce can crushed
  pineapple, drained
1 can coconut

Combine all ingredients in bowl; mix with spoon. Grease and line pan with wax paper. Bake in 9″ x 13″ pan, 350° for 50 minutes.

Frosting

5 tablespoons flour	**½ cup Crisco**
1 cup milk	**1 cup confectioners' sugar**
½ cup butter	**2 teaspoons vanilla**

Mix together flour and milk. Cook over low heat until thick. Let cool. Cream butter, Crisco, sugar and vanilla. Add to cool mixture. Frost cake and place in refrigerator until frosting sets.

Clint Nieweg
Upper Darby, Pennsylvania

WALNUT CAKE (KARIDOPITA)

Easy	*Makes: approximately 40 pieces*
Do ahead	*Preparing: 30 minutes*
Freeze	*Baking: 30 minutes*

This cake may be kept at room temperature for several days before it must be refrigerated.

Cake

14 eggs	**1 cup sugar**
3 cups chopped walnuts	**3 teaspoons baking powder**
1 cup bread crumbs	**2 teaspoons vanilla**

Syrup

2 cups sugar	**½ lemon**
2½ cups water	**1 stick cinnamon**

To make cake: Beat eggs and sugar at high speed in mixer until eggs are very light and fluffy (15 to 20 minutes). At low speed add remaining ingredients and put in 11″ x 17″ pan which has been greased with ¼ pound butter or margarine. Bake in 350° oven about ½ hour or until done.

Make syrup by adding all ingredients in saucepan and bring to a boil. Continue boiling for 15 minutes and then cool. Set aside until cake is baked. Remove lemon and cinnamon stick from cooled syrup and pour over hot cake. When cake is cool, cut into diamond shape pieces and serve.

Anne Lagos
Media, Pennsylvania

GRANDMA'S FRUITCAKE BON BONS

Average
Freeze

Makes: 7½ dozen
Preparing: 30 minutes
Baking: 20-25 minutes

1 6-ounce can frozen orange juice, thawed
½ cup molasses
3 cups raisins, 15-ounce package
2 cups mixed candied fruits and peels
½ cup butter or margarine
⅔ cup sugar

3 eggs
1¼ cups sifted flour
⅛ teaspoon soda
1 teaspoon cinnamon
½ teaspoon nutmeg
¼ teaspoon allspice
¼ teaspoon ground cloves
½ cup chopped walnuts

In saucepan combine juice, molasses and raisins. Cook over medium heat, stir constantly until mixture comes to boil. Reduce heat. Simmer 5 minutes. Remove from heat; add half of candied fruit. Reserve other half for garnish. Cream together butter and sugar. Beat in eggs, one at a time. Sift together flour, soda, spices. Add to butter-sugar mixture. Add juice mix and nuts. Line muffin tins with miniature paper baking cups. Place one tablespoon batter in each, garnish with one or two pieces reserved fruit. Bake at 350° for 20 to 25 minutes.

Mrs. Louis Blatterman
Costa Mesa, California

CHOCOLATE APPLESAUCE CAKE

Easy
Do ahead
Freeze

Serves: 12
Preparing: 30 minutes
Baking: 1 hour

½ cup melted margarine
15-ounce jar applesauce
1 cup chopped walnuts
1 cup raisins
2 teaspoons baking powder
1 teaspoon allspice
2 cups flour

3 tablespoons cocoa
1 teaspoon soda
1 cup sugar
1 teaspoon ground cinnamon
1 tablespoon cornstarch
½ teaspoon salt
1 teaspoon ground cloves

Mix margarine with raisins, nuts and applesauce. Sift dry ingredients together. Add to first mixture and mix. Bake 1 hour at 325° in bundt or angel food cake pan.

Charlotte DeMonte Phelps
Philadelphia, Pennsylvania

Shake raisins and other dried fruits with flour before adding to dough or puddings, so they will not sink to the bottom during cooking or baking.

SPANISH BUN CAKE

Average
Freeze

Serves: 9
Preparing: 30 minutes
Baking: 35 minutes

1 cup sifted cake flour
1 teaspoon baking powder
¼ teaspoon baking soda
1 teaspoon ground cinnamon
½ cup sour milk or buttermilk

¼ teaspoon ground cloves
⅓ cup butter
⅞ cup sugar
1 ounce bitter chocolate
2 eggs

Reserve 2 tablespoons flour; mix remaining flour, baking powder, soda, cinnamon and cloves and sift three times. In another bowl cream butter well; add sugar gradually and continue creaming until mixture is light and fluffy. Add reserved 2 tablespoons flour and mix well. Add chocolate which has been melted and cooled. Add well beaten eggs. Add approximately ⅓ of sifted dry ingredients and approximately ½ sour milk to butter-sugar mixture. Repeat until all dry ingredients and sour milk have been added, beating well after each addition. Pour batter into greased 7″ square cake pan. Bake at 350° about 35 minutes. If larger pan is used reduce baking time. This is better mixed by hand.

Mocha chocolate frosting

¼ cup butter
1½ cups sifted confectioners'
sugar

5 tablespoons cocoa
1 egg white
1 teaspoon strong coffee

The frosting is better if done in the mixer. Cream butter well; add 1 cup confectioners' sugar and cocoa gradually. Beat egg white until stiff; add remaining confectioners' sugar gradually and beat well. Fold egg white mixture into butter mixture. Add coffee and mix well. Frost top and sides of cake.

Mrs. Randall E. Copeland
Haverford, Pennsylvania

FLORIDA KEY LIME PIE

Average
Freeze

Serves: 10
Preparing: 1 hour
Chilling: 3 hours

1 tablespoon (1 envelope)
  unflavored gelatine
½ cup sugar
¼ teaspoon salt
4 egg yolks
½ cup lime juice, about 8
  limes or 12 Key limes
¼ cup water, or lime juice for
  a very tart pie

1 teaspoon grated lime peel
  (optional)
few drops green food coloring
  (optional)
4 egg whites
½ cup sugar
1 cup heavy cream, whipped
1 baked 9½" or 10" pie shell

Topping:

1 cup heavy cream, whipped
½ to 1 teaspoon grated lime
  peel (optional decoration
  for center)

lime wedges to garnish—10 for
  10 servings

Place two large bowls in the refrigerator or freezer. Largest bowl for egg whites. Thoroughly mix gelatine, ½ cup sugar and salt in saucepan. Beat together egg yolks, lime juice and water. Stir into gelatine mixture. Cook over medium heat, stirring constantly, just until mixture comes to boiling. Remove from heat; stir in grated peel. Add food coloring *very* sparingly to give a pale green color. Chill, stirring occasionally, until the mixture mounds slightly when dropped from a spoon. Beat egg whites until soft peaks form. Gradually add ½ cup sugar, beating to stiff peaks. Return egg whites to refrigerator and whip 1 cup heavy cream. Fold gelatine mixture into egg whites. Fold in whipped cream. Pile into cooled baked pie shell. Chill until firm. At this point the pie can be frozen and completed at the time of serving. If pie has been frozen, defrost. Spread with additional whipped cream (1 cup). Center with grated lime peel. Garnish with wedges of lime.

Mrs. Sidney Curtiss
Philadelphia, Pennsylvania

ABBY'S PECAN PIE

Easy
Do ahead
Freeze

Serves: 6
Preparing: 5 minutes, excluding crust
Baking: 45 minutes

1 cup white corn syrup
1 cup dark brown sugar
⅓ teaspoon salt
⅓ cup melted butter

1 teaspoon vanilla
3 whole eggs
1 heaping cup shelled pecans
1 9" unbaked pie shell

Mix syrup, sugar, salt, butter, vanilla. Mix in slightly beaten eggs. Pour into shell. Sprinkle pecans over filling. Bake in 350° oven approximately 45 minutes. Top with vanilla ice cream or whipped cream.

Abigail Van Buren (Dear Abby)
Beverly Hills, California

APPLE PIE IN BROWN BAG

Easy
Do ahead
Freeze

Serves: 8
Preparing: 20 minutes
Baking: 1¼ hours

Great conversation piece. Hard to imagine baking something in a bag and having it come out golden brown without burning the bag!!

Filling

4 to 6 large baking apples
½ cup dark brown sugar
2 tablespoons flour

¼ teaspoon nutmeg
1 tablespoon lemon juice
1 unbaked 9" pie shell

Topping

½ cup dark brown sugar
½ cup flour

¼ cup butter
¼ teaspoon cinnamon

Core and slice apples thinly. *Do not peel.* Mix with remaining filling ingredients and pile into pie shell. Spread topping over filling. Place in grocery store brown bag. Fold edge down and fasten in three places with paper clips. Bake at 400°, 1 hour and 15 minutes.

Patricia P. Davies
Claymont, Delaware

STRAWBERRY PIE

Easy
Do ahead

Serves: 6
Preparing: 30-45 minutes

Baked 9″ pie shell
2 (3-ounce) packages cream
  cheese
2 tablespoons cream
1 quart strawberries, cleaned
  and hulled

2 tablespoons cornstarch
⅔ cup sugar
whipped cream

Soften the cream cheese to a paste consistency with the cream. Spread on the bottom of the cooled pie shell. Select 1 pint of the most handsome berries and place them stem end down in the cream cheese. Mash the remaining berries. Combine cornstarch and sugar. Add to the crushed berries. Cook over low flame until thickened and clear. Pour over strawberries in the pie shell and let cool. Garnish sparsely with whipped cream when ready to serve.

Robert W. Crawford
Philadelphia, Pennsylvania

COCONUT PIE

Easy
Do ahead

Serves: 6-8
Preparing: 25 minutes
Baking: 25 minutes

1 14-ounce package of
  coconut
¾ cup water
1¼ cups sugar
2 egg yolks and 1 whole egg

1 tablespoon butter
9″ pie crust (optional: reserve
  some dough for a lattice-work
  top)

Mix ¾ cup boiling water and 1¼ cups sugar in saucepan. Boil for 5 minutes; add package of coconut and let boil another 5 minutes. Remove from stove. Add egg yolks and whole egg, beaten, and the tablespoon of butter. Let cool 5-10 minutes. Pour into pie shell. Cover with leftover dough for trim and bake until golden at 400°.

Mrs. Charles A. Pearce
Hingham, Massachusetts

BAKED CRANBERRY PIE

Easy
Do ahead

Serves: 6-8
Preparing: 15 minutes
Baking: 30-40 minutes

3 tablespoons butter
1 cup sugar
2 cups flour
3 teaspoons baking powder

dash salt
1 cup milk
1 teaspoon vanilla
1 cup whole raw cranberries

Sauce:

½ cup butter
1 cup sugar

½ cup cream
½ teaspoon vanilla

Cream butter and sugar. Into creamed mixture, add alternately the flour mix (flour, baking powder, salt) and the milk. Add vanilla and cranberries. Bake at 350° for 30-40 minutes in buttered pie pans or 8" x 8" square cake pan.

Mix and simmer the sauce ingredients. Serve hot.

Betty McWilliams
Spokane, Washington

MOCHA MACAROON PIE

Do ahead

Serves: 8
Preparing: 30 minutes
Baking: 30-45 minutes

1¼ bars German sweet
  chocolate
1¼ cups graham cracker
  crumbs
¾ cup chopped walnuts
6 egg whites

1 cup sugar
1 cup whipped cream
sugar to taste
1 teaspoon instant coffee
2 teaspoons vanilla
shaved chocolate

Grind chocolate and mix with graham cracker crumbs and nuts. Beat egg whites until stiff and gradually add cup of sugar, ¼ cup at a time. Mix egg mixture with chocolate mixture. Bake at 350° for ½ hour to 45 minutes.

Whip cream, dissolve coffee in vanilla and add to whipped cream. Top pie. Shave chocolate on top.

The Thomas Ryder House
Walpole Village, New Hampshire

LIME CURD TARTS

Easy
Do ahead

Makes: 2 dozen 1½" tarts
Preparing: Curd: 20 minutes
Shells: 45 minutes

Lime Curd:

4 eggs
1 cup sugar
½ cup lime juice (or lemon
    juice)

1 teaspoon grated lime peel
½ cup butter or margarine

Tart shells:

2 cups unsifted flour
¼ cup powdered sugar

1 cup butter or margarine

Curd: Beat eggs until light and mix in sugar, lime juice and peel. Put in double boiler. Add butter and stir constantly until filling becomes thick as mayonnaise. Cool and chill.

Tart Shells: Mix flour and sugar. Cut in butter until crumbs are very fine. Pat together into ball. Pinch off pieces size of walnuts; press into tartlet shell pans. Bake at 400° for 12 minutes, or until golden brown. Cool and fill with curd. Top with sprig of mint. I try to keep shells in freezer for emergency desserts. The curd may be kept for several months in refrigerator.

Mrs. Henry Wendt
Devon, Pennsylvania

FROZEN CRUNCHY STRAWBERRY PIE

Average
Do ahead
Freeze

Serves: 6-8
Preparing: 15 minutes
Baking time: 15 minutes
Freezing: 3 hours

Butter Crunch Crust

½ cup butter
¼ cup brown sugar

1 cup flour
½ cup chopped pecans

Filling

1 10-ounce package frozen
    strawberries
1 unbeaten egg white

½ cup sugar
2 tablespoons lemon juice
½ cup heavy cream

Crust: Mix together ingredients for crust. Heat oven to 400°. Bake 15 minutes in 13" x 9½" x 2" pan. Stir with fork occasionally. Save ¾ cup for topping. Press remainder into 9" pie pan and chill.

Filling: Beat together strawberries, egg white, sugar and lemon juice until thick, about 5 minutes. Beat heavy cream. Fold into strawberry mixture. Put into pie shell and top with reserved crumbs. Freeze.

Mrs. William M. Dow
Haverford, Pennsylvania

HOLIDAY EGGNOG PIE

Complicated
Do ahead
Freeze

Serves: 6-8
Preparing: 45 minutes
Chilling: 6 hours

1 9" graham cracker crust
1 tablespoon unflavored gelatine
¼ cup cold water
⅓ cup sugar
2 tablespoons cornstarch
⅛ teaspoon salt

2 cups fresh (or canned) eggnog
1½ squares unsweetened chocolate, melted
1 teaspoon vanilla
2 tablespoons rum
1 cup heavy cream, whipped

Prepare crust. Sprinkle gelatine over water to soften. Mix sugar, cornstarch and salt in top of double boiler. Gradually stir in eggnog. Cook over hot, not boiling water, stirring constantly until thickened. Remove from heat and stir in the softened gelatine until dissolved. Divide filling in half. Add melted chocolate and vanilla to one half. Set aside. Allow remaining half to cool. Then add the rum and whipped cream. Pour the rum flavored mixture into the pie crust; then pour the chocolate mixture on top. Chill at least 6 hours or overnight.

Topping:

1 cup heavy cream, whipped
¼ cup confectioners' sugar

1 to 4 tablespoons rum

Fold sugar and rum into whipped cream. Pipe onto the top of pie with a pastry tube. Sprinkle with chocolate curls, if you wish. Chill for several hours before serving.

Mrs. Harold McBain
Moorestown, New Jersey

ICE CREAM MINCE PIE

Easy
Freeze

Serves: 6-8
Preparing: 30 minutes
Chilling: 45 minutes
Freezing: 3 hours

1½ cups graham cracker
  crumbs
¼ cup sugar

⅓ cup melted butter
1 quart vanilla ice cream
1 cup mincemeat, well drained

Mix graham cracker crumbs, sugar and butter. Press firmly in greased 9-inch pie plate. Chill until set, about 45 minutes. Stir ice cream to soften; stir in mincemeat. Spoon into pie shell: freeze firm.

Mrs. Henry Bitler
Bryn Mawr, Pennsylvania

LEMONADE PIE

Easy
Do ahead

Serves: 8-10
Preparing: 20 minutes
Baking: 1 hour
Chilling: 4 hours

Meringue:

3 egg whites
½ teaspoon baking powder
1 teaspoon vanilla

1 teaspoon white vinegar
1 teaspoon water
1 cup sugar

Filling:

1 can condensed milk
1 small can frozen lemonade
1 pint Cool Whip

1 tablespoon grated lemon rind
  (garnish)

Whip egg whites until stiff. Add baking powder, vanilla, vinegar and water. Add sugar, one tablespoon at a time. Spread onto lightly oiled 10″ pie plate. Bake at 275° for one hour. Permit to cool in oven with door ajar. Mix ingredients for filling thoroughly. Pour into meringue crust; chill and garnish with lemon rind.

Mrs. K. S. East
Devon, Pennsylvania

MINCEMEAT CHIFFON PIE

Average
Do ahead

Serves: 6
Preparing: 45 minutes

1 envelope Knox unflavored
  gelatine
½ cup water
¼ cup rum
1½ cups prepared mincemeat
3 egg whites

⅓ cup sugar
¼ teaspoon salt
1 cup heavy cream, whipped
1 9-inch baked pie shell
Maraschino cherries

Sprinkle gelatine on water to soften in saucepan. Place over low heat, stirring constantly until gelatine is dissolved. Remove from heat and stir in rum and mincemeat. Chill in refrigerator, stirring occasionally until mixture mounds when dropped from spoon. Beat egg whites until stiff. Beat in sugar and salt. Fold gelatine mixture into stiffly beaten egg whites. Fold in whipped cream. Turn into a cooled baked pie shell. Garnish with Maraschino cherries.

Mrs. E. Edward Ludwick, Jr.
Gladwyne, Pennsylvania

SHOO FLY PIE OR CAKE

Easy
Do ahead
Freeze

Serves: 12 cup cakes
1 9″ pie
Preparing: 30 minutes
Baking: 25 minutes cup cakes
45 minutes, pie

3 cups flour
1 cup sugar
1 cup margarine, scant

1 cup buttermilk
1 teaspoon soda
1 cup molasses

Combine flour, sugar and margarine as for pie crust. Save 1 cup for topping. Dissolve soda in ¼ cup of the buttermilk. Mix all ingredients well. Pour into muffin cups or into pie shell. Top with crumbs saved. Bake in 350° oven.

Mrs. Andrew L. Lewis
Lederach, Pennsylvania

CHEESE CAKE CHERRY TARTS

Complicated
Freeze

Makes: 80 small tarts
Preparing: 30 minutes
Baking: 15 minutes

Tart

1 pint sour cream
1 can Borden sweetened condensed milk
3 8-ounce packages cream cheese

⅓ cup lemon juice
4 eggs
1 teaspoon vanilla

Glaze

2 cans red sour pie cherries, drained
1 cup of drained cherry juice
2 tablespoons and 2 teaspoons cornstarch
⅔ cup sugar

1 tablespoon butter
1 tablespoon lemon juice
⅛ teaspoon almond flavoring
⅛ teaspoon red food coloring

Tart: Blend first 3 ingredients in mixer. Continue to mix, adding eggs one at a time. Then add lemon juice and vanilla. Pour into midget foil cups until each is almost full. Bake at 325°-350°, 10 or 15 minutes, or until lightly golden and dry, when inserting cake tester. Refrigerate.

Glaze: Mix cornstarch and sugar; add to juice. Bring to boil and cook for 3-4 minutes. Remove; add butter, lemon juice, almond flavoring and red food coloring.

To fill tart: Put small amount of glaze in center, add cherry, (1 or 2) and cover with more glaze. Freeze uncovered till hard, then cover with foil.

Mrs. Robert C. Linck
Collegeville, Pennsylvania

CHOCOLATE BAR PIE

Easy
Do ahead
Freeze

Serves: 8
Preparing: 30 minutes
Chilling: 4 hours

1 Pet Rich 9″ pie crust, bake completely
1 teaspoon instant coffee
2 tablespoons hot water

1 7½-ounce milk chocolate bar with almonds
4 cups Cool Whip, thawed

Dissolve coffee in water and add chocolate bar. Stir until chocolate melts. Cool. Add Cool Whip and pile into cooled pie crust. Freeze for at least 4 hours. Garnish with additional Cool Whip, toasted almonds and chocolate shavings.

Mrs. Richard C. Bond
Bryn Mawr, Pennsylvania

"BLENDER" COCONUT PIE

Easy
Do ahead
Freeze

Serves: 8
Preparing: 5 minutes
Baking: 1 hour

4 eggs
2 cups milk
½ cup sugar
1 tablespoon brown sugar

1 teaspoon vanilla
½ stick butter
½ cup Bisquick
1 cup shredded coconut

Put all in blender. Mix one minute at low speed. Pour into greased 9″ glass pie plate. Bake at 350° for 1 hour.

Patricia P. Davies
Claymont, Delaware

DEEP DISH APPLE PIE

Easy
Do ahead
Freeze

Serves: 6
Preparing: 30 minutes
Baking: 40 minutes

6 large apples
2 tablespoons lemon juice
¼ cup water
½ teaspoon cinnamon

1 cup sugar
¾ cup flour
½ teaspoon salt
6 tablespoons butter

Slice apples into deep baking dish. Mix lemon juice and water; pour over apples. Mix cinnamon and ½ cup sugar; sprinkle over apples. Mix other ½ cup sugar, flour, salt and work with butter until crumbly. Sprinkle over apples. Gently press down like pie crust. Bake at 375° 40 minutes. Serve hot or cold; plain, with milk, or with ice cream.

Sam Gorodetzer
Cherry Hill, New Jersey

PINEAPPLE TART

Average
Do ahead

Serves: 6
Preparing: 25 minutes
Baking: Crust: 20 minutes
Filling: 15 minutes

Crust

1 cup flour
1 stick cold butter

3 tablespoons powdered sugar

Filling

2 cups crushed, unsweetened
  pineapple, drained
1 tablespoon cornstarch
3 tablespoons sugar

1 teaspoon lemon juice
1 tablespoon butter
2 eggs, separated

Topping

⅓ cup sugar
⅛ teaspoon salt

½ teaspoon vanilla

Crust—Mix in food processor, flour, butter and sugar, or blend with pastry fork. Pat into 9″ tart pan with fingers, on bottom and up sides. Chill. Bake blind—pat foil around crust, cover with beans, or rice. Bake 400° for 20 minutes till lightly browned. Can remove foil for about 5 minutes.

Filling—Combine cornstarch and sugar; add to drained pineapple along with lemon and butter. Cook on medium heat, stirring until thick. Separate eggs; beat yolks. Add a little of hot mixture to yolks, then remaining mixture. Return to stove to cook for another minute, until thickened. Pour into crust. Beat egg whites with salt, sugar and vanilla until thick. Spread on filling. Bake at 325° for 15 minutes. Then cool; and refrigerate until served.

Note: double recipe for 11″ tart pan.

Mrs. William H. McCoy
Wilmington, Delaware

If you yearn for a pecan pie and haven't any nuts, substitute crushed cornflakes. They will rise to the top, as with nuts, and give the same texture.

Bubbling juice from berry pies won't overflow if you cut drinking straws in thirds and insert them in holes in the top crust.

NO CRUST RICOTTA PIE

Easy
Do ahead

Serves: 12
Preparing: 30 minutes
Baking: 3 hours
Chilling: 6 hours

**2 8-ounce packages cream
  cheese**
1 pound Ricotta cheese
1½ cups sugar
6 eggs
juice of ½ lemon

1 teaspoon vanilla
3 tablespoons cornstarch
3 tablespoons flour
¼ pound butter, melted
1 pint sour cream

Cream together cream cheese, Ricotta cheese, and sugar. Add eggs, lemon juice, vanilla, cornstarch, flour and melted butter. Beat until smooth. Fold in the sour cream and put mixture in a 10″ springform pan. Bake 1 hour in a 325° oven. Turn off oven and let pie cool in the oven for 2 more hours. Place in refrigerator for at least 6 hours before removing sides of pan. Top with strawberries.

Mrs. Lucy Cucchi
Springfield, Pennsylvania

HEAVENLY PIE

Average
Do ahead

Serves: 8
Preparing: 1 hour
Baking: 1 hour
Chilling: 24 hours

1½ cups granulated sugar
¼ teaspoon cream of tartar
4 eggs, separated

5 tablespoons lemon juice
1 tablespoon lemon rind
1 pint whipping cream

Sift together 1 cup sugar and cream of tartar. Beat egg whites until stiff, but not dry; then gradually add the sugar mixture, continuing to beat until blended. Use this mixture to line bottom and sides of a 9″ greased pie plate, being careful not to spread too close to rim. Bake at 275° for 1 hour, cool. Beat egg yolks separately, then add ½ cup sugar, lemon juice and lemon rind. Cook in top of double boiler until thick, 8 to 10 minutes, remove and cool. Whip cream. Combine half with lemon egg mixture and pour on top of pie shell. Use remaining cream for top. Cool in refrigerator 24 hours.

Mrs. Donald O. Bailey
Wayne, Pennsylvania
Mrs. Frank G. Binswanger, Jr.
Jenkintown, Pennsylvania

MARTY'S CHOCOLATE PIE

Easy
Do ahead

Makes: 2 pies
Serves: 5-6 per pie
Preparing: 10-15 minutes
Baking: 40 minutes
Cooling: 2 hours

2 8-inch unbaked frozen pie
  shells
1 stick butter, melted
2 envelopes Nestle's
  Choco-Bake (premelted
  chocolate)
1½ cups plus 1 tablespoon
  granulated sugar

4 eggs, well beaten
3 tablespoons white Karo syrup
1½ teaspoons vanilla extract
pinch of salt
½ cup coarsely broken pecans
whipped cream for topping,
  slightly sweetened

Preheat oven to 350°. Melt butter in saucepan large enough to hold all ingredients of pies. Remove from heat. Add chocolate until mixed. Now add sugar, eggs, (beaten in another bowl), Karo syrup, vanilla and salt. Sprinkle pecans on bottoms of pie pans, then divide mixture evenly between two pie shells. Bake for 40 minutes. Allow to cool on the counter for at least 2 hours. Serve with whipped cream. Pie firms up somewhat with cooling.

Mrs. W. C. Lucas, Jr.
Malvern, Pennsylvania

When mixing cold shortening with an electric mixer, heat mixer blades in hot water for a few minutes.

SWEET POTATO PIE

Average
Partial do ahead

Serves: 12
Preparing: 1½ hours
Cooking: 2½ hours

1 9" or 10" pie shell,
  unbaked and chilled
4 to 5 baked sweet potatoes,
  enough for 4 cups purée
¼ cup melted butter
3 eggs
1 cup cream
1 cup milk

⅔ cup sugar
⅓ cup brown sugar
½ teaspoon salt
1 teaspoon nutmeg
1 teaspoon cinnamon
¼ teaspoon cloves, ground
2 teaspoons vanilla
¼ cup dark rum

Bake sweet potatoes at 350° for 1½ hours. Allow to cool, then peel and purée. Measure 4 cups purée into a large bowl. Add the remaining ingredients in the order given. Fill the pie shell. Will form a high dome. Bake on lower shelf in preheated 425° oven for 15 minutes. Reduce heat to 350° for 45 minutes.

The Commissary
Philadelphia, Pennsylvania

CHOCOLATE CORDIAL PIE

Average   *Serves: 8-10*
Do ahead   *Preparing: 3 hours*
                                                   Chilling: 2 hours

30 large or 3 cups miniature   **1 teaspoon vanilla**
  marshmallows   **2 tablespoons brandy**
¼ cup milk   **2 tablespoons crème de cacao**
1 package (6-ounce)   **3½ cups heavy cream that has**
  semi-sweet chocolate   **been whipped stiff, divided**
  pieces   **1 9″ crumb pie crust**

In a saucepan, stir together marshmallows and milk. Cook over low heat, stirring frequently, until mixture is smooth. Turn half of marshmallow mixture into a small bowl; set aside. Stir chocolate pieces into remaining marshmallow mixture; return to low heat and stir until chocolate is melted. Remove from heat and stir in vanilla; cool to room temperature. Stir brandy and crème de cacao into reserved marshmallow mixture; chill until mixture mounds slightly when dropped from a spoon. Fold three cups of whipped cream into chocolate mixture; spoon into crumb crust. Fold remaining whipped cream into chilled brandy mixture; spread over chocolate mixture. Chill until firm, at least two hours.

Mrs. Henry K. Justi
Wayne, Pennsylvania

COFFEE-TOFFEE PIE

Average

Serves: 8-10
Preparing: one hour
Chilling: overnight

Pastry Shell

1 package pie crust mix
  (enough for 1 pie shell)
½ cup light brown sugar,
  firmly packed

1½ squares unsweetened
  chocolate, grated
1 teaspoon vanilla
2 tablespoons water
½ cup chopped walnuts

Filling

½ cup soft butter
¾ cup sugar
1 square unsweetened
  chocolate, melted
  and cooled

2 tablespoons instant coffee
2 large eggs

Topping

2 cups heavy cream
2 tablespoons instant coffee

½ cup confectioners' sugar
chocolate curls

Preheat oven to 375°.

Pastry Shell: In medium bowl combine pie-crust mix with brown sugar, walnuts and grated chocolate. Add water and vanilla. Using fork, mix well until blended. Put in well-greased pie plate, pressing firmly against sides and bottom. Bake 15 minutes and cool.

Filling: In small bowl, beat butter at medium speed until creamy, gradually add sugar, beat until light. Blend in cooled chocolate, coffee and 1 egg. Beat 5 minutes, add remaining egg, beat 5 more minutes. Turn into cooled pie shell and refrigerate overnight.

Topping: Several hours before serving, combine cream, 2 tablespoons coffee and confectioners' sugar. Refrigerate 1 hour. Beat until stiff. Place on pie and decorate with chocolate curls or grated chocolate.

Mrs. Frank McKaig
Gulph Mills, Pennsylvania
Mrs. Thomas E. Wiener
Wynnewood, Pennsylvania

ICELANDIC PANCAKES

Average

Serves: 8
Preparing: ½ hour
Cooking: 2 minutes each

8 tablespoons flour
2 eggs
½ teaspoon baking powder
1 tablespoon sugar

1¾ pints milk
¼ pint cold coffee
4 ounces melted butter
A few drops of vanilla

Hand beat eggs in a bowl, slowly. Add flour and milk alternately, beating well. Add sugar, baking powder and vanilla drops. Lastly, add coffee and beat in melted butter. Bake on hot pancake pan; use just enough mixture to cover bottom of pan very thinly. Pancakes are turned over after approximately 1 minute. Serve rolled up with sugar or filled with whipped cream and jam.

Vladimir Ashkenazy
Lucerne, Switzerland

INDIAN PUDDING

Easy

Preparing: 10 minutes
Baking: 3 hours

This recipe is known to have been in use in the Davenport family in 1797, a truly American dish! It appears as it was in the hand-written cookbook given to the donor's mother in 1898.

1 quart sweet milk
5 tablespoons corn meal
⅔ cup molasses
salt to taste

piece of butter the size of an egg
½ teaspoon ginger
2 eggs, well beaten

Heat milk to boiling. Stir in corn meal, molasses, a little salt, butter and ginger. Mix thoroughly. Add two well beaten eggs. Bake 3 hours or more and eat with cream. It having a brick oven, bake all night.

Henry P. McIlhenny
Philadelhpia, Pennsylvania

APRICOT MOUSSE

Average
Do ahead
Freeze

Serves: 12-16
Preparing: 30 minutes
Chilling: 6 hours

20 lady fingers, split
1 8-ounce package dried
  apricots
¼ cup Grand Marnier or
  apricot brandy
2 8-ounce packages cream
  cheese, softened

1½ cups light brown sugar
4 eggs, separated
¼ teaspoon salt
2 cups heavy cream, whipped
½ teaspoon almond extract

Dry split lady fingers by placing in slow oven for 10 minutes. Cook apricots in small amount of water until just soft. Purée in blender with brandy. Mix cream cheese with 1 cup of brown sugar, then add egg yolks one at a time, beating well after each addition. Stir in apricot purée and almond extract. Mix well. Beat egg whites with salt and remaining ½ cup brown sugar until stiff. Fold carefully into apricot-cream cheese mixture along with whipped cream. Place lady fingers, cut side in, along sides and bottom of 10" springform pan. Pour in apricot mixture. Refrigerate at least 6 hours before serving. Unmold and garnish. Fresh strawberries marinated in Grand Marnier or apricot brandy are an optional garnish.

Mrs. Aram Jerrehian
Wynnewood, Pennsylvania

FROZEN LEOPARD

Easy
Do ahead
Freeze

Serves: 12
Preparing: 15 minutes
Freezing: 2 hours

3 cups crushed macaroons
1 cup sugar
1 cup half and half
pinch of salt

3 cups heavy cream (no
  substitutes)
1 cup brandy

Combine macaroon crumbs, sugar, half and half, and salt. Whip cream and fold into macaroon mixture. Gradually fold in brandy. Spoon into individual dishes and place in freezer. 15 minutes before serving, remove from freezer.

Juanita McKain
Rosemont, Pennsylvania

STRAWBERRY PRETZEL DESSERT

Easy
Do ahead

Serves: 10
Preparing: 45 minutes plus chilling time

2 cups firmly crushed
  pretzels
3 teaspoons sugar
¾ cups butter (melted)
1 8-ounce carton whipped
  cream cheese
1 9-ounce carton Cool Whip
1 cup sugar

1 6-ounce package strawberry
  Jello
2 cups boiling water
1 16-ounce package frozen
  strawberries (thawed)
1 16-ounce can crushed
  pineapple (drained)

Stir Jello in boiling water until dissolved. Add strawberries (including juice) and pineapple. Mix crust of pretzels, 3 tablespoons sugar and butter. Press into 9" x 13" pan and bake 10 minutes at 350°. Mix cream cheese, Cool Whip and sugar and spread over cooled crust. Pour strawberry mixture over all and chill until set. Cut into squares and serve.

Anne Fagan
Broomall, Pennsylvania

PORCUPINE APPLES

Easy

Serves: 10-12
Preparing: 10 minutes
Cooking: 30 minutes

6 large Winesap apples
1 lemon
1 10-ounce jar black currant
  jelly

toasted slivered almonds
vanilla ice cream

Peel, halve and core apples. In a large frying pan place apple halves, core side down. Fill with water to cover half of apples. Slice lemon and add to water, (don't waste any juice). Simmer, turning once until apples are slightly softened. Carefully lift apples from pan to serving platter, core side down. Stick toasted almond slices into apples to achieve porcupine effect. Add the black currant jelly to the water and lemon mixture. Boil down until it thickens. Spoon mixture evenly over apples. Serve with vanilla ice cream.

Mrs. Eugene Ormandy
Philadelphia, Pennsylvania

CHOCOLATE SPONGE

Easy
Do ahead

Serves: 6
Preparing: 20 minutes
Chilling: 3 hours

½ pound dark sweet
  chocolate
2 tablespoons butter
½ cup evaporated milk
4 egg yolks

4 stiffly beaten egg whites
1 teaspoon gelatine
¼ cup warm water
3 tablespoons whipped cream
  (optional)

Melt chocolate, butter and evaporated milk in heavy saucepan. Remove from heat and mix in egg yolks. Cook very slowly for 1 minute. Fold in stiffly beaten egg whites with gelatine which has been dissolved in ¼ cup warm water. Mold in a deep crock mold and set in a cool place. Serve either with whipped cream or regular cream. Dessert can also be put in individual little crocks.

Mrs. James S. Hatfield
Philadelphia, Pennsylvania

COCONUT MACAROON CRUST WITH ICE CREAM

Easy
Do ahead
Freeze

Serves: 8
Preparing: 10 minutes
Baking: 30 minutes

1 cup graham cracker
  crumbs
½ cup coconut
½ cup walnuts
4 egg whites

½ teaspoon salt
1 teaspoon vanilla
1 cup sugar
1 quart butter pecan ice cream

Combine crumbs, nuts and coconut. Beat egg whites with salt and vanilla until foamy. Gradually add sugar. Fold into coconut mixture. Put in a greased pan and bake at 350° for 30 minutes. Fill with butter pecan ice cream and serve at once or freeze.

Mrs. Robert P. Tyson
West Chester, Pennsylvania

URUGUAYAN CUSTARD

Easy
Do ahead

Serves: 4
Preparing: 35 minutes
Baking: 35-40 minutes

Caramel

⅓ cup sugar

Custard

½ cup sugar   **1½ cups milk**
3 eggs

Heat the ⅓ cup sugar in frying pan until it becomes a brown syrupy caramel. (Pour into baking dish covering bottom and sides.) Mix the ½ cup sugar, 3 eggs, and 1½ cup milk. Pour over caramel in baking dish. Bake in 350 degree oven for 35 or 40 minutes, allow to cool. To serve: place a large plate over custard and turn quickly upside down.

Mrs. Samuel Evans, Jr.
Bryn Mawr, Pennsylvania

ZAPPED APPLES

Easy
Do ahead
Freeze

Serves: 5-6
Preparing: 20 minutes
Microwave: 8 minutes

Especially for microwave.

7-8 apples, peeled and sliced   **1 teaspoon cinnamon**
½ cup sugar   **4 teaspoons cornstarch**
⅛ teaspoon cloves   **¼ cup raisins**

In a large bowl mix the sugar, cinnamon, cloves and cornstarch. Add apples and toss; add raisins, toss again. Place the apples in a covered casserole, cook in microwave on high for 4 minutes. Remove from oven and fold apples over several times to coat with juices. Return again to microwave for 4 more minutes. Remove and fold again several times. Ready to serve for dessert or for breakfast with milk, cream, or ice cream.

Eleanor Biles
Skytop, Pennsylvania

PLUM PUDDING

Average
Do ahead
Freeze

Serves: 16-24
Preparing: 1 hour
Steaming: 5 hours

Will keep one year refrigerated, but add more brandy.

3¾ cups suet or 1½ pounds
4⅛ cups flour
1¼ cups white raisins
1¼ cups currants
1 cup molasses
1¼ teaspoons salt
1 teaspoon soda
½ cup brown sugar
½ cup brandy, plus extra
   brandy to light at serving
   time

6 eggs, beaten
rind of one lemon
¾ pound citron, chopped fine
2½ teaspoons cinnamon
1¼ teaspoons cloves
1¼ teaspoons allspice
⅝ teaspoon nutmeg
⅜ teaspoon mace

Dissolve soda in molasses, add to beaten eggs. Add well mixed dry ingredients. Cut up and cream suet, and add. Add raisins, citron (dredged in a little flour, and spices). Pack in greased molds and steam, on rack, 3½ to 4 hours. Before serving steam one hour more. Makes 2 pudding molds, 1½ quart size. Each mold serves 8-12.

Mrs. William C. Scheetz, Jr.
Bryn Mawr, Pennsylvania

FRENCH MINT DESSERT

Easy
Do ahead
Freeze

Serves: 18
Preparing: 20 minutes
Freezing: 2 hours

1 cup butter (no oleo)
2 cups powdered sugar
4 4-ounce squares
   semi-sweet chocolate
4 eggs
½ teaspoon peppermint
   extract

2 teaspoons vanilla
2 cups crushed vanilla wafers (8
   ounces)
½ cup crushed vanilla wafers
   (topping)
½ cup chopped nuts

Cream together butter and sugar; beat well. Melt chocolate over warm water and cool. Set aside. Add eggs to creamed mixture; add chocolate, peppermint and vanilla; continue beating. Fold in vanilla wafer crumbs, adding more crumbs if necessary. Place in *small* muffin cups, or nut cups. Sprinkle vanilla wafer crumbs (½ cup) on bottom and nuts and crumbs on top. Freeze. Makes 18 muffin size cups. Remove from freezer a few minutes before serving to soften. This is a good recipe for serving a crowd. *Recipe can easily be doubled or tripled.*

Mrs. Richard E. Anglemyer
Anchorage, Alaska

PAT'S DESSERT PIZZA

Easy

Serves: 8-10
Preparing: 45 minutes
Baking: 15 to 20 minutes

Crust

1½ sticks butter
⅔ cup sugar
½ teaspoon salt

2½ cups sifted flour
4 tablespoons milk

Filling (Strawberry)

1 can (1 pound 4½ ounce)
  crushed pineapple, drained
⅔ cup flaked coconut

⅔ cup chopped pecans
1½ cups sliced strawberries
1 cup strawberry jam or jelly

In a mixing bowl, cream together butter, sugar and salt. Gradually add flour and mix in milk. Turn dough into a buttered 12" pizza pan. Pat out dough to cover pan, prick with a fork, crimp edges. Bake in a preheated 400° oven 15 to 20 minutes, until lightly browned. Cool on rack. Spread crushed pineapple on crust, sprinkle with coconut and pecans. Arrange strawberries on top. Drizzle melted jam or jelly over all. Let it set. Cut in wedges to serve.

Mrs. Neil W. George
Los Altos, California

LEMON MOUSSE

Easy
Do ahead

Serves: 6
Preparing: 1 hour
Chilling: 2 hours

2 lemons
4 eggs, separated
¼ cup granulated sugar
1 tablespoon gelatine (1 ounce)

¾ cup heavy cream
Garnish:
sweetened whipped cream
toasted slivered almonds

Grate rind of the lemons and reserve. Squeeze the juice and reserve. Combine egg yolks with the rind and sugar and beat vigorously until the mixture is light and lemon-colored. Stir gelatine into lemon juice and let stand for ten minutes. Heat mixture over low heat or hot water until gelatine dissolves; stir into egg yolk mixture. Whisk cream until thick and fold into mousse mixture. Whip the egg whites until stiff and fold them in. Pour into individual parfait glasses or bowls, or turn into glass 1-quart soufflé dish with buttered paper collar attached. Chill at least 2 hours. Decorate top of mousse with whipped cream and slivered almonds (or lemon shavings) before serving.

Mrs. Samuel R. Scott
Penn Valley, Pennsylvania

CALIFORNIA LEMON FREEZE

Easy
Do ahead
Freeze

Serves: 6
Preparing: 20 minutes
Cooking: 10 minutes

3 egg yolks, well beaten
¼ cup lemon juice
½ teaspoon grated lemon rind
¼ teaspoon salt

1 scant cup sugar
3 egg whites, beaten stiff
½ pint whipped heavy cream
1 cup crunched graham crackers

Combine egg yolks, lemon juice and rind, salt and sugar in top of double boiler. Cook until sugar is melted and mixture slightly thickened. Cool. Fold in beaten egg whites and whipped cream. Put half of graham cracker crumbs in bottom of ice cube tray. Pour in lemon mixture, cover with remaining crumbs, freeze.

Mrs. Norman Carol
Bala-Cynwyd, Pennsylvania

FRENCH CHOCOLATE ICE CREAM

Easy
Do ahead
Freeze

Makes: 1½ quarts
Preparing: 20 minutes
Freezing: 2-3 hours

¼ **cup sugar**
½ **cup water**
6 to 9 ounces semi-sweet
   chocolate pieces

4 egg yolks
3 cups heavy cream, whipped

In a small saucepan combine sugar and water. Bring to boil and boil rapidly for 3 minutes. Into a blender container put semi-sweet chocolate pieces (more for real chocolate lovers!). Add the hot syrup; cover, and blend on high speed until chocolate sauce is smooth. Add egg yolks. Stir to combine; cover, and blend for 10 seconds. Fold chocolate mixture into heavy cream. Spoon into plastic container; cover with waxed paper, and freeze 2 to 3 hours. This needs no stirring and will not form ice crystals no matter how long you store it in your freezer.

Variations:

1. add mini-chips for chocolate chip ice cream
2. add almonds for chocolate almond
3. add instant coffee to sugar-water for mocha ice cream

Michael Bookspan
Philadelphia, Pennsylvania

MINUTE MOUSSE

Easy
Freeze

Serves: 6
Preparing: 20 minutes
Chilling: 4 hours

6 ounces bitter-sweet
   chocolate
4 eggs, separated

5 tablespoons coffee, liquid
2 tablespoons Cointreau
   (optional)

Melt chocolate by putting mixer bowl over hot water. Into the same mixer bowl put coffee, egg yolks and Cointreau; blend 4 or 5 minutes. Whip egg whites until they peak. Fold second mixture into first mixture. Chill for at least 4 hours.

Peggy King Rudofker
Gladwyne, Pennsylvania

LILLET BAVARIAN

Complicated

Serves: 8
Preparing: 1 hour
Chilling: 3 hours

1 orange (grated rind)
1 tablespoon gelatine
6 ounces Lillet
1½ cups milk
9 egg yolks
½ cup sugar
¾ tablespoon cornstarch

½ cup heavy cream
5 egg whites
⅛ cup of sugar
pinch of salt
fresh raspberries or Mandarin
oranges

Sprinkle 1 tablespoon gelatine over 6 ounces Lillet (do not stir). Heat 1½ cups milk to boil. Whisk egg yolks, ½ cup sugar and cornstarch into orange rind. Pour milk over egg yolk mixture, whisking constantly, and return to stove. Mixture should reach 180° or should coat spoon. Pour back into bowl that rests on ice. Stir in gelatine and Lillet immediately. Make sure gelatine does not lump in the bottom of the bowl. Cool at room temperature. Whip heavy cream. Beat 5 egg whites until stiff. Add salt and ⅛ cup sugar. Fold cream and egg whites into cooled mixture. Pour into cups and chill. Serve with fresh raspberries or Mandarin oranges.

Michèle Haines
Spring Mill Cafe
Conshohocken, Pennsylvania

COFFEE CRUNCH DESSERT

Easy
Do ahead
Freeze

Serves: 6-8
Preparing: 30 minutes
Chilling time

1 cup vanilla wafers, (crumbs
of 24 wafers)
2 tablespoons melted butter
or margarine
½ cup butter or margarine
1 cup sifted confectioners'
sugar
3 egg yolks
2 teaspoons instant coffee
powder

1 1-ounce square unsweetened
chocolate, melted and cooled
½ teaspoon vanilla
3 stiffly beaten egg whites
3¾ ounces chocolate coated
English toffee bars, chilled and
crushed (½ cup)

Blend crumbs and melted butter. Press into bottom of 8" x 8" x 2" pan. Cream butter and sugar until fluffy. Blend in next 4 ingredients. Fold in egg whites; spread mixture over crust. Top with crushed candy. Refrigerate until firm.

Mrs. Paul Monaghan
Haverford, Pennsylvania

PAKLAVA

Easy
Do ahead
Freeze

Serves: 50
Preparing: 30-50 minutes
Baking: 1 hour
Final Cutting and Syruping: 15 minutes

Paklava—Pastry of the Middle East, Asia Minor and Balkan area. If to be set aside or frozen, the last step can be done at time of serving, after both Paklava and syrup are made lukewarm.

1 pound phyllo dough (Greek or Armenian Stores)

Group A:

2 cups butter (clarified)   **1 teaspoon cinnamon**
2 cups chopped nuts   **¼ cup sugar**

Group B: (Syrup)

3 cups sugar   **1 tablespoon lemon juice**
2 cups water

Mix ingredients of Group A in a bowl and set aside. Brush bottom of 11½" x 17"x2" pan with butter. Roll out phyllo dough and cover with towel to prevent drying. Arrange 10 phyllo sheets at the bottom of the pan, brushing each sheet with 1 tablespoon butter. Sprinkle with ⅓ of nut mixture. Lay 6 more sheets over the nut mixture, brushing each sheet with butter. Sprinkle with ⅓ of nut mixture. Repeat six buttered layers topped with remainder of nut mixture. Add remaining sheets buttered as before until all are used. Butter the top. Cut partially (into first nut layer) diagonally across the pan, making diamonds about 2" x 3½" in size. Bake in 300° oven for 1 hour. Meanwhile, combine ingredients for syrup in small saucepan. Bring to a boil and cook for 10 minutes. Cool. When Paklava is baked, cut through completely. While it is hot, pour the cooled syrup (Group B) over it.

Mrs. Dorothy Mahjoubian
Ardmore, Pennsylvania

PUMPKIN TORTE

Easy
Do ahead
Freeze

Serves: 16-20
Preparing: 20 minutes
Baking: 45 minutes

1 large can pumpkin (29 ounces)
½ teaspoon cloves, ground
2 teaspoons cinnamon, ground
2 teaspoons ginger, ground
1 teaspoon nutmeg, ground
½ teaspoon salt
¾ can evaporated milk (small can)

1 cup sugar
1 tablespoon vanilla
3 eggs, beaten
1 package spice cake mix
½ pound melted butter or margarine
½ cup chopped nuts

Mix first 10 ingredients and pour into a greased 9" x 13" pyrex dish. Sprinkle the package of spice cake mix over top. Drizzle melted butter over the cake mix and sprinkle the chopped nuts on top. Bake 45 to 50 minutes at 350°. Serve with whipped cream or dessert whip.

Mrs. Elmer D. Samson
Pasadena, California

BANANAS FOSTER

Easy

Serves: 4
Preparing: 10 minutes

Gleaned when we were with the New Orleans Orchestra. Prepare at the table.

½ cup brown sugar (packed)
¼ cup butter
3 to 4 bananas
½ teaspoon cinnamon

2 tablespoons banana liqueur
½ cup dark rum
vanilla ice cream

Melt brown sugar and butter in chafing dish or electric skillet. Add bananas, sauté until tender. (As with conductors, "too much stirring with the "stick," the bigger mess you make"). Sprinkle with cinnamon. Pour liqueur and rum over all and flambé until flame burns out, while basting. Serve over vanilla ice cream.

Stevens Hewitt
Philadelphia, Pennsylvania

ORANGES IN LIQUEUR AND CANDIED PEEL

Easy
Do ahead

Serves: 10
Preparing: 30-45 minutes
plus chilling time

10 large oranges

Grand Marnier liqueur

Candied peel:

peel of 4 oranges
1 cup sugar

½ cup water
sugar

Peel oranges, removing all white membrane. Divide into sections. Chill thoroughly. Just before serving, drain off juice and pour Grand Marnier over sections. Scatter with candied orange peel and serve.
Candied Orange Peel: (Can be made the day before.) Remove peel from four oranges in lengthwise sections. Cover with cold water and cook slowly until soft. Drain. Remove membrane and cut peel into thin strips with scissors. Put sugar, water and peel in saucepan and cook slowly until clear. Cool on plate and roll in granulated sugar.

Mrs. Byron Janis
New York, New York

BAVARIAN MELON

Easy
Do ahead

Serves: 12
Preparing: 10 minutes
Chilling: 1 hour

1 3-ounce package lime
   gelatine
1 cup boiling water
¾ cup cold water

1 cup heavy cream, whipped
3 medium honeydew melons
1 cup sliced strawberries
   (optional)

Dissolve gelatine in boiling water. Stir in cold water. Chill until partially set; then beat until foamy. Fold in whipped cream and strawberries. Cut each melon in half and remove seeds. Fill each half-melon with gelatine mixture. Chill until set. To serve, cut each melon half into 2 wedges. Garnish with berries.

The Committee

CHERRIES JUBILEE

Easy

Serves: 6-8
Preparing: 10 minutes
Cooking: 5 minutes

2½ cans Bing cherries (drain, reserve juice)
⅓ tablespoon butter
1 lemon (squeeze juice and reserve; grate peel, set aside)
1 orange (squeeze juice and reserve; grate peel, set aside)

3 to 4 tablespoons sugar
2 teaspoons cornstarch
½ teaspoon cinnamon
3 ounces kirsch
2 ounces triple sec
pound cake
vanilla ice cream

In a large pan, melt the butter. Add the sugar and ¾ of the juice from the cherries. Add the juices from the lemon and orange, the grated lemon and orange peel, the cinnamon, and boil for 2 minutes.

Dissolve the cornstarch in the remaining cherry juice. Add to sauce. Add cherries and boil for 1 minute until slightly thickened. Add kirsch and triple sec. Flambé. Serve over pound cake and ice cream.

Chef Gaspard
Riverfront Dinner Theatre
Philadelphia, Pennsylvania

To extract unbroken nut meats from shell, freeze nuts at least 48 hours and crack while frozen.

LINZER TORTE

Easy
Do ahead

Serves: 6-8
Preparing: 30 minutes
Baking: 45-50 minutes

2 hard-boiled egg yolks, sieved
1 cup ground roasted almonds (with skins)
1½ cups flour
⅓ cup sugar
1 teaspoon vanilla

⅛ teaspoon ground cloves
¼ teaspoon cinnamon
1 tablespoon grated lemon peel
1 cup butter cut into pieces
1 jar red raspberry preserves
1 egg
1 teaspoon water

Grind almonds in food processor. Add sieved eggs and remaining ingredients. Blend until dough balls up. Dust with flour and refrigerate for at least one hour. Butter a 9" spring form pan. Press in ⅔ of dough and raise up on sides about ¾ to 1 inch in height. Fill with raspberry preserves. Roll remaining dough, cut into strips and lay across top. Brush strips with 1 egg mixed with one teaspoon of water. Bake at 350° for 45 minutes.

Sally Roberts Kahn
Philadelphia, Pennsylvania

To peel citrus fruit, soak in hot water for 5 minutes, then peel. All the white membrane will come off along with the peel.

ENGLISH SHERRY TRIFLE

Easy
Do ahead

Serves: 8-10
Preparing: 20 minutes
Cooking: 10 minutes

10 lady fingers, plain
⅓ cup raspberry preserves
½ cup sherry, or less if you prefer
1 can fruit salad or raspberries (or whatever fruit you prefer)

vanilla cream pudding
1 cup heavy whipping cream
blanched almonds for decoration (optional)

Sandwich lady fingers with raspberry preserves. Arrange in glass serving dish. Moisten lady fingers with sherry and some juice from fruit. Arrange drained fruit on top of lady fingers. Make vanilla cream pudding. When almost cool, pour over lady fingers and fruit. Shortly before serving pile whipped cream on top. Decorate with almonds.

Vanilla Cream Pudding

⅓ cup sugar
2 tablespoons cornstarch
⅛ teaspoon salt
2 cups milk

2 egg yolks, slightly beaten
2 tablespoons butter or margarine, softened
2 teaspoons vanilla

Blend sugar, cornstarch and salt in pan. Combine milk and egg yolks; gradually stir into sugar mixture. Cook over medium heat, stirring constantly until mixture thickens and boils. Boil and stir 1 minute. Remove from heat and stir in butter and vanilla.

John Shamlian
Haddonfield, New Jersey

DUTCH APPLE FRITTERS

Easy
Partial do ahead

Serves: 6-8
Preparing: 45-60 minutes
Resting: 3 hours

2 cups sifted flour
2 cups beer, room
temperature
4 or 5 tart cooking apples
1 cup sugar

1½ tablespoons ground
cinnamon
oil for deep frying
confectioners' sugar

Three hours before serving, make batter. Sift flour into deep bowl. Make a well in the center and slowly pour in beer, stirring gently. Do not beat. Continue to stir gently just until smooth. Allow to rest at room temperature at least three hours. About 15 minutes before making fritters, cut peeled and cored apples crosswise into rounds about one-third inch thick. Place in a single layer on waxed paper. Combine granulated sugar and cinnamon and sprinkle evenly over both sides of apples. Heat about three inches of oil in a deep fryer or heavy saucepan to 375°. One at a time, dip apple rounds in batter and coat thoroughly. Deep-fry three or four at a time in the hot oil, turning occasionally, until lightly browned (about four minutes). Keep warm in oven in a shallow baking dish lined with paper towels. Arrange on platter and lightly sift confectioners' sugar over top just before serving. Makes about two dozen.

Sarah Casey, Food Editor
Evening Bulletin
Philadelphia, Pennsylvania

Buy almond macaroons and put together with chocolate icing for a quick festive cookie.

FROZEN PEACHES

Easy
Do ahead
Freeze

Preparing: 30 minutes
Chilling: 2 hours

2 quarts sliced peaches
1 cup sugar

4 ounces frozen orange juice, not
diluted

Mix and let stand at room temperature for 2 hours. Pack in containers and freeze. Delicious served plain or over ice cream.

Mrs. John V. Calhoun, Jr.
Devon, Pennsylvania

Suites

cookies, candies, and nuts

AMARETTI

Easy
Do ahead

Makes: approximately 1½ dozen
Preparing: 10 minutes
Baking: 5 minutes

½ **pound sugar**
¼ **pound blanched almonds**

½ **teaspoon almond extract**
2 **egg whites**

Chop and pulverize almonds. Mix with half of the sugar and extract. Beat egg whites until very stiff. Add balance of sugar and beat again. Add almond mixture to the egg whites; mix very well. Shape into 1″ balls or cookies. Place on greased cookie sheet, 1″ apart. Bake at 350° for 5 minutes or until lightly browned.

The Committee

APRICOT HEARTS

Average
Do ahead

Makes: 24 hearts
Preparing: 20 minutes
Chilling: overnight
Cooking: 10-12 minutes

Cheese Pastry
1 cup sifted flour
pinch of salt

½ **cup butter or margarine**
4 **ounces cream cheese, in**
   pieces

apricot jam
1 egg

sugar

Sift together flour and salt into a bowl. Add butter and cheese into flour mixture until well blended. Lightly shape into a ball. Wrap in wax paper and refrigerate until well chilled, or overnight. Heat oven to 400°. Lightly grease two cookie sheets. On floured board roll out dough to ⅛″ thickness. Cut into hearts. Place 1 teaspoon apricot jam on half of the hearts. Brush edges with beaten egg and cover with another heart. Press edges together to seal. Arrange on cookie sheets. Brush tops with beaten egg and sprinkle with sugar. Bake approximately 10 to 12 minutes.

Mrs. Eugene Ormandy
Philadelphia, Pennsylvania

BILLY'S CRUNCHY COOKIES

Easy

Makes: 6½ dozen
Preparing: 25 minutes
Baking: 10 minutes

1 cup butter
1 cup sugar
1 cup brown sugar
2 eggs
1 teaspoon vanilla
½ teaspoon salt

2 cups flour
½ teaspoon baking powder
1 teaspoon baking soda
1 4-ounce can coconut
4 cups corn flakes

Preheat oven to 350°. Cream together first five ingredients. Sift, mix, and add to the above, the next four ingredients. Add coconut and corn flakes; stir gently. Drop by teaspoonful on ungreased cookie sheet; 2 inches apart. Bake for 10 minutes, or until lightly browned.

Mrs. William G. Kay, Jr.
Bryn Mawr, Pennsylvania

MADELEINES

Easy
Do ahead
Freeze

Makes: 7 dozen
Preparing: 20 minutes
Baking: 15 minutes

3 cups flour (after sifting)
½ cup butter or margarine
  (melted and cooled)
3 eggs
1 teaspoon vanilla
2 tablespoons almond liqueur

rind of lemon, grated
1 cup milk
3 teaspoons baking powder
1½ cups sugar
confectioners' sugar

Put eggs in mixer and add sugar; beat well. Add melted butter, vanilla, almond liqueur and lemon rind. Sift flour and baking powder together and add alternately with milk to the above mixture. Put by teaspoonsful in well-greased Madeleine pan (use 2 if you have them). Bake at 350° for approximately 15 minutes. Cool and dust with confectioners' sugar.

Mrs. L. S. Heck
Mount Kisco, New York

PEANUT BUTTER CHEWS

Easy
Do ahead
Freeze

Makes: 12
Preparing: 10 minutes

½ cup corn syrup
½ cup sugar
1 cup peanut butter

2 cups Rice Krispies
½ teaspoon vanilla
pinch of salt

Melt in frying pan over low heat, the sugar and corn syrup. Add peanut butter. Stir until melted. Add Rice Krispies and salt. Stir well. Turn into 8" square dish. Cool, cut in squares and serve.

Mrs. Beezey Drake
South Pomfret, Vermont

PEANUT BUTTER-CHOCOLATE CHIP COOKIES

Easy
Do ahead
Freeze

Preparing: 15 minutes
Baking: 25 minutes

½ cup chunky peanut butter
⅓ cup margarine
¾ cup brown sugar
¾ cup white sugar
2 eggs
2 teaspoons vanilla

1 cup flour
1 teaspoon baking powder
¼ teaspoon salt
1½ cups semi-sweet chocolate
   morsels

Cream together peanut butter, margarine and sugars. Add eggs and vanilla. Then mix in flour, baking powder and salt. Add ½ cup chocolate morsels, and put in greased 9" x 13" pan. Sprinkle remaining chocolate morsels on top. Bake in 350° oven for 25 minutes. Cool and cut into bars.

Khris Hayes
West Chester, Pennsylvania

DAISY COOKIES

Easy
Do ahead
Freeze

Makes: 3 dozen
Preparing: 15 minutes
Baking: 10 minutes

1 stick butter
¼ cup sugar

1 cup sifted flour
any kind of jam or jelly

Beat together all ingredients except jelly. Make balls of dough using about 1 teaspoon per cookie. Place on greased cookie sheets, and depress each one in center. Fill with jam or jelly. Bake at 375° for 10 minutes. (I use larger end of melon baller instead of teaspoon. Use small end of melon baller for "dimple.")

Mrs. Frank H. Phipps
Villanova, Pennsylvania

THE BEST BASIC COOKIE

Easy
Partial do ahead

Makes: 24
Preparing: 50 minutes
Baking: 20 minutes

3 eggs, beaten
½ cup Mazola oil
1 cup sugar
1 teaspoon flavoring
(recommend almond or
brandy)

½ teaspoon vanilla
3 cups flour
¼ teaspoon salt
2 teaspoons baking powder

Add oil, sugar and flavorings to beaten eggs. Combine dry ingredients, sift and add to egg-oil mixture. Roll out on floured board, about ⅛" thick. Cut with floured cookie cutters into interesting shapes. Decorate or fill if desired. Bake on unfloured cookie sheets in 350° oven until edges are slightly brown (15-20 minutes). Batter may be stored in refrigerator in bowl, covered with wax paper.

Mrs. Myron E. Resnick
Broomall, Pennsylvania

POTATO CHIP AND CORN FLAKE COOKIES

Easy
Do ahead
Freeze

Makes: 8 dozen
Preparing: 5 minutes
Baking: 10-12 minutes

1 pound margarine
3½ cups flour
1 cup sugar

2 teaspoons vanilla
2 cups crushed potato chips
2 cups crushed corn flakes

Combine and mix well margarine, flour, sugar, vanilla. Add crushed potato chips and crushed corn flakes. Drop by teaspoon on ungreased cookie sheet. Bake at 375° for 10 to 12 minutes.

Jane Martin
Berwyn, Pennsylvania

BROWN SUGAR PECAN ROUNDS

Easy
Do ahead

Makes: 3 dozen
Preparing: 15 minutes
Baking: 10-12 minutes

½ cup butter or margarine
1¼ cups brown sugar,
  packed
1 egg
1¼ cups flour

¼ teaspoon soda
⅛ teaspoon salt
½ cup coarsely chopped pecans

Heat oven to 350°. Mix butter or margarine, brown sugar and egg. Stir in remaining ingredients. Drop dough from teaspoon about 2 inches apart onto ungreased baking sheet. (Dough will flatten and spread.) Bake 10 to 12 minutes or until set. Makes 3 dozen crispy cookies.

Mrs. Louis H. Bieler
Philadelphia, Pennsylvania

BUTTERSCOTCH-OATMEAL COOKIES

Easy
Do ahead
Freeze

Preparing: 15 minutes
Baking: 10 minutes

All steps may be done in food processor, except for butterscotch bits and oats.

½ cup butter or margarine
1 cup brown sugar
1 egg
¾ cup sifted flour
¼ teaspoon baking soda
¼ teaspoon salt

⅛ teaspoon baking powder
1 cup rolled oats
1 12-ounce package butterscotch
  bits (may use chocolate bits, if
  preferred)

Cream margarine and brown sugar. Beat in egg and add dry ingredients, which have been sifted together. Add oats and butterscotch bits. Drop from teaspoon on ungreased baking sheet. Bake at 350° for 10 minutes. (They will each look slightly underdone, but this makes them chewier.)

Mrs. Julius A. Mackie
Bryn Mawr, Pennsylvania

LIZZIES

Easy
Do ahead
Freeze

Makes: 7-8 dozen
Preparing: 1 hour
Baking: 15 minutes

3 cups raisins
½ cup bourbon
1½ cups flour
1½ teaspoons baking soda
1½ teaspoons cinnamon
½ teaspoon nutmeg
½ teaspoon cloves

½ cup packed light brown sugar
¼ cup soft butter or margarine
2 eggs
1 pound pecan halves
½ pound citron, diced (1¼ cups)
1 pound whole candied cherries

Soak raisins in bourbon for one hour. Sift flour, soda, and spices together. Cream butter and brown sugar until light; then add two eggs. Beat until fluffy. Beat in flour mixture and beat until smooth. Stir in raisins, nuts, and fruits. Drop from teaspoon onto greased cookie sheets. (There will be a minimum of batter, mostly nuts and fruits.) Bake in 325° oven about 15 minutes until firm. Store in airtight container or freeze.

Mrs. Dana Fernald
Malvern, Pennsylvania

CHOCOLATE LACE COOKIES

Average
Do ahead
Freeze

Makes: 3½ dozen 3-inch cookies
Preparing: 20 minutes
Baking: 6-8 minutes

1 cup oatmeal, 6 minute or
    quick variety
1 cup white sugar
¼ teaspoon baking powder
2 tablespoons plus 2
    teaspoons flour

1 tablespoon plus 1 teaspoon
    cocoa
¼ pound melted butter, or
    margarine
1 egg, beaten
1 teaspoon vanilla

Mix dry ingredients; add melted butter, beaten egg, and vanilla. Drop by teaspoon on waxed paper on cookie sheet, 4 inches apart. Bake at 300° for 6-8 minutes. Cool on waxed paper for 15 minutes. Peel cookie from paper. Dough can be made ahead and frozen.

Marilyn Costello
Philadelphia, Pennsylvania

GOOF BALLS

Easy
Do ahead

Makes: 2 dozen
Preparing: 20 minutes

1 stick margarine or butter
1 cup sugar
½ cup chopped dates
½ cup chopped walnuts

1 egg, beaten
½ cup chopped pecans
2 cups Rice Krispies
confectioners' sugar

Boil butter and sugar for 10 minutes. Add dates, beaten egg, pecans and 2 cups of Rice Krispies. When cool, make balls between palms and roll in confectioners' sugar.

Margaret Welliver
Albany, Oregon

BROWNIES

Easy
Do ahead

Serves: 12 or more
Preparing: 15 minutes
Baking: 30 minutes

¾ cup flour
2 squares Baker's
  unsweetened chocolate
¼ cup butter
2 eggs, slightly beaten

1 cup sugar
½ teaspoon baking powder
½ teaspoon salt
1 teaspoon vanilla
1 cup nuts, chopped

Beat eggs slightly; add sugar; beat very little. Add melted butter and melted chocolate. Stir just enough to mix. Fold in sifted dry ingredients. Bake in 8½" to 9" square pan at 350° for about 30 minutes.

Allow to cool in pan and cut into squares.

Mrs. Henry H. Bitler
Bryn Mawr, Pennsylvania

TRUFFLE COOKIES

Easy
Do ahead
Freeze

Makes: 3 dozen
Preparing: 15 minutes
Baking: 15 minutes

½ cup butter
3 tablespoons confectioners'
  sugar

⅓ cup Droste cocoa
⅔ cup sifted flour
extra confectioners' sugar

Cream butter, sugar; blend in cocoa and flour. Shape into 1″ diameter balls and place on teflon or greased cookie sheet. Bake at 325°, 15 minutes. Cool slightly; roll in confectioners' sugar; cool completely and roll again in confectioners' sugar, as the Droste cocoa makes them quite bitter.

Mrs. Henry Zenzie
Princeton, New Jersey

HELLO DOLLIES

Easy
Do ahead
Freeze

Serves: 20
Preparing: 10 minutes
Baking: 30 minutes
Chilling: 2 hours

1½ sticks butter, melted
2 cups graham cracker
  crumbs
2 cups chocolate chips
2 cups shredded coconut

2 cups walnuts, chopped
2 cans sweetened condensed
  milk
2 cups flaked almonds

Layer ingredients as listed in 9″ x 13″ pyrex pan. Bake at 350° for 30 minutes. Refrigerate for a couple of hours and cut into squares.

Pinchas Zukerman
New York, New York

CHOCOLATE COOKIES

Easy
Do ahead

Makes: 3 dozen
Preparing: 20 minutes
Baking: 10-12 minutes

½ cup butter
¾ cup sugar
1 egg
2 squares unsweetened
  chocolate, melted

¾ cup flour, sifted twice
¾ teaspoon baking powder
½ teaspoon vanilla

Cream together butter, sugar, egg and unsweetened, melted chocolate. Sift together flour, baking powder and vanilla. Combine ingredients. Drop by teaspoonful on ungreased cookie sheet. Bake 10-12 minutes in preheated 375° oven, until cookies are crunchy.

Mrs. Robert Alan Swift
Bryn Mawr, Pennsylvania

MUSHROOM MERINGUES

Average   *Preparing: 2 hours*
Do ahead   *Baking: 1 hour*

¾ cup egg whites, room   1½ cups superfine sugar
   temperature (whites from 6   ¼ teaspoon almond extract
   large eggs)   ¾ teaspoon vanilla
¼ teaspoon salt   unsweetened cocoa
¼ teaspoon cream of tartar   6 ounces semi-sweet chocolate

Beat egg whites in a large bowl until foamy. Beat in salt and cream of tartar. At low to medium speed of mixer, keep beating while gradually adding sugar. Add almond and vanilla extracts. Beat at high speed until stiff, 6 to 7 minutes. Place meringue mixture in a large pastry bag fitted with a ½" diameter tip. Cover 2 cookie sheets with parchment paper. Make mushroom stems first. Press out meringue while lifting bag, until stems are ½" to ¾" tall. (Do not worry if they fall over a bit.) Press out caps in rounds about 1" in diameter. Try to keep them high and puffy rather than flat. If caps have points on them, dampen a finger and press point flat. Sprinkle stems and caps lightly with cocoa. (I use a tea strainer.) Place cookie sheets in oven preheated to 225°. Bake 1 hour without opening door. At end of 1 hour, test to see if meringues can easily be lifted from parchment. Turn off heat and allow to cool overnight in oven. If you are in a hurry, leave oven door open and leave meringues in oven until cool, about 20 minutes. Cut points off stems with a serrated knife. Melt chocolate and allow to cool a little. Then spread melted chocolate on flat side of mushroom cap with a knife and stick stem on. Allow to cool upside down. Place in a mushroom or other pretty basket filled with crumpled wax paper and tie with a ribbon for gift.

Mrs. Louis Hood
Wayne, Pennsylvania

DELTA BARS

Easy   *Makes: 16 squares*
Do ahead   *Preparing: 20 minutes*
Freeze   *Baking: 30 minutes*

1 stick margarine   1 egg plus one yolk
1 cup sugar   1¼ cups self-rising flour
1 teaspoon vanilla (note: 1   2 egg whites
   teaspoon almond flavoring   1 cup brown sugar
   may be substituted if   2 ounces chopped almonds or
   almonds are the nuts used)   pecans

Mix at high speed in electric mixer, margarine, sugar, vanilla, egg and egg yolk. Fold flour in lightly. Spread this in a greased and floured 9" x 9" pan. Beat egg whites until stiff and add brown sugar. Beat. Spread on top of the dough mixture. Sprinkle with nuts. Bake 30 minutes at 350°. Cool before cutting.

Nannette Wendel
New Orleans, Louisiana

OLD FASHIONED BROWN EDGE COOKIES

Easy

Makes: 3 dozen
Preparing: 20 minutes
Baking: 10 minutes

½ pound butter
1 cup sugar
2 egg whites (unbeaten)

1½ cups flour
1 teaspoon vanilla
cinnamon and sugar

Cream butter and mix well with sugar. Add unbeaten egg whites. Add flour gradually. Add vanilla. Drop batter by teaspoonful on cookie sheet. Bake in 350° oven until edges are brown, (about 10 minutes, checking in five minutes). Sprinkle with cinnamon-sugar while still hot.

Caroline and Bob Custer

LEMON SQUARES

Easy
Do ahead

Makes: 12 squares
Preparing: 10 minutes
Baking: 45 minutes

1 cup flour
½ cup butter
¼ cup powdered sugar
2 eggs
1 cup granulated sugar

½ teaspoon baking powder
2½ tablespoons fresh lemon
 juice
dash of salt

Sift flour and powdered sugar into bowl. Blend in butter with fingertips until well mixed. Pat evenly into an 8" x 8" pan. Bake at 350° for 20 minutes. Beat together eggs, granulated sugar, baking powder, lemon juice and salt. Pour over the baked crust and return it to oven for 20 to 25 minutes longer. Cool on rack. Sprinkle with powdered sugar and cut in squares.

Mrs. Louis Hood
Wayne, Pennsylvania

SCOTCH BARS

Easy
Do ahead

Makes: 50 squares
Preparing: 20 minutes

Bars:

1 cup butter or margarine
½ cup sugar
½ cup brown sugar
1 egg
1 teaspoon vanilla

1 teaspoon lemon juice
1 cup uncooked oatmeal
1 cup flour
1 teaspoon baking powder
½ teaspoon salt

Frosting:

2 tablespoons Crisco
1 tablespoon butter
3 ounces Bakers chocolate
5 tablespoons hot milk

1½ cups confectioners' sugar
½ teaspoon vanilla
¼ teaspoon salt

Cream together butter, sugar, egg, vanilla and lemon juice. Stir in oatmeal, flour, baking powder and salt. Spread thinly in a 10″ x 14″ pan. Bake 20 minutes at 350° or until done. To make frosting: melt Crisco, butter and chocolate together. Add hot milk to confectioners' sugar with vanilla and salt. Then add chocolate mixture and beat until smooth. Spread on baked mixture. Top with 1 cup chopped nuts. Cut in squares.

Mrs. William Foster
Greenwich, Connecticut

BLOND BROWNIES

Easy
Do ahead

Makes: 2 dozen
Preparing: 10 minutes
Baking: 20-25 minutes

1 cup brown sugar
⅓ cup butter
1 egg
⅛ teaspoon baking soda
1 teaspoon vanilla
1 cup flour

½ teaspoon baking powder
½ teaspoon salt
1 cup chopped nuts
1 12-ounce package chocolate
   chips

Cream butter and sugar together. Mix the rest of the ingredients and add to sugar, butter mixture. Bake at 350° for 20 to 25 minutes.

Mrs. William G. Kay, Jr.
Bryn Mawr, Pennsylvania

SPICED NUTS

Easy
Do ahead

Preparing: 30 minutes

2 cups whole nuts (pecans or
  walnuts)
¾ cup sugar
3 tablespoons water
1 teaspoon cinnamon

¼ teaspoon salt
½ teaspoon nutmeg
1 teaspoon orange rind, grated
½ teaspoon cloves

Mix dry ingredients with water and cook to soft ball stage (when dropped in
cold water it will harden slightly). Add nuts and stir until mixture sugars. Turn
out on well buttered platter and allow to cool. Break up into individual pieces
when cool. Store in covered jar.

Mrs. George S. Fabian
Bryn Mawr, Pennsylvania

WEST INDIAN NUTS

Easy
Do ahead

Preparing: 15 minutes
Cooking: 1½ hours

2 cups sugar
3 tablespoons cinnamon
1 tablespoon ground cloves
2 teaspoons salt
1 teaspoon ground ginger

1 teaspoon nutmeg
1 egg white
2 tablespoons cold water
2 cups shelled nuts (almonds or
  pecans)

Sift sugar with spices. Beat egg white until frothy; add water. Place several
nuts at a time in egg-water, mix; then roll in sugar mix. Put generous layer of
sugar mix in shallow pan. Arrange nuts on top. Cover with more sugar mix.
Bake 1½ hours at 250°. Shake nuts in strainer to remove surplus sugar.
Store in tightly covered jar in a cool place.

Mrs. William P. Cashel, Jr.
Gladwyne, Pennsylvania

PLUM LEATHER

Easy   *Preparing: 30 minutes*
Do ahead   *Seasoning: 24 hours*

**2 pounds prune plums (fresh)   ½ cup sugar
   (about 5 cups)**

Slice pitted plums. Add sugar and in large saucepan bring to boil. Stir until sugar dissolves. Boil four minutes. Blend in blender until smooth. Strain and discard bits of skin. Cover two cookie sheets with plastic wrap and spread purée into ¼″ thickness. Dry in full sunlight or in gas oven with just pilot light. Drying takes a day. Fruit is dry when it lifts easily from plastic wrap. For storing roll up in plastic wrap. Keeps well. (If the kids can't find it.)

Stevens Hewitt
Philadelphia, Pennsylvania

PEANUT BUTTER CUPS

Easy   *Preparing: 1 hour*
Do ahead   *Chilling: 2 hours*
Freeze

**2 cups peanut butter (cream   6 ounces chocolate chips or milk
   style)   chocolate pieces
2½ cups sifted confectioners'   1 tablespoon margarine
   sugar
½ cup butter or margarine,
   melted**

Mix peanut butter and margarine. Add confectioners' sugar. Press into bonbon-sized baking papers. Melt chocolate chips and 1 tablespoon margarine. Spread a thin layer of chocolate over peanut butter cups. Refrigerate.

Melissa Watson
Charlotte, North Carolina

ALMOND BUTTER CRUNCH

Average
Freeze

Makes: about 2 pounds
Preparing: 1 hour

1 cup butter
2½ cups granulated sugar
1 cup chopped almonds
¼ pound semi-sweet
   chocolate bits

1 cup chopped almonds
1 teaspoon vanilla

Combine butter and sugar in pan. Cook, stirring until it comes to a boil. Remove, add 1 cup chopped almonds. Return to heat. Using a candy thermometer, cook over medium high heat until it registers 290°. Remove, add vanilla, and quickly spread out as thinly as possible on two large cookie sheets. Melt chocolate over hot water. Spread on one side of candy. Sprinkle with chopped almonds. Let cool. Turn over and do the same on the other side of candy. Cool thoroughly. Break into small pieces as evenly as possible.

Mrs. Norman P. Robinson
Haverford, Pennsylvania

APRICOT BALLS

Easy
Do ahead
Freeze

Makes: 20-30
Preparing: 30 minutes
Cooking: 30 minutes

1 10-ounce package dried
   apricots
2 cups sugar
rind and juice of 1 orange

1 cup chopped nuts (walnuts or
   pecans)
confectioners' sugar

Grind apricots with rind of orange. Combine with sugar and juice. Cook over gentle heat until sugar is melted and mixture has thickened. Cool, then add nuts. Form into small balls and roll in confectioners' sugar until well coated. Can be frozen, but omit confectioners' sugar until defrosted.

Mrs. George S. Fabian
Bryn Mawr, Pennsylvania

BAMA'S CARAMEL FUDGE

Average   *Preparing: 30 minutes*
Do ahead
Freeze

2 cups sugar   1 teaspoon soda
1 stick butter   3 tablespoons white Karo syrup
1 cup buttermilk   1 cup pecans
¼ teaspoon salt   1 tablespoon vanilla

In a large saucepan melt butter. Remove from fire and add sugar, buttermilk and soda. Return to fire. Stir frequently to soft ball stage, (234°). Add Karo, vanilla and nuts. Drop immediately by teaspoon onto waxed paper and cool.

Mrs. J. Mahlon Buck, Jr.
Haverford, Pennsylvania

MOCHA BALLS

Easy   *Makes: 50*
Do ahead   *Preparing: 15 minutes plus*
Freeze   *chilling time*

1 12-ounce package   2 rounded teaspoons instant
   semi-sweet chocolate bits   coffee
4 egg yolks   4 tablespoons brandy
1½ cups confectioners' sugar   2 teaspoons vanilla
1 cup soft butter   chopped pecans

Melt chocolate bits over hot water; let cool. Beat egg yolks: add sugar; beat until smooth. Beat in butter, a little at a time. Dissolve coffee in brandy and add vanilla. Combine with egg and butter mixture. Add chocolate and mix well. Chill. Shape into balls and roll in chopped nuts.

The Committee

AFTER DINNER MINTS FROM THE BARCLAY HOTEL

Easy   *Makes: 50*
Do ahead   *Preparing: 25-30 minutes*

3 tablespoons Virginia Dare   2½ pounds white sugar
   pure peppermint extract
   (add more to taste)

Heat and melt sugar. Add extract and mix thoroughly. While still hot, using a pastry bag, drop peppermints onto wax paper, on a cookie sheet. Let cool slightly. Pick off wax paper and serve.

Mrs. D. Jacques Benoliel
Philadelphia, Pennsylvania

PECAN TREATS

Easy   *Preparing: 5 minutes*
Do ahead   *Baking: 30 minutes*

1 pound shelled pecans   **½ teaspoon salt**
1 cup sugar   **1 teaspoon vanilla**
2 egg whites, beaten stiff   **½ pound butter**

Melt ¼ pound of butter in each of two 8″ x 13″ baking pans with sides. Beat egg whites until stiff. Add sugar gradually. Add salt, vanilla and pecans. Divide in half and spread on baking pans. Bake at 250°-275° for at least 30 minutes, stirring occasionally to absorb butter. When mixture turns brown, remove from oven and drain on paper towels.

Mrs. Theodore H. Ashford
Wilmington, Delaware

CURRIED PECAN HALVES

Easy   *Preparing: 25 minutes*
Do ahead   *Baking: 10-15 minutes*
Freeze

¼ cup butter melted in   **1 tablespoon salt**
** shallow pan**   **1 pound pecan halves**
1½ to 2 tablespoons curry
** powder, depending on**
** taste**

Stir curry powder and 1 tablespoon salt into melted butter. Spread pecans on cookie sheet. Coat pecans with curried butter and bake in 325° oven for 10-15 minutes, tossing several times.

Mrs. Henry K. Justi
Wayne, Pennsylvania

STRAWBERRY CONFECTIONS

Easy
Do ahead
Freeze

Serves: 10
Preparing: 1 hour
Chilling: 2 hours

**2 6-ounce packages
strawberry Jello
1 cup shredded coconut
1 cup finely ground pecans**

**1 can Carnation evaporated milk,
(5.33 ounces)
round plastic box red fine crystal
sugar**

Mix first four ingredients. Use just enough milk to make a pliable mixture, (less than full can). Refrigerate until easy to handle, (anywhere from two hours to overnight). Shape like strawberries and roll in red fine sugar. Refrigerate again, or put in freezer. To decorate use tube of green icing with decorating tip. Make two leaves on top. Chill before serving.

Mrs. J. Mahlon Buck
Bryn Mawr, Pennsylvania

VERY HEALTHY CANDY

Easy
Do ahead

Preparing: 10 minutes
Chilling time

**2 cups powdered skim milk
1 cup peanut butter**

1 cup honey

Additions:

**granola
raisins
coconut
sunflower seeds**

**sesame seeds
chopped nuts
carob chips**

Combine first 3 ingredients in a large bowl until well blended. Then stir in your choice of additions. The amount of additions should total about 1 or 2 cups. Divide mixture in half and place each half in a plastic bag. Shape into long rolls and fasten bags with twisters. Refrigerate until firm. Slice and serve.

Mrs. Frank Kaderabek
Bala Cynwyd, Pennsylvania

Virtuosity

gifts

WITH LOVE . . .
FROM YOU AND YOUR KITCHEN FOR:

THE HOLIDAYS

There are many ways to remember those kind and considerate friends, neighbors and tradesmen with more than the traditional card.

Mrs. Lawson's **Coffee Liqueur.** *Use your own label. Carafes with cork tops are ideal reusable containers. To the ribbon attach the recipe.*

Jar **Mock Mince Meat** in crocks or over-sized coffee mugs. Tie with ribbon and holly. Attach a recipe for Mrs. Bitler's **Ice Cream Mince Pie.**

Small loaves of Mrs. Ashford's **Cranberry Nut Bread.** *Easily wrapped in holiday paper. The addition of a small bread knife or a bread board makes it a special present.*

Spiced Nuts (your choice of one of our several good recipes). These can be offered in a variety of containers; jars, cans or nut dishes. To make a gift within a gift, place nuts in a covered pint jar. Surround the jar with upright candy canes held in place with a stout rubber band. Hide the elastic with a bow-tied ribbon. On your card, suggest the empty container be filled with greens for the holiday breakfast table.

Mr. Zukerman's **"Hello Dollies"** *is a rich Christmas cookie. These can be presented simply on holiday paper plates, or more extravagantly on a porcelain cookie plate of holiday design. Less extravagant would be the use of a cookie sheet. One can always use an extra.*

Mrs. Hagaman's **Sangria Jelly.** You might wrap the jars Mexican style in a straw place mat, tie with bright red and yellow ribbons.

Christmas Egg Nog could be delivered in attractive quart-size containers or a small punch bowl. Attach a nutmeg grater and fresh nutmeg.

THE NEW MOTHER

It's her first day home. Her arms are full, but her refrigerator is empty. An easily assembled casserole is Mrs. Anthony's **Another Chicken Recipe.** Add a fruit salad. Feel generous? Make the containing casserole part of the gift.

Tea-time cookies for the inevitable parade of "baby watchers." Make your choice from the many delicious cookie recipes.

A container of instant **Russian Tea** would be welcomed. Present it in a glass container intended for cotton swabs for the nursery.

THE NEW FATHER

Invite him for dinner and for recitation of baby statistics.

FRIENDS ON MOVING DAY

This is another empty refrigerator challenge. Lest we forget "the moving day blues," bring them cheer with Mrs. Kerson's **Spinach Tart,** a molded **Five Cup Salad** and a loaf of **Beer Bread.** Deliver these at the right moment on trays with your napery and silver. (Theirs is at the bottom of the barrel.) Or pack it in a basket, picnic style. You might add a bottle of chilled wine for additional cheer.

STRANGERS ON MOVING DAY

*Warmly welcome them with their first meal in the new house. Prepare Mrs. Kent's **Chicken and Hot Italian Sausage Casserole,** add a tossed green salad and **Bran Muffins.** Present with your list of local helpmates (butcher, baker, candlestick-maker, etc.). Add tickets for the next orchestra rehearsal.*

THE HOUSEWARMING

The traditional good luck gift of bread and salt can be nicely translated into **Different Banana Bread** and a box of sea or seasoned salt.

GRADE SCHOOL TEACHER

*An apple for the teacher? Why not Mrs. Davies' **Apple Pie in Brown Bag.** Include the recipe. Make the card in the style of a report card. Give her an "A" for patience, attendance, etc.*

THE SUBSTITUTE ON YOUR DAY FOR CAR POOL

Assuage your guilt with a **Dump Cake.** Effortless to make and certainly praiseworthy.

379

The "CARE PACKAGE SET"

These are those over-worked, far from home "A" students who deserve a batch of Mrs. Bitler's **Brownies.** (The "D" students need it even more.) Enclose a copy of the local Gazette.

YOUR BOSS

*Give him a tin of **Brown Sugar Pecan Rounds,** preferably following your two-hour lunch.*

YOUR HUSBAND'S SECRETARY

For the innumerable personal favors she's done for **you,** bake a **Carrot Cake.** Present it on a clear lucite tray that won't detract from the Chinchilla shrug in which you've wrapped it.

TRICK OR TREAT

*Save the ghosts and witches from themselves. Make **Very Healthy Candy.** Wrap portions in Halloween napkins.*

VALENTINE'S DAY

Fill those heart-shaped boxes or candy dishes with **Peanut Butter Cups.** The message to be your own.

YOUR BABY-SITTER

*Hide your Lady Godiva Chocolates and put out a tray of **Billy's Crunchy Cookies** beside a bowl of fruit.*

YOUR DEPRESSED FRIEND WHO JUST TURNED FORTY, FIFTY OR SIXTY

Invite her for a lunch of soup and salad. Omit the birthday cake, or at least omit the candles.

OUT OF TOWN GUESTS

*Send them on their way with a copy of **The Philadelphia Orchestra Cookbook** wrapped in a map of the city. A constant and practical reminder of their visit.*

THOSE FRIENDS WHO OWN THE POOL

Take batches of frozen cookies (not for your consumption, but for the next free-loaders). A large thermos of Mrs. Ahrens' **Super Lemonade** would be most welcome. Make a present of the thermos.

THAT LIVE-ALONE FRIEND

*Divide **Aunt Martha's Casserole** that you've made the day before. Cooking for one can be such a bore.*

THE CHURCH FAIR

Select from the many cake and cookie recipes that freeze well. Be ready for that call and adjust your halo.

THE FRIEND WHO TOOK CARE OF "GEORGE"
WHILE YOU VISITED MOTHER

*If she took extra good care of him take a burnt offering; if motherly care take a jar of **Hot Pepper Jelly**, a package of cream cheese and stoned wheat thins.*

THE "I NEVER COOK" TYPE

The one who thinks "pot luck" means ready ice cubes. Take a delicious **Caviar Pie** to compliment "whatever."

YOUR NEW DAUGHTER-IN-LAW

*First give her the gift of "laissez-faire" in her kitchen, and for your son's nutrition and palate, a copy of **The Philadelphia Orchestra Cookbook**.*

SURPRISE BIRTHDAY

Consult the "Cooking for a Crowd" section for your menu. For place cards substitute birth announcements. "It's a boy!" "It's a girl!" and fill in statistics."

YOUR SUMMER HOUSE TENANT

*After you've polished the silver, the furniture and the Gideon Bible, add a bowl of fruit. In the refrigerator leave a **Blue Cheese Ball** and a note of welcome. Be sure you have on your shelf a copy of **The Philadelphia Orchestra Cookbook**.*

THE FISHERMAN

Turn his catch into a gourmet presentation of **Fish Chowder.** Sustain his thrill of the first "bite" to the last spoonful.

YOUR HUSBAND

*Hasn't he always wanted a Ming dynasty soup tureen? Present it, with friends at table, filled with **Chinese Consommé.***

YOUR BROTHER-IN-LAW

The "Beau Brummel of the barbecue" deserves a generous quantity of **Spicy Sauce for Barbecue.** The container could be as unique as a special beer stein.

THE CONVALESCENT

***Gazpacho Blanco** is sure to perk up a faded appetite. Deliver it chilled with chilled clear glass soup bowls for now and future use. Add a small bouquet for a tray.*

THE BRIDAL SHOWER

Of course, a copy of **The Philadelphia Orchestra Cookbook.** List your favorite recipes. Attach a kitchen implement—anything from a wooden spoon to a food processor.

YOUR WEEKEND HOSTESS

*Take a crock of **Boursin** and a crock of Julia de Pasquale's **Cheese-Olive Spread.** Add a box of appropriate crackers.*

THE BACHELOR YOU WISH TO IMPRESS

Join the "casserole brigade," but make yours special with **Crab Après La Chasse.** Add a salad, a dash of charm and a pinch of reserve. Let him provide the wine.

THE MISS YOU WISH TO IMPRESS

*Take her to the best restaurant you can afford, but make her a present of **The Philadelphia Orchestra Cookbook.***

INDEX